CAMPGROUND COOKING

Edited by
CHARLES and KATHY FARMER

Follett Publishing Company / Chicago

Campground Cooking Staff

EDITORS
Charles J. Farmer
Kathleen Farmer

PRODUCTION MANAGER
Wanda Sahagian

ART DIRECTOR
Mary MacDonald

ASSOCIATE PUBLISHER
Sheldon L. Factor

About the Editors

Charles and Kathleen Farmer, husband and wife, live in the midst of Jackson Hole, Wyoming's rugged, awesome outdoors. Together they form perhaps one of the youngest, most prolific, full-time freelance outdoor writing and photography teams in the country. Individually and jointly, they have sold numerous articles and photographs to every major outdoor magazine. At 30 and 27 years old respectively, they have had two, full-length fishing books published. And, at the time of this printing, have two more books scheduled for publication in the near future.

Charles, born in New York City, has a journalism degree from Kansas State University and has worked for the Wyoming Game and Fish Department as a writer. He became a freelance outdoor writer and photographer in 1969.

Kathy, a native of Cincinnati, has a Master's degree in psychology. She started writing 3 years ago upon her marriage to Charles.

Copyright ©MCMLXXIV by Digest Books, Inc., 540 Frontage Rd., Northfield, Illinois 60093. All rights reserved. Reproduction or use of editorial or pictorial content in any manner, without express permission is prohibited.

The views and opinions of the authors expressed herein are not necessarily those of the editors and/or the publisher, and no responsibility for such views and opinions will be assumed.

Printed in the United States of America.

ISBN 0-695-80494-4   Library of Congress Catalog Card #74-80329

CONTENTS

Outdoor Meals to Remember
by Byron W. Dalrymple 4

Sourdough: Alaska's Gift to Outdoor Cooks
by Daniel D. McGrew 10

Campfire Magic
by Norman Strung 17

Cooking for Survival
by Bradford Angier 23

How to Ponass a Pike
by Thomas Hardin 28

Zapping the Spoilers
by Charles J. Farmer 33

The Awesome, Clawsome, Delicious Crawdad
by Helen Martin 40

Canoe Kitchen
by Mike Michaelson 44

Water
by Sam Curtis 50

Mister Pork & Beans
by Curt Gowdy 55

Care for the Little Critters
by Briggs Babbison 59

That Sweet Sap
by Jenny Reid 63

Feastin' Down the River
by Bob Hirsch 69

Dutch Oven Cookery
by Ed Park 75

Yukon Flavor
by Peggy Peters 82

Super Foods from Super Markets
by Jonathon Salazar 88

Chili: Greatest Invention Since the Campfire
by Adam Jackson 93

The Grub Box
by Beau Usher 99

Eating on the Move
by Jack Seville 104

As the Stomach Growls
by Kathleen Farmer 109

Pancakes at 10,000 Feet
by Paul Petzold 114

Beef Jerky: Short-cut to an all-purpose food
by James F. Daubel 121

Camp is Where the Stove Is
by Sam Curtis 124

Foiled Again
by Marvin Tye 130

A Bunch of Lunch
by Kathleen Farmer 134

Feathered Delights
by Helen Martin 142

River Running on a Happy Stomach
by Jim and Vicki Tallon 145

A Taste of Honey
by Charles Nansen 150

Backpack Foods Can Be Good
by Charles J. Farmer 158

Field Tasting
by Mark Sosin 165

Secrets of Streamside Cooking
by Dan Abrams 171

The RV Galley
by Jack Seville 175

The Long & Short of Finny Delicacies
by James F. Daubel 181

Off-Beat Stuff I Have Et
by Barney Peters 187

Home on the Campfire Range
by Norman Strung 192

Mushroom Munching
by Jane Barr 198

Seafood Southern Style
by Marvin Tye 202

Just Cooking in the Rain
by Charles J. Farmer 206

The Grand-Daddy of 'em all
by Sheldon Coleman 212

Berries for the Picking
by Bradford Angier 218

Fish Bones Need Love
by Helen Martin 223

Cooking My Mother Never Told Me About
by Vicki Tallon 227

Rocky Mountain Salads
by Jenny Reid 232

Cook Your Fish Where You Catch Them
by Dick Kotis 238

Chestnuts Roastin' on an Open Fire
by Charles J. Farmer 243

Coastal Smorgasbord
by Milt Rosko 247

Making the Most of a Mexican Cookout
by Vicki Tallon 252

Camp Cooks Are Soothsayers
by Kathleen Farmer 260

Going First Class
by Bob Hirsch 265

Squeaky Clean
by Kathleen Farmer 270

Good Field Care Means Good Eatin'
by Monte Sagge 273

Your Own Honest-to-Goodness Luau
by Peggy Peters 282

Suppertime and All is Well
by Kathleen Farmer 285

Author Byron Dalrymple bakes biscuits by means of a reflector oven.

Outdoor Meals to Remember

by BYRON W. DALRYMPLE

UNDOUBTEDLY the eating habits of most people are molded when they are young. They may be cultivated later, but the basic tastes are set during childhood days. When I was a youngster we lived out in the country in Michigan, and we were quite poor. Moneywise, that is. But we raised, and my mother canned, all our vegetables and fruit. Potatoes and carrots, squash and pumpkins went into the big dirt-floored root cellar for winter. Butter was churned with an old dash churn in the kitchen, and eggs, chicken, pork, beef, plus occasional turkey and goose, came right out of our yard and fields.

Thus we ate very well indeed. But simply. Everything was so fresh and good and in such ample supply there was no need—and no time or money either—to concoct all manner of fancy recipes. Not only was domestic food prepared in marvelously simple and delicious ways, but when my brother and I brought in rabbits, squirrels, pheasants, and even muskrats and raccoons from our trap-lines, they, too, were prepared very simply. You always knew what you were eating!

Later, when I had drifted into outdoor writing as a career—one that has held me for over 30 years now—my tastes in camp cooking, whether of game and fish or standard store-bought foods remained on the simple side. I've often chuckled to read the accounts of treks, let's say far back into the forest, perhaps where the City Dweller stumbles upon a cabin where lives The Oldtimer. There is always a haunch of venison handy, and The Oldtimer prepares it, hauling out a dozen different kinds of condiments he just happens to have handy and going through endless antics and seasoning voodoo rites. They wind up with a meal over which The City Dweller ohs and ahs. Savory scents waft throughout the log cabin, but nary a one distinguishable as venison—and they both go to bed to burp the night away.

We have a ranch of modest size nowadays in Texas, quite remote and rugged. Often we go down there to camp a few days. There are no buildings, no one lives there, and it is a true slice of wilderness. The creek bed is in some places solid flat rock, and wide enough so a portion of it is dry. The first thing I do is to gather downed wood and build a big fire, in preparation for one of our favorite meals. I pile the wood high and we go about our business while the fire over an hour's time metamorphoses itself into a large bed of coals and ashes.

Now from the big cooler we get the meat. It is chuck roast that has been cut into steaks a half-inch or three-fourths inch thick. We use them instead of a thick roast because we want everything to be done at once. These are salted and peppered, and a bit of margarine is spread on each side. Now whole carrots are peeled or scraped, and fair sized potatoes are peeled and cut in half the long way. These also get a bit of margarine. Several stalks of celery are added. Meat and vegetables are all placed on a large sheet of heavy foil that has been folded for double-wrapping. Last to go into the package are a few onion slices. Then the top is sealed by fold and crimp, leaving ample steam room inside.

This package is placed in a deep hole in the coals dug out with a shovel. And it is covered with ashes and coals.

Byron Dalrymple has been a free lance writer since 1945 with over 2500 articles in print. He has concentrated his efforts in the outdoor field both in writing and producing TV films (War-Dal Productions). He is just beginning his fourteenth book, which is naturally on an outdoor subject.

Now we can go do whatever we wish for an hour. When the package is gently dug out and removed, a whole meal is ready, the flavors of each ingredient blending with the others. It is eaten "tribe fashion," right from the foil, and bread is sopped into the juice as an additional treat. The only utensils used are knife and fork, the only supplies needed are salt, pepper, margarine, and the foil. If you're careful with it and clean it, the foil can be reused in a pinch. Obviously wild meat such as venison, elk, antelope can be substituted for beef for this excellent simple meal.

The best camp cooks I've ever seen in my travels over the continent on magazine assignments and on hunting and fishing trips have been the ones who cooked just that simply. A few onions and potatoes, a slab of chunk bacon or salt pork, flour, baking powder, salt, pepper. These are their basics and very little else is needed. Granted, today one can buy whole meals in plastic bags that require refrigeration—just toss into the pot and heat—and there are freeze-dried foods in infinite variety. Certainly these all have their place. Backpackers use freeze-dried items to advantage because of lightness, compactness, and no need for refrigeration. I have no quarrel with such foods when they are necessary. But I'd call these emergency and special-situation foods. And I'll just say that I wouldn't book with an outfitter on any wilderness trip who expected me to eat that way. Other "real" foods may be bulky, but the pack horse or mule doesn't spend much time thinking about it!

In any high-country trip even in summer, or northern treks at almost any time, temperatures are low enough so that butter or margarine can be carried. Or you can get along without it entirely by taking a can of one of the cooking oils that needs no refrigeration. However, oil is

Simple cooking is the key to enjoying outdoor cookery. Nothing simpler than broiled antelope steaks.

needed chiefly for frying, and the sign of a so-so cook is one who can think of nothing better to do than get out the skillet. Broiling, baking, or simmering is far better. Many memorable and simple meals have been put together this way.

As I write that I think of an evening when I was fishing a northern trout stream. Two of us had hiked in some distance to get into true wilderness water. We'd planned to get out earlier, but we came out of the stream ravenous and with a long way to go. On such hikes I always carry a small packsack. In it I had salt and pepper, a small, light, fire-blackened cooking pot, a couple of tin cans with the tops neatly cut out, some coffee, and—as I've often seen guides in Canada's bush do—a hunk of slab bacon wrapped in a cloth.

It was spring and the marsh marigolds were abundant, their new green leaves and stems bordering the stream in spots. We gathered a batch of them, tossing them into a landing net to carry them back to where we'd launched a fire. I sliced some bits of bacon into the cooking pot, added stream water, brought it to a boil and dumped in the greens. We cleaned trout, cut and trimmed green sticks, thrust them through the mouth of each fish and on into the tail near the vent. These were propped over coals. Presently we sat there gorging ourselves on roasted trout and spring greens flavored with bacon. Then I washed out the cookpot and made boiled coffee in it. A more enjoyable, delicious and simple meal outdoors is difficult to imagine.

Good cooking in camp is a marvelous balm for the spirit when irritations and frustrations occur on hunting or fishing trips. A couple of years ago I was high up in New Mexico's Sangre de Cristo Mountains on an elk hunt. There were plenty of elk, but we were having trouble finding one we wanted, for we were producing a TV film for Remington Arms and Redfield Scopes. In addition, the weather was rotten for filming and everyone was getting edgy. Jesse Williams, who is Information-Education Chief for the New Mexico Game & Fish Dept., was along doing the cooking.

On a drizzly, chill day with everyone irritable, Jesse made a motion that we forget elk and go fishing. We were at roughly 10,000 feet and above us another thousand feet he knew of a small lake supposedly loaded with big trout. Suffice to say that we made it to the lake, and that we caught some beautiful cuts averaging two and three pounds each. Irritations were forgotten.

Back down at camp, Jesse got a great mass of coals ardently glowing. He twined bacon strips around each trout, leaving the fish whole. Then he wrapped each in foil and placed them on a grill over the coals. Small trout, remember, can easily (and best) be cooked so the skin is crisp. With big ones it's difficult. I was a bit uneasy as to how these would turn out. They were absolutely superb. With them we had baking powder biscuits that Jesse made with canned milk and baked in a Dutch oven over the same coals. A simple, memorable meal indeed. In fact, there's an old saying: "Bad cooking ruins many a good camp; good cooking makes many a bad camp good."

For some years my family and I spent our summers in Wyoming and Montana, camping for at least two months, sometimes three. One of the truly great outdoor meals we looked forward to every year (and repeated often) was based on the fact that in many places along the streams and in the pine woods in those states morel mushrooms by bushels pop up during June and July. They're easy to identify from any book dealing with mushrooms, and they are unlike poisonous varieties.

While I went after the trout, Ellen and my two boys would take on the mushroom detail. A great heap of them was put into a large, deep skillet with only a tiny bit of margarine or cooking oil. Heating gently, the juice oozed out of the mushrooms. Soon the simmering skillet was half full of liquid plus tender, now-flattened morels, some half the size of one's palm. Meanwhile the trout, set on a small grill a few inches above the coals, had been broiling. When all was ready, Ellen thickened the mushroom gravy. Enormous quantities of mushrooms and gravy were heaped upon slices of bread on our plates. The trout? As any proper outdoor cook knows, broiled trout are best eaten from the hands, held by head and tail and attacked like an ear of corn.

I recall, too, that a block of wood has been our most precious and useful cooking utensil on a number of fishing trips. We had a rather primitive camp one time in Canada near an abandoned logging camp back in the bush. I had a cartop boat along and we were fishing for lake trout. Fishing had been poor, and we were right down to rock bottom for grub, so badly, in fact, that we were going to have to leave. Nothing was left but biscuit makings and one small onion.

But fortune of fortunes—late that afternoon I caught a trout of possibly 12 pounds. Just the one. We decided to run up a true gourmet meal before leaving. I found a two-foot section of a big birch log at the old camp, and split it, getting two big slabs out of the center. In our duffle and tool box were a few small nails and a roll of fine copper wire.

We built up a big fire and let it diminish to coals. Meanwhile I had gutted the big trout and split it lengthwise. Each half was laid skin side down on the fresh birch slabs. The perimeter of each was gently nailed in place and the copper wire was woven zigzag, nail to nail, across the fish to hold it in place. Now the small onion was split

The best camp cooks can do marvels with onions, potatoes, bacon, flour, baking powder and salt and pepper—maybe a little margarine too.

After a successful day of fishing, all the fisherman wants to eat is fish.

and half skewered to each tail section of fish, and the slabs then propped before the coals.

As the fish slowly broiled and the wood became scorching hot, juice from the onion dribbled in minute quantity down over the fish. Lake trout is of course oily and no grease of any kind was needed. Meanwhile Ellen was making biscuits in the Dutch oven. The boys had long previously discovered scads of ripe blueberries growing nearby. They were out raking in dessert. Broiled lake trout, biscuits, fresh blueberries—who could possibly need more?!

If I could have only one major cooking utensil to take on any camping trip, it would be an authentic Dutch oven, that fine old flat-bottomed, heavy cast-iron kettle with matching lid. Any kind of meat can be roasted, baked, stewed, or fried in it. It can serve for making bread, biscuits, pies. A miniscule fire will heat it and the heavy iron holds and distributes the heat. Our greatest meat-cooking use of it has long been for birds.

On several occasions I've made a camping venture out of dove shooting and also quail shooting. In my estimation it is little short of a crime to attempt to fry doves or quail. Or, to simply take out the breasts, a practice all too common among dove hunters. Here is how we cook them. The birds are shaken in flour while a modest amount of grease—as little as possible to brown the birds—is brought to rather high heat but not high enough to burn whatever kind you use.

The birds are now put in and quickly seared, or browned, with turning to make sure this is evenly done. Now the oven is taken off direct coals and propped on rocks or a grill a bit above the coals. Water is added, enough to roughly halfway cover the birds. Salt and pepper to taste is now used. The lid is put on and the pot watched to make certain the heat is so low the liquid just bubbles. The slower the cooking, the better. In a couple of hours the birds should be so tender the meat fairly shakes from the bones. Now the gravy is thickened—and the meal is ready. Whatever else you have with the meat and gravy course makes little difference. But if you have ample coals, try greasing baking potatoes, double-wrapping in foil, and burying them in hot coals halfway during the bird simmering. They'll be done in an hour, and the gravy poured over split bakers is superb.

I will admit that one of my weaknesses where the simplicity theme can break down might easily, is with wine. I've often carted along a bottle or two strictly for cooking. On several occasions we've cooked a wild goose whole, exactly as I've described cooking doves and quail, but have added a cup or more of vermouth. After trying the result, any martini lover might be tempted to give up and just stick with the goose!

To attempt to list even two or three per year of the memorable meals I've eaten outdoors over the years, most of them in one way or another involved with fish and game, would turn this into a fat book. It is certainly trite to say—as who hasn't?—that everything just seems to taste better when it is cooked and eaten outdoors. But it's true. And if you keep it simple, yet inspired and with a new twist here and there, the tastes it seems to me are not only delicious, but have a special savor of thorough authenticity.

Writing that, I cannot close without relating one more experience. One year I was on a vast ranch in Mexico, camped out with a companion and gathering material for several magazine assignments. Late one afternoon we came upon a line-rider camp of Mexican cowboys. They had, with the rancher's permission, killed a young steer. It was hung, excepting a whole hind quarter, in the shade of mesquite, and covered with mesquite branches to keep flies away. Now country Mexicans cook with utter simplicity, and also on occasion with great ingenuity. The one

A modern rendition of the old Mexican theme, these whole young steers baked for 24 hours over a bed of coals for a round-up lunch on a western ranch.

"Bad cooking ruins many a good camp; good cooking makes a bad camp good." The author demonstrates the foundation for good outdoor cooking—homemade biscuits.

who was cooking for this camp invited us to eat.

He went to a mound of earth a short distance from camp and began digging with a shovel. Soon mouth-watering fumes arose from the pit, and presently, with gloves on because of the hot earth, he gingerly pulled from the bottom of the hole a big package wrapped in burlap that was somewhat scorched. With great ceremony the armload was laid on a pile of mesquite wood at the camp, and the burlap was unwrapped. Inside was the missing hind quarter of beef. It was almost ready to fall apart. Everyone gathered around and ate with their hands, slashing off pieces with pocket knives or tearing them off. All it needed was a bit of salt and pepper and it was supremely delicious.

What he had done was to dig the hole the previous late afternoon and build a roaring fire in it. When the fire had burned for a couple of hours, earth was shoveled atop it. The burlap was soaked in water and the beef quarter wrapped in it, several layers. It was placed in the hole and the hole filled up with earth. There it had stayed in that scorching tomb, all night and all of this day. Since then I have eaten venison, elk, and even javelina prepared this way. Talk about setting the automatic electric oven to go on and off when you wish!

The cook told me in Spanish: "Range-killed unaged beef is bound to be tough. This cooking makes it like the finest hotel in the city."

How true! Most simple outdoor meals would wipe memories of any downtown gourmet cooking from even the most prejudiced of minds!

SOURDOUGH: Alaska's Lip-smacking Gift to Outdoor Cooks

by DANIEL D. "Dangerous Dan" McGREW

A BUNCH OF THE BOYS were whooping it up in camp one night and that isn't any wonder. Lew Baker had just bagged the biggest moose east of the Kenai and now in the gloom outside, frost crystals were forming on the meat and on the massive anglers which hung outside the cook tent. Inside it was all hilarity and celebration, warmth and the fragrant odors coming from a battered old bake oven which some prospector had abandoned on the site many years ago. With great ingenuity, cookie Ace Harper had restored it to working order.

But suddenly the celebration stopped when Ace pried open the oven door with a skinning knife and removed two steaming loaves of hot, golden-crusted sourdough bread. He placed these, along with a slab of fresh butter on the table. "Go to it, gang," he said, at the same time desperately trying to avoid the mad rush.

Perhaps never since the fishes and loaves incident of the Old Testament has bread ever vanished so quickly before a hungry man's eyes. And probably never has it tasted any better to a tired crew who had spent the afternoon hauling moose meat on their backs from a willow swamp several miles to camp. That is hard labor any way you look at it.

Almost certainly there were similar occasions all over Alaska that night—wherever sportsmen sat together in lonely log or canvas camps—because it was the first week of the open hunting season in the 49th State. Most of the hunters had gathered in such camps because here is one of the happiest hunting grounds for big game left on the face of the earth. But, as elsewhere, a good many of the outdoorsmen had come for other reasons as well—such as the companionship, to see old friends, a total change of pace and an escape from smog, Watergate and ringing telephones. But my friend Lew Baker, who often doesn't bring a gun, made no bones about his own reasons.

Dan McGrew explored Alaska before gold was discovered there. Living in Fairbanks with children and grandchildren, he scours the back country in his pontoon plane, which he shares with five neighbors. Being a man of few words, he writes only about things he loves.

Sourdough was invaluable to woodsmen in interior Alaska because of its tolerance to extremes in temperature.

"I come every year," he admits, "to eat good sourdough cooking three times a day." Most of us in camp knew just what he meant.

But exactly what is sourdough anyway? According to the new American Heritage Dictionary it is either "sour fermented dough used as leaven in making bread" or "an old-time settler or prospector, especially in Alaska or northwestern Canada." Of course both definitions are correct, but are by no means complete. The substance is used far more than to bake bread alone. And mystery still surrounds which came first—which was named after the other—the leavening or the pioneer Alaskan of the same name. I suppose that makes little difference today as long as plenty of the former is available—as it is in grocery stores, restaurants and particularly in gift shops all over our northernmost state.

At the turn of this century, sourdough was created of necessity and in fact made survival in a harsh, often frigid environment much easier—in some cases just barely possible. Baking bread, biscuits, pancakes, almost any pastry at all, would have been nearly impossible without it, simply because commercial yeast then available refused to "grow"—to make dough "rise"—in very low temperatures. But sourdough was more compatible to cold and this "starter" or "sponge" (as it was properly called for a long, long time) became a priceless possession of almost every miner, trapper or backwoodsman who ever ventured very far into the boondocks.

During the bitterest weather, a prospector might have carried his starter in a bag around his neck and tucked inside his shirt while traveling with a dog team. Some carried the sourdough atop their heads and under fur caps for safekeeping. At least one musher allowed his most reliable sled dog to carry the entire supply of starter in a pouch underneath the harness. When breaking camp it was the last thing to be packed and the first to be unpacked on arrival at a new site. It is therefore perfectly natural that sourdough remains as much a part of Alaskan lore as Nome and Cripple Creek, the Malemute and Red Dog Saloons, Joe Juneau and Soapy Smith, Robert Service and "The Cremation of Sam McGee." Nowadays sourdough hotcakes are featured on the menus of practi-

Sourdough is kept, along with meat, in bear-proof cache above camp.

Angler Bob Curtis duels with char on Tikchik River, Alaska. Some of the best sourdough pancakes in the state are served at the Tikchik Narrows Lodge.

cally all of the best restaurants from Ketchikan northward to Barrow and all points in between. Some of the recipes, and often the sourdough ingredients, date back to the earliest gold rush days. One original batch of sourdough can easily be perpetuated, perhaps forever. But let's go back to the beginning.

Assume you want to try sourdough baking. If commercial starter is not available or you prefer to make your own anyway, here's how. Mix together ½-cake of yeast with two tablespoons of sugar and ½-cup of flour. Some folks put in a couple of drops of vinegar or buttermilk. Add enough warm water to make a thin batter and allow this to stand at 65 to 75 degrees F temperature for four or five days—or until it smells sour, say like vinegar. It is then ready to use.

From this point onward you need never make any more starter. When preparing the dough or batter for anything, add the starter, but always hold out a cup of the dough to serve as the starter for the next baking project. And so on indefinitely. As mentioned above, some Alaskan families are (or claim to be) using sourdough which originated generations ago—and which might have been carried from Skagway in an oilskin over Chilkoot Pass to the Klondike. And more than a few of them claim it gets better and better (and more sour) with age. We'll certainly not dispute them here.

It is important to insert at this point that sourdough should be kept in a covered china, pottery, glass or plastic (*never* metal) container. When added to a batter of bread dough, it should be mixed with a wooden or plastic (*not* metal) spoon. When stored indoors, the refrigerator is the best place. The outdoor cook should seek the coolest place possible, perhaps storing the starter in a sealed jar underground or in the pool of a cold stream or spring. After a time, a bilious liquid may separate out (very old-timers may recall how this happened when making "homebrew" during Prohibition), but it is only necessary to stir this harmless stuff back into starter.

Sourdough survives today as far more than a convenience for camp cooks; it also produces the most delicious pastries any angler, hunter, camper or skier is likely to gorge on. Some folks even specialize in sourdough cooking and a good example is Col. Howard Clifford, an executive of Western Airlines which just happens to be a major carrier of travelers to Alaska. Here's how he makes his sourdough bread, which ranks with the best we have ever tasted.

Typical back country road house on Denali Highway, Alaska. Sourdough starter here is much older than the wooden house.

Sourdough pancakes make any outdoor experience memorable and worth talking about.

First, a cup of starter (Clifford's own formula) is allowed to stand overnight in a warm place. In the morning he adds two tablespoons of bacon fat or other cooking oil. At the same time four cups of sifted flour, two tablespoons of sugar and one teaspoon of salt are mixed in a large bowl. That done, the mixture is kneaded thoroughly into the sourdough starter (probably for 10-15 minutes). The dough is put aside in a greased bowl covered with a towel to rise for two to four hours, or until doubled in size.

Now Clifford dissolves ¼-teaspoon of baking soda into a tablespoon of warm water and kneads it thoroughly into the dough. Finally it is shaped into small loaves and set aside once more (in the sunshine when possible) until it again doubles in size. It is then baked in a hot (about 475 degrees F) Coleman camp oven for about an hour. Other types of outdoor ovens can be used, but the cook will have to rely on his own intuition as to when the bread is "finished."

One thing is guaranteed: Clifford's sourdough bread is a gastronomical experience as long as a crumb lasts. But it is never more delicious than when fresh out of the oven and plastered with fresh butter or strawberry preserves. That is also true of Clifford's sourdough wheat bread; the recipe for this substitutes two cups whole wheat flour

Supply of sourdough tucked inside shirt is also valuable to Alaskan hunter or trapper.

Harbor scene at Wrangell is almost as typical of Alaska as sourdough.

for two of the white flour. Adding a half-cup of cracked wheat is optional.

Another Alaskan (but now living in Moose, Wyoming) with a long and rich experience in outdoor and sourdough cooking is Margaret Murie. Mrs. Murie is author of the excellent books *Two in the Far North*, (all about Alaska) and *Wapiti Wilderness*. Her late respected husband, Olaus, was founder of The Wilderness Society. Following is Mrs. Murie's recipe for sourdough pancakes from the Jackson Hole Wild Game Cookbook, a delightful enough publication of the Jackson Hole (Wyoming) Art Association to have been reprinted three times.

The night before, two cups of flour (this can be whole wheat, corn meal or 100 per cent bran) are mixed with the starter and enough water to make the batter of the thickness desired. If you prefer thin cakes, make a thin batter. Or thicker to suit.

Next morning at breakfast, in another bowl, beat to-

Main street of Skagway where long trail over Chilkoot Pass to the Klondike began.

Old time sled dog mushers often carried sourdough inside their fur caps.

gether one egg, two tablespoons of molasses and ½-teaspoon of salt. After setting aside a cup of the starter for the future, mix everything together thoroughly, but "do not beat too much." When the griddle is heating, dissolve ½-teaspoon of soda into a little water and fold this into the batter. The batter will puff up and be about the consistency of whipped cream. The cakes should then be baked as soon as possible "on a real hot griddle."

Almost anything that can be said about Mrs. Murie's pancakes is understatement once you launch headlong into a stack drenched in any kind of syrup. If available, I suggest wild honey or maple syrup, both of which are discussed elsewhere in this book. But the simple truth is that nobody has a monopoly on genuinely fine sourdough pancakes. There are almost as many different recipes as there are sourdough fanciers—and a large proportion of these insist that theirs is by far the best. I submit the following historical example.

Flaming sourdough waffles of a very old origin are served at Wickersham House in Juneau, the capital.

Interior of restored Indian lodge at Saxman. Totems are even older in Alaskan culture than sourdough.

Sometime during the gold rush days of '98, the Malemute Saloon opened its swinging, latticed doors for business in Ester, not far from Fairbanks, Alaska. Every morning the cooks served up a brand of sourdough pancakes guaranteed to properly stoke and fortify a man for the day ahead, no matter how cold and dismal it may have seemed. The last I heard, they were still serving the same cakes to tourists and nothing succeeds as much as success and repeat business. So here's how they make the hotcakes where the original Dan McGrew bit the sawdust on the jackpine floor. The following recipe is meant for three adults or two hungry children.

Mix one cup starter, two cups flour, a dash of salt and enough milk to make a batter and allow the works to stand overnight in a warm place, of course. In the morning this should look like a large sponge, be full of holes and have a pleasant, yeasty odor.

After a cup of the batter is set aside as future starter, add two eggs, three tablespoons of melted fat, half cup of sugar and a teaspoon of soda. Never, absolutely never, add any more flour to this batter, which should be mixed well. It should be cooked quickly on a hot griddle and served with thick lumberjack syrup.

There remains an old story about an equally old sourdough who once staggered into the Malemute Saloon half-starved and more than half-dead. Several days before, after an encounter with a grizzly, a companion had left him for dead in the bush, after relieving the old-timer of his pouch of gold nuggets. But, bandaged and with a couple of stacks of pancakes under his belt, he was ready to hit the trail once more.

"Where you headed, Dad?" one of the dance hall girls asked.

"I'm going to shoot me a certain bear," the old man answered, "and catch the dirty $%&@ who stole my colors."

Also according to this story, the hotcakes the old man ate were only the "regular" rather than the "deluxe"—in other words they didn't contain blueberries which then were not in season. The imagination is boggled when one considers what might have happened say a month or so later with the blueberries ripe.

Sourdough pancakes and fresh picked blueberries! That just might be the greatest treasure to come out of Alaska since Seward skinned the Russians at their own game—even including the Nixon Wheat Deal of 1973 when they almost got even with us.

CAMPFIRE MAGIC

by NORMAN STRUNG

A grill is handy for open-fire cookery. This type of heavy duty grill is fine for pots, pans and skillets but would be inadequate for broiling steaks or hamburgers. For them you need a grate with rods spaced no more than a half-inch apart.

A campfire provides light, warms the spirit as well as the body, and cooks the chef's tasty morsels. Once you know how, the campfire is easy to build and adds an extra dimension to the outdoors.

THE MOST MEMORABLE chronicle of the difficulties involved in getting a match to catch flame was Jack London's classic, *To Build a Fire*, a short story of the frozen north where failure meant death.

Today's campfire cook doesn't face a test of such everlasting magnitude, but in many ways the task before him is a little tougher. Not only must he get a fire started, he must maintain that flame long enough to cook a meal, and at a level of heat that produces food done to perfection.

The effort and understanding required to turn out a top campfire meal is greater than what it takes to cook on a modern range, but it's by no means beyond the grasp of the average kitchen cook. Consider first, what makes a fire "go."

In order for a fire to burn, three things are needed: heat (more specifically, enough heat to raise fuel to kindling temperature), fuel, and oxygen. If any member of this trinity is not present, there will be no combustion.

By way of illustration, let's then look at these three factors at work when you start a fire.

Norman Strung is a book author and free lance writer, especially associated with the Rocky Mountains and his home state of Montana. His books include The Hunter's Almanac, Camping in Comfort *and* Deer Hunting in North America.

Tinder, kindling and firewood are classifications of the fuels you'll need. "Tinder" may be newspaper, an abandoned bird's nest, or charcoal starter. The important thing is that it have a low or quickly-realized kindling temperature, and that there be enough of it to, in turn, raise the temperature of the kindling above it to the point where it too bursts into flame. "Kindling" is generally pencil-thick to thumb-thick pieces of split wood or branch, and again, there must be enough of it to spark the firewood that is layered next. The firewood, in turn must be sufficient to create a bed of coals. Once this is done, the coals' heat will be enough to push any added firewood up to kindling temperature and combustion.

The tinder, kindling and firewood must, however, be loosely packed, with plenty of space for oxygen to enter. You can achieve this effect most easily by laying your tinder nestled between two wrist-thick logs. Stretch loosely-thatched kindling, from log to log, then lay down another level of kindling at right angles to the first. Firewood goes on top of that in the same pattern. With this arrangement, oxygen can easily get under the fire. This is the best point of entry for feeding the combustion process.

Author Norm Strung samples his favorite soup Private Stock. He favors the keyhole lay as the most versatile way of building a campfire. ▶

The heat is next, provided by the strike of a match. The touch of its flame is enough to raise the kindling temperature of the tinder and it catches fire. The tinder sets the kindling to fire, and the kindling the wood.

There are two notable additions to this fire-starting principle. Damp or downright wet conditions hold the kindling temperature of fuel down. If you're trying to start a fire on a wet day, you'll need double the normal tinder and a finer gradation of kindling, with levels of tooth-pick sized stuff to feed the pencil-thick wood, and so forth. We'll get into why in a second.

When starting a charcoal fire, the oxygen principle will be enhanced if you'll place your coals *on top* of the grill, building a kindling fire underneath it. You will be flabbergasted at how quickly the coals will begin to glow. As soon as they do, dump them into your firepit or the tremendous heat generated by the coals will warp the metal plates of the grill.

We now have the flickering beginnings of a "campfire range." But successful cooking requires more than a starting fire's sporadic heat; you have to control the heat's intensity and distribution. With a stove, you have the convenience and exactitude of carefully-calibrated dials and thermostatic control. This same kind of control must be exercised over a cooking fire, and knowing how makes the difference between uncommon eating pleasures and blackened pots and burned food.

Fuels are one means of controlling that heat, and that control is related to fuel types and fuel size. A pencil-thin piece of wood will reach kindling temperature faster than a log, and an equivalent weight of kindling-to-log will burn faster and hotter than one big log. This is because the many pieces of kindling expose more total surface area to the licking flames.

Neither pencil-size or log-size woods are suitable for cooking; one burns too hot, the other too cool.

Pieces of wood that fall between the diameter of a broomstick and that of your wrist will catch fire without a lot of prodding, yet sustain heat for a relatively long period of time.

Fuel types fall into two categories: manufactured and natural. Manufactured campfire fuels include things like charcoal briquets and natural charcoal. They're certainly the most efficient for cooking since they glow for a long, long while, and once kindling wood is burned away, they won't blacken pots. But these fuels are sometimes unavailable or impractical to bring along, say on a backpacking trip. Then too, there's a sense of joy that stems from the competence required to build and use a cooking fire of natural fuels that to me has always been a vital part of the pleasures of camping.

Natural fuels are divided into two categories too: softwoods and hardwoods.

Softwoods are coniferous trees—pines, spruces and firs. Because they contain a lot of resinous tars in their sap, they burn hot, fast, and create a lot of carbon, as well as a slightly piney, undesirable taste. They are rated as the poorer of the two.

Hardwoods are deciduous trees; trees that, for all practical purposes, lose their leaves each winter. They are considered best for campfire cooking because they burn long with little smoke. Some hardwoods are better than others for cooking. Hickory is surely the finest, imparting a salty, smoky-sugary flavor to the foods its flame comes in contact with. Cottonwood, on the other hand, unless it's bone-dry, imparts a flavor a little like the musky sweetness of rotting fall leaves. It's an interesting smell for sniffing, but I don't care for the flavor on my food.

When assessing cooking fuels and their importance, don't forget to include the way you're going to cook your meal. If you'll be boiling or foil baking over an open fire, very little if any flavor of the wood will reach cooked food. Reflector-oven baking and broiling lie at the other end of the scale—their taste can have a lot to do with the wood types you use in your fire.

Even though there is a hierarchy of preferred woods, you can use less desirable woods like pine and cottonwood for broiling. Use nothing but bone-dry wood that has been stripped of its bark (bark contains the most unpleasant smoke-properties). Then, burn that select wood to a point where it is largely black coals before cooking; where all the obnoxious smokes and grasses and resins have been burned or distilled away, you have what is essentially a homemade charcoal briquet. The easiest way to achieve these coals is by constructing the right kind of fire lay; "lay" being the design of your fireplace. More about lays in a minute.

The tasty woods, maple, applewood, cherry and hickory, don't require the attention of conifers. You can cook over a smoky fire of this stuff, and even a low, dancing yellow flame. But never forget yellow flame is that color because of unburned carbon. Too much yellow flame will blacken pots, and leave the same sour residue on broiled foods.

Ninety percent of campground situations will be satisfied by two fire lays—the tipi lay and the log cabin lay. The tipi lay finds rocks arranged in a circle, with wood stacked in a cone inside.

This lay finds the greatest rate of combustion up at the top of the cone, with a bright, enduring yellow flame that provides flickering light for friendly conversation, and a primary heat source close to the center of your body where warmth will do the most good. This is a "looking" fire.

The log cabin lay is squarish, with stacks and stacks of wood arranged at right angles to each other and spaced an inch or so apart.

In terms of combustibility, this type of lay tends to burn all at once with an even, all-consuming heat of equal intensity throughout the fuel-source. It doesn't throw much light, but, like the even tongues of blue flame on a gas range, or the coils of an electric stove, this well-distributed heat is most practical for cooking.

All this might seem a little disappointing; that there's one fire for heat and light and another for cooking, and never the twain shall meet. But therein lies the clue for easy campfire cooking. The keyhole lay is a matter of the two meeting.

To build the keyhole lay, begin a circle of rocks, but leave one-fourth of that circle open toward the direction from which the wind is blowing. Then build a square, three-sided rock wall for a log cabin lay that mates up to the three-quarter circle. Viewed from directly above, the pattern is that of an old-time keyhole.

Build a tipi fire in the round part and a log cabin fire in the square part. When the log cabin fire burns down to glowing embers, it's ready for cooking. Keep the tipi fire well-stoked with wood, and you've got light to cook by, heat for comfort, *and* a constant supply of cooking coals. Just rake them from the inside of the conical tipi configuration into your square cooking fireplace with a forked stick as you need them.

Ringing a fireplace with rocks is good safety practice. It's a means of setting limits on the potentially dangerous spread of flame. You'll even be safer if you dig the keyhole configuration down into mineral soil, then ring the upper rim with rocks. And safety isn't the only benefit you'll realize.

The type of fuel available is important to the type of cooking fire possible. Here at Willow Beach, Arizona, driftwood and dead willow branches produce a fast-burning fire.

If you'll save the duff and grasses carefully, then put them back into the hole when you leave the campsite, you'll cut any hint of your presence to a minimum, and help preserve a little piece of the outdoors for the next camper.

From a cooking point of view, you'll also have gone another step toward controlling your heat; you'll be regulating oxygen.

Perfect oxygen control does require a sealed environment. In old cooking ranges, the amount of air reaching the firebox came under close regulation by way of dampers. Once you learned how to use those dampers, cast iron stoves were as efficient and easy to cook on as modern ranges. Even today's stoves depend on this oxygen control; precise, automatic mixture of gas with air is what makes cooking with gas so turn-of-the-dial predictable.

This same kind of control can be approached in a campfire.

A fire in a pit must draw oxygen down to it. Since the fire warms the air, and warm air rises, there is a natural conflict that occurs, limiting the amount of oxygen that can get to a fire. However, if you'll dig a ramp on the upwind end of the keyhole lay . . . into the shortest straight side . . . you'll have provided an avenue for easy entry of oxygen, a draft if you will.

This draft will quickly fan glowing embers into searing hot coals. On the other side of the cooking coin, if you want less heat, block the draft off with rocks, a dampened log, or anything else that will reduce the oxygen drawn down. The coals will soon reduce the rate at which they burn, creating less heat. This can be a piecemeal thing too; say three rocks on the upper end. Keeping them in place will keep your cooking fire on "low" taking one rock away will raise the temperature to "warm," two will be "medium," and removing three gets you back up on "high" . . . just like a kitchen range.

While the type and size of fuel you select, and the degree of control you have over the oxygen reaching the fire are the primary ways to regulate heat, there are a few other emergency methods at the cook's disposal.

Raising or lowering the cooking grill is one. This can result in burned fingers and often does. Use a tool or glove to do this.

Throwing water on a fire cools it down in a hurry. Don't just dump a cup or can of water on the flames; all you'll succeed in doing is putting a portion of the fire out. Instead spray the coals via a hand-sprinkling. This cools them all down at once while preserving that necessary, even heat. Throwing water is often the only way to cool leaping yellow flames that result from fats dripping into the fire while you're broiling.

Dirt will also cool a fire, though this is the least desirable technique since it's smothering qualities are more or less permanent.

When wood has burned down to glowing coals, you have what is essentially homemade briquets. Coals or red-hot briquets are best to cook on.

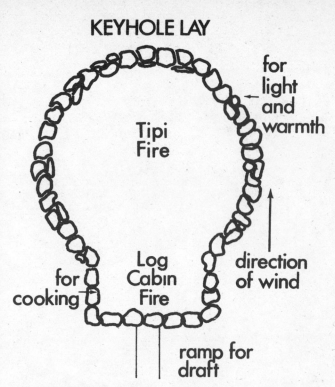

Keyhole Lay—A keyhole lay consists of a circle of rocks "mated" to a rock wall on the side from which the wind is blowing. A tipi fire is built in the round part of the keyhole; a log cabin fire, in the square part. In this way, light, heat and a constant supply of cooking coals with steady, uniform heat are all provided.

Support equipment for open-fire cooking begins with some sort of grill. In a pinch, you can arrange a triangle of rocks in the bed of a fire, but you're far better off with a criss-cross arrangement of steel rods. For car-camping and backyard barbecuing, I've found a grate that measures 18-inches wide by 30-inches long plenty big enough to hold food for six people. I also have discovered that it's wise to choose a grate with rods spaced no more than ½-inch apart. Several ashy steaks and burgers were the reasons why. A good source of these cooking grates is the shelf from an old oven or refrigerator, but always scorch these grills thoroughly before cooking food directly on them; they may contain oxides or coatings that will make your food taste bad or be out-and-out poisonous.

A bit more sophisticated arrangement is the grill designed specifically for the camper. The simplest and most fool-proof I've yet run across is a refrigerator-shelf-type grate with four folding legs that were sharpened at one end. To use it, you rammed the legs into the soil. This precludes a topple of supporting rocks or logs, and food landing in the fire.

Backpacking grates are a genre unto themselves, being extremely light and usually able to fold up into a tiny package. The most sensible one I've seen (and used) is a 14-inch by 5-inch quadrangular tube of hollow stainless steel that fits flat in the bottom of my pack. It weighs mere ounces, and easily holds the small pots and pans common to this form of camping.

Before leaving this subject, I feel honor-bound to point out two enemies of the campfire cook; *any* sort of stick-and-crotched-stick arrangement is out. They look nice in illustrations but they'll dump your food in the fire or dirt 80 percent of the time. Then too, they require green, hard-to-burn wood in their construction, and we've passed the point of frontier innocence where we can afford to kill living trees for a pastime.

The second abomination is Forest Service fire grates. These grates are too high for any kind of over-coal cooking and they're too low for a tipi fire. Draft control is difficult to achieve and, if they're fixed in place, adding wood in any sort of fire-efficient pattern is impossible without burning your hand. If they're hinged so they can be lifted up, you're in luck . . . sort of. Stand them on end and forget about them and build a keyhole lay in their bed.

If they're fixed, and it's permissible, build your cooking fire next to the provided grate. If not, build it on top of the grate. If you must build it inside the grate, try to raise the level upon which your coals will lie—but it will be a hassle.

I think a great deal of the flavors I know I'll enjoy as a result of cooking over a campfire. While building and using an efficient cooking fire isn't too difficult, it must be done right. The effort is worth it. After a little practice, you will find that a keyhole lay opens up a new world of outdoor sensory delights. With its flickering glow, soothing warmth and savory aroma, a campfire is ideal to bring friends closer and to transform common food into a banquet.

COOKING FOR SURVIVAL

Author Bradford Angier, expert on living in the wilderness and wild foods, cooks freshly caught trout on one of his "dry runs." He imagines his life depends on living off the land and sees how well he can get along. His knowledge is firsthand.

by BRADFORD ANGIER

ANIMAL FOOD WILL give you the most food value per pound. Anything that creeps, swims, crawls, walks, or flies is a possible source of food, although you should avoid toads. You've doubtless already eaten insects as contaminants of the flour, corn meal, rice, beans, fruit, and greens of your daily diet.

Ants, in fact, are excellent, particularly the large black variety that are to be found in rotten logs, as any bear will agree. If they are large enough, remove the head, the legs, and the thorax which is the middle of the three chief divisions of the body and which contains the heart, lungs, and esophagus. However, I've eaten fried ants whole, and they are fine. If you can find enough of the eggs, they're edible, too, although rather dryly bland. Termites are similarly eaten.

Some natives take advantage of the ants' formic acid by crushing them in water sweetened with berries or sap to make a sort of primitive lemonade.

In the same rotting log or stump you may be able to find another bears' delight, the white wood-burrowing larvae of beetles. Roast or boil these grubs.

Grasshoppers and locusts are regarded as delicacies in some parts of the world. Remove the hard wings and legs. Roast the remainder. It has a nutlike flavor. Cicadas and crickets are similarly eaten.

Should You Eat Your Shoes?

An animal's hide is as nourishing as a like quantity of its lean meat. Baking a trophy in its skin, although under some circumstances both convenient and savory, is for that reason something we should avoid when food is limited.

Rawhide is also rich in protein. The usual practice is to chew it raw in small bits until you tire of such mastication, then to swallow the slippery fragment, or to boil it. So cooked, it has even less flavor than roasted antlers in velvet and the look and feel of the boiled skin of a big fish.

The earlier Arctic explorers in particular tell of disputes as to whether or not leather, generally footwear or some other clothing such as gloves, should be eaten by the starving man. The answer is basic. If you are so located that you'll have to walk to safety, protection of the feet comes first.

If you are cold as well as hungry, you'll stay snugger wearing the rawhide than you could be offering it to your stomach in exchange for a scant bit of extra heat by metabolism. If the article is manufactured of commercially tanned leather, the solution will be even simpler. Such leather has little if any food merit.

Will You Have Yours Rare?

When rations are limited, all food should ordinarily either be eaten raw or cooked only enough to make it more palatable. The longer and hotter a food is cooked,

---

Bradford Angier has authored more than two dozen books, including Living Off the Country, Survival With Style, Feasting Free on Wild Edibles *and the new all-color* Field Guide to Edible Wild Plants. *He and his wife Vena reside at their home in Cambria, California but frequently return to the wilderness near Peace River, Hudson Hope where they built themselves a cabin.*

the greater are the losses of nutritive values. Even toasting bread diminishes this food's proteins and digestibility.

If you are living on meat alone, for example, overcooking will destroy the Vitamin C and make scurvy a possibility. Too, the overcooking of meat which is low in fat, like venison, makes the end result tough and stringy, besides wasting both flavor and nourishment.

Heart, liver, kidneys, tongue, brains, stomach lining or tripe, and even the eyes of all game can be used with the exception of the liver of the polar bear and of the ringed and bearded seals. These become so rich in Vitamin A at some times of the year that they are poisonous to both man and, incidentally, his dogs.

Don't overlook the marrow. The soft vascular tissue inside the large bones of an animal that was in good condition when secured is not equalled in caloric value by any other natural food. Too, it is the most delectable part of the animal. It is wasteful to roast such bones, as is often done, until they crumble. Crack them at the start, as with two clean stones. The less the marrow is then cooked, the more nutritious it will be.

If rations are meager, use as much of the blood as you can. Blood, which is closely similar to milk, is particularly rich in quickly absorbed vitamins and minerals. For example, you need iron. If you depend on eggs for this, it will take ten average-sized hen eggs to give you your daily requirements. Four tablespoons of blood will do the same thing.

One way to use blood is in broths and soups, enriched perhaps with wild onions and other free-for-the-eating vegetables. Under survival conditions, fresh blood can be secured and carried in a bag improvised from the entrails. Use it as soon as possible.

What About Ripe Meat?

Suppose you're starving and you happen upon the decomposing remains of a moose that has been killed by a fall into a canyon, for example, or by wolves or a grizzly? Don't some natives customarily eat meat that is so ripe that its odor is repugnant? In fact, don't many gourmets in our own country follow the same practice with their game birds? Where do you draw the line?

The most authoritative answer I found to this question was from a friend of the late Colonel Townsend Whelen who shot with him for ten years at a range in Washington, D.C., the Chief of the Meat Laboratory of the Agricultural Research Service of the U.S. Department of Agriculture, William L. Sulzbacher.

"While partially spoiled meat is not necessarily harmful, there are some precautions which should be borne clearly in mind," summed up Mr. Sulzbacher. "First of all, spoiled meat may harbour food-poisoning bacteria which could easily kill a man who was generally debilitated from starvation. Without going into detail, we can briefly state that the toxins of organisms like *Clostridium botulinum*, the causative agent of botulism, are quite stable and could easily resist any attempts to inactivate them which the wilderness dweller would have at his command. Secondly, there are some toxic chemicals developed in badly spoiled meat which would make our lost hunter very sick indeed.

"Another consideration is always temperatures and how the animal happened to die. Your example of the lost man finding a partially decomposed moose suggests an animal which may have died from some disease. Such a carcass is far less able to attain that 'age' or 'ripeness' and would be potentially more dangerous to eat than the carcass of an animal which had been shot, eviscerated, and hung. If I were sufficiently hungry, I would personally be willing to attempt to eat any carcass that had been slaughtered under more or less normal conditions.

"On the positive side," and this is all-important, "we are all familiar with the high degree of decomposition tolerated in meats by many aboriginal, and even civilized, people. If the temperature has been below 45° F., there is every likelihood that the better parts of your hypothetical moose—that is, any muscle which could be excised free of visibly decomposed meat—would be safe if thoroughly and briskly boiled for 30 minutes.

"Theoretically," advised this expert, "boiling for 30 minutes should inactivate most harmful toxins!"

This is, of course, at sea level. It is not true at high elevations where the boiling point is lower than, say 90° C.

The Spoiled Meat Problem

The general rule advocated to me by Dr. Sydney Anderson of the Museum of Natural History in New York, specializing in mammalogy and bacteriology, is to eat a little of the thus prepared meat, then to wait half an hour. If you don't feel any ill effects, you can safely dig in and eat to your heart's content.

Dr. Anderson indicates that virtually all malicious tox-

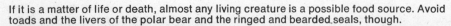
If it is a matter of life or death, almost any living creature is a possible food source. Avoid toads and the livers of the polar bear and the ringed and bearded seals, though.

Boiling is the most satisfactory way of cooking when you are subsisting on meat. It is more saving of fuel than other methods too. However, it is difficult at high altitudes.

ins et al will manifest themselves in less than a half-hour after ingestion.

The Most Satisfactory Way to Cook Meat

When you have large amounts of meat to cook or when you're subsisting on an all-meat diet, boiling is the most satisfactory way of cooking. You tire of the animal less quickly this way, and little of the nourishment is lost if you drink the broth. Too, boiling is more saving of fuel than other methods.

When meat is tough, boiling is the best way to prepare it for later broiling, roasting, or baking. It is difficult at high altitudes, however, and impractical at heights in excess of 12,000 feet.

Ideally, you'll have at least a large tin can for a receptacle. This can be made even more handy if you'll punch a couple of holes opposite each other just below the rim and loop a piece of light wire loosely through them. I've carried such cans with me for years whenever I'm in the bush, for the relaxation and refreshment of "boiling the kettle" at noon for tea.

Water can be boiled in vessels made of bark or leaves, but such containers burn above the water level unless they are kept moist or the fire held low. Half a green coconut or a section of bamboo, cut well above and just below a joint, can be used for boiling receptacles. These will not burn until after the water boils. Folded birch bark makes another container. Secure the sides with slivers of wood.

Indians used flammable receptacles, including baskets, for boiling by dropping hot stones into the liquid therein. A green stick bent back upon itself makes functional tongs. Water can be boiled in a scooped-out hole in clay, or in a hollowed log, by this method of dropping heated stones in it. Too, you can line a hole, scooped in the ground, with a bit of plastic or other waterproof material—or even the hide of the animal itself—and heat water this way.

Grilled Pheasant

A game bird such as a pheasant, trout or other fish, or something such as a rabbit can be cleaned and then impaled on a green hardwood stick. Or two sticks can be clamped over the meat and held together by a twisted root or vine. If, as with a rainbow trout, you are only going to cook one side at a time, an ordinary forked green stick will be sufficient.

Sear the meat first, thereby retaining more of the healthful juices, by thrusting it briefly into flames. Then cook it over a bed of seething coals, raking these to one side of the blaze if necessary. This way the meat will be cooked throughout without wasteful burning.

Planked Salmon

Salmon and other large fish can be opened, cleaned, and then pegged flat on preheated hardwood slabs with their skin against the wood. Remove the backbone if it is in the way. Turning the slab end for end occasionally, while it leans before a bed of glowing coals, will cook it throughout. As soon as the flesh flakes beneath a testing sliver, the fish is done and ready on its own hot plate.

Don't use softwood, or the resinous spruce or pine, as they will take away from the delicate taste of the fish. Too, when cooking calls for coals, burn one of the hardwoods such as the particularly sweet-smelling birch, as softwoods flame quickly to ashes and do not make lasting beds of embers.

Steamed Clams

Steaming can be accomplished without a container and is especially savory with foods, like clams and other shellfish, that require little cooking. Place your food in a pit lined with rocks that have been made sizzling hot in your campfire and covered ideally with live wet seaweed or, if you're not near the ocean, with wet green grass or damp green leaves. Put more seaweed, grass, or leaves over your victuals. Then force a stick down through the vegetation to the food pocket. Pack several inches of dirt over everything. Remove the stick and pour a small amount of water to the food through the remaining hole. Then block the hole.

Leave everything for four or five hours while you go about other tasks. For all its slowness, this method is delectable. All this can be accomplished most handily on a beach and is the basis of the ancient Indian clambakes.

Baked Rabbit

Small individual ovens can be made by covering the cleaned but not skinned rabbit, the cleaned but not plucked partridge, or the cleaned but unscaled fish with moist clay. Mix this clay with water to the consistency of stiff dough. Mold a sheet an inch thick. Then shape it around the food. Or if this is unhandy with what you have to work with, make a looser mixture with more water and dip and redip the food in it until it is satisfactorily encased.

Lay the moist article carefully in hot ashes over which a

Grilled pheasant will help you forget you are struggling for survival.

good fire is burning. An hour of such cooking readies a rabbit to my taste, to give you an idea for best satisfying your own palate. When you break away the brick, the hair will stay attached to it, leaving you a moist, clean, morsel with all the juices intact.

Baking in a Burrow

There's a handy way to make an oven when you're going to be camped in one place for any length of time. Start by pounding a sharpened stake, with about a four-inch diameter, straight down into a clay bank approximately a yard back from the edge.

Then some two feet down the side of the bank, far enough to make a rugged ceiling, scoop out the size oven you'd like. Dig as far back as the pole which you'll then withdraw to make the chimney. Harden the interior by smoothing it for several minutes with your wet hands. Then light a small fire inside to glaze it.

You can often find an old burrow to form the nucleus of such an oven. In any event, baking in it Indian-style is simple. Merely heat the oven by making a fire inside it. Rake out fire, embers, and ashes. Lay the food inside, perhaps on clean grass or leaves. Close both chimney and front holes. Then go about your usual activities. The food, which you can briefly check from time to time, will bake without any more attention.

Cooking in Ashes

This is a convenient way to prepare wild tubers. Just rake embers and ashes from a heated piece of ground. Lay the vegetables here. Cover them with ashes, then hot coals. Timing, as is the case with the majority of such cooking, is a matter of experimenting.

Breads can also be cooked cleanly in ashes after being rolled a bit more lavishly than usual in flour. When you realize that the white of hardwood ashes can be substituted part for part for baking soda, sodium bicarbonate, in making dough, this type of cooking may not appear to be so unusual.

Barbecued Caribou

When you have plenty of plump fresh meat, enough to make reasonable the sacrifice of a certain amount of nutrients in exchange for the lift of a barbecue, let a hardwood fire fall to coals in a pit. Then spread a grid of green hardwood poles over the mouth of the pit.

Lay on the chunks of meat, turning them over after the first few minutes to seal in as much of the juices as possible. These will be further protected if, instead of piercing the meat to turn it from time to time, you use sticks as tongs or spatula. The results will be more optimum if when flame curls up from the sputtering of fat, these are immediately dampened with a bit of water.

A couple of hours will generally do the job, although it's easy enough to cut into a slab of meat occasionally to make sure it does not become too done for your particular liking.

Parching

The Indians used to parch many of their grains and nuts. Just place the food in a metal container, or on a hot

Fish of any kind is nutritious and tasty. Roasted, baked or boiled, fish has saved many lives and lifted numerous spirits.

flat rock, and heat slowly until the seeds or such are thoroughly scorched.

Making Your Own Jerky

Cutting meat across the grain in quarter-inch strips, some six inches long and two inches thick, and drying it in the sun, wind, or smoke will produce the dry, hard, black, and incidentally sustaining and delectable jerky.

You can lay the strips of meat on a wooden grate and dry them until the meat is brittle. Use willow, alder, cottonwood, birch, or other hardwood for the fire, because the pitchy woods such as spruce and pine will blacken the meat and make it unpalatable. Never permit the heat to become great enough to cook the meat or to draw out the juices.

A teepee makes a good smokehouse when the flaps at the top are closed. Hang the meat high and build a slow, smouldering fire beneath it.

A quicker way of smoking meat is by digging a hole in the ground about three feet deep and a foot-and-one-half wide. Make a small fire at the bottom of the hole, and when it is burning well, add green fuel for smoke. Place an improvised wooden grate, to hold the meat, slightly more than two feet up from the bottom. Use poles, boughs, leaves, or similar handy material to cover the pit.

The Best Concentrated Food

The most nutritious of all concentrated foods is real pemmican, seldom obtainable commercially despite advertisements. Such true pemmican—by weight one-half well dried lean meat and one-half rendered fat—contains nearly every necessary food ingredient with the exception of Vitamin C. Eating a little fresh food, such as several rose hips daily, will supply the Vitamin C necessary to prevent scurvy. It takes five pounds of fresh lean meat to make one pound of jerky suitable for pemmican.

"To make pemmican you start with jerky and shred it by pounding," my friend and associate the late Colonel Townsend Whelen told me years ago. "Then take a lot of raw animal fat, cut it into small pieces about the size of walnuts, and dry these out in a pan over a slow fire, not letting the grease boil up.

"When the grease is all out of the lumps, discard these and pour the hot fat over the shredded jerky, mixing the two together until you have about the consistency of ordinary sausage. Then pack the pemmican in waterproof bags. The Indians used skin bags."

Baked rabbit, cooked in clay, requires no cooking utensils but much woodmanship.

how to PONASS a PIKE
(or a steelhead or a salmon or a snook)

This young angler's Indian father will prepare this pike according to his specialty—ponassing on green willow grills.

by THOMAS HARDIN

NO COUNTRIES on earth can claim so many species of great freshwater game fishes as the United States and Canada. There are so many, in fact, that some of the greatest are often overlooked or even considered as inferior. Consider just one example *Esox lucius*, the northern pike or jackfish.

Often it is not the fighting ability of the pike which is questioned; a big jack is a lot to handle on any kind of freshwater tackle. But since most game fish are also edible species, the pike seldom rates very high on anyone's list. In one well-known volume on fish cookery opened here before me is the following brief quotation: "Except in emergency, northern pike are seldom used by serious sportsmen. The meat is not tasty and it is infested with bones too tiny to be eliminated."

Well humbug, pure unadulterated humbug.

The northern may not exactly be as handsome a critter as, say, a fresh run salmon or a wild rainbow trout. It isn't a fish one associates with alcohol-clear and sparkling

---

Thomas Hardin takes fishing seriously. He has probably fought with more fish on the end of his line in the past five years than most men do in 20. He eats all the fish he catches and likes to help with the cooking too. His articles are usually seen in fishing and hunting annuals.

First step to ponassing is to catch the pike and the bigger the better.

streams where insects hatch on summer afternoons—and maybe this is the trouble. But unhandsome face and murky habitat notwithstanding, the pike of our evergreen north country is as delicious a food fish as any other that takes—no, that attacks—an angler's lure.

There remains that matter about the little Y-shaped bones, however. In small specimens they really are a nuisance, but small pike should be released to grow up anyway. In larger pike from seven or eight pounds and upward, it is possible to cope with the bones before cooking. And the best way of all to prepare a pike is to ponass it.

I have no idea about the origin or exact meaning of that word *ponass*. It isn't in any dictionary or cook book around our library and I've never even heard it used except in northern Saskatchewan and Manitoba where the pike fishing happens to be the very best. Probably it is Cree or Chippewyan and may mean nothing more than to cook—or to prepare as food. But it doesn't make too much difference.

More important is exactly how *does* an angler ponass his pike anyhow?

The first step obviously is to catch it and fortunately that is a very pleasant assignment. The best advice is to travel north, specifically to Manitoba, and check in at one of the fine fishing camps on Gods, Island, Kississing, Reed, Cedar, Cross or Nuelton lakes. All of these produce top candidates for the largest pike listed each year on Manitoba's Master Angler's List which commemorates all northerns taken in that province which weigh more than 18 pounds. A copy of the list (it also records top fish of all other species) can be obtained free from Wilf Organ, Director, Department of Tourism, 801–491 Portage Ave., Winnipeg, Manitoba, Canada R3B 2E7. Some of these blue ribbon pike waters (such as Reed, Cross and Cedar) can be reached by road; all the rest are accessible only by bush plane across the unbroken northern wilderness.

Pike fishing is a very exciting business in suitable waters because there are few dull moments. Locate a shallow bay fringed with lilies and smartweed, perhaps where a river flows into a large lake, and you have found a potential pike paradise. Almost any such location will contain some jacks—small to medium size fish at least—but the wise fisherman will keep exploring until he finds a bonanza bay where the fish run bigger. In any given spot, all pike tend to be of similar average size. So search for quality.

There are other pike hotspots, harder to find. Look especially for weedbeds which indicate shallow places far out in the center of a large lake; these are spots other fishermen hopefully will have overlooked. Cast first along the edges of the weeds—and then right into the center of the densest parts. Really big jumbos lurk in such vegetation which may become as thick as sauerkraut in summertime.

The outfit I prefer for big pike is a stiff, 5½-foot plug casting rod with a standard, revolving, plug casting reel filled with 18-pound-test monofilament. The stiff rod with backbone is necessary to set the hooks solidly into a hard mouth full of sharp, needle-like teeth. Even such heavy line can soon wear thin when casting very long in the salad. Large metal spoons, bucktail spinners and a variety of plugs will make suckers of pike and my tackle box always includes an assortment of such weedless spoons as the Arbogast Hawaiian Wiggler. There are times when it will "reach" pike where other lures only foul up.

However this is not an essay on how to catch pike. My purpose is simply to review a few basics necessary to catch the main ingredient, and one large enough, for ponassing. That is easiest done very early in the season (June to mid-July in Manitoba) and very late (from mid-September onward until freeze-up). Pike fishing often requires warm clothes as well as sturdy and reliable tackle. I always carry foul weather gear and insect repellent.

Having done a good bit of pike fishing which covered much sub-Arctic geography, I've met a number of skilled pike ponassers—all Indians—each of whom ponassed in his own inimitable way. But basically the method is the same. Perhaps the best ponasser was Edgar Redhead, who with his brother Byron was then guiding on Red Sucker Rapids on Gods River. We weren't fishing for northerns

A good place to find big pike is in the Reed Lake region of Manitoba's Grass River Provincial Park.

A big jack is a lot to handle.

at all (actually I was spin casting for eastern brook trout) when my small spoon fell into a deep backwater and immediately I felt a strong strike.

For a few moments I felt I'd hooked the biggest brookie in Canada until the fish surged to the top, where it was visible, and then raced downstream. "Big jack," Edgar said and then sat down to watch the contest. Somehow we got the fish out flopping onto a solid granite bank, without busting up any tackle. It weighed about 12 pounds, maybe a little more.

"That make us fine lunch," my unimpressed guide commented, as usual using as few words as possible.

First Edgar lopped off the head and tail of the pike. Then holding the body upright, he cut all the way down the back (*not* down the belly) just on one side of the backbone and neatly severing the ribs. That opened up the fish and after removing the entrails he was left with one single slab of meat. From that slab, with the point of his sharp filleting knife, he cut away as many of the Y-shaped bones as he could find.

Next in a rock crevasse, the guide built a fire of dead willow and alder. While that burned down, he selected several stout green willow sticks and formed these into an A-shaped frame with several cross pieces, all being lashed together in place with strips of green willow bark. The frame completed, Edgar tied (also with green bark strips) the pike flat onto the frame. Finally he rubbed salt into the fish and then tilted the frame over the smoldering fire so that it could be exposed both to the low heat and smoke.

Not exactly handsome, the pike is delicious.

To ponass the pike, Indian guide first dresses the fish. He cuts down one side of the backbone, producing one slab of meat.

"You go away fish for 'bout hour," he advised, "while I watch lunch."

During that hour I noticed that Edgar frequently turned the pike or adjusted the frame so as not to cook too quickly. Frequently he added fresh willow to keep the fire smoldering rather than burning brightly. When it became too hot, he added a handful of green leaves. Some of the Y-shaped bones which had been missed when dressing, now became blackened and charred from the heat; this made them easy to pick out and discard with the point of the knife. All the while the sweetly fragrant willow smoke curled around the pike, giving the dry, pure white, flaky meat a thin, crisp, brown, salty crust.

It is true enough that there beside Gods River I had worked up a positively ravenous appetite. I probably could have eaten one of the gulls, half cooked, which came to watch our feast and fight over the few tidbits which were left. But still that ponassed pike made an extraordinary meal; and all the ponassed pike ever since have been just as memorable.

Some other guides I have met preferred to carry along a small metal grid (instead of making a willow frame) for the ponassing. A few have brushed the fish with bacon drippings or other fat during the cooking. One other Manitoba guide, Charlie Macpherson, a leathery old Cree, used an herb powder mixture which he either couldn't or wouldn't identify for me. To tell the truth, it tasted something like Lawry's or some other seasoning salt available in grocery stores. Maybe he bought his at the nearest Hudson Bay post, but no matter, the finished product was delicious.

Obviously *any* large fish from shovelhead cat to channel bass caught almost anywhere can be ponassed. By sub-

The guide then spreads the fish on green willow frame, lashed together with strips of green willow bark.

The fish is then cooked very slowly over low smoky fire.

Catching the dinner can be plenty lively because the northern is a great game species.

Pike fishing is an exciting business with few dull moments.

Any fish can also be ponassed, as here on grill, with smoke curling upward to flavor meat.

stituting such hardwoods as green hickory, ash, apple or apricot branches, an even more attractive flavor might be smoked into the meat. The possibilities are without limits. You could ponass a fish wherever you catch it, in a forest camp somewhere, on an ocean beach or in the barbecue pit of your own backyard.

But I'll take mine far away in the air conditioned northwoods where loons laugh on damp spring mornings and the only other angler a man is likely to encounter is an osprey or an otter. Paddle quitely to a pike bay via canoe and you may meet a moose, flank deep in the rum-colored water, feeding on the same succulent vegetation in which giant pike are hiding. Pike fishing is great sport any way you view it; it is worth traveling a far piece to enjoy.

And so, I submit, is a properly ponassed pike.

zapping the SPOILERS

by CHARLES J. FARMER

Kathy Farmer demonstrates what can happen when cooler is neglected.

JIM AND BETTY Francis had driven a long way to reach Puerto Peñasco. But the end was in sight now and they both looked forward to dipping their toes in the fish laden Sea of Cortez. They had loaded up with groceries and supplies back in Tucson. Betty figured they had enough food to last ten days. She had chosen her meals carefully from a list that she and Jim had worked up. The couple had been camping regularly since they were married 15 years ago. They were sticklers for good menu planning and good food. Jim always made a point of telling me that the reason he liked camping so much was because food tasted so good outdoors. That was only half the reason though. He was one of the best salt water surf fishermen I knew. The triggerfish and cabrillas off Peñasco helped his appetite immensely.

For three days, Jim and Betty soaked in good Mexican fishing and plenty of sunshine. On the fourth day, Betty unhinged the lid of one of three camp coolers and a sickening aroma drifted into her nostrils. She called for help.

Shrimp, cabrilla fillets and lusty cheese toastadas topped with home-grown avocados had been remarkably delicious those first few days. Back in February, in their hometown of Dayton, the Francis's had craved the zest of fresh fish flanks and zippy Mexican morsels. They feasted on fresh things from the sea and land. Their stomachs bubbled with the joy of sweet, plump limes and tomatoes so fat and ripe they nearly exploded with the first eager bite. But with the exception of the egg, cheese, fruit and drink cooler, Jim and Betty had let their most expensive food investments run hot . . . and sour.

33

A good ice cooker (food chest) is the nucleus of good camp eating.

Shade canopy for cooler doubles ice life and discourages spoilage.

Frequent lid opening melts ice fast.

Friends of theirs from Phoenix had urged them to purchase two additional 28-quart, heavy-duty coolers for their seven-day Mexican campout. They purchased the extra coolers—a wise investment considering the March heat south of the border and the scarcity of ice. In addition to the large, 44-quart cooler they already had, one cooler could be used to store ice and the other for non-meat perishables. The plan worked out well . . . until they had underestimated the power of the Mexican sun, and failed to check their cooler every day.

The T-bone steaks that Betty planned for the fourth day were tainted. Chicken legs, hamburger and a two-pound package of sliced ham also smelled sour. She figured that some of the meat could have been cooked well and eaten. But in Mexico, she and Jim decided not to take any chances.

The water from the melted ice was hot to Jim's touch. "No wonder that stuff spoiled so fast," he sighed. "Just as I was starting to crave steak again," he added. "I sure thought this cooler would hold ice better than that."

All of the coolers that Jim and Betty owned were good, popular brand models . . . the best on the market. What they did not realize was that the temperature hovered in the mid-90s their first three days in Mexico. They had

Cooler should be located in handy place in shade.

failed to provide a shade screen for the coolers. Ironically, Betty was provided with a warning jolt at noon the second day out. Wearing shorts, she sat on one of the coolers and immediately let out a sharp "Ouch." "Boy, that metal is hot!" Jim, selecting some feather jigs from his tackle box, was intent on getting down to the water where some gulls were pouncing on bait fish. He scarcely heard Betty yell.

Good camp coolers are wise investments for good eating in the outdoors. There are, however, quite a few considerations to think of when purchasing an ice chest. The best overall suggestion, is to consider your personal needs such as the size of your family; hot-warm-or-cool weather camping; and how much use you expect to give a cooler.

Types of Ice Coolers

Coolers range from the styrofoam containers to welded steel boxes with long life spans. Padded canvas sacks and plastic insulated material are also shaped into food and beverage coolers. I have seen simple coolers in hunting and fishing camps made from wood-framed wire mesh. These are constructed and hung in spots that are free (or nearly so) from long periods of sunlight. They work fairly well in cool and cold climates and for specific needs.

Coolers should be constructed to keep perishables chilled. The box should also be sturdy enough to endure many camp outings; built so it does not leak—and sealed in such a way that it protects food from dirt and insects and at the same time insulates against heat and cold. For winter camping there are times when a good cooler keeps food from freezing. Most of us, however, look for boxes that "keep" ice for a long time.

The above qualifications of a good camp cooler eliminate some types of coolers almost immediately. The styrofoam cooler, a fine insulator and good for weekend picnics, is not sturdy enough for most camping needs. One family I know went through 10 styrofoam chests in a single summer. They claimed they were cheap enough so it did not matter if they only lasted a short time. At $2.98 a crack, though, that same family could have invested in a 28-quart, metal cooler that would last at least 10 years.

Canvas coolers, insulated plastic bags and other contraptions may be fine for limited purposes, but not for modern, family camping and outdoor cooking. I compare them to tents without floors and leaky air mattresses. They are outdated. Better equipment has replaced them.

While the wood-framed, wire mesh cooler might serve a

good purpose in the remote hunting camp, it is strictly a "make the best of what you have" affair, and not really suited to the mobile camper and outdoor chef.

In my opinion the best camp coolers on the market today are steel cased and insulated with polyurethane foam. Heavy duty plastic interiors are easy to clean and should not leak. Some interiors resist food stains and clean up easily. There will be some spilling inside the cooler, so this is a practical feature to look for. The lining of the cooler should be so molded in the corners that food or liquid is not trapped in sharp corners and can be easily wiped clean.

Just as it is important to make sure your refrigerator at home closes with a positive, cold-saving seal, it is vital that a camp cooler have a well designed, yet easy to open and close latch. In selecting a cooler, work the latch—opening and closing the lid—several times. Make sure the seal formed between the lid and upper lip of the box is tight and even. A simple test of latch and seal effectiveness is to put your lips to the seal and try to suck in air. If you can't get any, with the latch in the closed position, the seal is a good one. Test all sides of the box and don't worry about who's looking. A particular cooler can be the best constructed, but fall short at the seal and latch.

Size and Weight of Cooler

The bigger the better is not always the best adage, especially when choosing an ice chest for your needs. For example, a 60-quart cooler may provide all the cooling room a camper needs. When that cooler is loaded to the lid with ice and food however, weight becomes a factor. I put one such cooler on the scales and decided that most campers would balk at loading and unloading 50 pounds of insulator to and from the camp site. At least I would. Items tend to get lost in a cooler that big or bigger. And I feel two or three smaller coolers are better for most needs than one super large one.

I'll never forget my introduction to camping about 15 years ago. My mother had just packed a 20-quart styrofoam cooler to the hilt. This model had the popular, stiff wire handle positioned at either end of the box with steel grommets. Dad, eager to load the car for a weekend camping trip, bent slightly at the knees . . . grabbed the handle like a weight lifter and thud. About a foot off the ground, the grommets and the wire handle had ripped through the styrofoam. The cooler collapsed on the concrete . . . apples rolled down the street and a two-pound jar of homemade strawberry preserves burst with a mushy thud all over the fried chicken and fresh picked tomatoes. Dad never used a styrofoam cooler again. After a short but loud delay (to the sporting goods store), we finally got underway.

Some super large coolers have limited uses like feeding little league baseball teams. But for the camper, one, two or three 20- to 30-quart coolers are the handiest for outdoor cooks. Loaded with a ten pound *block* of ice, the cooler yields quick, thorough chilling and with a normal load of food will weigh around 25 or 30 pounds (much easier to load and move around in the family station wagon.)

How to Pack the Camp Coolers

For at least 10 years, I have packed all perishables into one, 28-quart cooler and got along just fine. With the addition of a family, and more and more outdoor trips under our wheels, the addition of a second 28-quart cooler made things a bit more convenient. But most of you will probably stick to one cooler and for all reasonable camping excursions, that is all you need.

To a 20- to 30-quart chest, I add a 10-pound block of ice (the kind sealed in a plastic bag that lives most commonly in vending machines). I have yet to do an experiment,

Insulator, such as Space Blanket, can cut down sun's direct heat.

and don't know of anyone else who has performed one, on whether ice melts faster with or without the plastic bag. Usually, I leave the block enclosed in the bag and place it flat in the middle of the bottom cooler compartment. On all sides of the ice, I position beer or pop cans so the ice stays in the middle of the cooler. Early in the trip, this helps to distribute the cold more evenly around the box. As I need cold drinks, I replace them with extra warm ones . . . in a way so that the ice continues to be held in the center. As the food supply is used up, and the drinks too, this trick is not as important as when the box is loaded. But it helps.

All can goods are loaded around or on top of the ice as are the rest of the heavy, unbreakable foods and containers. Lighter items, meats and fragile foods like tomatoes and grapes, for instance, are packed near the top so they won't get squashed if there is a shift in weight inside the cooler.

In the tray (and a tray is helpful in one-cooler camping situations) place packaged meats, butter and all foods that you want to be handy. Many times, when traveling and camping, my wife Kathy will make sandwiches in the morning and store them in the tray section of the cooler. When we eat the sandwiches are fresh and in one piece.

Meats and other perishibles should be well packaged and placed on top.

Block ice will last as long as a week under average conditions.

The reason for not placing meats in the cooler's midsection or bottom is that they could become ruined or soggy in the chest's melt water. Or they can drip over other food and beverage items causing a real mess. A properly insulated cooler, with a good seal and a large chunk of ice, will chill the foods in the tray compartment almost as well as those near the bottom.

One of the best reasons for owning two coolers is that one can be used for beverages. From experience, I have found the drink cooler is opened twice as often as the food chest. The ice melts faster in the beverage chest. When the kids are along especially, ice and cold can be conserved to a significantly greater degree when there is a separate chest for soda pop. There is less tendency then for meat and food to spoil.

An extra ice chest is great for side trips when the main cooler stays back at camp. It is also ideal for boat use when it can be packed along and used for cold drinks, sandwiches and freshly caught fish.

Ice

You will have a choice of crushed, cubed or block ice at a vending machine, supermarket or ice house. Block ice is definitely best for the camp cooler as it lasts longer. Crushed ice is the worst you can buy and cube will do in a pinch if block is not available.

If you have a large enough freezer at home, you can freeze your own ice in one or two-quart cardboard milk containers. The container is merely a mold. Cut it away when the ice is solid. If you have extra ice . . . and an extra chest, store it in the beverage container and use it in the food box as needed. The average price for a 10-pound block of ice is 75 cents. Under normal conditions, 70- to 80-degree temperatures, a block of this size will last me about four days. I have had a block of ice nearly disappear in one day (Lake Obregon bass fishing in Mexico at 124 degrees) and in Wyoming during 40-degree stretches of spring and fall camping, several blocks have lasted as long as a full week. You can increase the efficiency and longevity of your ice supply by following a few tips.

Adding Life to Cooler Ice

Many camping situations provide enough natural shade that strategic positioning of the cooler can extend ice life. Unfortunately "spot" shade may shift as the sun arcs in the sky and good, shady spots may not be the most convenient

Cooler also acts as insulator against freezing foods.

Foods kept fresh in cooler insure good nutrition for outdoor sports.

Space Blanket is good insulator for cooler canopy and can add ice life.

for the camp cook. Moving the cooler or coolers to and from the shade gets tiresome . . . especially when they are heavy. So tips for longer ice life can apply to either wooded areas or those prairie, desert or beach areas that may be devoid of natural shade.

For the purpose of providing cooler shade where it is handy I have devised a small, lightweight nylon tarp with grommets that provides enough room and shade for three large coolers and several jugs of water. Four, thin metal stakes, long enough to hold the tarp securely in sand, yet stout enough to push or hammer into dry, hard ground, hold the tarp approximately a foot above the highest cooler. Even in the hottest weather, with the sun beating down, the shaded air space between the cooler lid and the tarp is a good enough insulator that ice life can be extended as much as three days as compared to coolers unshielded by the tarp.

This may seem insignificant until a camper craves a very cold drink, or a crisp, cool salad would boost morale. The novice camper, in fact, might not understand this tender,

Coolers come in all shapes and sizes.

loving care of ice—at first. But a trip cut short because the ice has run out, or a long drive in search of ice will soon illustrate ice mania in a very short time.

The sun tarp adds efficiency and ice life to any cooler. It can prevent food spoilage. The tarp has been ignored or lightly regarded in most camping articles, yet for the small space it takes up (about three feet long and barely three inches wide when rolled up like a flag), and the cost of about two dollars for tarp, grommets and rope, it is a valuable commodity under the sun.

A Space Blanket makes an excellent cooler tarp when an air space is provided. And I have also found that the same Blanket, when folded to the size of the cooler's opening and laid on top before the lid is closed, also adds ice life.

One area that especially drains the size of a block of ice is the car. Ordinarily when the vehicle is moving, or the air conditioner on, the outside of the cooler remains cool. But it just takes one or two hours with the windows closed, and the cooler exposed to the sun through the car windows, to cut an ice block in half.

One suggestion is to drape a nylon tarp (or blanket) loosely over the top of the cooler and crack the windows a half inch or so. This will cut down ice melt and possibly food spoilage.

Here are some other basic tips for cooler use. Drain coolers frequently. Water in the bottom adds to weight and might ruin foods that happen to fall to the bottom. If you keep the cooler clean inside, there will be less chance of food odors. Plastic bags can keep individual fruits, vegetables and meats in order—clean and fresh. In case they do find their way to the bottom, the bags will protect them. And most of all, avoid excessive opening and closing of the cooler. Plan what you need from the cooler and limit the times when the lid is up.

I never realized how precious ice could be until I started camping regularly. Now I pamper those 10-pound blockheads.

THE AWESOME, CLAWSOME, DELICIOUS CRAWDAD

The crawdad. So ugly to view; so delicious to eat.

by HELEN "TIGER" MARTIN

TO A DEDICATED ANGLER, the crawfish can be one of two extremes . . . either a choice bait with which to tempt a trophy-sized bass, channel cat, or other gamefish prize; or, if the crawdad is not purposely impaled upon a hook, it is often a "dad blamed" bait stealer which greedily gobbles worms, nightcrawlers and minnows. Fishermen either love the crawdad, or they cuss him.

To a gourmet cook, however, the lowly common crawfish is a taste treat that is perhaps better known by the glorious name of *des ecrevisse*. He's a tasty critter that can be served up in a variety of toothsome ways. Easy to catch, simple to prepare, and sumptuous when served, the crawfish can add hours of fun and enjoyment to a family outing.

Finding crawdads is a simple task. With over 100 varieties of the critters creeping and crawling throughout the United States, you will find them in almost any type of

---

Helen Martin complements her husband Jim, field editor for Outdoor Life Magazine, *with outdoor writing/photography. Known to her friends as Tiger, she and her family literally live outdoors in northern California.*

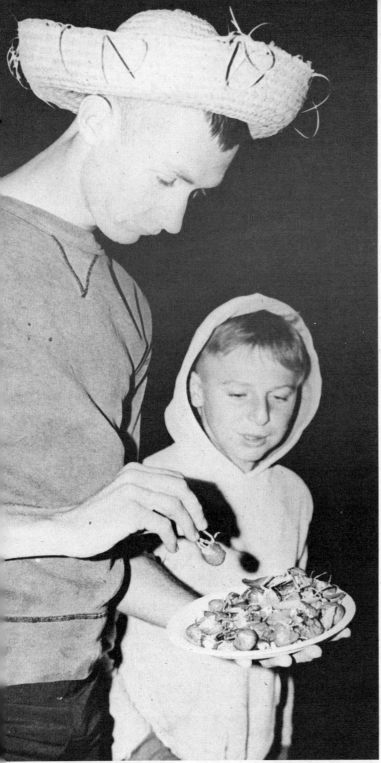
Crawdads taste extra good when eaten right at the spot.

water from the brackish Southern bayous to crystal high mountain lakes. If you haven't already pinpointed a likely crawdad hole, an inquiry at a local bait or tackle shop should produce several leads.

That familiar folk song about getting a line and a pole and heading for a crawdad hole is as applicable today as it was when originally composed. A cane pole and a short length of string, coupled with a chunk of raw meat is all you need to start in business. You don't even need a hook ... just fasten the meat to the end of the line. Crawdads possess voracious appetites, and will readily accept almost any type of bait that is dangled in front of them.

The catching technique is elementary. Just drop your baited line in the water close to a submerged log, rocky shelf or any other spot where a crayfish can find concealment. If a crawdad is present, he'll soon come creeping out to investigate. He'll first latch on to your offering with his large claws, after which he will start to eat. Once the crawdad is busy chomping, you can slowly lift the pole to bring him towards the surface. He'll probably do a bit of back flipper work in an effort to carry the bait back towards the bottom, but he will seldom let go unless you lift him from the water.

My husband and I often catch crawdads as a team, with one person working the line and a second wielding a long-handled net. Once the mudbug is lifted from the water, the net is placed below him. One netter can usually keep up with two or three fishermen, and the scene is always lively.

The lazy man's way of catching crawfish is to set out baited traps. This can be highly productive, but it is certainly not as much fun as the line and pole method.

During the summer months we sometimes go after crawdads at night by searching for them with flashlights while wading in the shallows. Crawfish leave their hiding places after dark and crawl around in search of food. You can easily pick them up with the beam of a flashlight. Then it's a quick grab and you have meat for the pot, which is already boiling on the shore. A tip to keep in mind is that crawdads swim backwards when frightened, so be prepared for a rear action retreat when you make your grab. A small minnow net can be a big help in cutting off such escapes.

My husband, Jim, and our ten-year-old son enjoy craw-dadding while skin diving. The trick is to turn over rocks and logs on a lake bottom where the critters are hiding. Once exposed, the crawfish stands up on his legs ready to fight. By wearing cotton gloves for the grabbing, both Jims manage to score quite well picking them up.

Fixing crawdads for the table is almost as easy as the catching. Cotton gloves come in handy here, too, for those somewhat frightening front pinchers are always a threat. Awesome and clawsome, that's the crawdad.

Since the sweet meat section of the tail is the only edible portion of the crawdad (except for an exceptionally large claw), we like to remove this part and discard the rest before doing any cooking. The result is more meat with which to work, and no foamy kettle of gunk such as occurs when the crawfish are boiled whole. So step No. 1 is a quick snap to remove the tail. The rest of the body is then buried in our mulch pit.

It's also far easier to clean the tails while they are still raw. Here's the no-strain way of so doing.

Notice that each tail has three sections at the end. Take the center flange between your thumb and forefinger, make a half twist, then pull. This will devein the gut string to leave the meat ready for the pot.

Boiling is the easiest way to cook a mess of crawfish. I use a large pot filled with water, salt and red-hot peppers, although for variety I sometimes employ a ready made spice bag especially concocted for shrimp boils. Crawdads should not be over cooked. From five to seven minutes, until they turn bright red, is about right. Cool, then peel and eat either plain or with a sauce. If you have the will-power to hold off the munching until you can peel up a batch, they can be served with a seafood sauce as a cocktail.

To many families, the simple boiling process represents the only way to fix crawfish. I'll not argue this claim. Yet for cooks who enjoy experimenting, *des ecrevisse* offers a fertile field for culinary practice.

Diving for crawdads is a novel summertime sport.

Crawdads can be utilized much the same as shrimp. Here's a family favorite.

CRAWDAD SCAMPI

Plan to use from 12 to 18 crawdads per serving, depending upon the size and the family appetites. Separate tail from body, devein tails, then peel. Arrange on broiling rack, then brush with melted butter. Prepare sauce from the following ingredients.

    ½ pound butter or margarine
    1 large clove garlic, minced or pressed
    4 tablespoons chopped parsley
    2 teaspoons fresh lemon juice
    ¼ teaspoon salt
    ¼ teaspoon prepared mustard
    ½ cup dry white wine

Blend the above ingredients, then cook in a heavy skillet for 5 minutes. While sauce is simmering, place crawdads under broiler for 5 minutes. When crawdads are cooked, remove to shallow serving dish and cover with above sauce, which has been strained. Serve with rice.

Crawdad Bisque is a delicious luncheon soup that is easy to prepare.

CRAWDAD BISQUE

Devein, then boil crawdads. Peel enough tails to equal one cup.

Blend the following ingredients in a three-quart saucepan.

    1 can tomato soup
    1 can bouillon
    1½ cups extra rich milk

Bring liquid ingredients to a slow simmer then add the crawdads, plus ½-cup chopped ripe olives. Cook for one minute more to make sure the crawdads and olives are heated through, then serve with chopped chives.

A crawdad Louis (or salad) is another summertime favorite.

CRAWDAD LOUIS

Prepare a bed of crisp salad greens. Decorate the edge with tomato wedges and slices of hard boiled egg. Pile chilled, boiled crawdads in the center, then top with a regular Louis sauce such as the following.

    1 cup mayonnaise
    ½ cup chili sauce
    2 tablespoons lemon juice
    1 tablespoon Worcestershire sauce
      dash Tobasco sauce
    1 tablespoon minced chives.

Louisiana is famous for its Cajun Creole cookery—and rightly so. Although many recipes are as authentic as word of mouth can make them . . . and equally delicious . . . some recipes have been copied and saved for posterity. Jambalaya is one of the most famous and is as exotic tasting as it sounds. I don't recall the derivation of the word "Jambalaya," but it might well mean "all jumbled and cooked together."

CRAWFISH JAMBALAYA

    1½ cups cubed ham
    4 cups crawdad tails (uncooked but peeled)
    2 tablespoons olive oil
    2 tablespoons butter
    2 large onions
    3 cloves garlic
    3 large tomatoes (peeled and chopped)
    1 bell pepper (finely chopped)
    1 cup uncooked long grain rice
    1 quart consommé
    ½ cup red table wine
    ½ cup sherry wine
    salt, pepper and a bay leaf

Coat bottom of Dutch oven with olive oil. Heat, then add ham and raw crawfish. Sauté lightly. Add butter, onions, minced garlic, rice and seasonings. Continue to sauté until rice turns golden brown. Bring consommé to a boil in a separate saucepan, then combine with ingredients in Dutch oven. Add tomatoes and pepper and seasonings. Mix, then bring to a boil. Reduce heat and allow to simmer until rice is cooked (approximately 30 minutes). Add wines and simmer for 10 minutes more. Serve in bowls.

Crawdadding time is beach party time.

Basically the same ingredients used for Jambalaya can be blended for another old-time favorite called:

CRAWFISH PIE

 2 cups uncooked crawdad tails
 2 cups cooked long-grain rice
 1 can condensed cream of mushroom soup
 1 cup water
 ⅓ cup finely chopped celery
 2 egg yolks (hardboiled and chopped fine)
 ½ cup buttered bread crumbs
   salt, pepper, paprika

Combine cooked rice, crawdad tails, soup, water and celery in a bowl. Salt and pepper to taste. Spread in a greased casserole dish. Sprinkle surface with egg yolk and top with buttered crumbs. Season with paprika, then allow to bake uncovered in a 350 degree oven for 30 minutes.

Crawdad Thermidor is a popular dish for families who do not relish the more spicy dishes described above.

CRAWDAD THERMIDOR

 2 cups crawdad tails (cooked)
 2 tablespoons butter or margarine
 2 tablespoons finely chopped onion
 1 4-ounce can sliced mushrooms
 2 tablespoons flour
 ½ cup extra rich milk
 ½ cup chicken stock or broth
 ½ teaspoon Worcestershire sauce
 1 egg yolk (uncooked)
 2 tablespoons cooking sherry
   salt and pepper to taste

Melt butter in a cast iron skillet; add onions and sauté until tender. Blend in flour and seasonings, stirring constantly. Using a French whisk, slowly add milk, chicken stock and Worcestershire sauce. Continue beating over low heat until mixture comes to a boil. Add egg yolk, sherry, crawdad tails and mushrooms. Pour mixture into a well buttered casserole dish; top with buttered crumbs; and allow to bake at 400 degrees for 15 minutes.

Catching crawdads in the old fashioned way with line and pole.

Another "quiet tasting" dish is Crawdad Newburg.

CRAWDAD NEWBURG

Prepare two cups of medium white sauce. Rapidly beat in two egg yolks. Add two tablespoons cooking sherry. Stir in two cups deveined cooked crawdad tails. Serve hot over rice, noodles or hot biscuits.

It's easy to see how crawdads can be substituted for shrimp in many ways to add an exquisite gourmet touch to menu planning. A little experimenting with your favorite sea food recipes can also be rewarding. Yet even good things can be overdone when served in large doses. If you find that the crawdad grabbers in your family are returning home with more than you can put to good use immediately, the surplus can be frozen.

To save crawfish for later use, twist off the tails, devein and place them (uncooked) in water filled milk cartons for freezing. When the miseries of the extended winter months seem to overtake me, I merely remove a carton from the freezer and fix a spicy Creole dish that's guaranteed to banish my chill.

Nighttime crawdadding can be productive. Crawdads are spotted in the flashlight beam and grabbed up before they have a chance to go in hiding.

by MIKE MICHAELSON

Mike Michaelson is the editor of Canoe *magazine and author of a bimonthly column called "Canoeside Cookery." He is the co-author of a comprehensive consumer guide to canoeing published by Henry Regnery Company. With his English accent, wife Ina and two children Glynis and David, Mike explores the Great Lakes and Midwest.*

SOME 300 YEARS ago the legendary French Canadian voyageurs joined the Indians on the great water routes of North America as the earliest practitioners of canoeside cookery. These short, stocky men with overdeveloped chests and atrophied legs (with inboard canoe space at a premium, maximum height for a voyageur was about 5'6") paddled 18 hours a day with or against the current, travelled an average of 30 miles a day and existed on a monotonous diet of stew and pemmican, the latter a frontiersman's version of the spaceage energy bar concocted from dried buffalo and grease. The stew, usually the staple fare for breakfast and evening meals, was a thick, spoon-standing mixture of beans, bacon and bread.

Latter-day canoeists seldom travel such prodigious distances in a single day and usually create a more varied and appealing diet. Nonetheless, the corollary is not altogether inappropriate. Today's concentrated foods provide good

CANOE

A canoeing family can plan vacations where portages are avoided. Then the canoe kitchen can be equipped with all the necessities and a few luxuries. My wife Ina bastes steaks after a day on the river.

nutrition while eliminating weight, bulk and problems of spoilage—just the characteristics that made pemmican the choice of early paddlers. And certainly beans, bacon and bread remain campside favorites while stew—along with chowder, soups and other one-pot meals—are practical for the canoe traveller.

Beans, of every stripe, are a good source of protein as well as being relatively inexpensive and easy to tote and prepare. Baked beans are a perennially popular choice of outdoor chefs, perhaps because they evoke memories of childhood days at camp when they inevitably were teamed with chopped frankfurters. Nonetheless, the plebian bean has numbered among its admirers such eminents as the late Presidents Kennedy and Eisenhower, both of whom introduced their favorite recipe for baked beans into the White House menu.

John F. Kennedy preferred the classic Boston-style dish with Worcestershire sauce and ketchup added to the traditional ingredients of navy beans, onion, salt pork, dry mustard and sugar or molasses. Dwight D. Eisenhower liked his baked beans served Midwestern style with heavy dark molasses, tarragon, vinegar and pepper added to the basic ingredients.

While Boston did much to popularize the baked bean, these sturdy New Englanders borrowed the idea from those original North American canoeists, the Indians. In the early 17th century the Pilgrims observed that their Indian neighbors softened beans by soaking them and then baked them overnight over hot stones—mixed in a clay pot with deer fat and onion.

Modern canoeside chefs can follow this tradition, substituting, for convenience sake, canned baked beans as a base to eliminate the traditional overnight soaking. The following recipe, courtesy of *Camper's Catalog,* can be

KITCHEN

Our daughter Glynis and son David enjoy cooking outdoors and doing kitchen chores. Somehow "roughing it" works miracles. What was distasteful at home suddenly becomes a pleasure.

The tantalizing aroma of steaks and hotdogs broiling over coals brings the family together, mouths watering, waiting for the feast to begin.

cooked over the coals or prepared beforehand to be reheated at camp.

KETTLE BAKED BEANS

3 1-lb. cans baked beans
⅓-cup molasses
2 tbs. prepared mustard
1 tbs. lemon juice
½-tsp. black pepper
2 onions, chopped
1 clove garlic, crushed
½-cup cooked bacon, crumbled
¼-cup strong black coffee
¼-cup rum

Mix ingredients and bake at 350 deg. F. for one hour or over coals for 1½ hours. Leftovers can be reheated in the same manner. Makes 6 to 8 servings.

When it comes to sophisticated outdoor cooking equipment, the canoe cruiser who elects not to include grueling portages in his trip itinerary has a considerable advantage over his backpacking outdoor compeer or the canoeist whose trip will entail overland hauling of boat and equipment. While, of course, it always is prudent to keep the load as light as possible, the canoe cruiser who doesn't need to be critically concerned about weight can afford to pack a two- or three-burner propane or white-gas stove as the basis for a versatile canoeside galley. At the other extreme, are the tiny white-gas stoves favored by backpackers. They weigh somewhere around 20 ounces, are small enough to fit into the palm of the hand and yield enough heat in a single half-pint tankful to prepare several meals. These Swedish-made stoves—the Svea, Optimus, Primus—are ideal for the paddler who wishes to travel light.

A good compromise of convenience and lightness is the one-burner propane stove. Coleman has a model that utilizes a 16.4-ounce disposable fuel cylinder as one of its legs and which closes flat for storage and portability to 11 inches long by seven inches wide by a mere two-and-one-half inches high.

Whichever type of stove the canoe chef chooses, the new wilderness ethic suggests that, wherever possible, the portable stove supplant the traditional camp cooking fire. With increasing pressure on our remaining natural resources, there must be serious doubts in any recommendation of the use of campfires. Certainly, there is an inherent cheerfulness about the cherry glow of a crackling campfire, especially at dusk on a dark, damp dreary day. And no one can deny the camaraderie of a campfire gathering on a group canoe trip (it just is not the same sitting around a glowing propane stove). So perhaps a tenable compromise might be to limit campfires to designated areas, to use fireplaces already established by earlier campers and to use only deadwood for fuel.

But even these reasonably diligent parameters have their purist critics. As Jerry Sullivan and Glenda Daniel reason in their fine book, *Hiking Trails in the Midwest* (Great Lakes Living Press, P.O. Box 11311, Chicago, Ill. 60611): "... the campfire these days is going the way of the pine bough bed. There are so many people using the woods that fires are just too obtrusive. They use up dead wood that should be rotting back into the soil. They leave ugly black rings..."

Assuming you confine your fire to one of those ugly black rings and decide to use it for cooking, use hardwood for fuel whenever it is available. Making a trench for your fire will help to concentrate its heat. And remember that a fire that has burned down to hot embers is ideal for the camp chef's griddle and that a small fire with concentrated heat will provide the best medium for cooking. If you are canoe/camping in an area that is used by many campers, it probably is a good conservation measure to improve an established fireplace, adding boulders, forked cooking sticks and other refinements and thus encouraging campers who follow to use this ready-made fire cradle rather than despoil another section of the wilderness.

In selecting cooking utensils, those familiar attributes of lightness, compactness and versatility offer convenience at the campsite and a less wearying load on portages. Nesting saucepans with interchangeable handles meet all of these criteria. Add a skillet (in some nesting sets the skillet doubles as a lid for a large pot) and a coffee pot and you have the means for preparing some ambrosial camp meals.

Heavy-duty aluminum foil also is a versatile tool in the hands of the improviser (with outdoorsmen, of course, born to improvisation) that can be fashioned into all manner of cooking implements from bread pans to muffin cups to pot lids. We use it to wrap whole tomatoes that have been cross-cut and dressed generously with butter, Worcestershire sauce and seasonings. Cooked directly on the coals or in a reflector oven these foil-baked tomatoes make a fine accompaniment to steak and other meat, fish and fowl entrees and also create a zesty sauce. We bake them on a portable barbecue—the type that can be bought at a variety store for less than $2 and that makes a nice luxury on a canoe trip when portaging does not exact a premium on extra weight and bulk.

For those baked beans, for baking bread and biscuits

Beans are a good source of protein yet inexpensive and easy to tote and prepare. Nesting pans are ideal cookware for canoeing. They are light, compact and versatile.

and for roasting, a folding reflector oven is an item worth considering. Canoeists who also are handy in the home workshop will have little difficulty in making one from sheet aluminum. In fact, with some aluminum or steel rods and some sheets of heavy-duty aluminum foil, one can put together a simple but effective reflector oven. We've seen this kind used to bake scrumptious trail pies from fresh-picked blueberries and for performing culinary wonders with newly-caught trout. A friend once used his homemade aluminum job to whip up a multi-layer cake in celebration of his daughter's birthday while they were on a trip in the northern Canadian bush.

For best results, keep a reflector oven well polished and maintain a lively flickering fire—in contrast to the smoldering coals that are best for direct-heat cooking. And be sure not to underestimate the amount of heat a reflector oven produces—it can be deceivingly intense and result in burned food.

Tough plastic plates and cups serve as durable eating utensils for the canoe cruiser, while those ubiquitous Tupperware containers combine strength and lightness with leakproof seals (the latter a desirable feature for paddlers who prefer their breakfast syrup sans split peas). For those who travel fast and light, aluminum cooking/eating kits are a popular choice, with a cup doing multiple duty for coffee, soup, stew, desserts and many main dishes, too. The so-called Sierra-style cup is widely used this way (but has a wide, shallow shape that promotes too-fast cooling of hot food).

For toting this gear—and keeping it dry—many canoeists favor those black rubber waterproof bags that are obtainable at surplus stores. They provide a container that is expandable enough to cram in gear and that is reliably waterproof while riding out the heaviest waters. A version of this bag, made especially for canoeists, utilizes heavy urethane-coated nylon canvas and cement-seal seams and is waterproof under all but extreme capsize conditions. Another idea is to custom-build your own equipment containers, using plywood and fiberglass to mould them to fit the contours of the canoe. These are watertight and add flotation. Such waterproof methods of stowing gear render obsolete the traditional canoe traveler's trick of lining the floor of the canoe with tree boughs to keep a duffel raised clear of sloshing bilge water.

When the canoeist is travelling light, with only a one-burner stove, one-pot meals are a practical necessity—but no reason to abandon creativity. Many a memorable camp dinner has been coaxed out of a tiny, self-priming stove.

Omelets provide fast, appetizing meals and offer virtually limitless variations—when filled with mushrooms, cheese, combinations of freeze-dried vegetables and crumbled bacon bar (that tasty, versatile creation that should be automatically included on every canoeist's provisioning list). For a hearty meal-in-a-skillet that can be prepared in about 20 minutes, try this suggestion for Wayfarer's Omelet from R.T. French Company. It is a combination of ground beef and eggs flavored with a prepared onion seasoning.

A favorite with our family is tangy tomatoes. These foil-baked tomatoes are great accompaniments to steak.

WAYFARER'S OMELET

1 lb. ground beef
6 eggs
½-cup milk
1 envelope ground beef seasoning with onions
Slices of tomato and onion, if desired

In a 10-inch skillet, brown ground beef; pour off excess fat. Beat together eggs, milk and contents of seasoning mix envelope. Pour over ground beef. Cook over low heat until eggs are set, lifting edges of omelet with spatula to allow uncooked egg to flow to bottom of skillet. If eggs are not done on top, cover and cook until top is set. Loosen edges and fold omelet. Garnish with tomato and onion slices. Makes six servings. (If preferred, substitute a 12-oz. can of corned beef for ground beef. Heat in skillet until softened before adding egg mixture.)

Perhaps even more variable is soup and its cousins the bisque and the chowder. They provide hot nourishment after a hard day's paddling that is particularly welcome during early- and late-season paddling when the evening air has a bite to it. They are adaptable to the canoeist's larder in that they often can combine whatever ingredients happen to be available. A chowder, for example, is a good way of using up cooked fish remaining from last night's bountiful dinner (yesterday you hit that fabulous fishing hole; today, you didn't even get a nibble).

It is not a new idea, of course, to use fish leftovers in this fashion. Potluck chowder long has been a dietary staple of seafaring folk. It all started when French fishermen, back from hard, dangerous days at sea would contribute part of their catch to a communal pot and the village would cook up a rich stew to celebrate the safe return of its menfolk. The massive copper pot used to make this fish soup was called *la chaudiere,* a name later corrupted to "chowder." The following recipe comes courtesy of Coleman Company's Thayne Smith and Pillsbury Publications, who offer, as a serving suggestion, fish chowder complemented by squares of hot cornbread (use that reflector oven, here) for a cool evening's supper.

EASY FISH CHOWDER

1 lb. fish, cooked and cubed (about 2 cups)
2 cans (10½ oz. each) condensed cream of potato soup
1 soup can of milk (about 1 cup)
4 to 6 slices crisp bacon, crumbled
1 can (1 lb.) sliced carrots, drained
2 tbs. instant minced onion or ½-cup chopped onion

Combine all ingredients in a large saucepan. Heat through. Makes six to eight servings.

Finally, another chowder, this one from Mercury Outboards, is offered on the premise that, while trout and plump bass often may be elusive, crappie, sunfish, perch and other panfish are abundant in many areas. The following recipe is designed to serve six to eight paddlers.

Tupperware containers combine strength and lightness with leakproof seals. They keep salads fresh and crisp. The author and his wife enjoy a glass of wine before dinner. Little things, like a bottle of wine, add a gourmet dimension to outdoor canoe cookery.

No matter how fancy adults want the cuisine to be, kids prefer basics—like a hotdog on the end of a fork.

A canoe trip topped off with a simple meal is what childhood memories are made of.

PANFISH CHOWDER

6 to 8 lbs. fish, cleaned
2 chopped onions
1 bay leaf
1 stalk minced celery
2 teaspoons salt
4 cracked peppercorns
3 potatoes
2 slices bacon fat
2½ cups milk
1 cup evaporated milk

Place ingredients in pot and cover with cold water. Bring to a boil, reduce heat and simmer 5 minutes. Strain broth into a saucepan, add three potatoes (peeled and sliced) and bring to a boil. While potatoes cook, remove skin from fish and flake flesh from the bones. Dice two slices of bacon fat, saute until crisp. When potatoes become tender add bacon, fish, 2½ cups milk, and one cup evaporated milk (or heavy cream). Include the fat from the skillet in which bacon was fried. When pot is simmering again remove from heat and serve chowder with crackers. Serves six to eight.

by SAM CURTIS

Sam Curtis is a licensed Montana guide and an outdoor writer/photographer. He has camped the U.S., Canada and Europe. He has taught in the classroom as well as on mountain and desert trips the fundamentals of camping skills and has helped instill an appreciation of the environment. He is working on a book entitled Whitewater.

WE SELDOM THINK about water when preparing a meal at home; it's as near as the kitchen sink, and the supply is unlimited. But the outdoor cook doesn't have that convenience. He has to plan for his water needs and know whether he'll be able to find a source or whether he'll have to carry his own.

No matter where you'll be camping with a vehicle, it's always a good idea to carry some water—I'd say at least five gallons. If nothing else, you've got a reserve for cooking and clean-up, eliminating the need to run back and forth to the stream or spigot every time you want a cup of coffee.

When it comes to large containers, there are three common choices you can make:

• Steel jerry cans are virtually indestructable, but they are disadvantageous in that they rust and flavor the water. I'd call them the least desirable.

• Collapsible heavy plastic jugs offer the seeming convenience of foldability and easy storage, but they puncture pretty easily. Don't forget, five gallons of water weighs over 40 pounds. Rest that kind of weight on anything sharp, and you're sure to get a hole.

Nothing tastes as good as water directly from a mountain stream. Drink slowly, a little at a time. Savor it.

Wilderness streams that tumble over rocks in the sun are safe water sources.

that gallon adding a hefty weight to his pack. If you must pack your own water, carefully consider how much additional weight you can comfortably carry, and plan the length of your trip around that water supply.

Your water can be carried in any number of containers —aluminum canteens with canvas covers, plastic canteens, polyethylene bottles, wineskins (botas), even half-gallon chlorox or whisky bottles. Safety against spillage is the first concern in selecting a container. Choose one that will not leak around the cap and won't puncture or wear out easily. Aluminum is the most sturdy and puncture-resistant, and when dampened the canvas cover provided with this canteen will cool the contents by evaporation. Polyethylene bottles are very durable and inexpensive; and botas, because they're soft, will conform to the inner contours of your pack.

The size of the containers makes a difference when you carry large amounts. You don't want eight pint bottles to carry a gallon of water. A hiker or skier packing a gallon will find it most convenient to use two half-gallon containers or a half-gallon and two quart containers. This will allow equal weight distribution in your pack.

A problem often facing the camp cook is not the lack of water, but doubt over its purity. If you're in a remote area where clear water tumbles over rocks in the sunlight, chances are it's safe to drink. Sun and aeration are powerful purifiers. Any clear, cold water in real wilderness with

• Solid, sturdy plastic jerry jugs are what I feel are best. They can crack when it's extremely cold, but otherwise, I've found them to be tough, light when empty, and they don't impart any flavor to the water.

The amount of water you'll need to carry for cooking and living skyrockets, however, when you plan on being in desert or dry country where water isn't readily available. In this situation, figure on bringing three gallons of water per person per day. You could, of course, get by on the limited supply common to the desert backpacker, but when you've got wheels under you, weight isn't too important, and this amount will keep you within the bounds of comfort without any real sacrifices.

When you leave the roads and head for the foot trails in the back country however, you've got to lay your plans *very* carefully. First, ascertain whether there is any water to be had, and be positive about your information.

You should familiarize yourself with the country you plan to camp in. Areas with moderate to heavy rainfall will probably have lakes, rivers, and streams; topographical maps will show you where. Don't depend on mapped springs. They have a nasty habit of being dry when you need them most. In arid country, don't count on *any* map to assure you of water sources. Water may be around, but probably not where the map indicates. Always check with local people about the current water situation, if you don't know the area personally.

When the availability of water is doubtful in your proposed camping area, you'll have to carry your own.

An individual's daily water consumption varies with the temperature, humidity, amount of physical exercise and perspiration, and his own physical make-up. Experience will give you a clear sense of your own needs. But as a general rule, one gallon a day per person is sufficient for cooking, drinking, and a little washing. This is not a Spartan amount, but the supply must be used carefully. You can carry more, but water weighs eight-and-a-third pounds per gallon. For the RV'er or animal packer, the extra poundage isn't a burden, but the backpacker will find

A wide-mouthed plastic bottle tied to 12 feet of nylon cord provides a safe means of getting water from a partially frozen stream.

Water you've purified tastes flat because it has lost much of its oxygen. Renew its natural taste by pouring it from one container to another five or six times.

an abundance of aquatic life is probably safe to consume over short periods of time, even though a thorough lab test might label it contaminated. Several years ago I had the spring that fed my cabin tested. The results indicated contamination, so I asked the local health officer to come out. After reading the test findings, he chuckled, "You know, 90 per cent of the folks in the U.S. drink water that's not half as pure as yours. That spring is fine."

Water that's brackish, stagnant, or strange smelling should be distrusted though, and the only safe solution to your distrust is to purify the stuff.

At sea level, water boiled for ten minutes will be safe to use for cooking or drinking. But the boiling point of water decreases one centigrade for every 1,000 foot rise in elevation. This means that water needs to be boiled longer for purification at higher altitudes; 15 minutes at 5,000 feet and 20 minutes at 8,000 feet, for example. It also means the chef will have to boil food longer to cook it thoroughly; many a gooey mess has been served by the innocent because of this altitude differential.

I find purification tablets more desirable than boiling. They save fuel and fussing. Halazone tablets are effective. Drop two tablets into a quart of water, wait half an hour, and it's ready to drink.

With both methods the water ends up tasting flat. Freshness will be restored if you'll pour the water from one container to another five or six times. This process puts oxygen back in the water that purification removes.

The trickiest water problems are posed by two widely divergent camping situations—desert camping and snow camping. Each has its own peculiarities.

The water problems arising from camping in the desert or the dry canyon country of the southwest are clear—there isn't much or any water. Several week-long hikes I've planned in the canyons of southeastern Utah have been turned into two-day trips because of the lack of water. Campers in this kind of country should realize that they must carry enough water to get them into their campsite *and back out, too.*

Water can be found however, particularly in arid country that is rocky. One good place to look is in rock potholes. Potholes provide natural leakproof containers that catch rain water and empty only from evaporation. But don't underestimate the power of evaporation in these hot, dry regions. A quart of water can be sucked into the sky in an hour. For this reason, potholes which are shaded from the sun are more likely to contain water. These holes aren't always immediately visible; they may be hidden under outcroppings or on top of ledges above your head.

Several years ago, friends and I had been hiking for three days in the remote country of Utah's Canyonlands National Park. We were almost resigned to cutting the trip short because of our dwindling water supply. So when we came to a spot that looked as though it might yield some, we combed the area for half an hour. Nothing. I sought the shade of a nearby ledge and, putting my hand above my head to lean against the rock, found what we needed. Purely by chance, my fingers found the lip of a protected pothole that held enough water to fill all our containers.

Large rocks and boulders in a dry stream bed often hide waterholes. When the water is flowing in these streams, it undermines rocks and causes deep holes on their downstream sides. The holes remain shaded by the rocks and hold water long after the rest of the stream is dust dry.

A final possibility is digging for water. Wherever you find areas with moist sand, usually under rocks or ledges, there's a good chance of finding water simply by digging a hole. The water will be muddy, but that's no problem when you really need it. If you're fussy, you can always let the suspended particles settle before drinking or cooking with it.

Survival manuals suggest ingenious ways of getting water in desert country. One is to dig a hole with sloping sides in the sand. A pan is placed in the hole with a plastic sheet anchored over to the sand above it. A small rock is placed in the center of the sheet to form a shallow cone that has its point over the pan. What moisture there is in the underlying sand will form as condensation on the inside of the plastic sheet and roll down the incline to drip in the pan. If you're dying of thirst, and you have the plastic sheet, and you have the patience, you might get enough blood from that stone to live to tell about it. The camp cook however, should rely on more sure-fire methods to prepare his culinary delights.

Cooking in the snow represents the other extreme. Water is everywhere, on you, under you, and on top of you (if you decide to build a snow cave or igloo), but it isn't much good in its crystalline form. The process of melting snow for water has drawbacks that I'll get to in a minute. For starters, you're better off finding the liquid form to begin with.

Deep snows and cold temperatures sometimes make water as difficult to find as it is in the desert. Canteens should be filled whenever the opportunity occurs. Take advantage of any open streams and take the edge off your

Almost any clear, cold water with an abundance of aquatic life is safe for consumption when you are in remote areas.

When it is necessary to melt snow for your water, old snow will yield the greatest amount.

Aluminum canteens, polyethylene bottles and plastic jerry cans are among the most effective water containers.

thirst while you're there. Drink cold water slowly; it may feel good going down, but your stomach has the job of warming it up. You'll get a bellyache if you drink too much too fast.

Often all but the deepest pools in a stream will be frozen or snow covered. Use extreme caution when approaching these pools; the snow may give away and drop you in the drink. It's an uncomfortable and dangerous experience. Approach the hole with skis or snowshoes on in order to give your weight greater distribution. Instead of trying to climb down to the water, tie a 12-foot piece of nylon cord to a wide mouthed plastic bottle and toss it into the pool from a safe distance. Other containers should be filled from this water-retriever.

Frozen lakes can be hard to chop through, but if you're camped near one your original hole can easily be reopened for repeated water runs. Be careful of high mountain lakes, however. Heavy snows coming before a good freeze in the fall often leave these lakes covered with a layer of slush that never freezes solid because additional layers of snow act as insulation. The slush can support the weight of the snow, but a man would sink through it. Test such lakes with a pole or rock before venturing onto it, and then go only as far from shore as is necessary to get water.

When you stop for lunch in the middle of a sunny day, water can be obtained by spreading a dark colored ground cloth or tent over a sweater or jacket placed on the snow. The clothes insulate the waterproof tent from the cold, and snow sprinkled on the tent melts quickly from the heat absorbed by the dark material. Cup the material slightly with one side lower than the other; a pot placed at the lower end will catch the water.

There will come a time when all of these methods fail to produce the water needed for your cooking and drinking needs, and you'll have to resort to melting some of that white world you're living in.

There are two drawbacks to melting snow—it's both time and fuel consuming. When you're snow camping, you'll have to cook on a stove because fuel for a cooking fire will be buried. Like water, stove fuel is heavy and an extra amount must be carried when you know you'll have to melt snow.

I've spent many an hour over a snow pot, but I've never actually timed the melting process or measured the yield. So for the purpose of obtaining some specific figures I recently tried an experiment. I filled a ten-cup pot with firmly packed old, wet, corn snow from outside my cabin and put it on a backpacking stove with the burner wide open. In 17 minutes, I had six cups of boiling water. Then I put six cups of creek water in the pot and put it on the same stove; it boiled in eight minutes. Melting the snow took twice as long and consumed twice as much fuel to yield the same amount of boiling water. Actually, the time and fuel consumed in usual winter conditions is greater because the snow is dryer and lighter and therefore has less moisture content.

Once on a ski mountaineering trip, five friends and I spent three hours over dinner. Water was required for every item on the menu, and we only had one stove. Despite my grumblings and experiments, the three hours were pleasant. It was dark outside by five, and there wasn't much to do but sit inside the snow cave with the cheerful sound of the mountain stove puttering under the pot. Our meal was delicious, and we could savor each dish separately. Water was there for the taking—hundreds of square miles of it—we just had to be patient with its ways.

Rock potholes often provide the only water sources in the arid canyon country of the Southwest.

"The simplest recipes are often the best," says Curt Gowdy. "Breakfast got us off to a good start."

MISTER PORK & BEANS

by CURT GOWDY

ONE OF MY favorite simpler things I have loved in the out-of-doors ever since I was a little boy is a can of pork and beans. My mother used to say I was the greatest pork and beans eater in America. When I went fishing with my dad, we always took along an extra supply.

The simple meals in the outdoors are the best, at least for me. Fish are my favorites. Although I usually release most of the fish I catch, one or two small trout, that can be cooked at streamside, make for memorable meals. For me, trout taste best when fried in butter, and lemon. I also add chopped onion to the skillet and a dash of pepper. This really tops off the feast. And there is nothing better than eating the fish fresh from the stream.

Beef barbecues outside are fine. And steaks cooked over the coals can't be beat. But the meals I remember most are the ones I shared with my dad as a boy . . . outdoors. And even today, outdoor feasts, with good friends like Phil Harris, are the highlight of many fishing and camping trips.

Curt Gowdy means an easy-going voice broadcasting sports to fans throughout the country. Born and raised in Wyoming, he is an avid outdoorsman as well. The streams and mountains of Wyoming helped shape his character. Annually he returns to the Rocky Mountain west to renew his close touch with nature.

55

Fishing and outdoor cooking seem to go hand in hand.

Besides fish, I make a hunter's stew at home in a big pot and take it along on hunting and fishing trips. The stew is good and thick, rich with big chunks of meat, potatoes and vegetables. There is nothing like that stew after a day in the field or on a stream. Really caps off the day . . . especially when good companionship goes along with it.

I do quite a bit of upland game bird and waterfowl hunting in Maine. Just the right time and place for good soup. Often, I make the soup ahead of time—lots of it. Prepared with a good chicken stock, a couple of meaty bones and plenty of vegetables, I rate the soup pretty high on my list of outdoor foods that add to the zest of a fishing or hunting experience.

Cooking in the outdoors is enjoyable for me. It is a pleasant break from the busy schedule of broadcasting. In fact, I feel cooking is part of the fun of a fishing or hunting trip. And that is the way we plan and prepare meals for our outdoor adventures. Without good food, and the smell and tradition that goes into open fire cooking, a trip seems incomplete. Some of the best lunches I can remember, for example, have been produced on float trips when we beach the boats and the culinary magic begins. Topped off with a nice bottle of wine, the shore lunch makes sportsmen stop, enjoy the great beauty around them and share it with their fellow outdoorsmen. That experience, to me, is a vital chunk of the outdoors. I need it. And cooking and eating makes it happen.

My friend Phil Harris, the entertainer, is one of the biggest boosters of outdoor cooking. He is a master of producing mouth watering meals. We have done seven outdoor shows together on the American Sportsman television series and he constantly brings up the point that we should do more cooking on the show. He says people really like to watch other people cooking and eating in

The results of a morning on the stream—a few trout for the pan.

the outdoors. He believes in the theme that a shore lunch, or coming in for dinner after a day out of doors, adds to the fun of being together. Sportsmen share the events of the day. The fishing or hunting pace is finally slowed down so that communication flows.

Outdoor cooking should not be considered a lot of work. If it is, then it is a burden, rather than a pleasant break. Some foods and complete meals can be prepared or pre-cooked at home to save time. And these can be enjoyed outside. Meals do not have to be complicated. In

Shore lunches, good fishing and companionship are among Curt Gowdy's favorite memories.

addition to feasts built around meat and fish, vegetables and fruit add nutrition, variety and good taste. I'm a firm believer in fresh foods, both at home and out of doors.

It is a pleasure to watch good, outdoor cooks in action. One of my friends, Jack Dennis, a fishing guide in Jackson Hole, Wyoming, produces outstanding shore lunches. Fresh cutthroat trout are the main ingredients and Jack has several great recipes for them.

Phil Harris is probably the best all-around cook I've been around. He makes biscuits and bread in Dutch ovens. That's his specialty. When we did a chukar partridge hunting show in Idaho about five years ago, he cooked the birds. He wrapped the chukars in aluminum foil with some celery and onion to keep them moist inside. He also added a bit of parsnip. Phil baked pies for dessert. And that great Harris meal was topped off by some German white wine. It was one of the greatest meals I have ever eaten. He prepared the whole thing himself. It takes a certain knack, and Phil Harris has that. His pancakes just float on air they are so light. He is definitely the great-

Outdoor cooking should not be a chore and steps can be taken to make it fun.

Curt Gowdy likes good food and plenty of it outdoors.

est all-around outdoor cook I have ever been around and I don't think many people know that about Phil Harris.

I enjoy just about any meal cooked in the outdoors. My mother taught me a simple recipe for veal that I'm particularly fond of. Before I leave on a trip I buy some very thin veal. I also pack along a can of mushroom soup. During a shore lunch, or after a day's fishing, we get a good fire going. The veal is cooked in a big, iron pan and then the mushroom soup is poured over it. That is all there is to it. Simple, but delightful. And one that I have enjoyed outdoors many times. It is really tasty.

When it comes to outdoor cookbooks, I rate James Beard's *Outdoor Cookbook* as one of the best. Some of the dishes are a bit on the fancy side for me. But the man is a master and I have enjoyed his recipes often.

I just can't tell you how enthused I am about cooking in the out-of-doors. And I highly recommend it for everyone who loves being part of the wilds. But the outdoor trip, and the cooking experience, is especially suited to fathers and sons. That is the big kick I used to get when my dad started me fly fishing when I was eight or nine years old in Wyoming.

We would eat my mother's soups and stews for lunch and dinner. But one of my greatest thrills was frying eggs and bacon in the morning over an open fire. Dad made his coffee in a charred, metal pot that would sit in the middle of the fire. We would toast our bread over the flames. Eat some fruit or freshly picked berries. And then get ready for a long day of fishing. We'd always have a big, whopping breakfast. That's the way dad and I started our day. And those are still some of the dearest memories of my life.

Skinning grouse—They have already been field dressed and washed immediately after shooting.

Care for the Little Critters

by BRIGGS BABBISON

AN OLD TIMER—a genuine, consistent pursuer of those feathered, little bombs that like the tangles of multiflora rose and eye-level ragweed patches—once told me that no cook could ruin a bobwhite quail, or any quail for that matter. For a long time, I believed him.

Then, a couple of years back, I sunk my upper bridge into a delicate appearing, but leather-like morsel, that the head chef called "Quail under Glass." It must have been under there for quite a while. And aside from residing for some time under the finely cut crystal, the oven, where it

---

Reared on Kansas quail hunting, Briggs Babbison has stalked game birds from Canada to Mexico, and small game from California to Maine. Writing from his comfortable farm near Wichita, he thinks the "little critters" are sometimes overshadowed by the more exotic species of big game. Eating-wise, the "small ones" can not be beat.

baked, roasted, simmered, marinaded, soured, sweetened, had thoroughly killed it. A ruined quail.

Not so long ago my mouth watered with the anticipation of a ruffed grouse dinner that some friends invited my wife and me to. There was no way of ruining a freshly killed brace of grouse whose craws bulged with pea-sized aspen leaves. Unfortunately, immediately upon entering the house of grouse, a rather sour smell hit us right between the nostrils. I cringed. Absent was the wonderful aroma of slow roasting birds basted in butter. That pungent odor was not immediately diagnosed. But halfway through the effort, as I picked politely at the wasted meat on my plate, I remembered the time when I left two cottontails, ungutted, in my game bag overnight. A sad mistake . . . but true. Not wanting to waste the rabbits, and feeling terribly guilty about my mistake, I tried to salvage them. It had been cold the night before and the meat would still be edible.

That was the smell! The taste and aroma of innards. I was able to cast the tainted rabbits off as a lost cause and a good lesson. But the grouse? My wife and I are just too polite. We picked ever so gingerly. I had to refuse a second helping which was a first (or second) in my culinary experience. And there was no way I was going to ask our host if he had neglected his field care duties. That was quite evident.

There is a lot of emphasis placed on proper field care when big game animals are involved . . . and rightly so. But somehow, the fact that small game animals and game birds should be handled in a similar, efficient manner, is often neglected. Perhaps the prime reason for this is that, compared to an elk or moose let us say, a rabbit, squirrel or pheasant is a cinch to field dress and "pack out." It is far easier, and less messy, to stuff a day's limit of quail or cottontails into a game sack, uncleaned, than it is to clean them as they are shot or during a mid-day break. Easier, yes . . . but not better.

A common excuse used by some hunters is that the rabbit or pheasant must have been "an old, tough bird to begin with." This is the built-in alibi that blames age for toughness and poor taste. The fact that some game can be shot as early as seven in the morning and not cleaned until eight or nine that evening, has little to do with taste and toughness. But oh how it does! Even the big old bomber birds and squirrels on their "last barks" can be good eating. One of the first, and most important of thoughts for preparing small game for the table is to consider any and every bird or animal harvested as a potentially great meal. If you do this, you will find yourself field dressing game as you hunt; skinning, plucking and thoroughly washing game that same day; and taking care to insure cooling and protection for birds and animals.

One of the most well-perpetuated myths of bird hunting occurs in the western, sage grouse states. "If you can, try to shoot the small birds, the younger grouse. Those old bombers are not worth a hoot on the table," one grouse hunter told me. "If you cook an old B-49 grouse with a redwood plank for two hours in a pressure cooker," a

Sage grouse hunting is a real test of good field care when shirt sleeve hunting temperatures reach 80 degrees. Prompt field dressing and washing insure great eating back at camp.

There might not be much meat on a snipe . . . but what there is will be improved with quick field dressing and washing.

guide quipped, "you throw away the grouse and eat the board. It will be a lot better eating." The joke was sort of funny at first. But when I discovered, after hearing it for the 100th time, that the story tellers were serious, I began to defend those veteran grouse.

First of all very few grouse live to be old. They rarely survive the number of years it takes to get tough. And just any bird, with the exception of that spring's hatch, will be big. So you, as the hunter who can (with the proper frame of mind) put uncomparable meat on the table, must accept the sage grouse as it is. The bird is naturally big and slow on the take offs, and, in comparison to a downwind teal or bramble bush bunny, rather clunky moving (like a bomber) and relatively easy to hit. On the table, whether the bird is fresh from the egg, or a veteran of one or two hunting campaigns, the flesh can be delicious, when two steps are taken in the field.

With a pocket knife make a three or four inch slit across the bird's vent, just behind the breast bone. With your fingers, reach in and pull out *all* the entrails. This is easily and quickly (five seconds) done for any game bird. A belt canteen, especially when the day is hot, will not only quench thirst, but a small dose of water can wash the body cavity. Pour the water directly into the cavity and use your fingers to wash out most of the blood. This on the spot treatment can mean the difference between poor or great eating. A rag, which you can carry on your

There is a tendency among waterfowlers to leave field dressing and washing until the end of the day. Yet there is plenty of time to dress and wash ducks and geese inside the blind. This improves their flavor immensely.

belt or in the game bag, can be sprinkled with water and used to clean your hands.

The cleaned bird can be placed directly into a game bag. Or, better still, hung on a bird loop carrier from the belt. Air can then circulate into the cleaned body cavity promoting cooling, even on the hottest days. A plastic bag is the worst thing you can use to carry birds in the field or when transporting them home. Cotton mesh game sacks allow air to circulate around game, and soak up blood.

The same field care techniques used for sage grouse can be used for any warm or hot weather bird shooting. Whether you carry water with you in a canteen, or have it readily available back at the car, washing can prevent meat from being tainted by blood and entrails fluids.

On cool or cold days, it is still a good idea to pull out the entrails immediately after shooting. Washing should be done when possible. Snow can be used to rinse out the body cavity or soak up blood. A nearby stream serves the purpose nicely.

Possibly one of the greatest areas of field care neglect occurs in the duck blind or goose pit. The flavor of waterfowl can be enhanced by basic, on-the-spot field dressing and washing. Ironically, the very nature of duck and goose sport is conducive to practical field care. About a minute's worth of time, inside the blind, while waiting for the next flock of ducks is all it takes to pull out the entrails and rinse out the body cavity. More likely than not, water will be handy for washing out the blood. Inside the blind, ducks or geese can then be hung from a game carrier for quick cooling and better table flavor. Despite the cold weather face of waterfowl hunting, the brunt of good shooting, even in the northern states, often occurs when temperatures are around 50 or 60 degrees. Prompt field dressing should be a must.

Regardless of the temperature, I field dress rabbits and squirrels immediately after shooting. If water is handy, I thoroughly wash the body cavity. For the past three years, I have added another on the spot step—skinning. In fact my field care procedure varies little from the steps taken in care of deer meat. It is much simpler to skin a rabbit or squirrel immediately after shooting it, then to wait until the end of the day. Skinning promotes cooking. It eliminates the chore after a long stalk in the fields. Rabbits and squirrels can be wrapped in cotton mesh game sacks (the same kind used for big game) where the flesh will be protected from dirt and insects. The head can be removed during the skinning procedure. At the end of the day, all that is required is a thorough washing and drying of the game before it is cut into serving pieces for the pan or oven; or before it is wrapped and frozen.

Upland game birds like quail, pheasant, grouse and partridge are naturally tender and delicious. Choose recipes that bring out, rather than disguise their flavor. In general, you will cook them as you would a good, frying chicken. Of course, size and weight, determine cooking times. And many of these cooking times, despite what the recipe books say, will be determined by frequent checking and personal experimentation.

It is my opinion that heavy sauces or marinades should be saved for poor quality meats. And since none of the above birds fall under that category, you will do better with simple frying, broiling or roasting techniques. Salt and pepper; bacon grease for frying; butter or margarine bastes and your favorite seasonings will give you the taste of great meat, not sweet toppings.

Basic frying or roasting methods for rabbit and squirrel will often result in tasty, but somewhat stringy, tough meat.

Even the lowly jack rabbit, scorned as too tough by many, can, when properly dressed, washed and cooked, be a delight on the table.

Nothing like a good squirrel stew or fry to set the taste buds watering. Prompt field dressing, washing and cooling will make these bushytails a delight in the pan.

My wife treats both varieties of small game alike.

Pressure Cooked Rabbits and Squirrels (add seasons and chopped onions to taste)

1. Brown pieces in olive oil (or cooking oil).
2. Pressure cook for 20 to 25 minutes at 15 pounds pressure—game is cut up into frying pieces as you would chicken.
3. Water or wine can be used as liquid in pressure cooker.
4. Meat is done so it is tender and falls off bone.
5. Serve with rice topped with pressure cooker gravy; home fried potatoes and onions . . . a mugful of cold beer or light, chilled Rhine wine.

Ducks and geese can also be prepared pressure cooker style for excellent tenderness and flavor. But another fine method of cooking calls for the slow oven technique.

1. Brown cut up pieces in olive oil (salt, pepper, oregano, garlic salt can be added to taste).
2. Take out of oil and drain. Place in baking dish in single layer.
3. Cover meat with wine (or melted butter, or bouillon and add spices like mentioned above to taste).
4. Cover the baking pan and place in oven at 300 or 325 degrees F.
5. Bake (according to size of pieces) for three to five hours; basting with its own sauce until done. When leg joint moves freely it is one sign of being done.
6. Serve with baked yams, homemade biscuits, fresh spinach and chilled Rosé wine.

Aside from good field care, which will insure fine flavor, the serving of small game as soon after the kill, eliminates freezer staleness or burn. Freezer life should not exceed six months. As with big game meat, small game is better preserved in the freezer when wrapped in a good grade freezer paper . . . then bagged in plastic. Too often, leg or wing bones punch holes in plastic bags inducing freezer burn. Identify the package and date it according to the kill date.

If you are a stickler for good field care, and your buddies are not, keep your bird or small game separate. There is no sense in your suffering the penalties of tainted meat. You will appreciate your efforts (and your family will too) the next time you sit down to a small game feast.

OUTDOOR COOKS and for that matter, outdoor eaters, consider the clambake, a Texas beef barbecue, a potlatch and a "sugaring off" party as strictly American culinary treats. And they're right. America, of course, is not the only place where beef cattle are raised or salmon run, nor is it the site of the mother lode of maple trees as most would assume. It is instead Eastern Asia. Although nowhere in Chairman Mao's little red book is maple syrup, maple sugar or even the tree mentioned, we can hope that the Asian peasant has discovered the delicious possibilities of the liquid which annually flows through each and every tree. We can hope that somewhere there exists the Cult of the Maple. There must breathe one Chinese who wonders if there isn't something somewhere beyond Column A and Column B.

The maple family *(Aceraceae)* has nearly 150 species, about a dozen of which are native to the United States. There are also a number of foreign species introduced here as ornamentals. No matter where you find yourself in this country there is some type of maple in the area.

The distinctive leaf is one of the first children learn to recognize and the glorious reds and golds which appear when the nights are frosty and the days warm are the principal reason for our spectacular autumns. Everyone should also recognize the maple leaf as the emblem of Canada.

My New England block couldn't have been the only one on which kids broke in half the winged seeds in spring to press the sticky end to our faces for a "pixie nose." These seeds, if they safely weather the onslaught of children early in the season, ripen and become edible in the fall. The Indians boiled the larger ones and enjoyed them in prodigious amounts.

Wild turkeys, quail, grouse, and prairie chickens eat maple buds, twigs and seeds. Black bears, rabbits, beavers, and squirrels feast on every part of the maple—flowers, seeds, twigs and bark. Before storing the nuts for winter use, squirrels often remove the husks and wings—in the interest of conservation of space, no doubt. Even big game animals such as elk, moose, deer and mountain sheep devour maple twigs and foliage.

Cabinet makers cherish fine pieces of "curly maple" or "birdseye maple" for their craft and fireplace aficionados love the fine hardwood for a warm, steady blaze. Theirs, of course, is a one-time-only use, while the person who merely taps some of the sap for maple syrup and maple sugar does the tree no harm. He can return year after year to his "sugar bush," as a grove of sugar maples is called, and even century after century.

Back in the late 1700's, one Mathew Hueston, a military man, served under General Anthony Wayne in southwestern Ohio. When the Indians were finally pretty well settled down, Hueston visited the fertile slopes of Four Mile Creek (now Acton Lake) and thereafter bought land in what is now Butler and Preble Counties. He set aside part of his virgin forest for future generations and this still remains for public enjoyment. Should you visit the Hueston Woods Sugar Camp during March and explore the Sugar Bush Trail you can see the maple sugar exhibit and learn how the sap is turned into maple syrup.

Long before Hueston arrived on the scene the red men were using the sap. The first settlers to venture along the Atlantic seaboard were introduced to the wild sweet by the

---

One of the leading female outdoor writers, Jenny Reid was born and raised on the East coast. Being bred a city girl, she quickly adopted country ways when introduced to birds, wildflowers and game animals through a school friend who lived on a New England farm.

Ranger at Blendon Woods (Columbus, Ohio; Metropolitan Parks System) demonstrates how maple sap is drawn from trees.

THAT SWEET SAP
by JENNY REID

Here the sap is boiled, yielding mouth-watering vapors.

Indians who caught the sap in birchbark containers and in tightly woven baskets and skin vessels. They had cut a V-shaped gash in the lower trunk and drove an elderberry spout apex. The sap ran out the tube and into the containers. (The making of the spout was another task entirely: a straight elderberry limb was cut in the spring, dried, and then the soft lining of the center was pushed out with a hot stick.) To produce the syrup the First Americans employed the same principal we use today: evaporation.

According to Indian legend, Nokomis, mother of the earth, was the first user of maple syrup. At that time it was not sap which ran from the trees, but the syrup itself. Nokomis, in the fullness of time, became a grandmother of the sort of boy rarely seen today. This boy, Manabush, felt that his grandmother had made it too easy to gather the syrup. "People must work for this syrup," he sermonized, "or they will form bad habits and become lazy." We must assume that Granny concurred, as Manabush climbed to a maple's crown and sprinkled it with water so that the syrup was diluted to sap. Ever since that sad day man has had to work hard for his maple products.

The Indians poured the sap into a hollow log and added hot stones to evaporate the water. Later they used earthen vessels set in the fire and these were followed by the metal kettles of the white settlers. Today's stainless steel automatic evaporators are more sophisticated, but the process remains unchanged.

Making your own syrup and maple sugar is not at all difficult; you needn't even bother with the elderberry spout, just bend the top of a smoothly cut can into a shallow V. Select your trees at any time of the year rejecting any that are less than 10 inches in diameter. These should not be tapped. The sap begins to rise in the trunk sometime between mid-February and mid-March depending on the area and temperature conditions. Using a ⅜-inch or 7/16-inch wood bit, drill a hole two or three inches deep, two to four feet from the ground. The larger the tree, the more holes may be drilled. A smallish tree, from ten to 15 inches in diameter, would only have one. One 15 to 19 inches, two; 20 to 24, three; and 25 or more, four.

Next, attach your can lid, or use a spout of "spile" which you've bought. It would seem natural to suspend the pail from the spout. Don't. Hammer a nail into the trunk instead and use that. The collection of the sap is the most laborious of all the syrup making operations. In commercial sugar houses, this accounts for at least one third of the entire cost

After evaporation in the old, traditional method used for many generations, what is left is the syrup.

of production. Collect the sap daily and store it in a cool place. Allowing it to sit in the warm sun promotes the growth of micro-organisms which spoil it. (Don't you wish Nokomis had insisted Manabush stay out of that tree?)

After the collection, it's just a matter of boiling the sap and skimming as necessary. Boil it outdoors and inhale the delicious vapors as outdoor cooks have for so many years. How much sap will you need? Well, a lot. The sugar content in the sap is the surplus food the tree made the previous summer and stored as starch. A good summer for the tree— a greater sugar content the next spring. However, even at best you'll need between 30 to 35 gallons of sap to boil down to a gallon of syrup. At worst, 40 or 45. Strain this carefully and there's your finished syrup.

For maple sugar just continue boiling until what candy-makers will know as the "soft ball" stage is reached. The soft ball stage is that point at which a tiny piece, say less than a teaspoon, forms a soft ball when dropped into cold water. Now remove the batch from the heat, beat with an egg beater and pour into dry molds. If you have a really large quantity, use a regular sugar beater. I find that tiny molds are best for two reasons. One, the sugar breaks easily when lifted from a large one; and two, maple sugar is so sweet that just a small piece is sufficient for even the sweetest tooth in the crowd.

My alma mater is Mount Holyoke College, a small, institution for females not only in, but of, New England. The dietitian, whose accent would remind you of the Kennedys' (sorry Miss Smith), included many traditional dishes in the menus. I must, in all honesty, report that the New England boiled dinner did not bring raves from most of the students, but we all loved Indian pudding and Boston brown bread and of course, real maple syrup on our breakfast hot cakes. What I really remember best though, was maple toast.

On cold, blustery Massachusetts days when spring seemed an eternity away and a gray-blue gloom settled over the campus, there was only one thing to do. Eschew the noisy pack at the College Inn and go with one understanding friend to the Book Shop's Tea Room down the street. Order a pot of tea and maple toast. The building dates from Colonial times and has wide, tilted floor boards, braided rugs, tiny, wavy window panes and a warm snugness. To settle here quietly for an hour sipping steaming tea and munching maple toast was Nirvana. I recommend the combination for anyone in need of warmth of any kind and that would include hunters, anglers, campers, anyone outdoors.

In Ohio maple sap usually begins to "run" at the same time the open season on ruffed grouse—the state's greatest game bird—ends.

Later on, the white-eyed vireo is a common nesting bird in Midwestern and Eastern maple forests.

Great horned owl is another important nester and resident of maple woodlands.

Severe cold snaps and ice storms of later winter seem to trigger the flow of sap in sugar maple forests.

Allow two or three pieces of toast each. Place the slices of white bread on the broiler pan, toast until golden and remove. Butter the other side and strew it with maple sugar and dust with cinnamon. Return to the heat and just as soon as the top is slithery, put the pieces on a small, warm serving dish and serve to a weary husband, a camping companion or enjoy with a convivial neighbor.

You might like to make **maple muffins** with your syrup. Beat an egg with ¼-cup of milk. Sift together 1¾ cups of all-purpose flour, 3-teaspoons of baking powder, and ¼-teaspoon salt. Stir this into the milk mixture, along with ½-cup maple syrup, a bit at a time. Then fold in ½-stick melted butter or margarine. Bake in a warmed, greased muffin pan in a preheated moderate 350 degree camp oven for 20 minutes or until done.

Here's a delicious idea for **biscuits with maple syrup.** Sift together 2 cups all-purpose flour, 2 teaspoons baking powder, ½-teaspoon salt, and ¼-teaspoon cream of tartar. Cut in ¼-cup shortening. Add enough milk, about ½-cup, to make a soft dough. Roll this out about ½-inch thick and cut a dozen small biscuits. Place them in a shallow, greased pan and top each with several chips of butter or margarine and a slight dusting of cinnamon. Have a cup of maple syrup bubbling on top of the stove. Pour this over the biscuits. Place at once in a pre-heated hot 425 degree oven and bake 15 minutes or until done. Serve hot with either whipped cream or with scoops of butter pecan ice cream.

Maple sauce, delicious over squash, apple, pumpkin and blueberry desserts is easily made. Whip a cup of heavy cream into soft peaks. Then tip ¼-cup of maple syrup across the top and carefully fold it in. Season with a grating of nutmeg.

On snowy mornings when all hands need something warm inside before tackling the drifts, use another version of the sauce over hot cereal, French toast or waffles. Crumble ½-pound maple sugar stirring in 3 tablespoons boiling water. Heat at a bubble until all the sugar is dissolved. Add a sprinkle of nutmeg. Then remove from the stove and mix

In Quebec from mid-March to late April, some 22 million trees are tapped. At "sugaring off" parties everywhere, a sweet taffy is made by pouring the thick, hot maple syrup over pans of white snow.

in a stick of butter. The B vitamins, calcium, phosphorus, and enzymes are refined right out of today's cane and beet sugar, but maple sugar has them all.

From the sugar bushes around Mt. Gilead, Ohio comes this recipe for:

MAPLE SYRUP PUDDING SAUCE

¾ cup maple syrup
¼ cup water
2 whites of eggs
½ cup cream
1 teaspoon lemon juice

Boil maple syrup and water until it will spin a thread. Pour it slowly into the stiffly beaten whites of eggs, mixed with cream and lemon juice, beating constantly with an egg beater.

Bradford Angier, author of *Feasting Free on Wild Edibles* (Stackpole), widely quoted here, tells of his first sugaring-off party and I feel it's a fitting end of any piece on maple syrup:

"... I remember as a small boy riding out to a hillside maple bush behind two glistening horses in a pung. Syrup was already bubbling in the sugar house with an elusive and marvelous odor, and they gave me a small pitcher of it and an old fork.

Everything must have been ready, for when I strung this amber liquid out in a fine line of fresh snow, it hardened. Even before it was cool enough, I twined the string on my fork and transferred it gingerly to my mouth. This I repeated until all the syrup was gone, and then I got some more. The flavor was indescribable, except that there was the aroma of the forest in its sweetness—the fresh wind blowing, the branches swinging overhead, and all the free, rich wildness of the mountains themselves."

Feastin' Down the River

There's plenty of room on a houseboat—both inside and out— so you can cook almost anything you like.

by Bob Hirsch

IT WAS DAYLIGHT, but just barely. The big 40-foot houseboat rode gently at anchor, tucked back in a small canyon of the Escalante River arm of Lake Powell. The bow of the boat was tied to a big tree that poked out of the water and occasionally the rail bumped against it softly. It was 70 miles back to the marina and civilization but only about seven feet beneath the surface of the water to the schools of crappies we'd been catching for three days. It was fishing time but the sleeping bag was warm and I snuggled down, intending to spend another half hour in the sack.

Then I suddenly remembered it was the last day of the trip and we'd have to start back in just a few hours. Apparently the rest of the crew got the same message about the same time. There was movement inside the boat and the three sleepers who shared the top deck with me all awoke and began to dress. Nobody wanted to wait for breakfast. In ten minutes only my wife Mary and I were left aboard. The other five couples on our floating fish safari were all out in small boats stalking the crappies.

"I've eaten so well on this trip I really should just skip breakfast," Ken Meyers said as he shoved his small boat away from the mother craft. "I'll probably change my mind later. Right now I want a last chance to load a stringer of fish."

The 12 of us were sharing the cost of the four-day outing. Mary and I were the unofficial captains, since we'd made similar trips a couple of times before. Both of us were temporarily 'fished out' so we stayed aboard and had a leisurely breakfast. An hour later I climbed to the top deck of the houseboat and checked on the anglers. I could see the four

---

Bob Hirsch is a free lance writer, headquartered in Phoenix. He appears weekly on TV to inform sportsmen of the latest fishing, hunting and camping news. He is the author of Arizona's Seven Rim Lakes and is currently writing a book on Arizona fishing. He and his wife Mary have five children (ages 11 to 18) and spend at least one-third of their time cooking in the outdoors.

Propane stove and oven are standard in all the larger boats so the cook is not limited in food preparation. Only lack of storage is a consideration in planning menus.

small boats, all prospecting among the brush tips that showed above the blue water. None seemed headed back and when I rejoined Mary in the cabin for a second cup of coffee, I told her it looked like the morning was going to be 'fishing first, eating second.'

"I'll bet some of those gals are dying for a cup of coffee about now," Mary said. "Let's take our cartop boat and make a mercy run around the cove with the pot and some hot doughnuts."

"That's a fine idea, except for the doughnut part. What store do you plan on visiting?"

Mary opened the icebox and took out a can of ready-to-bake biscuits.

"There's plenty of these left and that's all I need. Stand back."

In a few minutes there was a skillet on the stove with an inch or so of hot oil bubbling in the bottom. In the meantime the biscuits had been opened and now she poked a hole in the middle of each and dropped it in the pan. The big iron skillet held eight at a time, she turned them once with a pair of tongs, then lifted them to a paper towel to drain.

"O.K., you've watched long enough," Mary told me as she put the second batch in the pan. "Sprinkle some sugar in a paper bag and shake those finished doughnuts."

So breakfast that morning was served "en boate" as Mary and I rowed around the little niche in the red rock and passed out cups of hot coffee and handfuls of warm, sugared doughnuts.

It's not hard to see why the popularity of houseboating has zoomed in the past few years. The combination of comfort and adventure is nowhere so well represented. Marinas with houseboats for rent are always located on large lakes and those who buy the floating palaces generally moor them on big bodies of water, where there's plenty of cruising

This is the crappie canyon on Lake Powell. The houseboat was tied to the tree at the foot of the sheer red rock cliff and it served as home base for 12 hungry fishermen.

room. So you can fish or swim or explore or simply pull back in a quiet cove and unwind. Whatever the activity, you have to eat, and aboard a houseboat (with a few exceptions) there's no limit on the kind of food or fixin's you can enjoy.

After half a dozen excursions, Mary and I have reduced the cooking problems to a minimum, without sacrificing on either meal variety or quality.

Unlike smaller boats, where the galley is a tiny, cramped affair, houseboats have plenty of room. Most are equipped with both a stove and oven, fueled by propane. A few also feature propane refrigerators but the three different models we've used all had iceboxes instead. In any case, the cold food storage facilities are almost always inadequate for the number of people aboard. Our trips have ranged from a low of three couples on a 32-foot model to a high of 14 eaters on a 40-footer. With meat and vegetables and fruit and soft drinks and beer for a crowd like that, we include three or four extra ice chests. If your outing is also a fishing adventure, the extra ice chests (hopefully) will fill with fillets as they empty of food.

There's also a limit to the amount of food storage space available, so it pays to plan ahead and write down menus—rather than buy boxes and boxes of food and hope appetites and shopping lists come out even.

Planned menus are a must. If your trips are anything like ours, breakfast and dinner are the two meals that get the most attention. Lunches are generally taken 'on the run' and the informality of a houseboat fits in perfectly with easy to fix sandwiches, soups, fresh fruit or similar snacks. So provide plenty of nibbling-type food. If you bring too much of anything, let it be in this category. And don't be surprised if 'picky' eaters raid the grocery supply four or five times a day.

As well as a number of houseboat trips with other couples, Mary and I have also taken two family voyages with our five children. Whoever is aboard, we simply let everybody know where the 'fixins' are and let lunch take care of itself.

If one of the kids can sweet talk mom into fixing a cup of soup and a grilled cheese sandwich—so be it. Most of the time it's every man for himself. We provide lots of chips, assorted lunch meats, cheese, pickles, single serving instant soups (we used to get these at a backpack store but now soup by the cup is a regular grocery item), apples and pears and jillions of cookies. The cookies are usually homemade and we pack them in reusable plastic bags. When the goodies are gone the bags can hold leftovers or fish fillets.

Harold and Alice were along on the trip that combined great crappie fishing and the biscuit-doughnuts and they brought a big bag of hydroponic tomatoes, grown in a backyard greenhouse that Harold constructed. They were the tastiest tomatoes any of us had ever eaten and lunches on that voyage were extra special.

We try to keep breakfast items together in one cupboard or ice chest, lunch fixings in another and dinner groceries in a third. There's some intermingling—especially in the icebox provided on the boat—but this system saves a lot of searching when meal time rolls around. Cooking duties usually rotate meal by meal and the new chef can thus find the chow and pots and pans in time to feed the crew and avert a mutiny.

The first day aboard the boat is a hectic one. You run down a checklist of switches and buttons with the marina attendant, load impossibly large heaps of gear and grub and somehow manage to stow everything and get underway. It's certainly not a time to spend much effort on cooking. So we traditionally have big bowls of chili and lots of Indian fry bread. The chili is fixed at home and toted along in a pressure cooker. It doesn't need this kind of cooking, it's simply

Compact, well equipped kitchens like this make the chef's work easy. Here Mary is ready with more coffee. The pot is always on.

a good, spill-proof way to transport it. Heated and served for dinner the first evening, along with a tray of 'finger food' —carrots, celery strips, sliced tomatoes and cucumbers— the chili is a big hit. So is the fry bread, an Indian staple used by a good many tribes but most often credited to the Navajos.

NAVAJO FRY BREAD
6 cups unsifted flour
1 tablespoon salt
2 tablespoons baking powder
½ cup instant non-fat dry milk
Lukewarm water

In a bowl, combine flour, salt, baking powder and non-fat dry milk. Add just enough lukewarm water (about 2¾ cups) to make soft dough. Knead thoroughly. Pinch off a ball of dough about the size of a large egg. Shape it round and flat, with a small hole in the middle. Then work it back and forth from one hand to the other, making it thinner and thinner. Navajos slap the dough back and forth between their hands in much the same way that Mexicans make their thin flour tortillas. Don't forget to make a hole in the middle. It makes all the difference in how your bread will cook.

In a frying pan, have ready hot fat at least an inch thick. Navajos use lard, we prefer liquid cooking oil. Drop the thin round of dough into the hot fat and fry to a light brown on one side, then turn and brown the other. As it fries the bread puffs and becomes light and crisp. Drain each on a paper towel. Serve hot (on a paper napkin) with butter, jam or honey. You can also put powdered sugar in a paper bag, add a piece of hot bread and shake to coat the bread with the sweet covering. This recipe makes about 18 pieces, each as big as an eight-inch plate.

If our houseboat trip includes some fishing—and they always do—at least one night is scheduled for a fish fry. Bass and crappies are the fillet candidates and a boat full of hungry anglers can put away an amazing amount of slaw, hot biscuits and deep fried boneless fillets—and that's about all we serve. Simple food but lots of it.

Every angler has a secret way to fix fish. My favorite begins with a boneless fillet—bass, crappie, walleye (oh yes!), perch or catfish. Usually it's one of the first three. If the fish are large, slice the fillets so none are more than about half an inch thick. Now chill the fillets thoroughly. If the fish are going directly from the lake to the pan, I like to put some cracked ice on the pan of fillets, so when they hit the hot fat they are ice cold.

After much experimentation with crackers and beer and corn meal and flour, I've settled on a simple method that lets the natural superb flavor of the fish alone. In one bowl, whip two eggs with a fork and add half a cup or so of milk. The second bowl should contain half pancake flour and half cornbread muffin mix flour. Now—the cornmeal muffin flour is *flour,* not cornmeal. It's simply been ground fine but the flavor is still there. Regular cornmeal, long a favorite with fish fryers, is too gritty for my taste. The pancake flour adds some 'rise' to the fillet coating. Pancake flour all by itself is too pasty. I told you I've experimented!

Now heat oil (peanut is best) in a deep iron skillet. Only several sessions of frying will teach you just how hot to get

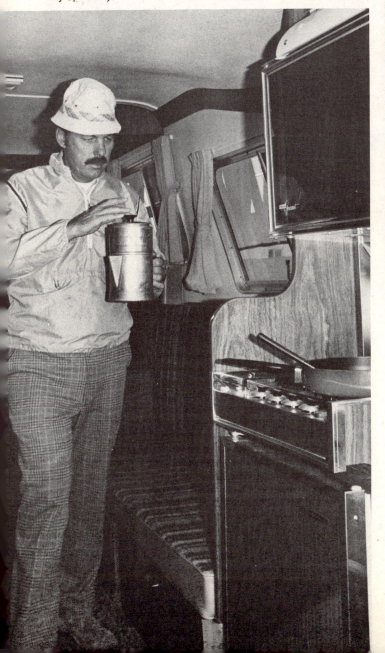

I even take a turn occasionally, although frying fish fillets is my specialty.

The oven can fix a ham, bake a casserole or keep the biscuits warm—all while you enjoy life on the boat. Built-in iceboxes are too small for a big crew. We always add a couple of ice chests to our carry aboard gear.

it and keep it, but the fillets should cook quickly. Dip the fillet in the egg and milk, coat it well with the flour mixture and pop it in the pan. The importance of the very cold fish meat is that now the fillet is steaming inside the coating we've added. The colder it is, the quicker it steams, assuming the oil is nice and hot. The fillet shouldn't take more than two or three minutes to cook. You can turn them once with a pair of tongs, then lift them out to drain for a moment on a paper towel. They won't have much oil to get rid of. The inside will be hot and flakey but not greasy. The outside will be crisp and light brown—and also not greasy. If you take it easy and pace yourself, you can keep eating fish fillets cooked like this for at least two hours.

If your recipe is different, tough. Never argue with the chef, lest you get sent to the end of the line.

Concentrate on one-dish meals aboard your boat. Easy, quick and filling is the watchword. The new hamburger

The rear deck of the houseboat is a good place to get those fish fillets ready. Crappies and bass are the fish being cleaned. Fifteen minutes from now they'll be in the pan—and two hours later the crew will still be eating!

helper products are just the kind of thing to bring along.

Here's an especially filling recipe we like. It can be served with nothing more than a relish dish or a tossed salad.

OLE' CHILI PIE

5½ cups corn chips (Fritos)
1 large onion,
2 cans of chili
2 cups of grated cheddar cheese

Place two cups of the chips in a baking dish. Arrange chopped onion and half the grated cheese on the chips. Pour in chili and top with remaining chips and cheese. Bake at 350 degrees for 15 to 20 minutes. If your gang is real hungry, grate some extra cheese and sprinkle over big corn tortillas. If the boat has a broiler, slip them under that; otherwise a frying pan will do. This will serve eight if they eat a lot of tortillas along with the chili.

We often take a ham along on our houseboat journeys. It can be baked in a low oven during an afternoon spent fishing or cruising or exploring ashore. Add pineapple slices and canned yams the last half hour or so, while you toss the salad and set the table. The leftover ham can be used in a potato, cheese and ham casserole, fried as a deluxe accompaniment to an omelet, or starred in sandwiches at lunch time.

Notice that cheese is mentioned often. We like it and it's extremely versatile. So is sour cream or one of the non-dairy substitutes. It can be used for salad dressing, as a final touch on baked potatoes (wrap them in foil and bake them ¾-done at home, so they can be quickly heated and finish cooking on board) and combined with dry onion soup mix to form a tasty dip for the cocktail hour.

Other easy to use products include instant breakfast juice, variety pack cereals that can be eaten right from individual boxes, hard salami 'sticks' that don't need cooling and, of course, biscuits. Good old biscuits. Besides being served 'as is' for breakfast or dinner, you can try the doughnut trick, use them as dumplings on stew or as tiny sandwiches at lunch time.

Travel aboard a houseboat is a continuing delight. Eating underway with the blue water sliding under the bow and the sun shining through the dining alcove windows is classy. So is a quiet meal in a quiet cove with your family or friends to share the special joys of this kind of outdoor cooking.

Try—whenever possible—to be at the wheel when lunch time rolls around. That way you pass along a special request to the galley slaves. Ring your bell or toot the horn and let the entire boat know that the captain urgently requests a beer and a sandwich. Rank, after all, has its privileges.

"**THIS IS THE LAST** time I'm going to hunt elk!"

Those were the first words my hunting buddy, Lew Dyer, had uttered in the past hour—but come to think of it he hadn't been very vocal all day. Sure, he'd done some muttering about the ancestry of his horse when it slid and stumbled down a muddy bank—and almost dumped him—and then earlier that day there had been a few excuses when he muffed a shot at a nice bull, but basically he'd been silent.

I really should mention that in between all this, a storm had moved in and drenched us with heavy, wet snow. We learned to our dismay that I'd goofed by failing to put the lunches in the saddlebags that morning. And of course, on the way back to camp we somehow got mixed up and drifted into the wrong canyon.

Yes, it *had* been one of those days!

Ed Park, a freelance writer and photographer, concentrates on the western states, Mexico and Alaska. Trained in fish and game management, his articles speak with authority about the habits and idiosyncrasies of game fish and animals. He and his family spend weeks each year camping and cooking outdoors.

DUTCH OVEN COOKERY
by ED PARK

My wife, Lue, seasoning a new Dutch oven by coating with grease prior to "baking" it in oven.

A new Dutch oven, coated with grease, is then cooked in our home oven.

By the time Lew and I dragged ourselves out of the wrong canyon and into the right one, and finally down the hill to camp, it was dark. We were soaked, hungry and weary beyond belief, and at that point I was ready to agree with him that there certainly must be something better to do than stumbling around the mountains looking for elk.

At camp we unsaddled, fed and picketed the horses, kicked the snow off the tent and took care of our rifles and other gear. By then we were about done in and there was a great temptation to forget dinner and just crawl in the sack to get some badly needed sleep. But, both of us knew a bit of food would improve our outlook on everything.

It was my night to cook and I'm sure that if I'd had to start from scratch right then, I'd not have made it. Golly I was beat!

But fortunately I didn't have to begin fresh. Instead I merely took the shovel and scratched carefully around in the snow-dampened earth where we'd had our morning's campfire. Soon I took our small camp broom and brushed away the last of the dirt and burned-out coals that covered the recessed lid of a large cast-iron pot, and lifted the pot out of the still-warm ashes that encased it.

I hauled the pot inside, set it on the dirt floor of our tent, beside our sheepherder's stove (which Lew had roaring already with a quick kindling fire) and got some silver and a couple of plates. Tea water was on the stove so I sliced some bread for each of us—and sat. Dinner was ready!

When I lifted the lid on that pot, the hot-sweet smell of a delicious all-day stew hit us and revived us enough to want more. Silently I spooned out generous helpings for each of us and grinned as Lew dug in with gusto. We both ate without saying a word, topping off the meal with hot tea and jam on bread.

As Lew slicked up the last of a third big helping and laid his plate aside, he asked, with a grin, "Can I change an earlier statement?"

"Sure."

Oven on grill over campfire.

Use of the dingle stick over campfire.

(Above) Lue fries eggs on Dutch oven lid.

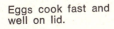

Eggs cook fast and well on lid.

Eggs ready for eating after being fried on lid.

"I guess I'll keep on elk hunting. Some parts of it are too good to miss."

Lew was his old self again—as was I. A half-hour earlier both of us were about ready to flick it all in, but in the brief span of those 30 minutes we'd been able to change into dry clothes, get warmed by the stove, sit long enough to rest a bit—and fill our bellies with a delicious, hot stew—without going to a lot of fuss and trouble.

The key to our survival was the food. And the key to that meal was the heavy cast iron pot with the recessed lid—our Dutch oven.

Those who enjoy the outdoors, but who have not yet learned something about the joys and romance of the cast iron Dutch oven, have a delightful surprise coming. Campfire cooking just doesn't seem complete without a Dutch oven someplace in the scene.

One of the blessings of a Dutch oven was forcefully demonstrated by our elk hunt meal, that all-day stew.

That morning we had planned ahead a bit by building a good hot campfire. We kept it roaring while we fixed and ate breakfast, got the lunches ready (which I left behind), readied our gear and saddled the horses. In between I found time to brown some cubes of venison (the results of an earlier hunt) in a bit of bacon grease in the bottom of the Dutch oven.

Then I cut up some potatoes, carrots, onions, green peppers and celery. I put all this in with the meat and added the right amount of water. A sprinkle of salt, some pepper, a couple bay leaves, some allspice and a dash of lemon juice topped off the ingredients.

As soon as it was ready I set it at the edge of the fire to begin heating up while we did other chores.

Just before we left for the day's hunt, I shoveled away the burned wood and dug an oven-sized hole down in the middle of the deep layers of hot ashes. Then I lowered the Dutch oven into this hole, shoveled more hot coals on top of it and covered the whole works with more coals and burning sticks. Then covered all this with warm dirt. That night's dinner was already cooking!

All day long, while Lew and I let those elk make fools of us, our dinner was slowly cooking. The heavy cast iron Dutch oven, plus the hot coals and earth packed around and over it, held the heat and kept the juices simmering.

Ed Park stirs a Dutch oven stew.

And inhales aroma of his famous stew.

Our daughter, Kelly Urback, adds dumpling to stew.

Lue bastes dumplings.

Nothing beats homemade Dutch oven dumplings on stew.

Anyone who has enjoyed an all-day stew, cooked for a long period of time at a low temperature, knows how tender and flavorful such a meal can be. Add to that the magic of cast iron cooking and the bone-weary business of hunting big game—and you can begin to imagine how very welcome that meal was.

If a person has yet to get involved with a Dutch oven, a few tips will help.

To begin with, know what you are looking for. The true campfire Dutch oven is a big, heavy, rather squat cast iron pot with sloping sides and three legs. The lid is tight fitting, slightly domed, and has a rim around the edge. The lid has a small, cast-iron handle while the pot itself has a bail handle.

Don't be misled by salesmen in some fancy fireplace stores, or elsewhere, who will try to sell you what they'll call "modern" Dutch ovens—no legs, rather ugly, and having a lid with no rim around it. These are also cast iron and would be all right for cooking in your electric or gas oven at home, but they aren't what you'll want for campfire cooking.

A relatively new innovation is the aluminum Dutch oven. It is built just like the traditional cast iron oven, except it is made of aluminum. I'll have to admit I've had no experience with aluminum, but somehow I just don't trust them. Maybe I'm too much a traditionalist.

True, the aluminum ones weigh a heckuva lot less than cast iron (my six-quart Dutch oven weighs just over 16 pounds), and they are rustproof, but I'd think it would be very easy to overheat one. The resulting warpage would ruin it.

One of these days I'll have to break down and try an aluminum one, but, golly, when my cast iron one does things so beautifully, why court trouble with those "new-fangled contraptions?"

In many parts of the country just buying a Dutch oven can be a chore. In the West, where I live, you can often just drop into a sporting goods or hardware store, even in a small town, and just buy one. In other areas, espe-

Ready for eating—possibly the best stew a person could ever eat.

Ed Park buries a Dutch oven in coals and ashes of hot fire.

cially the East, you'll probably have to order one, and don't be too surprised if the store clerk doesn't know what you're talking about.

My current oven is made by the Lodge Manufacturing Co., South Pittsburg, Tennessee 37380. It is the 12-inch size and currently sells for about $14.

Dutch ovens may also be purchased from Griswold or Wagner Manufacturing Companies, now both part of General Houseware Corporation, Cookware Group, P. O. Box 4066, Terre Haute, Indiana 47804.

The new aluminum Dutch ovens can be purchased from Scott Foundry, 3159 West 68th St., Cleveland, Ohio.

After you get your new oven, a few things have to be done to it to prepare it for use.

First off, give it a good cleaning with hot soap and water. The factories coat the new ovens with waxes to protect them, so of course this must be washed off. Do a really good job of washing, for it may be the only time you'll ever thoroughly soap-clean your oven.

Once the new oven is clean, well rinsed and dry, it is time to season it. Seasoning is nothing more than saturating the metal with grease. This can be accomplished by deep-fat frying food the first couple times you use it. Or seasoning can be done as a separate step.

Smear all inside surfaces, including the lid, with a heavy coat of grease, then set the oven in your home oven to cook. Get it hot and let the grease cook into the metal. Use a swab of some kind to smear the melted grease. Be sure all inside surfaces get a good seasoning.

This can be a smoky process, so keep that kitchen fan going, or open a few windows.

Once your oven is seasoned it won't have to be seasoned again—unless some unknowing, overzealous cook decides it looks a bit raunchy and hence needs washing!

The correct way to clean a Dutch oven, or any cast iron cooking utensil, is to merely wash it with hot water. A bit of scouring with a soapless pad is alright to dislodge cooked-on stuff, but stay away from soaps—especially the strong detergents. If you over-clean your oven you'll have to go back and start at the beginning and reseason it again.

If you don't ruin your oven by washing too well, it will continue to get better with each meal cooked in it.

Another thing to avoid is cold water on a hot oven or lid. Let cast iron cool well before wetting, or warpage could put you in the market for a new oven.

Now that you know where to get one and how to prepare it for use, what do you do with it?

There is something special about meals cooked in cast iron. Even fancy cooks who can afford the most expen-

80

sive of frying pans know that an inexpensive, heavy cast iron skillet is the best for stove-top cooking.

Cast iron roasting pans are cherished, as are cast iron pots of all kinds. They are simple, cheap, homely—but they do the job as no other cooking utensils can.

One reason is their weight. They are heavy, so they take the heat more slowly, distribute it more evenly, and hold it longer. I may use those thin, lightweight aluminum things when weight is important, such as when back-packing, but there are few better ways of ruining food with too hot and uneven heat. For camping by car, horse, canoe (or anywhere where something else carries the load) I insist on cast iron.

This great value of cast iron holds doubly true for the Dutch oven. It is designed for cooking over an open fire, an uneven source of heat at best. Your fire flares up, burns down, gets hot coals, then flares anew with more fuel. There is no selector dial on a campfire.

The Dutch oven can be used for cooking on top the fire, just as you'd use a pan on your kitchen range. Set it right on the burning wood, on a bed of hot hardwood coals, or use it on a grill just above the flames. The three sturdy legs will allow you to set it on the ground, just slightly above a bed of hot coals. The bail handle can be hung over a dingle stick, if you prefer this method.

And although a regular cast iron skillet will do a better job, the lid of your Dutch oven can be used as a skillet. Just lay it on the fire, bottom-side up. Your "pan" will be slightly concave, so your eggs will tend to drift toward the center, but you'll manage.

One of the places a Dutch oven really shines is when you bury the oven and let your meal cook for a long period of time, such as we did with our stew on that elk hunt.

In this case you want a good hot fire beforehand. You need to heat up the soil and rocks thoroughly. Keep a roaring fire going as long as you're in camp in the morning.

Meanwhile, prepare the stew and set it by the fire to begin cooking. This also heats the oven and its contents, so when you finally do bury it, it will start out hot.

Then just before you leave camp, dig a hole in the center of the fire area and set the Dutch oven down in it. The tight-fitting lid will keep excess dirt out.

Then cover the top of the oven with more hot coals and earth. Finish by burying the whole works. Your meal is cooking!

Hours later, when you return to camp, the meal will be done.

Immediately questions will pop to mind. I said earlier that you add "... the *right* amount of water." How much? I mention leaving the oven buried for several hours. How many hours?

For those of us accustomed to set recipes, regulated heat and timers on our stoves, this business of estimation can be frustrating. But I know of no other way of doing it, other than by experience. Just try something—then remember how it turned out. The odds are good you'll do well, for cast iron has a way of making up for a lot of errors.

For one thing the tight-fitting lid will keep in the moisture, so meals will not dry out and burn. The shape of the slightly-domed lid will baste your meats, making it unnecessary for you to look in at all. Do what you can. Bury it and have faith!

In time you'll learn which woods produce the best coals (oak, hickory, maple, alder) and which burn up quickly without many coals (pines, firs, cedars). You'll learn that rocks, once heated, hold the heat a long time. They are good to place in the hole next to your Dutch oven.

You'll also learn such things as using care when you dig up the oven. That lesson may come hard the first time as you knock the lid loose and let a shower of dirt and ashes flavor your meal.

Recipes could fill many cookbooks, as indeed they do, so we'll not belabor the point of what to put into your Dutch oven. The stew already mentioned is a natural. Other one-dish meals also fit the Dutch oven's design. For indeed it was made to be an all-in-one cooking utensil.

A roast, cooked slowly and long, is another Dutch oven favorite. Pre-heat the oven and lid, put in a bit of grease and heat until it smokes, then sear the meat on all sides. Slowly add a bit of hot water, season to taste, maybe add a few carrots, potatoes, onions, or whatever, and cook.

Various bean dishes, chowders, soups or chili are just some of the types of meals well suited to the Dutch oven. In fact a person would be hard-pressed to find things that can't be cooked in this versatile pot.

Another place the Dutch oven shines is in baking bread. If you aren't a sourdough fan, you're missing a real treat. But that's another complete story.

For any kind of bread in camp—sourdough or otherwise—the basics are the same. Pre-heat the oven and lid. Have your bread dough ready and grease the hot oven and lid thoroughly.

Put in your bread dough—in chunks for biscuits or whole for bread. Brown the bottom of the dough. Once browned, turn it over and put the lid on the oven. Your oven is setting on hot coals and you shovel more hot coals on top the lid. The raised flange around the lid's rim was designed to hold the coals.

Baking time again is a matter of experience. Maybe 10 to 15 minutes for biscuits, quite a bit longer for loaves of bread.

Dutch oven cooking—or any campfire cooking—is basically an art of trial and error, logical thinking and experience. Sure, you'll have some disasters, as even the home cook does. But the victories will be extra sweet because they have been flavored with the smoke of a wood fire, the exhilaration of outdoor experiences and the romance and utility of your cast iron Dutch oven.

Buried Dutch oven is great for all-day cooking. Note lipped lid made for holding coals on top for all-around, even heat.

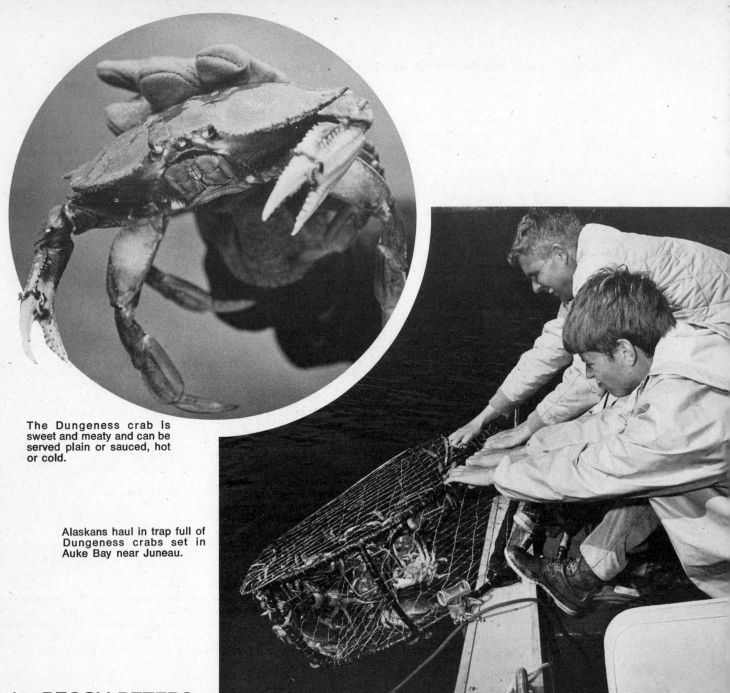

The Dungeness crab is sweet and meaty and can be served plain or sauced, hot or cold.

Alaskans haul in trap full of Dungeness crabs set in Auke Bay near Juneau.

by PEGGY PETERS

THE LOW GRAY CLOUDS squeezed random drops on my husband Joe and me as we walked a little stiffly down the small plane's ramp to finally settle our feet on the soil of Yakutat, Alaska. Yakutat is a tiny settlement (395 persons) at the far end of the Alaskan panhandle. Past Juneau, before the Malaspina Glacier, and about 50 miles from the Yukon border as the guillemot flies. "Nowhere," you may say. "Heaven," is the reply from anyone who loves forested scenery, the outdoor life and most especially from anyone who loves fine seafood.

A native of the Ozarks, Peggy Peters was fishing almost before she could walk. Raised on bluegills and channel cats, she now includes salmon, marlin and dolphin in her fishing repertoire. She can out-fish most men but she does not take pride in that fact. She writes for the fishing lover—male or female, they are her kind of people.

Our friends and hosts, Phil and Dessa Baker, are residents of Yakutat and awaited us in the tiny air terminal building. Phil is a meteorologist whose still-blushing first love is fishing the waters of Yakutat Bay with Dessa in their fine 24-foot craft, the Fuzz Buzz. When the local cannery is operating the Bakers might sell part of their catch as is the local custom, but for the most part what they land, they eat. Joe and I were to spend a few days fishing with our friends before joining a group of travel writers in Juneau. Those days with the Bakers were my introduction to the magnificent seafood of Southeastern Alaska.

That first night's dinner at chez Baker featured scallops. Fresh, firm, enormous scallops. Dessa held up her plastic bag full and said, "Peggy, just look at these." The two of us talked seafood—well, Dessa talked and I listened (she's the expert!)—as we rolled the scallops in beaten egg and

YUKON FLAVOR

Tour boats and fishing cruisers dock near Glacier Bay Lodge. Here is where some of the best Alaskan seafood is served.

then in crumbs, getting them ready for the frying pan. These chunks are so large that Alaskans figure only eight to the pound. "Phil and I don't like 'em fancy . . . no French sauces." Dessa continued, "They're so flavorful they don't need any help from Escoffier and very little from me." Dessa sauteéd batch after batch and the platter's mound grew to an astounding height before dinner was announced. Firm textured, sweet flavored and perfectly cooked, those scallops! I've had bay scallops and sea scallops in the East, but I have never had any like those of Alaska. I'd like to relate what other dishes graced the Bakers' board, but I honestly remember nothing but the scallops.

All tales you have heard about the high cost of everything in Alaska are true, and especially true of perishable products—produce and meats from "the lower 48." In consequence Alaskans use their own seafood in great quantity and also wild meats. Alaskan school children are regularly excused from school during hunting season and it's a rare family which doesn't have a moose (butchered, of course) in the freezer. Most of the meat is allowed to hang for a week or more before preparation for the freezer and Phil showed Joe and me the "hanging shed" outside which had just recently had a new layer of heavy wire mesh fencing added to discourage marauding bears.

Judge James Wickersham, a venerable old Alaska hand, dead lo these many years, didn't always sit on the bench —he had a fine, adventurous life, part of which he spent on the Yukon River. Alaskan food was just one of his interests. In his *Old Yukon* he describes a "rabbit stew" he encountered in a log tavern on the river which illustrates the importance of local products:

The stew was prepared in a large kerosene can on top of an ancient Yukon sheet-iron stove set on the

Glacier Bay Lodge is home base for sightseers, bird watchers, wildlife photographers, anyone who appreciates the untainted outdoors.

dirt floor and held in place by a low, rough frame of logs. In this can the famed rabbit stew always simmered. As hungry guests reduced its contents, more water, rabbit, caribou, bear or lynx was added. From early November when the first ice permitted travel on the great river highway in the front of (the landlord's) door, until the following May break-up, the odor and steam from this ragout of wild meats permeated the tavern, glazed the half-window with beautiful icy patterns, and filled the two-inch air-hole above the door with frost.

It was May too, when Joe and I and the Bakers ventured out on the deep green waters of Yakutat Bay in the Fuzz Buzz. It was here that I caught my king (or chinook) salmon. In all truth, it was a beauty, lured to its death by a sardine bait.

After the incomparable scallops of the night before and with my beautiful salmon lying in state on crushed ice, my interest in Alaska's seafood increased manyfold. Dessa, while whipping up a snack featuring her own moose paté (which is a story in itself!), filled me in on the Alaskan's way with salmon. She assured me that strange as it may seem, one of the most popular ways of fixing the smaller types of salmon is to bake them whole in a paper bag.

The cook seasons the very fresh fish with salt and pepper, butters the outside and just slips it into a brown paper bag closed with paper clips and bakes it! Served with sour cream and dill it's almost traditional in our 49th state.

The question of how long to cook the fish has pretty much been settled by the Canadian Department of Fisheries. They state that no matter what kind of salmon is yours, and no matter how it will be cooked, its thickest part should be measured in inches and that number multiplied by ten minutes. If the fish measures three inches at its widest diameter, it must be cooked for 30 minutes. According to the Bakers, even if the formula did come from Canadians, it works.

Another way in which a salmon of four to five pounds might be baked is stuffed using either a shellfish concoction or breadcrumbs and wild mushrooms which abound in Alaska. Others barbecue their catch. It is first cut into manageable cubes, then placed in a wire grill and continually basted with melted, herbed butter while cooked over coals. Prepared in this way the salmon is crusty on the outside and hot, tender and moist inside.

Probably the best known feast of salmon was the "potlatch," a celebration of giving once common along the Pacific shores from California to Alaska. At a potlatch the host fed vast hordes of guests from a menu of even greater proportions. He also gave away all of his worldly goods. Gifts ranged from canoes to animal skins, and though these were distributed according to the recipients' rank in the social order, no one, no matter who he was, ever left a potlatch empty handed—or hungry. Of course the host's home wouldn't remain bare for long—only until the next potlatch was given.

The menu at a traditional potlatch featured salmon of course, and old accounts also grandly mention halibut, roasted or boiled; herring or salmon roe eaten with young sprouts of berry bushes; acorns and fern root, etc.

The missionaries who attended several celebrations were less than lyrical in their descriptions. One wrote: "First came berries preserved in grease and mixed with snow. Then came dried salmon and halibut which the guest was expected to eat with oil, accompanied by boiled seaweed mixed with fish and fish oil. This course was followed by a dessert of bitter berries."

Indians' and early settlers' main concern after catching the salmon was to preserve it. Salting was the most common method and earliest. Smoking was, and is, widely practiced and many also pickle a portion of the catch.

Toward late afternoon on our last day aboard the Fuzz Buzz we decided to suspend our fishing and cruise over to the cove where the Bakers have their shrimp pots. Now I had always thought of shrimp as occurring in the Gulf of Mexico, but never in the cold waters of the Gulf of Alaska. Seldom have I been so wrong. Our craft drifted among red and blue floats scattered across the cove. Phil was on the prow with a boat hook snagging, one after the other, all the floats marked "Baker." Joe noted others were labeled with the Bakers' neighbors' names.

A tour boat brings sightseers to the edge of Muir Glacier.

Large halibut caught in Glacier Bay. When fresh this is among the finest food fishes of all.

Weather was settling in and a stiff, cold breeze cut across the water as Phil hauled them up hand over hand. With his wet, gloved hands he poured each load of shrimp into the boat's buckets. Several times when the top of the shrimp pot broke the surface of the water Phil grabbed a Dungeness crab off the line and popped it into the ice chest. No fish entrails or heads go to waste on the Fuzz Buzz; they are all used as bait to attract both shrimp and those meaty, delicious crabs.

Most of us from "the lower 48" are more familiar with the Alaska king crab than the Dungeness but that may be because the former freezes and ships so well. There are many who testify vehemently that the Dungeness is the finest of all. They may well be correct. It's sweet and meaty and can be served plain or sauced. Dessa says they like them best cold with home made mayonnaise and cold brew.

Also in Yakutat Bay a crab pot yields enough Dungeness crabs for a typical Alaskan seafood dinner.

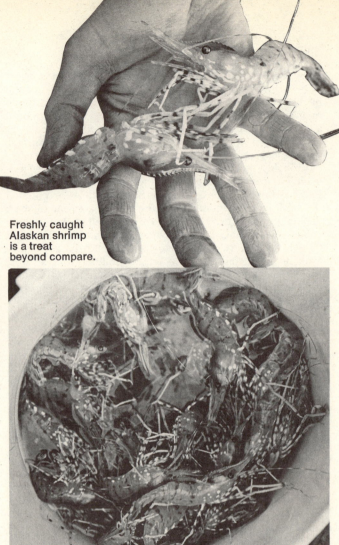

Freshly caught Alaskan shrimp is a treat beyond compare.

Phil Baker lifts trap from deep in Yakutat Bay and is rewarded with haul of delicious large shrimp.

The best way to prepare shrimp is the simplest—boiled and then dipped in a little melted butter.

On our last night in Yakutat the bounty of the Bakers reached seafood's culinary heights. We ate shrimp. Did we eat shrimp! Joe and I sat on the kitchen floor "heading" the little creatures. Those fellows are very lively, perhaps seeking to avoid the pot at any cost. We had to be quick to grab one and soon learned just how to snap the head off in one quick jerk. Heads in one pile, bodies in the other.

Whenever I found one shrimp too prickly of leg or thick of neck to tackle I tossed it (unseen, I hoped) into Joe's pile. He retaliated by tossing two into mine (he'd spotted me after all). When finally all were ready and we had all but finished off Phil's special libations for the evening, Dessa tossed the shrimp (we tried to avoid the head pile) into boiling water by the handful. Just as they turned pink and rose to the top of the water, she skimmed them off and deposited them into an enormous heated bowl.

Using two pots the process didn't take long; soon the four of us were diving into the bowl and devouring these magnificent morsels. Sometimes we paused to dunk one into melted butter or to swallow from a foamy stein of beer, but mainly ours was literally a hand-to-mouth meal. Dessa had one thing to say as we slowly began to clear away the debris later: "Simplicity of preparation; that's

Cruising aboard the Fuzz Buzz in Yakutat Bay produces prize salmon.

the best way." How right she was.

It may sound as though we had savored all the seafood delights Southeastern Alaska has to offer, but there was one more. Several days after we left Yakutat we found ourselves at Gustavus Airport after a half-hour plane ride by Alaska Airlines from Juneau. From here we were driven in the limousine (it was really a battered VW bus) the seven green miles to Glacier Bay Lodge. We arrived at Bartlett Cove, a spectacularly beautiful area of Glacier Bay National Monument. It appeared that the entire land mass was upholstered in a deep green moss. The evergreens towered thickly into the sky above our heads.

The lodge settles comfortably into its surroundings. It and the surrounding guest rooms are raised above ground level and are constructed of glass and timbers. Huge windows look out over the bay where a launch takes guests on day-long cruises. Mountain goats are easily seen, as are porpoises, bald eagles' nests and occasionally a whale. Bird watchers love the puffins, murrelets and white-winged scoters. Best of all though, is being taken right to the edge of one or more of the 16 glaciers which feed into the inlets. The ancient ice looks milky and opaque and then suddenly a deep aqua-blue as the light reflects through a crevasse. Occasionally one can hear a muffled "woompf" and actually see an iceberg born as a section of glacier "calves" into the water.

The alert visitor might note one of the crew gathering ice from the water on the return trip and storing it in tubs. Any questions are answered later over cocktails sipped in front of the wall-wide stone fireplace. "The ice in your glass", notes the host Frank Kearns "is ice-age old. It was compressed over the centuries by the glacier's own weight and so is far more dense and melts far more slowly than ordinary ice."

This appeared to be true as dinner was a bit late that night and we had an opportunity to test out the theory. The reason for the tardiness was that the fishing boats bringing the main course to the kitchen were overdue. Any wait was forgotten when dinner was announced and we could sample one more of Alaska's great seafoods. Halibut, this time. Absolutely fresh, cut in two-inch chunks and deep fried in an egg batter containing oregano, chili powder and beer. Any interested patrons are cheerfully given the recipe. Halibut flourishes in these waters and fishermen have caught hundreds of pounds of the flat bottom-dwellers. Try it yourself—fishing excursions are easily arranged from the Lodge which, incidentally, contains the finest accommodations in the entire state. It is served by Alaska Airlines.

No discussion of Alaskan seafood is complete without mentioning what might accompany it on the menu. Of Alaska's 350 million acres only about 17,000 acres are used to grow vegetables and most of these are in the Matanuska Valley, south of Talkeetna where enormous and flavorful cabbages, beets, turnips, radishes, etc. are raised. Any of these would be common on the table during the season. Traditionally dried apples are made into pies and no one should over-look sourdough (look elsewhere in this book) products. The breads are best with a firm texture and hardy, slightly tart flavor. Alaska's cooking is unique, and for an area with so few people, special recipes are numerous indeed. A representative list might include caribou Swiss steak, baked ptarmigan, red and blue huckleberry pie, sweet kelp relish, braised bear paws and beaver haunch.

We have no doubt that any of these would be interesting; perhaps even tasty, but would never concede that any area of Alaska's cooking and eating could compare with her seafood. And we ought to know.

Dessa Baker proudly shows the lingcod she caught in Yakutat Bay. Despite strange appearance, the lingcod is a superb table fish.

Lipton dinners, not designed specifically for the camper, are a big hit due to the speed in which they can be prepared and their good taste.

Super Foods from

by JONATHON SALAZAR

"THIS IS FUN," my wife Gail bubbled as we strolled down the aisles of our neighborhood supermarket. "I can't believe how many foods were just designed with the camp cook in mind," she added. "But they really weren't," I chipped in. "It is just that modern dehydrating and freeze-drying techniques, along with easy preparation and serving methods, are a bonus to the camper who has good nutrition and a minimum of weight in mind."

A retired Air Force colonel, Jonathon Salazar with his wife Gail has traveled to all sections of the country during the past five years. Vagabonding means adventure to them. Wintering in the South and summering in the North, they experience the best of each part of the country.

She picked off a box of Lipton's dehydrated Beef Stroganoff from the shelf. "Take this meal, for instance. A camper or backpacker can shed the contents of the outer box. Inside are individually packaged noodle, sauce and garnish ingredients that weigh 6¼ ounces, and yet when cooked with three cups of water will produce two adult-size main dishes. That's terrific! And what is even better is the entire meal, not counting the time it takes to boil three cups of water, can be cooked and ready to serve in 15 minutes. One pot does it. I can't think of anything better after a long day fishing for bass or hiking the trails."

My wife had a point. New and better supermarket foods, not specifically designed with the outdoorsman in mind, are helping the camp cook produce a variety of easy to fix, one-step meals that add variety and good taste to fish, burger, hot dog, beans and bread basics. And just about every supermarket has them.

Along with lightweight, dehydrated, freeze-dried or

For hot cocoa mixes, just add hot water and stir.

Super Markets

powdered foods and drinks designed primarily for home use, many supermarkets now stock specially packaged foods for outdoorsmen. Better known as backpack foods, these complete, lightweight meals fill the gap, where conventional, heavy, many-step meals fail in the outdoors. But regardless of whether your local supermarket has a stock of commercially prepared backpack foods or not, it is possible to build breakfast, lunch and supper menus entirely around the new, lightweight foods found on market shelves. These foods can be the foundation to good meal planning. Combined (or used separately) with fresh fish or game, wild edibles, Navajo bread or other special creations, the super foods have added a new dimension to camp eating.

Let's take a walk down the breakfast aisle. I won't argue the merits of bacon and eggs sizzling in the camp skillet. But there are some breakfast variations that offer good taste and nutrition. And for the "lightweight" camper or the backpacker, where pounds are critical, these breakfast choices are definitely more practical.

An egg substitute? What in the world would the chickens say? There is one, you know. Relatively new on the market shelves . . . at least for the general consumer. Some brand names are Egg-Stra and Egg-Beaters. Defrost and you have the makings of a good tasting scramble or omelet. Backpack food manufacturers offer powdered eggs and omelets, some spiced with chopped peppers and onions, that are good. All you add is water, stir and cook.

Instant hot cereals—individually packaged, are remarkably good. Just add boiling water and stir. Some cereals feature honey, maple, raisin and brown sugar extras. I think they are all tasty. And after the water is boiled, a minute's worth of stirring means a hot breakfast.

Instant breakfast drinks require the addition of milk. The drinks can be a good change of pace. Before an early morning fishing trip, they taste good and supply the

89

Plastic bags replace standard packaging for most campers making food items compactable and lighter in weight.

(Left). Powdered breakfast drinks can be transferred from bottle to plastic baggies and used as needed for good hot or cold drink anytime.

(Below). Squeeze tube foods, like honey, are just right for grub box or stuff bag.

needed nourishment. I have found that by making instant milk the night before, it is well mixed (my wife and I use a two-quart plastic jug for storing and mixing) and can be kept cold. Mix in the powdered instant breakfast for a good drink.

For lightness, Tang crystals can be transferred from the jar to double plastic sacks before the trip. When water is added, either for individual cupfuls or larger quantities, a healthy orange or grape drink can be enjoyed with breakfast.

Instant hot chocolate can be purchased in bulk and plastic bagged or bought in individual servings. I have tried Carnation and Swiss Miss and found them both good. Again hot water does the trick. You can even get hot chocolate with its own supply of miniature marshmallows.

You can also make your own instant hot chocolate from cocoa, powdered milk and sugar found on market shelves.

Bacos, or soy bacon bits can be eaten separately, like bacon, or added to scrambled eggs or omelets.

Camp lunches can be simple and light. There are plenty

of supermarket foods that qualify in this department. Instant soups, by the cup or potful, are made with boiling water. Or you can use bouillon cubes and spices to create your own quick soups. Either way, a fast, economical soup-based lunch can be a fine mid-day pick up.

Smoked salami is a favorite of mine. It keeps well and adds some zip to lunches. Cheese fits the same bill. Both items are a bit heavy for some types of backpack trips, but they are worth their weight.

During mid-day, liquids usually play a big role. Most instant fruit and flavor drinks, are fortified with vitamin C which is a good idea. The pre-sweetened drinks are the most convenient for camping trips. Kool-aid, instant tea (or coffee) and a wide variety of fruit flavors are now available.

Supper is no problem. You have a choice of dehydrated or freeze-dried beef, ham or chicken dinners—complete with noodles and garnishes. The Lipton Company did a fine service for campers when it brought out their complete dinners. For about 80 or 90 cents for two healthy servings, the dinners have inside packaging which makes them compact, light and easy to stuff into a pack or food bag.

Kraft complete spaghetti dinner, everything you need for a tasty Italian dinner in one box, is one of my favorites. A camper has a choice of mild or zingy spices. Either way, it fills a need for a zippy meal. One box can feed four when used as a side dish. Or the same amount can offer two generous main course servings for a couple of adults.

Another Kraft product that is a favorite of ours is their quick and easy macaroni and cheese. Makes two large servings from one box or four side servings. As side dishes the macaroni and cheese goes wonderfully with crispy walleye or perch fillets.

Instant puddings, made with instant milk, are quick, fast-setting desserts that help fill the craving for something sweet. Produced in just about every flavor imaginable, the pudding can be mixed in a one-quart kettle. And one small box will yield about four generous servings. The pudding can be eaten as is. It can be topped with some instant milk. Or it can be used as a pie filling when poured into a plate or pan lined with a mixture of graham cracker crumbs and brown sugar. A smaller cobbler version of the pie can be created into a gourmet dessert when wild berries for the picking are in seasons. Served hot or cold,

(Above). Instant soups are good for lunches, snacks and adds before supper. All that is added is hot water.

(Right). Old reliables like sardines, although heavier than most specialized pack foods, add taste treats to camp diets.

the fresh cobbler, made with instant pudding, graham crackers, brown sugar and ripe berries could very well be the highlight of any camping trip.

The foods already mentioned are just a sampling of relatively new, lightweight ingredients that can serve the camper. By the time you read this, new and better products may be finding their ways to supermarket shelves. But one thing for sure, the old standbys, the ingredients that have produced many a camping feast, will be around.

There is nothing, in my opinion, that beats a plastic sack full of Bisquick. With it, I can whip up light pancakes for breakfast, turn out some pretty fair drop biscuits (laced with honey) for lunch and use it as the main ingredient for that evening's fish frying batter.

A camping trip without pork and beans? Hardly ever. The only thing that holds back the old fashioned variety, thick with molasses and brown sugar, might be a backpack over its weight limit. But for the car camp, horse pack or RV galley, the pork and beans seems to have been born in the outdoors.

There was a time when tiny, relatively lightweight canned goods made up the bulk of a camper's grub box or food sack. Sardines nested in mustard or tomato sauce made good lunches and quick snacks. And, for those who like them (I don't) Vienna sausage fits some needs. Canned Spam can be sliced for sandwiches, or it can be fried in the morning as breakfast meat. Stew and hash, although never equaling the fresh kind brewed and mixed in camp, has a place in the can—and in camp.

The Extras

One of the handiest items to come along recently, at least as far as the camper (backpacker) is concerned, is liquid margarine. In a plastic squeeze bottle, it cannot be beat for pancakes, hot biscuits, Indian bread and many other uses that margarine has. It can be used as cooking oil, although considering it as a luxury, especially on a backpack trip. I would tend to substitute regular cooking oil that can be carried in a plastic squeeze bottle.

In fact, a lot of extras—luxuries of sort—can be safely carried in plastic squeeze bottles. Not only are such things as pancake syrup, honey and cooking oil lighter, there is less hazard of breakage with plastic bottles. And, whether they are used from a vehicle camp or when backpacking, they are easier to pack.

Fruit really cannot be considered an extra. Conventional campers, with the aid of modern ice chests, can stock up on a hefty supply of fresh fruit and be assured it will keep reasonably well. The backpacker too, has a fine selection of supermarket fruit. Those dried or freeze-dried packages of apples, apricots, peaches and other varieties have been so welcome on the back woods trips I have taken, that I have saved the best for last. Eaten as is for snacks, or steamed for breakfast or any after meal desserts, the market dehydrated fruit selection is a good one.

Other healthful nourishment comes in bags of raisins, figs and dates. Nuts of all varieties are rich in protein. Shredded coconut is good for you. And sweets—plain, simple candy bars, may not get the high rating of professional nutrionists, but they have given me plenty of energy and psychological lifts during tough hikes.

Simple as it may seem, there are some men and women, some mothers and fathers, some teenagers, who are stymied when it comes to their selection of camping food from the local market. These same persons may efficiently, confidently and wisely shop every week for a family of four at home. But when it comes to food for the outdoors, they are lost.

Look for the new quick, lightweight, one-step meals first. Chances are you have used them at home. Add some of the old favorites like beans and fixin's. Keep enough fresh fish to spice the store bought menu. Add wild food where you safely can. And you have the makings of great eating.

Lightweight supermarket foods are ideal for boat-kayak camping too.

Cooked slowly, lovingly in a Dutch oven outdoors, chili con carne is Mexico's greatest contribution to the abundant life.

CHILI

...GREATEST INVENTION SINCE THE CAMPFIRE

by ADAM JACKSON

MY OLD FRIEND and hunting buddy Sam Houston Brown isn't likely to be recalled among the heroes of the Lone Star State as is his namesake and second cousin twice removed. But anyone who ever spent any time outdoors with the old pioneer isn't likely to forget the experience. His motto and happy philosophy was "all's well that ends well."

No matter whether it was a deer hunt, a dove shoot or simply jug fishing for channel catfish on the Rio Grande, Sam would always bring to camp a certain homemade ambrosia to top it off. No, it wasn't corn likker or sour mash or even tequila. However it *was* a surefire remedy which more than made up for any suffering from cactus punctures, sore behinds, missed shots at the biggest whitetails or being suddenly drenched by gully-washing downpours.

It was, believe it or not, a large iron pot of the best chili con carne brewed west of . . . well, anywhere.

As far as I know, Sam went to the grave without leaving behind any recipe or instructions on how he made the stuff. That is unfortunate, in fact, tragic. But when the hallowed subject of outdoor cooking in general, or chili in particular, pops up, I can't help thinking immediately about the old Texan. Writers have described many different meals or dishes as being fit for the gods, fit for a king, etc. But let me go one step further; I submit that chili is

---

Adam Jackson has hunted most parts of the country and has tested each area's specialty foods. His culinary tastes reflect his unique life style. The best food is wild; the best cook is a better improviser than a reader.

"The aroma of good chili should generate rapture akin to a lover's kiss."

fit for the American outdoorsman. And I am not alone.

Will Rogers always judged a new town by the quality of its chili and said he never met a chili-lover he didn't like. The Texas prison system may not be exactly a new land of milk and honey for the inmates, but the chili served is memorable enough that ex-cons frequently write to the wardens requesting the recipe. Barry Goldwater once said he would rather have a good bowl of chili than the best strip steak in town (always the politician, he didn't say which town) and Lyndon Johnson served up prodigious amounts of what he called Pedernales River chili at his ranch. On his 103rd birthday recently, a Kinney County, Texas, rancher observed that he owed his longevity "to being a bachelor, to not smoking, to indulging only in good clean bourbon and chili without grease that Nan (his sister) cooked."

Jesse James would not rob a bank in McKinney, Texas, because his favorite chili parlor was next door. W.C. Fields said that chili was the best reason he could think of for sitting down very long at a dinner table. John Pershing, who probably tasted his share of it while shooting up the Mexican border, noted that a cavalryman could go farther on a meal of chili and a canteen of water than on any other ration of similar weight. It should be noted in all fairness that some of his horse soldiers did not share that notion.

There is even a club, the International Chili Appreciation Society with headquarters in (where else?) Texas, which meets annually to test, compare, rave about and otherwise wallow in the wonders of that delicious elixir. Part of the Society's slogan states that "the aroma of good chili should generate rapture akin to a lover's kiss." If that seems too camp or conservative nowadays, remember that it was composed quite a long time ago when a lover's kiss was wow!

◀ Chili is as Mexican as an old mission in Sonora.

Anyway, here we have the finest dish ever invented; Julia Child, Escoffier, Cantonese and French cooking to the contrary. So let's see how, why and where it originated.

It may come as a surprise to many cooks that the source of any genuine chili is really a fruit. It grows on the woody plant, *Capsicum frutescens,* which thrives very well in arid environments of northern Mexico, especially of Sonora and Tamaulipas, and the southwestern United States. When the reddish fruit pods are picked, completely dried in the sun and powdered, we have what is often called molido—the delicious, distinctively pungent flavor. It should be noted here that there is considerable difference in molidos. Depending mostly on where grown, the flavor may range from very hot to mild. Some even have a sweet taste. Those sold under various brand names tend to be fairly uniform so that a cook can select what best suits his own taste.

Chili con carne—chili with meat—originated with poor people in northern Mexico and almost certainly out of necessity. The Sonoran (Coues) whitetail deer was the most abundant, most available source of protein there and venison was used as the meat. Dusting this meat with chili powder was a method of preserving it in the sometimes intense heat as well as flavoring it. Incidentally venison is still the best base, bar none, for making the best chili because it is very lean and nutritious. Furthermore the least desirable and even the toughest cuts from neck and shank can be used. Nor does the size and age of the deer make much difference. By the time it has undergone sufficient, slow cooking under the influence of chili and other

95

Working Mexican men hurry home for a delicious, nutritious lunch of chili, made from molido, a reddish fruit pod.

seasonings, the venison will be absolutely tender and irresistable.

Much research has been done to discover the original, traditional chili con carne recipe—if just one actually existed. Perhaps the following will come as close as any other, having been used for at least a half-century to feed a dozen hungry ranchhands on one old estancia.

Chop up four to five pounds of venison into small pieces say the size of marbles. Over an open fire, in a large enough cast iron Dutch oven, brown the meat in a minimum amount of lard, a small quantity of venison at a time. When all is browned, drain off excess fat and mix the meat with three or four teaspoons of chili powder— molido. Let this flavoring cook into the meat for 20 minutes or so on a low fire, stirring it occasionally.

Next remove the oven from the fire and add just enough water to cover the venison. Stir in one teaspoon of oregano, a pinch of cumin, two cloves of chopped garlic, one teaspoon of salt and two large chopped onions. If you happen to like a very hot chili, this is also the point to include three or four small, hot pepper pods. But do so with caution because most afficionados do not prefer a very hot chili. But with or without, cook the mixture slowly for at least an hour, stirring all frequently. The chili will then be ready to eat. But wait . . .

Let's assume there is no great hurry. In that case allow the cooked meat to cool and then carefully skim off any fat which congeals on top. Set aside the pot in the coolest possible place overnight—perhaps just leave it outdoors or maybe set it in a cool spring or brook. Let it freeze if it gets cold enough outside. Next day or the day after, simmer it again with loving care for about an hour. It may be necessary to add a little water. Then gorge on the most exquisitely robust stew ever devised by hungry humans— hopefully along with a cold beer or two.

Paradise Found!

Still—let's keep things in perspective. Not all outdoorsmen agree on what kind of chili is best. Some like it hot;

The pause that more than refreshes. A skillet of chili will make this outdoorsman fairly fly over the roughest country.

probably most prefer it mild. Some don't mind a little grease; others abhor it. Of course venison isn't always available, but keep in mind that elk, moose, antelope and bear are fair enough substitutes. Even beef can be used and the cheaper and leaner the cuts, the better. Although original chili con carne recipes call for diced meat, many chili fans would rather use ground meat.

Even the solid, militant, old International Chili Appreciation Society is racked with a certain amount of dissension; one hard core faction insists that beans—no kind of beans whatever—can be a part of any chili dish. Others reply "why not?" Aren't beans delicious, inexpensive (that's another great thing about chili; it's comparatively cheap, even today) and protein-rich. I should insert here that Sam Houston Brown leaned slightly toward the affirmative and so do I, but not *too* heavy on the legumes if you please. Better even than kidney or any other red beans, by the way, are lentils. My wife Jenny (who is looking over my shoulder) says to be sure and add that.

Strange as it may sound there are even opposing factions over whether wine goes with chili or not—and if so, which wine. But all, according to the most recent concensus, agree that tomatoes have positively no place in chili. Sure you usually get tomatoes in some restaurant chili (even in Brownsville, El Paso and Laredo) or when they celebrate South of the Border night at the PTA or Elks club. But tomatoes are out and that's the end of it. The chili powder itself takes care of any red color that your sensitivity requires. No need to add an Italian touch to Mexico's greatest contribution to the abundant life. A few—a very few—have even added rice to chili, but let's do more here than just mention such a questionable practice. It's like dipping raw oysters in chocolate sauce.

Now men naturally make the best outdoor cooks and that goes double when you're talking about brewing up a proper chili. Which nobody can deny. Just the same Jenny has her own recipe and anyone who ever sampled it would have to admit that it belongs in this article. She calls it her "respectably hot but not scorching chili" and that is an appropriate description for it. I call it her "how to keep the menfolk at home harmony formula." Anyhow here goes:

To start Jenny needs the following which normally are on hand at the Lazy B, especially the three or four pounds of venison. Also required are five tablespoons of peanut oil, two cups of onion chopped coarsely, four chopped garlic cloves, four tablespoons of chili powder, 1½ teaspoons each of oregano and cumin, one teaspoon of crushed red pepper, two cups of beef broth (or dissolved beef bouillon), two cans of red beans and/or one cup of dry lentils cooked, one tablespoon salt, one teaspoon sugar, one or two tablespoons of yellow cornmeal.

First ingredient for cooking chili is a deer—venison—but remember that any big game or even beef will suffice.

Trail camp in the Gila Wilderness—and guess what's cooking in that big iron pot.

Jenny sears the meat, which is cut into ½-inch cubes, thoroughly in the hot cooking oil, using a wooden spoon rather than a fork to do it. When browned the venison is put aside in a separate bowl. She then wilts the onion and garlic in the remaining fat before adding the chili powder, oregano, cumin and peppers which are well stirred with the onion.

The beef broth is added next, then the salt, sugar and beans, broth and all, mixing everything thoroughly together. That done, Jenny returns the meat and cooks the whole works for about an hour or until she determines that the meat is tender. Satisfied that it is, the chili is left to cool overnight or even longer until needed.

When eventually ready to serve it, Jenny simmers the chili, adding just enough of the cornmeal so that all is not too soupy or runny to be ladled out in an evergreen woods, beside a cool blue lake somewhere, or even across the tailgate of our jeep. Sometimes she also produces a guacamole salad (avocados, minced onion, fresh lime juice, chili powder, pinch of salt) and always there is Coors beer on ice in the chest. My wife has never won any blue ribbons for this masterpiece, but that is easily explained; she has never entered any competitions. And I'll take no chances with that high-falluting Chili Society trying to steal her away.

Maybe—hopefully—I've made a point in all the above. You'll go a long distance and maybe completely around the world trying to match a good bowl of chili. But for a hearty outdoor meal you just can't beat it. Even some of the concoctions (yes, even *some* brands of canned chili) which would make Sam Brown restless under his tombstone are not all that bad in a tight pinch.

Summed up: our Mexican friends surely hit the jackpot when long ago they first discovered the chili plant and how to make the most of it.

Amen, brothers.

the GRUB BOX

by BEAU USHER

Homemade grub box can be used as food preparation table as well as for storage.

CHUCK WAGON COOKIE had one. And the boys riding herd on the steers from Abilene to Amarillo would have been plumb upset if the grub box wasn't stocked plumb full of good fixin's. But the grub box or chuck wagon was more than a traveling grocery store. It was more like a mobile kitchen. With the turn of a wooden latch, the trail cook could uncover a highly organized, efficient kitchen, so clean and well stocked that Betty Crocker would kick her heels with joy.

Originally from Cincinnati, Ohio, Beau Usher visited Santa Fe, New Mexico 15 years ago on a vacation and has not returned home since. His infatuation with the West has grown deeper and may now be called adoration. Being a practical man, he believes that camp cookery is a matter of common sense. To him, the surrounding country is more important than what you eat.

Meal planning, food preparation and eating played vital roles on the trail drives of good cow and horse outfits. If the food was good, nine times out of ten the morale would be too. A trail cook was hired by the foreman of the drive with just as much, if not more, care than a seasoned drover. The outfits that hired their cooks in the saloons, the night before the drive started, usually paid for their hazy, hasty choices in erratic eating schedules; poor menu planning; stomach-aches and gas pains. Morale suffered just as it does when today's modern camp cook fails at the job.

Smart outdoor cooks, those who kept the cowboys full and happy, and modern day camp chefs, learned that a compartmented grub box was often the key to prompt, well organized meals. But amazingly enough many novice campers, and some veterans too, are missing a grub box in their basic stock of camp gear.

With the exception of size, grub boxes have changed

99

Recessed drawers hold individual packets of soup, coffee, tea, sugar, salt, pepper and spices. Note spaces for pots and utensils.

(Below). Food and supply check list keeps grub box stocked regularly.

little over the years. Cattle drive boxes were big ... often as wide as the chuck wagon itself. With the number of men that Cookie had to feed, pots, pans, utensils and the basic supplies of salt, sugar and coffee were always the economy size.

Grub boxes today are built to fit into the back of station wagons or the trunk of cars. They are smaller in size than the chuck wagon boxes, but basically the same. The best ones are still homemade from wood and designed for specific, personal needs.

The most important function the modern day grub box performs is keeping the basics of camp cooking and eating ready in one, handy, mobile kitchen. It eliminates the need for searching for such culinary staples as salt, pepper, sugar, coffee, tea, cocoa, powdered fruit drink, ketchup and mustard. The box guarantees that the can opener, bottle opener, spatula, forks, spoons, knives, matches, pots, pans, canned heat, plates, cups and toilet paper will not be forgotten at home.

The grub box is a second kitchen. When it is independently stocked with the items above and always ready, it can save at least two hours of packing and unpacking time on each trip. For the spur-of-the-moment, weekend camper or the two-week vacationer, the grub box is a reliable insurer for peace of mind. You may forget the caviar, but you won't forget the mustard—it is in the grub box. The box is stocked with the items that are most commonly left behind . . . the roots of good outdoor cooking. And that is why the grub box is so important. With the little, but vital items taken care of, more time can be spent on trip planning; packing the gear; and making sure the tent, sleeping bags, cooler and stove are in good order.

My grub box is made of exterior, ½-inch plywood. The four recessed drawers and molding are constructed of ¼-inch exterior plywood. The box is held together by finishing nails and glued in all joining sections. Exterior corner brackets give a final touch of durability.

The box is sealed with caulking compound which makes it as waterproof as a wooden box can be. The caulking also protects the contents from road dust which often works its way into a vehicle. The sealant keeps even the smallest insects out. The grub box can be placed directly on the ground and still keep all undesirable elements out. One or two coats of exterior enamel gives further protection to the wood . . . and makes the box virtually weatherproof. Clear shellac or varnish add a nice finish to natural wood and also give protection. Some outdoorsmen add sport decals, like game animals, fish and birds to liven up the box.

Grub box hardware includes carrying handles on either side. The swing out lid is held in place by chains making the lid a sturdy work shelf. And two latches hold the lid securely closed when not in use. Wooden knobs for the drawers can be cut and carved from scrap wood or commercially purchased, screw-in knobs can be used. The drawers are recessed with ¼-inch molding to insure they stay in place on rough roads or when the box is loaded and unloaded. The molding is held in place by glue and brads.

The grub box is 2½ feet wide by 2½ feet high and 2 feet deep in its deepest part. Empty, it weighs about 15 pounds; full, it can weigh as much as 50 pounds depending on what is stored in it. The grub box is definitely not an item that should be loaded, unloaded and moved around frequently. It can be constructed however, to be set in a suitable place in camp . . . and left there regardless of the weather.

In the four recessed drawers, items such as matches, can openers, extra lantern mantles, individual packets of soup, coffee, sugar, tea, salt, sugar, pepper, non-dairy creamer, instant gravy and spices can be safely and securely stored. One drawer can be set aside for utensils—knives, forks, spoons—just like home.

The grub box I have also has enough open, spacious compartments for the larger items. The bottom section of the box, for example, is not compartmented at all. I keep small and medium size fry pans there. A two-quart kettle; one-quart kettle and coffee pot; plates; two lids and drinking cups that are calibrated as measuring cups. For awhile, I stored a week's supply of army C-rations in the bottom compartment for emergencies. But due to their weight and space, I have since switched to dehydrated and freeze-dried foods that weigh considerably less and take up little room. Those foods sometimes fill in nicely for fishless or gameless days—or just for some variety.

Remaining shelf space, all of which is "lipped" by ¼-

Space Blanket cover and insulator is good for keeping non-perishables cool and clean.

Large quantity of dehydrated and freeze-dried foods can be kept in stuff bag.

Backpacker's answer to grub box is food stuff sack that keeps things in order.

inch molding to keep items from sliding out, is used for a supply of paper plates and cups; canned heat (Sterno); plastic squeeze bottles of cooking oil, mustard and ketchup and larger cooking utensils like spatula, fork, pot handles; single burner stove and aluminum foil. Extra space can also house such luxuries as transistor radios, flashlights, aspirin, toilet paper, toothbrushes and vitamin pills.

Since none of the items usually contained in the grub box can spoil, they can be stored there. My wife typed and taped a basic check list to the inside lid of the box. When we are low on certain items, she checks them off with a red pen that we keep inside the box for that purpose. The next time she goes to the grocery, she replenishes grub box supplies, making sure they are put in the box and not on our kitchen shelves. This way, we know we are ready to go at a moment's notice.

We have discovered that by storing the entire box in the back of our 4WD, more overnight camping trips have resulted. The reason being, I feel, is that we have all the basics already, and that the addition of a few items like bread, eggs, meat and liquids will give us enough food stock for great eating. The box has even come in handy for weekend drives into the country when sudden bursts of appetite make us turn to the grub box for soup, cocoa, crackers, sardines or other snacks. It is just plain handy.

In camp, the grub box set on logs, camp table or picnic bench is the center of the outdoor kitchen. During a camping stay of one week or more, it provides the backwoods chef with a tool for organization. At his or her fingertips are the basic ingredients and tools for every meal. The box also provides counter space—something that camp stove chefs never seem to find enough of.

A handy addition to the grub box, especially in areas devoid of trees or shade, is a nylon or canvas drop cloth. One end of the cloth can be tacked to the back of the box. The other end, with enough material so that it can be draped loosely over the box, can be weighted with a stick or a couple of fishing sinkers. With a rock, or another stick, positioned on top of the box, and the cloth draped over it, air space and shade are provided. This keeps the contents inside the box cool. Although grub box items should not be the perishable variety, things like mustard, ketchup, bread (on occasion) and any items that could melt, can be kept longer.

Stuff bag handle and construction should be tough enough to easily support filled bag (about 25 pounds here) so that it can be suspended from tree in bear country.

Backpacker's Grub Box

It stands to reason that a conventional grub box is out of the question for the backpacker. Therefore food or grub sacks take the place of the rigid wooden box.

Grub sacks are made of heavy, nylon material. The best ones have heavy duty plastic zippers that run the length of the bag, usually 24 inches or so. When filled the bag stands about a foot high. The zipper opening, rather than a drawstring opening on top, makes it easier to select foods from the bag. Some food sacks are divided into three compartments by canvas or nylon dividers sewn into the bag. The dividers have a purpose. They can separate breakfast, lunch and dinner, for instance. Or they can make it easy for the cook to find such basics as salt, pepper and commonly used spices. Complete packaged dehydrated dinners can be stored in one compartment. Things like cheese, dried salami, jerky and snacks can be stored in another compartment. Like the wooden grub box, the main function of the food sack is to organize foods and cooking tools.

A complete ten-day food sack may weigh as much as 20 pounds depending on the nature of the backpack trip. The sack should have a sturdy, sewn or riveted-on nylon or canvas carrying handle. The whole works, when filled, should fit into a backpack compartment. Ordinarily, the food is divided by packers into several food sacks. After a day's hike the sacks can be placed near the eating area and that day's cook has all the meal makings at the fingertips. Different sacks can be marked as to what they hold.

After use, sacks can be zipped and hung if need be (in bear country) or stuffed back into the pack. Foods carried in the sack should be packaged in soft, plastic bags . . . sometimes double sacked, and fastened with a plastic tie-wrap. This keeps food sack contents pliable for stuffing into packs. It prevents sharp-edged aluminum packages from ripping or puncturing plastic bags. The food sack protects food and utensils from moisture, animals, dust and insects. Mainly though, the sack is an organizer—a convenient way to pack food. There are some excellent food sacks sold at sporting goods and camping supply outlets.

Whether the grub container be soft or hard, good, well-planned, "on-time" meals usually result.

EATING

Eating on the move at rest stops and picnic areas not only breaks the monotony of the road but offers ideal opportunities for sightseeing and an exquisite snack.

ON THE MOVE

by JACK SEVILLE

I FIND, like my contemporaries, I have been growing more discriminating about my diet. Aging suggests itself as contributory; an increasing relish of fine food accompanying a decline of other appetites. But I dismiss the premise.

It is a fact, however, that when dining out we search for a restaurant which specializes in local fare or complicated dishes which we don't often attempt on our own. On the road, we assiduously avoid the gastronomical gamble of stopping hit-or-miss at roadside beaneries.

Instead, on trips by passenger car, we slake our thirst from an insulated jug—with cold water, in deference to our dog. *Sans* dog, it might be iced tea or water spiked with the juice of a lemon—to increase its quenching quotient. Often another vacuum bottle contains hot coffee or bouillon. An ice chest contains the makings of a quick snack or an ample picnic.

Snacking is made easy with a box of crackers, a block of cheese and a small hard salami which does not require refrigeration. On the other hand, a picnic can be as noble and as varied as time and imagination will allow. How much more enjoyable than a soggy sandwich is a cold roast chicken and a half-bottle of chilled wine!

We have friends who are addicted to spur-of-the-moment picnics. The only "camping gear" they own is a well-honed jackknife and a box of plastic spoons kept in the glove compartment.

When the spirit moves, they point their station wagon to the nearest town, passing up the neon-lit fast-food emporiums for the neighborhood shopping center. There they purchase delicatessen sandwich meats, cheese, cole slaw, and pickles. They'll pick up chilled cans of soda and some fresh fruit. If there is a bakery, they'll add the luxury of fresh-baked bread and pastry. On the edge of town or back on the highway, they'll locate a secluded spot where they can spread a blanket or beach towel and enjoy a feast *alfresco*.

A real boon for roadside cooking and eating is the increasing number of roadside rest stops. The more enlightened states, like my own state of Virginia, provide attractive oases with clean restrooms, drinking water, picnic tables, grills, trash containers and public telephones. Some have a visitor-information staff, and all are patrolled by police and maintenance crew.

They are provided in the interest of safety as well as convenience. A rested driver is obviously a safer driver. Those who are urged on by the how-many-miles-you-can-make syndrome, should consider that by making a rest stop

---

Jack Seville, Recreational Vehicle editor for Sports Afield, *runs his free lance writing business from Onancock, Virginia. A long-time devotee to the outdoors, becoming a true outdoorsman is a never-ending art to his way of thinking.*

---

the meal stop, they've saved time—as well as money and the probability of a bellyache—by avoiding the drive-in "Greasy Spoon" further down the road.

All you need to be nominally self-sustaining is an ice chest. Even the least expensive styrofoam box, which remains one of this century's best bargains, will suffice.

And there is no need to stop there. Eating on the move need not be limited to cold foods. At improved roadside rest stops any motorist can be a gallivanting gourmet. All one needs is a bag of charcoal briquets, a can of fire-starter and a roll of heavy-duty aluminum foil. The foil, of course, performs multiple services—fashioned into pans and plates, as well as a cocoon for vegetables (like buttered corn on the cob) cooked in the coals.

When you become hooked on the idea, you'll go one step farther and add a portable camp stove for quicker, cleaner and more sophisticated cooking. Today's camp stoves are as easy to use and as efficient as your kitchen range. You will, however, have to contend with the variables of ambient temperature, altitude and wind. And, you do have to make a choice of fuel—either gasoline or liquid petroleum gas. Safety as well as convenience should be considered.

White unleaded gasoline, sold at some service stations, has been the common fuel for camp stoves, but most stove manufacturers recommend the specialized liquid fuel produced for those appliances. This highly refined light petroleum naphtha contains no lead and almost no sulfur, and it's better for burning in stoves because anti-rust and anti-gum compounds have been added.

Although slightly more expensive, liquid petroleum (LP) gas is more convenient. It is available in 14-ounce disposable canisters (about the size of a quart bottle) as well as in the larger refillable tanks used to fuel appliances on recreational vehicles.

Used as directed, all of these fuels are safe and efficient, but misuse can be hazardous. Gasoline, naphtha, fire starter and stove fuel should be stored in leak-proof steel containers, plainly marked and tightly sealed. Because the fuel cans should be kept away from direct sunlight and out of enclosed areas where heat will cause the fuel to expand and leak out around the cap, they are not ideal for use when car camping.

LP gas will also ignite on contact with a flame or spark. The gas vapors are heavier than air and refillable tanks should always be stored outside or isolated in ventilated compartments. But, because the 14-ounce canisters have self-closing valves and a limited quantity of fuel, they are the least hazardous. Small, lightweight and with an ample fuel supply for one outing, they are ideal for picnicking or camping by car.

A two-burner stove and a 14-ounce canister of LP gas

For quick but elegant roadside meals, self-sufficiency is a must. This calls for careful planning and foresightful buying and not depending on stopping next to a supermarket.

will take up no more space than a small overnight bag, in fact, they fold down to the size of a small suitcase and have a convenient suitcase-type carrying handle.

By using disposable cooking and eating containers and utensils, you of course eliminate the need for dishwashing and thus the need for a sink. However, some of the so-called disposable items can be used again if handled with care—especially the heavy aluminum-foil ware. And there is an ingenious plastic container in the shape of a shallow sink—you carry a supply of water in it and when turned on its side, it serves as a sink.

Anyone who really gets hooked on do-it-yourself eating on the move sooner or later will devise his own portable kitchen kit, food locker or grub box, whatever it might be called in your area. If you are not handy with tools, the mail-order houses catering to campers have them ready made.

Today all forms of recreation are suffering from increased pressure with camping and picnicking among the most popular. As a result we often have to substitute artificial or controlled conditions. We see it in put-and-take fish for the angler, pen-raised birds for the hunter, sometimes trailer sites by reservation and camping by permit.

And there is an accompanying evolution taking place in the equipment we use, with plastics and man-made fibers substituting for the materials that had been Nature's raw products.

All of this isn't bad, mind you. On the contrary, in many respects we have more opportunity for recreation, it's closer

The type of eating you do while on the road is limited only by your tastes and ingenuity. Here a family turns a short stop into a feast with salami, cheese and white wine.

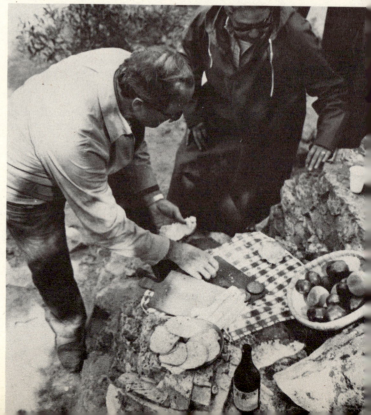

When you become hooked on the idea of cooking outdoors while traveling, you will probably add a portable camp stove for quicker, cleaner and more sophisticated cooking.

To be a gallivanting gourmet, all one needs is a bag of charcoal briquets, a can of fire-starter and a roll of heavy-duty aluminum foil. Then, even hotdogs take on a special flavor and more meaning when roasted over coals in the outdoors.

at hand, and we're outfitted a lot better than our grandfathers ever were. But the point to be made is that for the most part, our efforts until now have been to duplicate or preserve at least a facsimile of grandfather's forms of recreation. But times are changing.

As an example, in all of the outdoor books written before the last few years, the emphasis was on campcraft, woodcraft, woodsmanship. You'd get brownie points by living off the land, knowing which trees to fell for the best firewood, which ones to chop down to construct shelters, how to make a soft, aromatic bed of fresh-cut boughs, and how to bury your tin cans in the woods.

Now the challenge is to avoid using anything of Nature's but to take in and bring out everything needed to survive in comfort, and to leave no sign of our intrusion.

Certainly among life's little pleasures are the aroma of wood smoke and satisfying a lusty appetite with a hearty meal cooked and served at the campfire. Fortunately, there remains a time and a place to indulge the yen. But our increased awareness of ecology has caused the indulgence to lose status and often appear to be over-indulgence. It might even be argued that the pleasures of creative campfire cooking are more ritualistic and sensual than elevating.

Our original pattern was to emulate the nomads who travelled with no excess baggage. That aspect is still fundamental, and it's easier to do today than it ever was. We have lightweight, low-bulk food as well as featherweight equipment. But no longer can we live off the land like the nomads. We cannot waste a tree to prove our woodsman-

Do-it-yourself eating on the move not only is more enjoyable but it sharpens your outdoor skills, builds independence and helps you escape the crowds and pressure of the city.

ship. Nor should we bury our tin cans and plastic wrappers —we carry them in full, we certainly can carry them out empty.

Nowadays, the emphasis is on thoughtful planning and skillful use of proven equipment. Today, that's what separates the tenderfoot from the surefoot.

Anyone who can read can learn to cook; anyone who can cook can cook outdoors. There is something pathetic about the grown person—man or woman—who protests he (or she) "can't boil water," and is perfectly willing, if not entirely satisfied, by a meal at any old hash house.

The best way to learn is by doing. This publication is for the doers and contains all anyone needs to know to get started or to become proficient. Before going on to the next article, some parting tips:

Cooking with charcoal takes a little longer—about 20 or 30 minutes before it has burned to glowing embers. Until it is reduced to embers, it produces less heat and will leave soot on the pots. Glowing embers on the other hand, will not soot the pots.

The cure for soot, when cooking over a wood fire, is to first smear soap or detergent over the outside of the pot. After use, it will easily wash off. If you've neglected this precaution, use sand and wood ashes to scour pots that have become blackened.

Work gloves make good pot holders. Tongs are handy to move hot coals and to shake off the gray ash which reduces the heat because it insulates the hot center of the coal.

Careless dishwashing can result in spread of germs and a quick outbreak of diarrhea. That's one good reason for using disposables. But if you do wash dishes, use hot, sudsy water and rinse well with boiling water.

In remote areas, where sanitary facilities are not available, don't dump dishwater in lakes or streams. Instead, pour it, along with waste food scraps in a brushy or rocky area where it will either be cleaned up by wildlife or harmlessly disintegrate.

Before drinking any water obtained from questionable sources, boil it for at least 10 minutes or treat it with Halazone tablets.

as the stomach growls

Nothing soothes growls like sizzling eggs and bacon outdoors.

by KATHLEEN FARMER

THE SCENE LOOKED too perfect to be real. An opal-colored nylon mountain tent shimmered in the sun, competing with its neighbor the high country lake for blinding brilliance. Taking in both tent and lake at the same time, an observer would have to shield his eyes from the diamond-shaped reflections bouncing off the surface of each. The wind wrapped the sleeping campers in a soothing, liberating lodgepole fragrance. Pine squirrels argued with a bold Gray Jay (nicknamed Camp Robber) and a persistent Uinta ground squirrel for crumbs from last night's hot dog buns.

Nature had singled the couple out at this moment for special treatment. She was treating them to the perfect show. But they were somewhere else dreaming.

"GGGRRROOOWWWWLLLL! GGGRRROOOWWWWLLLL!"

Gertrude bolted upright and then slowly and quietly laid down again. Wide-eyed, adrenalin pumped and pulsated, readying her body for action. She waited to hear it again. Afraid, she tried to hold her breath but succeeded only in gasping for air. "Who knows," she thought, "it might be my last."

"GGGRRROOOWWWWLLLL!"

"Oh, George, your stomach almost scared me to death."

Rubbing his eyes and rolling over in his pillow-soft down bag, he intended to ignore his growling stomach. The cuddly comfort, like being enveloped by a floating cloud, seduced him into a cat nap immediately.

"GGGRRROOOWWWWLLLL!"

"That does it. George, you must be starved. I'll get up and start breakfast. Can't have my pioneer husband suffering from lack of food."

While Gertrude wiggled out of her mummy bag, George muttered a lazy, "Hhmmm."

Gertrude dressed quickly into jeans, wool sweater, a vest stuffed with Dacron II, two pairs of wool socks and her vibram-soled hiking boots. "Brrr. These chilly mornings sure get ya moving fast." Gertrude zipped open the flap of the backpack tent and rolled over the elongated lump next to her which she knew to be her oblivious-to-the-world husband.

"Uuuuggg," he grunted. She giggled. She enjoyed waking before George for a change. Usually, she was the one sacked out. This morning things would be different. She would fix breakfast for him.

Today was the end of their backpacking adventure. They would break camp and hike the six miles back to their waiting car and civilization. George had treated her like a queen. The enticing aroma of frying bacon forced her out of the tent each morning. Being an experienced

Nutritionists say that breakfast is a good foundation to correct eating habits. In the outdoors, it is not only important, but fun.

"How did you know I'd like camping?" she asked him last night over the smoldering coals after finishing her third hot dog. (She customarily ate only one weiner but the outdoors increased her appetite immensely).

"I was lucky I guess."

"But how did you know? I sure didn't know if I could lug a 20-pound pack on my back over six miles of trail." She recalled the apprehension churning her insides right before they started on the hike. She imagined herself giving out half way to the campsite. She feared she could not do it.

"You love the novel and the different. You are in good physical shape because of your infatuation with tennis. You like fishing and the outdoors. It wasn't hard to predict you'd take to backpacking."

Crawling out of the tent, she felt like an old veteran of the rugged mountain life. She knew how to start the fire and carried wooden matches—the kind that strike anywhere—in a waterproof plastic bag. "Thank goodness, it's not raining," she mumbled under her breath. She was not that confident yet about her woodsmanship.

Before this backpack vacation, she considered breakfast to be a waste of time. She would rather sleep longer than get up early and prepare a meal. She would habitually arise 30 minutes before Martha picked her up for work at the ad agency. She would race to the bathroom and put on her makeup while dressing piecemeal. Brushing her hair, she would sip coffee intermittently. Hearing Martha honk the horn of the sporty Mustang, she skipped down the stairs, jumped into the front seat and they were off. A leisurely week-day morning was unheard of and unwanted by Gertrude. On weekends, she would sleep late and eat a sandwich for brunch. That was before she married George.

George awoke two hours before he left the house for his

Perhaps there is no finer smell in the outdoors (man-made) than bacon and eggs frying on a sunshine morning.

outdoorsman, George knew little tricks about building fires and cooking that she had found fascinating as well as ingenious. Like the morning it was raining. He broke off tiny branches found near the base of pine trees. "Twiggies," he called them. He placed them carefully into a tepee-shaped pile and held a lighted wooden match underneath the twiggies. Suddenly, they caught on fire.

"A one match fire. Not bad, heh?"

Gertrude could not believe her eyes. "Why aren't they as wet as everything else?"

George explained, "Twiggies are protected from moisture by the large limbs. Twiggies are close to the trunk and near the bottom of the pine tree and are shielded from rain and snow. You can always count on them. It's a good idea to carry an extra supply along in your pack in case you camp in an area with no pines. Twiggies produce a fast, hot blaze. Then, you slowly add bigger pieces of firewood. If they are damp, it doesn't matter that much, once the fire is already started."

Gertrude was amazed. This being her first backpack trip, everything was new to her. She knew nothing about the wilds but thanks to George she was learning fast. She loved it. Their marriage was only six months old. She thought she knew George pretty well yet this outing revealed another side of him—one she had never seen before.

job at the state Game and Fish Department. He showered, shaved, read the newspaper, listened to the news and sports on radio, sometimes watched the Today Show on TV. He enjoyed waking up completely before he arrived at work. George and Gertrude tried hard to adjust to each other's habits.

George's waking up so early was a point of irritation to Gertrude—that is, until this outdoor experience. She now understood why he relished the morning hours. In fact, she was beginning to enjoy and value the conversations and plans that they discussed over the steaming hot eggs and bacon. By plotting out the day's activities, she found herself looking forward to the day. The daylight hours became less humdrum and routine. She wondered if this fresh positive attitude would carry over to her working days as well as these relaxing vacation ones.

The firewood having burned down to glowing embers, George's words echoed in her mind. "Stomach growls are particularly ferocious when camping. Breakfast is the only known cure for them. Without breakfast, the condition will only worsen." How true. Never in her life had Gertrude been so hungry. She seemed to be craving food most of the time. At night, her dreams revolved around snacks, like guacamole dip with tortilla chips or popcorn —things that a backpacker would not include on his menu. Luxury items—treats that most people take for granted.

Gertrude filled the one-quart kettle with water. George had discovered a spring about 75 yards from camp. From this, he scooped the earth-dew into the one-gallon, heavy-duty plastic water bag. He hung the sack on the limb of a tree near the fireplace. There it was handy. Water is the basis of most backpack dinners. And while the meal cooks, the campers can alleviate severe stomach pangs with a bubbling cup of hot chocolate, instant tea or Tang.

Bacon is readied for the pan.

Kathy Farmer pours hot water into cupful of instant cocoa.

An instant drink that tastes good icy cold will double in flavor when mixed with hot water. George's motto is: "Cold outside, drink hot; hot outside, drink cold." The hot drink not only warms the innards. It stimulates warmth in the hands from holding the hot cup and bathes the face in heated steam rising from the liquid.

"The first step in fixing breakfast," Gertrude repeated to herself, "is to boil water for a hot drink to appease the stomach growls temporarily until you can prepare some 'real' breakfast." Instant oatmeal or dry cereal is okay if you are in a hurry to fish, hunt or explore. But the pain of an empty stomach is bound to strike again within the hour unless you have a heaping, honest-to-goodness breakfast. When a limited amount of time forces you to skimp on breakfast while camping, you will find yourself nibbling all day on snacks that never satisfy the hunger pangs. By suppertime, the growls will have intensified. Since you ignored them while they were located in the stomach, they will have moved upward until they reach your head. There they will stay until you meet their demands. This ailment more than any other chases campers back to civilization sooner than they had originally planned. And all because of not spending a little time and effort to prepare and eat and relish a nourishing breakfast.

Because this was Gertrude's first backpack expedition, George decided to break with the tradition of packing only

Kathy makes hotcakes in fry pan. Two burner skillet is even better.

Pancakes are a treat and can be enjoyed with a "flip" in the outdoors.

Early morning kayak ride . . . then a hearty breakfast back at camp.

dehydrated and freeze-dried food. He wanted Gertrude to bask in the wonders of nature yet still have some of the culinary pleasures of home. She would be ready for the entire backpack package of strenuous exercise, instant food and spectacular scenery after two or three trips. For right now, though, the rigors of the outdoors would produce enough challenges. He did not want Gertrude to feel overwhelmed. He therefore included bacon, a commercial type of egg substitute and bread. On the next trip, he would bring a freeze-dried bacon bar, dehydrated eggs and a plastic bag full of Bisquick for biscuits.

There is no fragrance that compares to bacon sizzling, spitting and curling in a skillet over an open fire. This experience alone can transform a city-slicker into a die-hard outdoors lover. Gertrude too fell under the spell. She learned not to drain bacon on a paper towel like she would at home. On a crisp morning, this produces cold, cardboard-like bacon. Instead, push the bacon to one side of the skillet. Then add the eggs.

A motorized camper can carry regular eggs without problem. However, a backpacker usually ends up with cracked eggs seeping throughout his pack. One alternative is a cholesterol-free egg substitute, like one brand called Egg-Beater. It is found in the frozen food section of the supermarket. When defrosted, it is a liquid, one container equaling four eggs. For easy stuffing into a pack, it is best to transfer the liquid from the carton to a plastic squeeze tube. Once Egg-Beater is defrosted, it should be used within seven days. But it is nutritious and fat-free.

Another choice for backpackers is dehydrated eggs. Easy to prepare, tasty and simple to store in a food bag, a wide variety of egg dishes is available, including Western omelet and scrambled eggs with bacon bits.

For a bacon and egg breakfast, toast is next. Find a

It is easy to appreciate a scene like this on a contented stomach.

Kathy believes a good breakfast starts the day off right and most campers agree.

Gertrude licked her lips thinking of the delicious breakfast George served her two mornings ago. Rainbow trout fillets wrapped in a crisp Bisquick batter and pancakes with honey. "Fish for breakfast?" as she wrinkled her nose in distaste. That would have been her reaction if they were comfortably sitting in their snug kitchen at home. "Snugness opens the door for smugness," she thought with a half smile. "I have been cured of that affliction. Now I'm game for anything. What shall I concoct for breakfast this morning besides bacon? Something unusual that George will like." She flicked through a mental card file of her recipes. "An omelet—just the thing. And we haven't had one for ages. Why don't I whip up a mushroom and mint omelet? With the luscious snow mushrooms we found yesterday and the spearmint leaves we collected, it will be an unforgettable dish."

In the pampering softness of the sleeping bag, George was reliving a thrilling catch he made at his softball game two weeks ago. The score tied. The home team was up. The third batter hit a looper towards the center field fence. Back, back he went, climbing the fence with his left foot. Stretching . . . he caught it. The last out. Now they would go into extra innings . . . "Wait a minute. What's that spicy, entrancing smell? It's making me light-headed."

forked stick. It does not have to be green since it will not be placed that close to the flames. Place a piece of bread on the fork part and hold it about one foot above the flames. (This can be done on a gas or propane stove as well as open fire). How fast the bread toasts is surprising. Flip the toast. And in about five minutes at the most (depending on how long it takes to find a forked stick), you will have superb toast. This procedure can be used to toast sandwiches too. A cheese sandwich, especially on a snowy or rainy day, is truly a gourmet treat when it is toasted in this manner, melting the cheese in the process.

Instead of toast, biscuits are always welcomed. Bisquick is a handy mix for biscuits—all you add is water. Divide the dough into silver dollar size pieces and place them in an aluminum foil cocoon. Unless you have the even heat of a camp stove, be careful not to burn the bottom of the biscuits. It is easy to do.

"Are you awake already, George?"
"What are you cooking? Filet mignon?"
"Almost as good. A mushroom omelet with spearmint."
"Don't do anymore until I get out there. I want to witness the whole thing—from greasing the pan to gobbling it up. You are making outdoor cooking history. You must be."

A hearty breakfast is just the beginning. It sets the pace for the rest of the day. If breakfast is memorable, what will be in store for you during the next 24 hours? Something exceptional, that's for sure.

IT SEEMS LIKE ONLY yesterday that my brother Curley and I made the first winter ascent of the Grand Teton in 1936. Most people think a person is a little nuts to climb a mountain in winter today. They thought we were completely crazy in those days. The general comments around Jackson Hole, Wyoming among the cowboys were, "What the hell does the GD fool want to go up there for? How could he think about going up there when he could be drinking in the Cowboy Bar!"

But it wasn't so crazy. I had learned outdoor dressing techniques from some of the old trappers around Jackson Hole, who really dressed quite well. When I look back now, they knew a lot about conservation of energy. They thought that a person shouldn't go on an extended trip in cold weather in the hills unless he had bacon. One can understand that, because we know now that in order to

---

Paul Petzold has been a mountain climber and wilderness guide most of his adult life. The National Outdoor Leadership School is his way of acquainting people of all ages with the wild mountains and streams that he loves. His motto is: By showing outdoorspeople how to treat and live in the untamed parts of the world, these invaluable areas will be untainted by ignorance and neglect—thus unchanged.

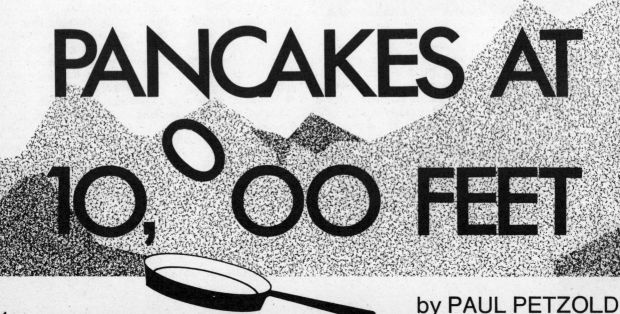

PANCAKES AT 10,000 FEET

by PAUL PETZOLD

keep warm you have to take extra amounts of salt. This salt is really necessary to keep your blood volume up and keep blood flowing to your extremities, like your ears and fingers. We know that lack of salt tends to dehydrate the body and draw the blood into the vital organs, leaving the extremities subject to frostbite. They didn't know that in those days, but they knew that you had to have salty bacon. The bacon provided some fat too, which helped them keep warm. Those old trappers always carried a lot of salt and salted their food rather heavily.

Of course, we didn't have the variety of food that we have today, but it was great. We took along elk steaks, homemade bread, candy, coffee and tea. Actually, as I look back on it, we haven't made a great deal of progress since that time. It seems very strange to me to see how the little knowledge that the old trappers had has been lost in the present generation. We are now teaching winter outdoorsmanship, how to be comfortable and warm in any weather—almost a new thing for most people.

I founded the National Outdoor Leadership School in 1965 in Lander, Wyoming because people were interested in the outdoors, conservation, winter camping and mountaineering, but no learning program existed that combined all these skills into a united, coordinated course of practical study. Now, we turn down about 2,000 applications a year, we have so many individuals trying to enroll in our school. Most of them are young and vitally concerned over the environment and how to experience it without destroying it.

Our school is a non-profit organization which trains qualified outdoor leaders and teaches people to conserve and enjoy the wild outdoors. As a result of experimentation, we have learned a lot about outdoor cookery.

In the outdoors the National Outdoor Leadership School (NOLS) teaches to eat often and never become hungry or thirsty for maximum health and energy development. Eat when you want and what you want. The following is what we have found successful from experience with hundreds of students of all types and from all backgrounds. We teach students how to plan rations suitable for backpack-

Winter camping requires special planning, clothing and equipment. If you know what you are doing, camping can be even more exhilarating in the winter than during the summer.

ing and within most people's budget and how to prepare meals that are both nutritional and taste terrific.

Fat's Not Ugly—It's Energy

The importance of good nutrition can not be overemphasized. Good nutrition has many elements—energy, nutrients and a good balance of salt and water. Energy keeps the body functioning at rest, does muscular work, maintains warmth and fights disease. Proteins, vitamins and minerals are needed as building blocks to repair tissue and build muscles. Water and salt maintain fluid balance and contribute to vital electrochemical reactions.

Food can be divided into three basic types: carbohydrates, fats and proteins. One gram of pure fat liberates nine calories of energy when burned. One gram of pure, dry protein and one gram of pure, dry carbohydrate both liberate four calories of energy. Because food must first be digested before being burned for energy, the energy loss due to digestion must also be taken into consideration. Simpler molecules are more easily digested than more complex molecules. Proteins are the most complex molecules; fats more complex than carbohydrates; and carbohydrates the simplest. Although both carbohydrates and proteins produce four calories on burning, carbohydrates lose less energy due to digestion. Therefore carbohydrates are more efficient energy foods than proteins.

Author Paul Petzold instructing a group of students at his National Outdoor Leadership School.

During strenuous activity greater than normal amounts of energy are needed. Fats and carbohydrates are the most efficient foods to supply this energy. Sugars and starches (carbohydrates) are quick energy foods supplying needed energy soon after eating. Energy in fat is more slowly released thus longer lasting. Fats eaten before retiring at night will help you sleep warmer.

The amount of calories needed varies with body build, activity and climate. Supply at least the number of calories normally eaten at home. Through trial and error, NOLS has established a ration of 3,750 calories per person per day for summer backpacking. For winter, approximately a 20 percent increase in calories is added making 4,500 calories per person per day. If dry rations are used, this will be about two pounds per person per day.

Man Does Not Live by Calories Alone

Calories alone will not maintain a healthy body. Since muscles and body tissue are mainly proteins, proteins must be added to rebuild the body. Likewise, vitamins and minerals are essential to good health. Generally, a well balanced diet will be sufficient. Nutritionists commonly use the method of the "Four Basic" food groups to insure adequate vitamins and minerals. The food groups are: 1) Meat, fish, poultry and meat substitutes; 2) Cereals and grains; 3) Milk and milk products; and 4) Fruits and vegetables. Two servings of each per day is recommended in addition to one stick of margarine and additional sweets for extra energy.

A complex interrelationship of salt and water regulates many body functions. The body needs both salt and water in balance. Water is a major component of the body and salt helps the body retain liquids.

Exercise, hot weather and altitude deplete one's salt supply. Lack of salt contributes to headaches, nausea, loss of appetite, muscle cramps and dehydration. The resulting dehydration further causes susceptibility to frostbite and hypothermia plus, if continued for any length of time, it will damage the kidneys. Altitude sickness or its milder form "mountain sickness" can be reduced by a proper water-salt balance.

Individual requirements vary. At NOLS we have found that salt tablets bought at drugstores have strong dosages that are disagreeable to some people. We use rock salt crystals which give a much broader range of dosages for differing individual requirements. Rock salt can be obtained at any supermarket. Let individual sweating determine the dosage. People who sweat very little will need only 3 to 5 crystals a day even when doing heavy exercise. Some people need as much as 15 crystals a day. The goal is to replace salt lost through sweating as overdosages of salt can also be detrimental. Maintaining one's salt requirement will help reduce mountain sickness, but is not a panacea. A slow ascent, sufficient water, rest, avoiding exhaustion and well-balanced meals are also needed to minimize altitude or mountain sickness.

A conscious effort must be made to drink sufficient water. Summer requirements range from two to three quarts per day. Winter and high altitude requirements range from three to four quarts per day. Thirst is a signal; so drink whenever the urge strikes. If water is unavailable along the trail, be sure to carry plenty.

Fixing Food on Top of the World

Rations have to be adjusted for high altitudes and winter. The higher the altitude, the less oxygen is available to metabolize food. The more complex foods, molecularly speaking, such as protein and fat, are harder to digest and utilize than simple sugars and starches. Keep proteins to

Obtaining water becomes a major task in the winter. This stream, fed by warm springs, does not freeze over but is polluted. Melting snow is therefore necessary for drinking and cooking water.

Winter camping demands top physical conditioning.

daily minimum requirements. Fats are still very important sources of concentrated energy at high altitudes, so take enough but do not overdo it. Low altitude (below 10,000 feet) winter expeditions do not have the digestion problems of high altitude, so rations should simply be adjusted to add more energy.

Most food in the winter should be easy to prepare, instant and of the one-pot variety. It takes 15 to 20 minutes to melt snow into water and another 10 to 15 minutes to boil the water—25 to 35 minutes before cooking can even begin. Avoid foods that need more than 15 minutes to prepare at sea level. Altitude doubles the problem. At 15,000 feet, water boils at 184 degrees F and will not get hotter without a pressure cooker. A meal that takes 30 minutes at sea level will never get cooked at high altitudes.

Because liquid intake is so important in the winter or at high altitudes, add extra soup bases and drink mixes to your rations.

Generally, no baking goods are taken except for pancake mixes. Allotted poundage in flour and cake mixes can be substituted with ready-made breads such as fruitcake. A few simple desserts perk up appetites. These should be desserts that can easily be made on a stove.

Alcohol if judiciously used can also enliven winter feasts. A spoonful per quart cuts the bland taste of snowmelt water. Flaming desserts are also possible. But a few simple guidelines must be followed. Do not drink alcohol in place of water during the day. Do not use alcohol to "warm up." Alcohol promotes circulation in the extremities reducing warmth in the core and may promote frostbite if given to an already cold person. In all cases, drink moderately.

Obtaining water becomes a major task in the winter. Melting snow is a tedious and time consuming job that must have top priority. Snow can be scorched if a pot of solid snow is set directly on a high flame. A bit of water in the bottom of the pail or slow heating with constant stirring will prevent this. After each meal, melt an extra pot of water for water bottles. Warm water bottles wrapped in a mitten or bootie when carrying will not freeze yet are readily available. Have both water and food available at night; for thirst and hunger are major reasons people sleep cold.

At high altitudes in the summer, the sun's radiation provides energy that can be utilized for obtaining water. If spending a day in camp, put a dark colored plastic tarp or rain parka in a hollow in the snow. Then place a small amount of snow in the tarp. The sun's energy absorbed by the dark color will melt the snow. Bail out the water and fill water bottles. Large amounts of water can be obtained this way.

Be sure to eat the food you carry. Generally, a real effort has to be made to eat 4,500 calories per day. A good rule of thumb is to eat and drink a certain number of cupfuls at each meal. Use a large 1½ to 2 cup capacity cup. Have one cupful of hot drink before breakfast, one to two cupfuls of solid breakfast and another cupful of hot drink after breakfast. Before supper, have one cupful of hot drink (soups are good), two to three cupfuls of solid supper and one cup of hot drink after supper. An extra cup of hot drink before bed is also recommended. Melt at least a pint of water to take to bed and sip on this at night and eat trail food when hungry. Leave about a cup for melting snow in the morning. Do not cut down on liquid intake to avoid getting up at night. If proper amounts of water are consumed, getting up at night is the norm. A full bladder will rob warmth and cause restless sleep. It's not so bad; stargazing is at its best at 2:00 a.m.

Coffee and other diuretics should be used in moderation in the winter. Diuretics do not allow water to be absorbed and dehydration results, even with sufficient liquid intake.

Clean Camp, Clean Spirit

Sanitation is important in campfire cooking to prevent plagues of diarrhea. Cooking gear should be cleaned after use and, *each time* before using, should be sterilized with boiling water. Do not use soap on dishes because diarrhea results if not rinsed properly. Boiling water will do the job. Scouring pads of any kind are not recommended because they collect germs. Pine needles and pine cones work as well and are disposable.

Avoid sharing personal eating utensils as much as possible. Use a large wooden spoon for stirring, not your own spoon.

If water is of questionable quality, use water purifiers. Halozone is very effective, killing everything except hepatitis virus. The safest method is to boil water to a rolling boil for 7 to 15 minutes. This kills all germs. In an area of good water, avoid stagnant ponds and water directly downstream from horse crossings. Be careful in your own camp so you are not the polluter of pure water. Do not wash dishes directly in streams; do not bathe directly in streams; place latrines well above the water table and away from streams and use biodegradable soaps.

Save Wilderness, Use a Stove

Where the wood supply is limited, stoves should be used. Stoves are convenient and absolutely necessary at high altitudes and in the winter. We highly recommend stoves for all wilderness use. If dead wood is plentiful, you can supplement with fires.

Several kinds of backpacking stoves are available. Kerosene or gasoline stoves are reliable in a wide range of conditions. Kerosene is less combustible, therefore safer, but more complicated to light. Gasoline stoves burn white gas or special lamp fuel, *not* automobile gasoline. Svea, Optimus and Ender are good brands of backpacking stoves.

At NOLS, we use Optimus 8R's for summer and 111B's for winter. These have proven to be reliable, efficient and able to withstand repeated use, although they are heavier than other models. Parts are easily obtained and repairing in the field is not impossible.

Where Beginners Flop

Burned, bland, overcooked and undercooked food is common of beginners and can be avoided. Cook on low heat. Start with sufficient water and check often to see if more is needed. Stir thickened foods often. Cook in clean pots to avoid burning old food stuck on the bottom. Use salt. A bland "soapy" taste most often is due to lack of salt.

Backpacking in the snow is strenuous exercise. A camper should be certain to eat 4,500 calories per day. Eat and drink whenever hunger or thirst strikes.

Salt brings out flavor in everything, but if overdone can make food inedible. Oversalting usually is a result of not accounting for the saltiness of flavor bases—so taste before adding salt. Overcooking is usually caused by poor timing of multiple ingredients. Generally, add freeze-dried food first, boil 10 to 15 minutes then add rice or pasta. Thickeners, milk and cheese should be added just before the dish is done—they tend to burn if added earlier. Cook pasta and rice until done (it is done when it tastes done).

Start most dry foods in boiling water as starches put in cold water tend to become gooey. Avoid draining as water soluble vitamins are lost this way. If you drain, save the water for soups.

Think of a backpacking stove or fire as a home stove. Most food made at home can be made while backpacking. Stoves and fires have controllable heat so utilize this quality. Cook on low flames with a stove and on coals barely burning with a fire.

Secrets from the School of Hard Knocks

Breakfasts: Powdered forms of food sometimes do not dissolve well in cold or boiling water. If mixed in lukewarm water (one part powder to one part water) into a paste and then added, lumping is minimized.

Oat and wheat cereals are nutritionally superior to rice and barley cereals.

Baking Goods: Pancakes are made of a pourable batter of biscuit mix and water with a small amount of margarine in the batter to prevent sticking. Pancakes are cooked by frying one side and flipping.

Cakes are basically pancakes with sugar added and a little more margarine to give good texture and are baked instead of fried.

Biscuits and muffins are stiff doughs. Biscuits are like stiff pancakes and muffins like stiff cake dough. Both are baked.

Cookies are a stiff dough with margarine instead of water as the main liquid ingredient and more sugar added. Sugar and margarine are creamed together and the flour and cereals are worked into this.

Brown sugar is slightly more nutritious than white sugar, more versatile and easier to pack.

Powdered eggs can be added to all baking goods to make them lighter and of better texture, but are not necessary.

Supper: Cheese becomes stringy when boiled or when added to dishes with lots of water. If you desire to add cheese to a soup, melt it in a white sauce first, then add. Cheddar is good for cooking and keeps well. Other varieties are good for new tastes, but generally do not keep as well as cheddar.

Several thickeners are available. If no more than three to four spoonfuls of flour are added, a good thickener is one part flour to one part water. Potatoes, cream of wheat, cream of rice, MPF and wheat germ are also thickeners.

Pasta and rice are interchangeable in most recipes. Pasta —a variety of spaghetti, egg noodles and macaroni—will form a major part of your diet with meat and sauces added for flavoring. Sugar is interchangeable with fruit drinks, pudding and gelatin mixes when low on sugar. Dry soup bases are good salt substitutes.

Powdered milk and margarine are not essential to most recipes but are added as nutritional boosters. Real butter may be taken in the winter in place of margarine. Take off all wrappers as butter freezes into a very solid block with the paper embedded. Butter will not keep without refrigeration, so margarine is used for summer backpacking. Margarine is added to almost everything and is the most concentrated energy food available. Take all wrappers off

A pioneer in winter camping and mountaineering, Paul Petzold feels outdoorspeople should feel at home in nature during winter as well as summertime.

as is done with butter. Margarine can be carried in plastic bags or in wide mouthed plastic bottles.

Nuts are excellent in main dishes and go well with vegetables. Most nuts are salted so cut down on regular salt.

Freeze-dried vegetables are major sources of vitamins and minerals. Sulphured fruit has more vitamins and minerals than "organic" dried fruits. Freeze-dried fruits are very expensive and are not necessary when dried fruits are included in the rations.

Wheat germ and MPF are nutritional boosters to be added to everything you cook.

Desserts: Dry gelatin desserts make excellent hot drinks and will gel if set out overnight.

If you choose to use candy, do so in addition to an already nutritious diet. Candy wrappers tend to stick to the candy with repeated freezing and thawing so remove before bagging.

Spices: Rock salt can be crushed between two spoons and used as regular salt.

A good basic selection of spices is: cinnamon, nutmeg, curry, oregano, chili powder, garlic and pepper. To this add any spice you particularly like. Liquid extracts and soy or Worcestershire sauce are also useful. Bouillon cubes or dry soup bases are used for flavorings.

Re-rationing: Two weeks is the extent of most people's pleasurable carrying capacity and in the winter extra fuel will also have to be accounted for. If an extended trip is planned, a method of resupply must be found.

Condensed by permission of Paul Petzold and the National Outdoor Leadership School from the "NOLS Alumnus" (Volume 2; Number 1) and *NOLS Cookery*, edited by Nancy Pallister and published by the Teachers College Press, Emporia, Kansas, 1974; price, $1.95.

Camp "smoked" beef jerky, hard-boiled eggs and a flask of fresh water are the makings for a quick lunch while wading a favorite trout stream.

BEEF JERKY: short-cut to an all-purpose food

by JAMES F. DAUBEL

THE TALL GRASS was soft and cool as I leaned back, feet dangling in the trout stream, for a short break under a warm May sun on Michigan's Manistee River. I had creeled two rainbows of unspectacular dimensions and had considered foregoing a lunch break until I began to feel my legs tiring from the strain of wading on this first trout outing of the year.

Upper reaches of the Manistee in Michigan's central Lower Peninsula offer some of the state's most picturesque surroundings. Glistening white birch trees stand at attention at river's edge. Deer can be seen drinking at the shoreline and grouse are heard drumming from nearby woodlots in early spring. I treasure the 15 minutes I spent watching from a discreet distance as a whitetail doe, immersed to her neck, laid cooling herself in a calm backwater in scorching August heat.

There are few pursuits in the outdoor world that beckon

James F. Daubel is a freelance writer and photographer. He is Executive Editor of the Fremont News-Messenger *and covers the latest outdoor happenings in Ohio, Michigan and the surrounding area. In addition, he writes a weekly outdoor column for the Associated Press of Ohio.*

me more persuasively than does trout fishing. But I live in Ohio where trout water is limited, so my fly-fishing is confined to the occasions when I can get free for a few days to make the six-hour drive to my favorite Michigan streams worthwhile.

To capitalize on the available time, I have devised a system for fishing several flies-only stretches on major trout waters like the Manistee. Assuming that I am camped some distance from the river, I park near the downstream limit of the section I plan to fish then hike by road to an entry point far enough upstream to provide sufficient water for a day's wade back to my car.

I usually begin fishing at mid-morning, working wet flies or streamers downstream until I pass my parking place near dusk. By that time I have scouted the most likely spots for dry fly fishing in the general vicinity of where I will exit the stream, preferably close to my car, after dark. At the first sign of the evening hatch, I switch to dries and work back upstream, fishing well after the sun sets until leaving the river for the short walk to my car.

I was at about mid-point in one of those day-long wades when I reached the familiar flat grassy bank and decided to sit for a spell and attend to lunch. I peeled off my fishing vest and smiled as I recalled the load I used to tote around with me all day.

Years ago when I initiated my excursions, I thought I had to pack a wide range of provisions, including a virtual kitchen, in order to survive a day away from civilization. Fully loaded, I resembled an overstuffed Mae West with legs.

Eventually I pared down to the basics and have even managed to improve my diet and reduce pack space in the process, thanks to a unique variation on preparing one of the oldest "convenience foods" in existence—beef or venison jerky. My luncheon menu now invariably consists of a couple of hard-boiled eggs, a flask of water and self-made jerky which is easily done in the camp oven.

The convenience of dried meat is considerable. I can prepare large batches at one time and it will keep indefinitely. Jerky is light, compact and it requires absolutely no fuss or time in preparation when I'm on the go. In fact, I often munch it as I wade, thereby avoiding any break in my fishing.

Dried meat known as "jerky" no longer is the food staple it was in days before modern refrigeration. But the passing of time has not diminished its value in terms of nutrition, portability and overall convenience in the out-of-doors. Those are important factors when you can't take prepared foods with you or when you don't want to interrupt fishing, hunting, backpacking or other outdoor adventures to cook.

Jerky is red meat that has been salted, dried and often smoked. It has fed man for generations. It served the Indians and pioneers so well because it could be stored or transported for long periods without spoiling.

There are many ways of making jerky but they all boil down to this: moisture is drawn out of the meat and salt is added as a preservative.

Most methods of making jerky are not feasible for the average sportsman. Traditional processes, aside from being complicated, call for elaborate equipment or time-consuming attention to detail.

That is why commercial jerky has become a novelty food, prohibitively expensive for most of us except for infrequent snacks. When I first conceived of the notion to pack only dried foods, I visited a specialty store near home with intentions of stocking up on jerky. I was rudely awakened. On a per-pound basis, the cost exceeded 30 cents an ounce! I learned later that homemade jerky is hard to find, and in stores that do stock it I've never seen the cost below $4 a pound.

In recent years, several processors have begun marketing a meat that is prepared like jerky and sold in cellophane packets. Displayed at grocery checkout counters and in taverns along with the salty sausage sticks, that type of jerky also is expensive, usually figuring out to 10 to 20 cents an ounce.

I was about to resign myself to toting sandwiches when the subject of deer hunting came up in conversation with Allan Wolter on a recent outing. Al is a ranger with the Wayne National Forest near Ironton, Ohio, and an accomplished bow hunter.

I had just bagged a deer in Texas and had the meat processed there and air shipped to Ohio. We were discussing cuts of venison and how to prepare them when Al suggested making jerky from the usually dry, tough cuts like the round steaks, butt or shanks. Much to my delight, he volunteered a recipe for making jerky in camp with only one ingredient that you would not routinely have on hand —liquid smoke, the secret to simplified, true flavor jerky.

Among our staples the next time afield were several

A wide knife helps cut thin strips off flank steak. Cutting is even easier if meat is partially frozen.

Two parts water to one part liquid smoke is the mixture that is brushed on beef to give it the smoky taste. Do not be too generous with the liquid or the taste will be too strong.

Salt is a preservative and adds flavor to beef jerky. Sprinkle it liberally on both sides of the meat strips.

Beef strips are put in oven for slow curing.

Salted and brushed with marinade, beef strips are placed on camp oven rack and "smoked" at about 100 to 150 degrees F for at least six hours.

packages of frozen venison and my folding camp oven, the type that fits on almost all standard gas-fueled or propane stoves.

Making jerky is easy but it does take time, although your attendance once the "smoking" begins is not mandatory. And though you needn't have the credentials of an outdoor Julia Childs to make a success of it, several fundamental rules should be kept in mind.

First, select only lean red meat for making jerky. Trim off any fat before processing and go over the dried meat again after smoking to remove whatever slivers of fat that may remain. Fat turns rancid and will taint jerky regardless of how well it has been dried.

Don't waste money on expensive cuts of beef and there's no need to use the better pieces of venison. The round or flank steaks, boneless brisket, butts or shank cuts all cure better (they usually contain less fat) and compare favorably with better cuts after processing.

The meat should be cut into thin slices. Thick chunks are hard to dry. Slice the meat in inch-wide strips about six inches long and from 1/8 to 3/16 of an inch thick. Slice across the grain with a wide knife.

To make slicing easier, I freeze the meat I'll use in camp before leaving home and bury it in ice to keep it at least partially frozen until I'm ready to use it. Slightly thawed meat can be sliced paper thin rather easily, although you don't want it quite that thin for jerky.

Begin by assembling your materials. In addition to the meat, you'll need a camp stove and oven, a bottle of liquid smoke (available in most supermarkets), table salt, slicing knife, brush, cup (for mixing), foil wrap and a heavy weight such as an iron skillet.

Slice the meat and stack the strips in layers, first in one direction then cross-ways, until it is all in a more-or-less orderly pile. If you're doing this in the open air, keep the meat covered to protect it from flies. When all the meat is cut and stacked, weight it with the skillet overnight. This helps press out moisture and reduces drying time.

The next day, brush the meat lightly on one side with a mixture of one part commercially bottled liquid smoke and two parts water. You may need to experiment with this phase a bit. Too much liquid smoke imparts an offensive taste; too little leaves the jerky without the real "smoked" flavor.

Salt each strip liberally and evenly—but not heavily—on both sides. Here again, some experimenting may be necessary to accommodate individual tastes.

Lay the strips across the wire racks of the camp oven. Line the bottom of the oven with foil to catch the salty drippings, which are much more easily prevented than removed.

Adjust the flame on the camp stove to low heat so the oven temperature is between 100 and 150 degrees. Allow the meat to dry for at least six hours. Keep the oven out of the wind so the temperature is maintained as constant as possible. Beyond insuring adequate fuel throughout the curing period, you need devote no further attention to the processing until it is almost completed.

Moisture is a breeding ground for bacteria which cause spoilage, so meat should be dried thoroughly but not to the point that it becomes brittle. Toward the end of the drying period, test the meat for doneness by bending a strip. When the jerky has thoroughly browned and is stiff, but bends before snapping, it is sufficiently dried.

As long as it is kept dry and air is allowed to circulate around it, the jerky will keep indefinitely, although that is not a likely necessity once you taste its pleasant smoky flavor and become accustomed to the convenience it represents afloat and afield.

CAMP IS WHERE THE STOVE IS

by SAM CURTIS

Tailgate stoves allow you to prepare a quick breakfast without fussing with a fire.

Competing in popularity with white gas stoves are propane models which run off refillable tanks.

ONE OF THE PLEASURES we associate with camping is the aroma of wood smoke and the attraction of sinuous flames. Fresh trout seems to sizzle more pleasurably and taste sweeter when it's cooked on the open fire.

There are times however, when a camp fire is neither convenient nor enjoyable. The motorized camper who's on the move doesn't want to take time to produce glowing coals just to make a quick breakfast. A cross-country skier with wind rattling his tent poles may wish he were home by the fire, but he certainly isn't going to try to build one where he is. Also, camping areas may be closed to open fires because the surroundings have been stripped of dead wood or because the forest fire danger is high.

Conservation and convenience finds the use of camp stoves increasingly widespread. Besides their nonexistent impact on the environment and their minimal fire danger, they have advantages that can't be found in the camp fire. They supply instant heat—no need to wait around for morning coffee—their flame is constant and adjustable, and they can't drive you away with choking flame and flying ash.

Like the wood fire, the basis for a stove's heat is its fuel. Gasoline, kerosene, alcohol, butane, and propane are all used in various stoves, and each has its own advantages:
White gas is the traditional fuel. The Coleman Company has been making stoves which use this fuel for decades, and many featherweight backpacking stoves burn it. White gas is inexpensive and easily obtained throughout the U.S., though not in foreign countries. It produces a hot flame, but stoves using it must be primed or pumped to produce the tank pressure needed for operation. This fuel, being liquid, is easily spilled and very flammable.
Kerosene is used for some backpacking stoves. It, too, is inexpensive and can be found throughout the world. It has the further advantage of not igniting easily if spilled. Priming or pumping is required.
Alcohol isn't a popular fuel because of its low heat output, but it's still used in situations where safety is the prime consideration, particularly on boats where there's no way to escape a fire except by going overboard. This fuel is volatile and evaporates quickly when spilled. An alcohol fire can be put out with water.
Butane is used in small disposable containers for a few light weight stoves. It can't be spilled and requires no pumping or priming, but it has drawbacks that make it undesirable for all but limited use. It's expensive and will not burn when its temperature drops below 32 degrees Fahrenheit.
Propane vies with white gas in current camp cook popularity. It comes in refillable and disposable containers with the refillable tanks more economical to operate. Once the fuel container is attached to your stove, turn on the burner and put a match to it—just like a gas range in the kitchen. Propane can be found in many countries and comes under the name "Camping Gaz" in Europe.

Camp stoves themselves fall into two categories: tailgate and backpacking. Tailgate stoves are used by motorized campers who aren't greatly concerned with weight or

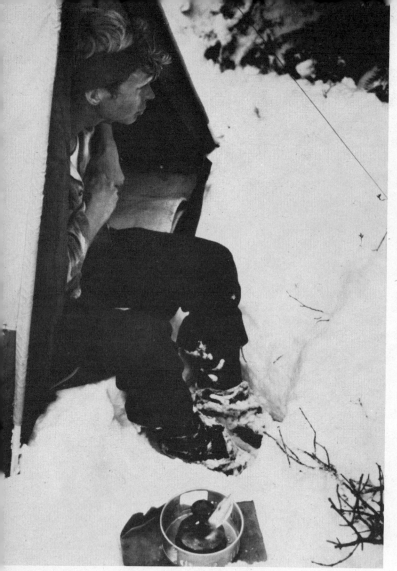

Self-pressurized stoves should be insulated from the cold and protected with a wind-screen when used in the winter.

bulk. Backpacking stoves are light and compact for the person who carries his home on his back.

When shopping for a tailgate stove, look at prospective buys with an eye toward adaptability and convenience. Three-burner models allow you to cook several courses at once, or a meal for a large group, though they're heavier and more bulky than the two-burner stoves. Remember, however, that the cooking capacity is not determined by burners alone. Two burners on one stove may accommodate two large pots very easily; another model may have a smaller grid over the burners which makes the use of two big pots unsafe. Check the dimensions of various stoves to see if they'll hold the cooking ware you want to use.

Stoves should be easy to clean. The grid that holds your pots should be easy to remove to facilitate interior washing. Many stoves have grease or splash trays under the grid which can be removed to make clean-up even easier.

The grid itself should be tough enough to resist the heat-warping temperatures of the stove's burners. In addition, it should be designed to support pots and pans safely with no chance of slipping or tipping.

All stoves should be equipped with panels which protect the stove burners from wind, since wind greatly reduces a burner's efficiency. This is usually achieved with tops that stand up to form back and side wind screens. When the stove isn't in use the top closes over the burners to make a small suitcase. The closing clasp on the top should be easy to operate and lock down securely. The carrying handle should also be convenient and sturdy.

Propane stoves have an advantage over white gas models in that adapters can be used. In this way, other propane appliances can be connected to one fuel source. Along with the stove you can run a lantern, a heater, even a portable refrigerator.

Different manufacturers offer various unique features and stove accessories. The Traveler Titan made by Zebco has a broiler-grill combination. Dishes can be simmering on top of the stove while bacon cooks in the broiler pan underneath the burners. The Coleman Company offers a folding camp oven which is placed over a burner for baking. The same company has a cast-aluminum griddle with Teflon coating. Another handy item is the propane conversion kit put out by Paulin. This kit enables you to convert white gas stoves so they operate on refillable or disposable propane containers. By selective shopping done through manufacturers' catalogs, you should be able to find the stove and accessories to suit your cooking quirks and needs.

The question of fuel consumption bothers many campers operating tailgate stoves for the first time. The beginner usually ends up bringing too much or too little fuel. To avoid this, look at the manufacturer's catalog. For white gas stoves, the burning time for a tank-full of fuel will be listed for each model. Figure the number of meals you'll be preparing over the stove and the average cooking time required for those meals. You'll come up with a good estimate of the fuel you should bring.

The method for figuring out your propane needs is somewhat different. Heat output is measured in BTU's—British Thermal Units. Propane stove manufacturers indicate the number of BTU's per hour each burner on a stove will produce. For instance, a two-burner stove with both burners rated at 6,400 BTU/hr. will produce 12,800 BTU/hr. when both burners are operated on high. Since a pound of propane will supply approximately 21,000 BTU's, multiply 21,000 times eight—if your fuel tank holds eight

White gas stoves have been made for decades and are the first choice among many outdoor cooks.

A backpacking stove that fits into nesting cook pots adds compactness to your kitchen.

pounds—and divide the result by 12,800. Your eight-pound tank will operate the stove for about 13 hours with both burners wide open.

The BTU rating listed for both propane and gas stoves not only allows you to compute fuel needs; it also indicates the heating power of the burners. A burner listed at 6,400 BTU's will not cook food or boil water as fast as one with a 10,000 BTU rating. Heat output should be a consideration when buying a stove.

A backpacker, cross-country skier, or mountaineer has to have a different perspective than the motorized camper when it comes to his stove. If you're going to carry it yourself, you're particularly concerned with bulk, weight, and the amount of fuel you'll have to carry. Beyond this, you should look for a stove that is easy to operate and stable to cook on. Unfortunately, all the features which go into an ideal backpacking stove haven't yet come together in one model. The lightest and most compact stove requires the nuisance of priming. On the other hand, the most easily operated stove runs on butane, which is expensive, heavy and useless below 32 degrees F.

White gas stoves are the most popular among people who travel light. The fuel produces a hot flame and it's inexpensive. These models must be pumped or primed to produce pressure for operation. For priming, a small amount of gas is poured in the priming cup and ignited. This flame heats the fuel tank causing vapor pressure to force gas through the burner when it is turned on. If you time the operation carefully, the last bit of flame from the priming cup will provide just enough heat to start the burner. Turn on the stove as the flame is about to go out and the fuel escaping from the burner will ignite.

In windy or cold weather, gas stoves may have to be primed more than once to produce the needed pressure. When the burner is started however, its heat will sustain pressure for operation until the stove is turned off.

Self-pressurized stoves are affected by extreme cold and heat. These models must be insulated from snow during winter use. A small piece of ensolite is ideal for this purpose. Place a piece of this closed-cell insulation under the stove. In very hot weather, too much pressure may build up

Camp stoves complement campfires. For convenience and even heat camp stoves are tops. For the romantic camping atmosphere, like here on the beach, the campfire sets the mood.

The camper has a wide range of brands and models to choose.

Here is a setup that would please most outdoor chefs.

LP Gas cartridge gives life to compact pack stove.

in the fuel tank and be blown off through the safety valve in the fuel cap. The pressure can be brought down by splashing some cold water on the stove.

Kerosene stoves are good for situations where cooking must be done in confined areas; it's less volatile than white gas and therefore safer. These stoves require a separate priming fuel, usually alcohol, and must also be pumped to maintain pressure.

Butane stoves are by far the easiest to operate, but should only be chosen when there is no chance of freezing the fuel. On long trips butane stoves are weighty and bulky because all empty fuel containers have to be carried out.

Several of the large mail order catalogs specializing in backpacking equipment, like Recreational Equipment, Inc., of Seattle and Eastern Mountain Sport, Inc., of Boston, carry valuable comparative statistics on a wide range of lightweight stoves. Information is given on stove weight with and without fuel, burning time of a tank of fuel, average boiling time, and fuel cost. In addition, the stoves are evaluated for their stability, ease of operation, compactness, and suitability for cold weather use. By using this information, you can get a clear sense of the pros and cons of various models and then make a wise buy.

Accessories for light weight stoves can enhance efficiency, compactness, and ease of operation. Some stoves are designed to fit inside a compact set of nesting cook pots, an arrangement which greatly reduces the bulk of

Steady, constant heat of modern camp stoves insures fast perking coffee.

Propane grills like this are good for picnics and camping.

your kitchen articles. Wind screens are a must, and should be purchased if not supplied with the stove. Small plastic funnels make refilling fuel tanks easier, and some cooks carry a plastic eye dropper to fill the priming cups of stoves requiring the operation. Fuel flasks should be sturdy and leakproof. Check the screw cap for a tight fitting gasket. Cleaning needles, a thin piece of wire in a jack-knife-like container, should be carried for cleaning the orifice of gas stoves. Aluminum pot lifters which grip the edge of hot pans eliminate bulky handles and add safety to the kitchen.

Whether cooking with a tailgate stove or a backpacking stove, safety is important. Use stoves in well-ventilated spaces as they, like any fire, consume oxygen. Refuel stoves away from flames. When the fuel tank can't be removed from the stove, wait until the stove has cooled before refueling. For safe and efficient operation, stoves should be kept clean and filled with recommended fuel only.

Although stoves are a must when fires are impossible, don't overlook their compatibility with a well-made campfire. Many a gourmet meal has been the result of this combination. Use the fire for chops and steaks spiced with the subtle flavor of apple or hickory wood, and perhaps roast potatoes in the coals too. But for sauces and vegetables, nothing beats the flame control, the stability, and the efficiency of a good camp cook stove.

by MARVIN TYE

MY HOME in the suburbs of Atlanta, Georgia, is little more than a mile from the entrance to Stone Mountain Park. In just a few minutes we can leave the roar of interstate and commuter traffic and the other stresses of civilization behind and find ourselves in a peaceful setting of tall trees and quiet lakes.

My wife, Mary Elizabeth, and I like to drive out to the park on an afternoon for a picnic and perhaps a little fishing. Rather than being bothered with an assortment of pots and pans and other bulky items, we do most of our cooking with aluminum foil.

On a recent trip to the park we made ¼-pound patties of ground beef wrapped around the edges with bacon. We placed each patty separately on a sheet of aluminum foil and added slices of potatoes. We wrapped the package so that one large crease and seal were formed across the top. After folding this down tightly, we folded each end of the package back toward the center and pressed them until they were also sealed tightly.

Atop Stone Mountain, Georgia, Marvin Tye writes about outdoor recreation. Specializing in archery and salt water fishing, he is a field editor for Southern Outdoors.

At the park we built a fire in one of the picnic sites and allowed the hard wood to burn down to coals. The packages were then placed directly upon the coals and turned occasionally with wooden sticks so that they would cook evenly on both sides. In about 30 minutes we had a meal that could be eaten directly from the foil using it as a plate. We had brought along a pitcher of iced tea and paper cups to drink it with. After the meal was completed there were no dish washing chores to be done. The cups and our combined cooking utensils and plates of aluminum foil were discarded. If we had used plastic forks as well there would have been no utensils at all to wash.

Aluminum foil is an item that has many cooking uses indoors, in the back yard, on a picnic, or deep in the wilderness. It is particularly useful in backpacking or other wilderness activities where weight can be a problem. A small package of aluminum foil will fit easily into most packs. It can be removed from the package and the roll flattened to take up less space or it can be wrapped around a flat sheet of heavy cardboard or simply folded and placed into a pocket. This last method can be recommended only for a very short hike where little foil is needed.

In camp, foil has many uses. With a coat hanger or other heavy wire it is easy to combine foil in order to make

One of the author's favorites—ground beef wrapped in bacon—is placed on a sheet of foil with sliced potatoes and onions added. This can be assembled before leaving home.

through the foil. I have found that it is also a fairly simple matter to poach eggs on an aluminum foil pan such as this by first adding water to the bottom of the pan, letting it come to a boil and then putting an egg on top of the water. In just a few minutes you can have a poached egg of the same quality as that prepared in a poacher at home.

Some campers like to make a smaller pan. I have found that either size works sufficiently well for poaching. In addition the larger pan is better suited to being used as a plate after the egg has cooked. I usually make two pans. One is used for frying bacon and the other for poaching eggs. The eggs and bacon can be placed on one of the pans and that pan can be used for a plate.

As a quick substitute for a hot fire, canned heat does a good job of frying or poaching eggs. It can be placed under the pan and left unattended briefly while the camper busies himself with other chores.

The camper should be careful not to puncture the foil while frying bacon or similar foods because grease can leak out into the fire and cause it to blaze up or the fire could come through the pan and cause the grease to burn.

Heavy duty foil is best for outdoor cooking. The light weight foil tears more easily and will not support as much weight when fashioned into cooking utensils. Foil can also be used for frying food by placing a sheet of it over a wire grill above an open fire. The foil should be well greased before placing the meat upon it. This method of frying is handy when no frying pans are available. It can also be an effective way to cook when the camper desires to keep the food simmering after it has cooked. This can be accomplished by raking the coals to one side leaving a hot portion of the foil for cooking and a slightly cooler portion where the food can be moved after cooking to be kept simmering until everyone is ready to eat.

Foil can also be used as a reflector in the preparation of bread and pies. One example would be to place a tent shaped strip of foil over bread being cooked on a grill in a frying pan. The foil reflects heat down on the bread while it is also being heated from below.

a frying pan. Simply bend the coat hanger or wire into the desired shape and place foil over the wire and crimp the edges so that it will be held in place securely. Food placed on the foil will cause it to sag in the middle and thus prevent grease or food from spilling off.

The pan can either be hand held over a fire or held in place by stones placed around it. It is possible to fry just about any food in this manner so long as you can keep the weight reasonably light enough so that you will not break

For such a dish, the foil is folded so that there is a crease to seal it at the top and two similar creases at each end.

Fish, game birds or wild meat can be substituted for hamburger in this recipe and be cooked to perfection.

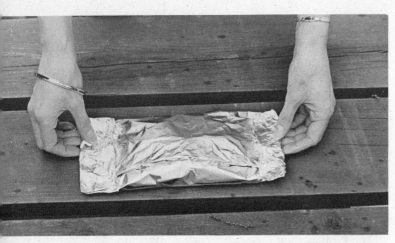

A good rule of thumb when cooking with foil: Wrap meats tightly to brown evenly; wind foil around vegetables loosely to steam them.

The foil package is placed on the coals. It should be turned over so that it cooks evenly on both sides.

Besides a cooking utensil, foil can be used as a mixing bowl. Here a salad is being tossed to highlight a riverside fish fry.

A large sheet of heavy duty foil can be crimped over the back and two sides of a grill to make a hood. This also reflects heat upon the food from above while it is being cooked from below. This is useful for cooking all manner of food including vegetables, meats, bread, biscuits, pies and cakes. The hood also serves as a wind screen if placed properly and will prevent particles of dirt or insects from being blown into the food.

In addition to its uses for cooking, foil can also be used to wrap knives and forks while packing, to store spices and other foods and to make cups. If the cups are to be used for drinking coffee or other hot beverages, the camper should be sure that it is sturdy enough to hold the beverage without tearing apart and spilling it. Cups can be made by wrapping the foil around your fist and then twisting the edges to make a handle or by wrapping it around a piece of coat hanger wire or similar material that has been twisted to shape with a pair of pliers. A double thickness of heavy duty foil might be desired to insure sturdy construction.

A pan for baking can be fashioned simply by folding a rectangular sheet of foil into the desired shape and crimping the edges. The foil may be used as a plate when other cooking utensils have been used to prepare the meal. This prevents the necessity of having to pack heavy dishes into the campsite.

Foil can be used to cook game birds, fish or wild meat in the same manner described at the beginning of this article for the cooking of ground beef patties. The hunter or fisherman can simply take a bit of foil, spices, vegetables, and bacon into the field with him and if successful add wild meat to the package for cooking. The successful fisherman will place a slice or several slices of bacon, depending upon the size of the fish to be cooked, on a piece of foil. Then he can add the cleaned fish, slices of potatoes and onion, more bacon and seasoning, seal the package and cook on the coals for a period of time determined by the size of the fish and the heat of the fire.

A similar procedure can be followed for cooking game birds. After you have cleaned and plucked the bird, place an onion in the body cavity, tie legs and wings, and tuck in a few strips of bacon. Season as desired, roll tightly in foil and roast on the coals for about an hour. The package should be turned over frequently.

In cooking meats on the coals it is best to place the shiny side of the foil inside. Time involved in cooking varies with size of the package and the heat of the coals. A large fold can be placed to one side of the package instead of on top of it. This will allow a more even cooking of top and bottom. In many cases this makes little difference and so one method of fold is as good as another. The fire does not have to be too big, just so there are enough coals to cover the entire area being cooked and to supply sufficient heat to do the job. That's all that is necessary.

Some campers prefer to have a large number of coals and to first place the package on top of the coals and then place additional coals on top of the package so that it will be cooking on both top and bottom at the same time.

I have found that one piece of foil used to wrap a package such as this is sufficient. Some campers prefer to use two pieces of foil so that the inner piece will be clean after cooking. They believe that this will leave a package that can be used as a plate with no danger of getting ashes or soot into the food. This is true, but cleanliness can be achieved with only one wrapper if the cook is careful when opening the package.

Potatoes and other vegetables can be cooked in much the same manner but it is not necessary to place them directly in the fire. Potatoes can be wrapped in foil and

The author's wife Mary Elizabeth bends a coat hanger to make a frying pan from aluminum foil.

Eggs can be poached by first adding water to the foil frying pan and then bringing it to a boil.

placed at the edge of the fire while it is still blazing. They need to cook for approximately an hour. They should be turned frequently during this time. It is possible to cook them while coals are being formed for cooking other components of the meal. Potatoes can be baked in this manner, then sliced open and filled with butter after they are done. You can vary this procedure by peeling each potato and cutting it into thick slices before cooking. They can be buttered and reassembled, placed in the foil and cooked in this manner.

Sweet potatoes cooked in a similar manner add a delicious variety to the usual camp fare. Squash, onions, carrots, apples and a variety of other fruits and vegetables can be easily prepared with foil.

Generally speaking it is best to wrap meats tightly and to use a rather loose wrapping when cooking vegetables. This produces a pressure cooker type effect on the vegetables. It allows steam to blend the flavors of the vegetables together. In cooking meat, close contact between the meat, the foil, and the fire helps to brown the food evenly.

Aluminum foil has long been accepted as a handy cooking item by the housewife. The camper and outdoor cook will find many uses for this material as well. With a little imagination the ideas stated here can be improved upon and enlarged.

Aluminum foil cookery promotes relaxation; the time to fish, sightsee and just to sit back and breathe in the fresh, clean air. No dish washing!

Instant hot or cold, Vitamin C enriched liquids are good tasting and add energy.

LUCILLE IS A LUNCH PERSON. From sunrise to noon she plans and prepares the midday menu. Last spring on an Ohio River houseboat trip from Cincinnati to Louisville, the party of four couples docked near Rabbit Hash. They intended to fish a little, explore the unknown shore and have fun stretching their seafaring legs in some frivolous activity—maybe skipping rocks.

Lucille refused to leave the boat. "But it will be like going on a spree—like finding land after four days afloat." Nothing doing. She would stay on board, scour the galley and have lunch ready when they returned. Sam whispered to his wife Laura, "But what if we don't want to come back here for lunch? It's 9 o'clock now. That allows us only three hours before lunchtime." Laura shrugged her shoulders. What can you say when a friend wants to sacrifice and serve her companions?

At 12:43, the group approached the houseboat exhilarated. Feeling like children caught by a disapproving adult, they quieted down. Shuffling their feet and smiling sheepishly, they waved at Lucille. But the enticing aroma of frying chicken quickly dissolved the tinge of guilt that was slowly descending on them. They licked their lips and hastened their pace. With all the excitement of catching a six-pound walleye and the line breaking right after Ken brought him ashore, they had not realized the aching emptiness of their innards.

The tradition of mouth-watering Kentucky fried chicken was proudly upheld at that banquet-size midday meal. Accompanying the crispy moist chicken were top-of-the-stove dressing, mashed potatoes with gravy, cranberry sauce and string beans with sliced almonds. Every morsel was devoured. "I didn't know I was so hungry," was repeated often over the apple pie a la mode and coffee.

After a hearty breakfast, most people predict that they will not need much lunch. With so many plans and so much to do, campers frequently let the noon meal slip their mind. "The time goes by so fast that it will be suppertime before we know it. Why waste any part of our short two-week vacation on lunch? We came this far to hike, smell wildflowers and fish—not just to eat." In addition, the outdoors stimulates appetites to such an extent that many weight-conscious individuals believe they should skip the midday snack. Otherwise, they may be faced with a strict, crash diet when they return home. These misconceptions can be barriers to appreciating the outdoors completely.

You are lucky if your circle of travel companions includes a person like Lucille. One who values a nutritious lunch. In fact, Europeans still consider the noon meal to be the most important. After a short siesta or period of complete relaxation, they are ready to meet the challenges of the rest of the day. This pause half-way through the daylight hours provides an opportunity to regroup and rejuvenate resources. If it has been a bad day, the midday

by **KATHLEEN FARMER**

Nothing like a roasted hotdog break, and hot cider to add to the pleasures of ski touring.

A BUNCH OF LUNCH

The canoe picnic is a great way to enjoy a leisurely lunch.

When the sun is high, and the fishing slow, the best thing for campers to do is fix a nourishing lunch. It gives them new direction.

The common hotdog has spiced many a winter-time outing.

Scenes like this inspire healthy appetites.

break is the chance to turn the tide. By asking, "Why did everything go wrong?" an aggravating morning can be transformed into a profitable afternoon.

On a vacation or weekend trip, lunchtime slows you down and offers the moment to relish the morning's happenings. Americans' chief complaint is "Not having enough time." But there is plenty if only the person knows how to use what he has. One way of making "enough time" is simply to do nothing for an hour or two around noon, eat and see where you have been and where you are headed. That is the purpose of lunch. Without it, not only does the stomach feel grossly neglected, but the day is a jumble of activity, lacking definition and direction.

To action-oriented sportspeople, the midday meal is an art that has to be learned. To them, eating breaks the day's continuity, like an unwelcomed interruption. But once lunch is included as a worthwhile portion of the trip, it is anticipated with eagerness and adds to the total experience.

On the night before a trip, I prepare a chuck roast or round steak by simmering it in onion soup for two or three hours. Before bedtime, I slice the meat very thinly and make as many sandwiches as possible (usually three to six hefty ones). Wrapped in sandwich size plastic bags and refrigerated, they are ready to store in the tray of our cooler early in the morning when we leave on our outing. These sandwiches have been unspeakable morale-builders on the first day of the vacation when things are not going as planned. By stopping and eating them, our outlook suddenly becomes more positive and accepting, "We'll make the best out of whatever happens."

I remember elk hunting season last Fall. By dusk the

day before the season opened, we had chosen a backpack camp far enough off the road, we thought, to avoid other hunters. We figured we were in an area where road hunters would spook elk to us instead of away from us. We selected a cozy spot about three-quarters of a mile away from camp under a trio of Douglas firs to sit and wait for our "big bull" next morning before sunup. It overlooked a clearing surrounded by pines, covered with tall grass and cut by a trickling stream. "Cover, food and water. Everything a bull elk would seek on the first day of hunting season."

We decided to arise, dress and be at our hunting spot by 5:00 am. At 3:00, we were jarred awake by glaring headlights aimed directly at our backpack tent. The sound of the 4WD slamming, banging, bumping over sagebrush and watermelon-size rocks would chase bedded-down elk out of the area. Seeing no elk, the driver wheeled the vehicle back towards the road, his radio whining a mournful song. Angry, disappointed and temporarily frightened, we held a hasty conference. "We have over three hours until legal shooting hours." "Let's have some hot chocolate and warm up."

By about 4:00, we were positioned in our secluded hunting spot, waiting for daylight and the appearance of the elk of our dreams. I carried a small nylon backpack full of food and a thermos of hot chocolate.

At daybreak, we heard shooting from the north. We held tight. Hunters could scare elk towards us. Two hours later we spotted a hunter on foot stalking the thick pines to our right. No elk will come from that direction now. An hour and a half after that, two hunters stood on the rise behind us overlooking our clearing. They had moved through the pinon forest on our left. Elk would steer clear of that section too now that human scent had permeated it. Our perfect plan had fallen flat. We now had to rediscover a likely place to wait for elk and it was 9:30 am. The morning of opening day—the best time to find a respectable bull—was over. Not moving from our chosen spot, we hoped for a miracle to occur—an elk to appear in front of us out of nowhere.

I unwrapped the sandwiches and poured the steaming hot chocolate into Sierra cups, which fogged up our glasses—if an elk walked through the clearing we would not be able to see him. The food and drink brought warmth back into our bones. We whispered about what our next plan of action should be. We resolved to return to the road and hunt the timber on the other side which was thicker, more difficult to hunt and thus would attract less hunters. After that had been discussed and the sandwiches were filling up the void that had developed inside us, we were able to chuckle over the astute hunters we had seen who had not spotted us even though we wore blaze orange vests. We shot two nice elk that afternoon. I thank the sandwiches. They gave us the energy to plot and carry out a second plan.

Home-cooked meat sandwiches can not be beat for a healthy, happiness-inducing lunch. These types of sandwiches can be produced throughout the trip if you have an oven and a well-equipped kitchen, commonly found in recreational vehicles and houseboats. Baked ham is a favorite of mine. Spiced with whole cloves and slices of pineapple, it makes supper special. Next day, made into sandwiches, it imparts the comfortable flavor of home. The following morning, diced ham can perk up an omelet for breakfast. The same is true of turkey or roast pork. With the cooking conveniences of home, the chef has only to exercise ingenuity and selectivity. Choosing meats that are simple to prepare (I consider baking to be the easiest method) and versatile so the leftovers can be stretched to fill one or two lunches and breakfasts, this is the secret to successful outdoor cookery.

For campers without ovens and who are on the move most of the time, a smoked sausage, cheese and crackers lunch is most attractive. No cooking is involved. And the fixings can be stowed into a day-pack without weighing more than five pounds. Smoked sausage, like pepperoni or salami, or smoked fish requires no refrigeration and stays fresh indefinitely. A hard cheese, such as cheddar, keeps fairly well within a two-week period without refrigeration —if kept reasonably cool. The saltiness imparted by both

Break for lunch at this Wyoming camp.

Early morning fishing usually means big lunchtime appetites as these boats head for shore.

the cheese and sausage is needed by a body involved in strenuous activity. Of course, this also produces a strong thirst.

The outdoors induces a craving for sweets, as much psychological as it is a demand for more calories. And water does not seem to satisfy a thirst as well as an instant fruit drink. We always include Tang and Kool-Aid (sugar already added) in our camping staples. Bring twice as much as you think you will need. You never seem to get enough of sweet drinks while camping. Tang should be pre-packaged in a heavy-duty plastic bag before you leave home. This facilitates stuffing into a small backpack and prevents breakage. Kool-Aid does not come in individual-serving packets. You may estimate how much Kool-Aid one cupful may require or you can mix the entire package. One container of Kool-Aid with sugar makes two to four quarts of drink. Since carrying a pitcher along is impractical, a recommended way of dissolving the Kool-Aid in water is in a heavy-duty, four- to six-quart plastic bag. These are easy to pack, burnable and relatively inexpensive. If all the Kool-Aid is not consumed, a knot tied to close the plastic bag and to attach the bag to your belt will keep the thirst-quenching liquid handy for the next stop.

Last summer we discovered a third type of instant drink we really liked. Instant tea with sugar and lemon already added is delicious both hot and cold. In fact, it hits the spot in the morning for a change instead of hot chocolate.

The uncomplicated midday snack of sausage, cheese and a sweet drink offers another bonus to the cook—no cleaning up after. The meal requires only three utensils: a pocketknife, a spoon and a Sierra cup. A pocketknife is a must for an outdoorsperson. My husband Charlie and I carry ours everywhere. It has come in handy during informal steak cookouts where steak knives are not available. And it opens well-wrapped packages in a flash. A common remark from a person who observes you whipping out your pocketknife is, "You must know a lot about the outdoors." The outdoor guide's way of serving sausage to his clients is by spearing the slice with his pocketknife and aiming it at the client—"Untouched by human hands."

A spoon is a nice tool but not a necessity. A twig can stir just as well with less noise and sometimes bestows a delightful spicy taste of pine to drinks. Measuring is what the spoon does best. But when concocting a sweet drink for lunch, exact measurements do not always insure quality. Sometimes, too much mix is preferred by the camper.

A Sierra cup has been the object of much discussion. True, the Sierra cup is shallow with a wide mouth. One group of campers say that as a consequence, the liquid in the cup cools too quickly. I, however, drink or eat the

Navajo fry bread is fixed on houseboat stove.

contents before it has a chance to cool off. I prefer this type of cup to a paper one or any other type because its handle hooks onto your belt and will not fall off in heavy brush. It is always there if you want a drink. You do not have to rummage through the backpack to find it. Also, after you drink or eat from it, you simply rinse it and put it back on your belt to dry. It will not tear, fall apart or crush like a paper cup. And you need not burn it after it has been used.

I know I should eat sausage and cheese for nutrition. However, I tend to speed through and gulp the main part of lunch down as fast as I can. Because after the sausage and cheese comes Gorp. Gorp is a trail snack which is addictive. It is sold commercially by backpack foods manufacturers but I prefer the kind we make at home before our trip. In a huge bowl, mix M&M candies, raisins, Spanish nuts and shredded coconut. Divide into double-sacked sandwich-size plastic bags and twist-tie shut to keep the Gorp fresh. Stash these bags into any extra place in the food bag or pack. You and your family will eat all you have and clamor for more.

A good camp, and good morale is usually the result of three well-balanced meals.

Trailer lunches are good for stomachs as well as re-grouping the family for late afternoon and evening activities.

One of the reasons for storing Gorp in small bags is to conserve your supply. I know of one backpacker who ate a two-quart plastic bag of Gorp at one noon stop and could not move from there for 24 hours. Gorp pushes you onward with energy when you think you can go no farther. It brightens a rainy day. It helps you forget about sore calf muscles and a strained back. Unlike the oldtime, cure-all tonic, it does nothing for baldness but it usually paints color onto a pale forehead.

Backpack food manufacturers offer a variety of trail foods which are tasty and are like peanuts in that they are salty and you can not stop eating them. Rainbow Fruit Chips, Chunky Pineapple Waikiki, Crunchy Banana Chips, Pemmican Fruit Bar, Tropical Chocolate Bars are just a few that are full of energy, nutrition and add variety if you happen to be one of those poor souls who do not favor Gorp.

Lunch outdoors is taking the time to enjoy the simple things. A hunk of sausage, a few slabs of cheese, some stream water mixed with instant sweetness and most important . . . the time to inhale your surroundings.

Kathy Farmer fixes soup for lunch at Lake Mead.

The secret to cooking wild game birds, like this chukar, is to bring out the natural flavor of the bird rather than masking it under harsh, heavy spices.

FEATHERED DELIGHTS

by HELEN "TIGER" MARTIN

AMONG THE NUMEROUS rewards awaiting the hunter/angler is the opportunity to savor the fruits of his efforts at the dining table. A wide variety of fish and wild game have commanded positions of respect on the Martin tableboards ever since my husband, Jim, introduced me to the outdoor way of life shortly before our marriage. Over the years we have dined regally on a sumptuous array of gourmet wild game dishes. We find the flavor of wild game quite delicious, providing it has been properly prepared. But this can be a big IF, and a problem that often presents itself to persons who are unfamiliar with wild game.

After more than 15 years of my being official camp cook, I have learned that there are two basic ways of readying fish or game in preparation to its cooking. You either ask your husband to perform the de-scaling, de-furring, or de-feathering; or, you do the job yourself. My husband will accomplish this task quite willingly, and sometimes enthusiastically; however the job is frequently not completed to my satisfaction. One might say that while Jim may earn a gold star for rough field dressing, he seldom makes the honor roll for the finishing efforts.

To cope with this situation, I have developed cooking methods that go along with his lazy-daze ways. When preparing wild fowl, I employ a skin and dip process, a method which eliminates the time-consuming chore of plucking pinfeathers, yet provides an end product that tastes "out of this world," if I can place credence in the accolades of friends who have shared a meal with us.

Here's how I prepare a pheasant, one of the most popular game birds found in northern California, and certainly a epicurean delight when served. The same technique and recipes, by the way, can be used on ducks, grouse, chukar and even wild geese. Let's pick up the process just after I have received the field dressed bird from Jim. Field dressed, incidentally, means he has gutted, skinned, beheaded, dewinged and removed the lower legs from each bird, and presumably accomplished a fair to middling job of washing the carcass.

If the bird has been badly shot up, you can remove the blood by soaking it in a pan of cold, fresh water to which salt has been added. A handful of salt to a gallon of water is about the right proportion. Then rinse the carcass, pat it dry, and prepare to cut it up as follows.

Lay the skinned bird on its back on a cutting board. Using a sharp knife, cut along either side of the breast bone and remove each breast. Set these two large chunks aside.

Next, remove the leg and thigh at the hip joint.

This leaves the bony body with a few scraps of meat adhering. Place this in a pressure cooker, together with a coarsely chopped onion and a couple of stalks of celery, plus three cups of water. Add the heart and gizzard, too, if you have saved them. Add a half teaspoon of salt and a dash of pepper; close the lid; then cook under pressure for 30 minutes.

This completes the skinning process; now let's get ready to start dipping. The legs and thighs come first.

Rub these with olive oil, which has been seasoned with oregano, salt and pepper. Dip or shake each leg in flour, then place in a hot frying pan which has been coated with a slight amount of light cooking oil. Brown on each side.

When richly golden, drain excess oil and add ½-cup of strained broth taken from the pressure cooker, together with ½-cup of red table wine. Simmer until tender, which should take approximately 1½ hours. Then add one tablespoon of tomato paste to the gravy, together with flour if additional thickening is required. Stir and season to taste.

While the legs are simmering, drain the rest of the broth from the cooked carcass, then pick off the bits of remaining meat from the bones. Thoroughly rinse one cup of long grained white rice in cold water, then place it in a heavy sauce pan together with two cups of the pheasant broth. Add the meat scraps and one tablespoon of butter. Bring

Wild goose is such a prized culinary treat, no part should be wasted.

After 15 years of experimenting, the author has developed a method of preparing wild game birds, including duck, that highlights each part of the bird.

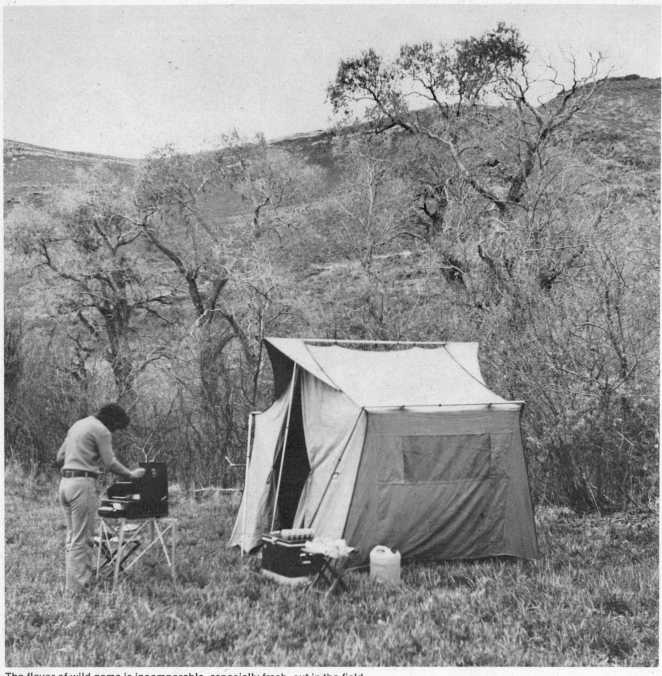
The flavor of wild game is incomparable, especially fresh, out in the field.

the mixture to a rapid boil, stir, then reduce heat to simmer for 15 minutes. Turn off the heat and allow the rice to steam to a fluffy dry.

As the rice is cooking, return to the two pheasant breasts. Using a slim, sharp knife, cut each side into thin fillets—as thin as possible. Each breast should yield a minimum of four fillets—more if the bird is large. Individually dip each fillet in a mixture of beaten eggs which has been thinned slightly with a tablespoon of cream. Coat each fillet with unseasoned bread crumbs, then brown in a frying pan containing a slight amount of hot cooking oil for from 30 to 45 seconds per side. Serve fillets with lemon wedges.

Prepared in this manner, the pheasant provides both sliced fillets and tender legs. In addition, you have a tasty rice dish. Served with a fresh vegetable and a salad, a single bird should satisfy three hearty eaters, or four diners with less demanding appetites.

I prepare other large game birds in the same manner as I do pheasant. Two large ducks will generally serve four persons. In the case of smaller waterfowl, I use three.

Geese can be cooked in the same manner, although I occasionally find a tough old bird. Should the honker appear sinewy during the filleting process, I simply make each slice of breast a bit thicker than usual, and place it between pieces of waxed paper and pound with a meat hammer. This tenderizing process enables me to cook the fillets as described above.

Of course, more time should be allowed for cooking a goose than pheasant, and less for duck, but I assure you the end product will be equally delicious.

RIVER RUNNING ON A HAPPY STOMACH

Near Havasu Creek in Grand Canyon, John Cross, river pilot and cook, whips up steak, eggs and toast for breakfast on a hotplate he built himself.

by JIM and VICKI TALLON

DURING THE PAST DECADE we have had the fortune and misfortune to make a number of river runs, with the most notable being the Colorado River through Grand Canyon and the Salmon River in Idaho. The terms "fortune" and "misfortune" are not wantonly picked to describe the adventure level of these trips, but are dictated by our stomachs. Yes, that old adage about an army traveling on its stomach applies to river runners as well. If you don't eat properly on an outdoor trip, any outdoor trip, it may seriously damage the outing as a whole. And a thing that could be great pleasure becomes but a torment to live through.

Unfortunately, potential river runners select outfitters with a certain degree of blindness. I mean, how can you tell grub variety and taste from a brochure? It may indicate that fine food will be dished up, but an outfitter's interpretation of that may be entirely different from what is needed by you and your stomach to exist and stay in a pleasant frame of mind. Experience has taught us lessons about float trip outfitters, and we have learned from both good and bad. In turn, we have applied what we learned, partly to make future float trips more palatable, but largely to our everyday camp trips and cookout ventures. You can do the same.

Consider first that most river runs, or float trips as you may choose to call them, span several days. Two of our three trips through Grand Canyon took nine days. Now you can put up with poor grub for a day or two, but after that it becomes a test to see how many days you can hold out before hanging the camp cook and/or outfitter up by his heels over a green wood fire.

On one of our trips, the cook-river pilot was as innocent as we were. While his outfitter-boss ate comfortably in the posh restaurants of Salt Lake City, Utah, we gagged through four days of chicken-flavored Spam. For the first five days we lived well with breakfasts of bacon, eggs, fried potatoes, Dutch oven biscuits, pancakes, and even French toast; lunches consisted essentially of a wide selection of cold cuts and cheeses; and dinners included fried chicken, pork chops and steaks. The ice boxes were constructed of sheet metal and wrapped with a canvas-covered batting for insulation; the ice went in a hurry and our fresh food spoiled. We found that the outfitter had purchased a whole freight-car load of chicken-flavored Spam at a bargain price and that represented the emergency food. We ate it for breakfast, lunch and dinner, hot and cold.

In contrast, we made another trip through Grand Canyon with an outfitter who had an eye out for future business. His iceboxes were sufficiently insulated and filled with dry ice. We had fresh foods to the end of the trip and ice left over. Nothing spoiled. For what it's worth, this outfitter quickly sells out for his quota of passengers allotted to him by the National Park Service for float trips through Grand Canyon. The other outfitter is no longer in business.

Now I suspect that a skilled outfitter could lose all his ice and still satisfy the stomachs of his passengers. We personally would manage to eat excellently on our outdoor

---

Jim and Vicki Tallon are a husband-wife outdoor writing/photography team. With their daughter Rachel, they have specialized in the southwest and Mexican fishing and camping. Recently they moved to Helena, Montana to discover how the other half lives.

trips whether our ice melted or not. We have an emergency stock of freeze-dried, canned and packed convenience foods stored in our camper. But we rarely get into this supply and I can not remember when we lost our ice.

A smart river pilot has plenty of outdoor knowhow and uses it constantly. He can prolong the life of ice by keeping pop and beer out of the iceboxes; they can be hung over the side of the raft in a gunnysack and cooled in 50-degree Colorado River water. Even with air temperatures reaching into the high 90's, the drinks taste good and cold.

All river running outfitters I have traveled with were experts at complete utilization of space available in the rafts. Gear and grub went into the midsection, on the fulcrum, where they rode better in the big rapids—some to 25 feet high in Grand Canyon. Food not relegated to iceboxes was kept in neoprene and plastic bags, and waterproof metal cases. Three of the outfitters keyed these bags and cases to the menu by numbers or letters, or both. They located the key on the menu, and went directly to the bags or cases that contained the food for that particular meal. No aimless rummaging; no waste of time.

Next to the icebox and fresh foods, the success of river runners' meals hinges directly to the Dutch oven, grill and hotplate for cooking; and the source of heat. For the latter, I understand that in the past year, some Grand Canyon outfitters carried propane stoves. Much of the driftwood in the Canyon has been consumed by past expeditions and is getting very difficult to find. However, on every float trip we have made, wood served to cook food and heat our bodies on chilly nights. Our guides started the cookfires about one-half hour before breakfast or dinner (lunches were eaten cold), and allowed to burn down to coals. Dutch ovens were placed directly in the coals, and the bed of coals was usually large enough that a mesh grill or hotplate could be used as well. Steaks were broiled on the mesh grills and pots and pans simmered on them. One river runner-outfitter has taken a piece of diamond-plate sheet metal about two feet wide and three feet long, and with the diamond side down, heated and hammered up the edge so it would hold a shallow layer of cooking oil or bacon grease. It makes an excellent hotplate, essentially a very large skillet. Our guide could fix eggs, bacon, fried potatoes and the like for about 20 people easily. And the food that came off the hotplate tasted better than any I have been able to get out of a skillet. For awhile I assumed it was our guide's cooking skill, but food tasted just as good when I did the cooking. And that's the ultimate test.

The Dutch oven is the most vital piece of cookware because you can bake and boil and even fry in it. Dutch oven biscuits rate tops with me and I have tasted Dutch oven cakes that perhaps excelled those done in a modern oven, certainly they bested store-bought cakes. On river trips, part of nearly every hot meal is cooked in the Dutch oven. One outfitter carried several Dutch ovens cast in aluminum; he had designed them himself and the cost must have been quite high. Today, aluminum Dutch ovens are available on the outdoor cooking market. Although our cook did a superb job of cooking with them, most outfitters prefer the cast iron models. They complain that the aluminum Dutch ovens get hot too fast and cool off too fast; they just don't hold the heat.

At the risk of being knocked down by teetotalers, I consider beer an enjoyable part of a float trip. But in moderation of course. On Grand Canyon and Salmon River trips, the rivers themselves serve as the source of drinking and

Hell-bent for dinner. Whatta way to go between meals. With this kind of action in the rapids of Grand Canyon, boaters need substantial meals, and the professional outfitter gives them to his passengers.

In Grand Canyon, river runners make use of rocks and boulders as chairs and tables for eating an outdoor dinner.

The fantastic utensil, the Dutch oven, sees use at nearly every meal. Here a batch of eggs are about to be scrambled in a Dutch oven. This mesh grill also serves for broiling steaks, sliced ham and pork chops.

On the Salmon River, it's trout and eggs for breakfast.

cooking water. You may start out with a crystal clear stream, but it takes only one thunderstorm to turn these rivers into muddy waterways, especially the Colorado River. On the Colorado, river pilots add several packages of Kool-Aid to pails of river water and call it "goopy grape." The Kool-Aid disguises the muddy taste of the water, but it fails to hide the grit of sand and soil. Considering the space limitations of the rafts and the length of most river trips, canned beverages rate low on the list of essentials.

Other psychological treats can include chocolate bars, peanuts, fruit (most river runners carry apples and oranges), olives stuffed with pimento, a bottle of cream sherry—such things that most river runners don't put on their menus. When you are pinned in Grand Canyon for nine or ten days, knowing that the only catering service would have to be done by helicopter, such little things are priceless; they take on a new worth far beyond their cost.

The mainstay of many river runners is one-dish meals. I've never been on a float trip where they didn't have at least one steak dinner, but such bill-of-fare every night would greatly push up the cost of river running. The one-dish meals are generally prepared in Dutch ovens and some have been so good that I would have passed up a steak for them. One river runner-cook started cooking a roast in a Dutch oven immediately *after* dinner. The roast was planned for lunch the next day, sliced cold for sandwiches, which beats to pieces the idea of bologna sandwiches.

Too, most river trips include plenty of green salads and desserts. On our own trips we're heavy on salads but light on dessert. But in the depths of Grand Canyon, try resisting homemade . . . er, maybe "river-made" in this case, ice cream. About five days away from civilization, our pilot produced a hand-crank ice cream freezer and all the necessary ingredients for ice cream. Dark had turned off Grand Canyon's spectacular colors and temperatures were shirtsleeve warm; someone played a harmonica. Everyone wanted a chance to crank the freezer and for an instant my mind did a flicker-flashback—back further in time than I'd want to admit, when warm feelings and lasting friendships were cultivated around a hand-crank ice cream freezer. It's this kind of treat that re-vitalizes body and mind on an outdoor adventure.

Pitching in and helping are important parts of the long river run. This means mainly loading and unloading the rafts, finding firewood and burning and crushing cans for sacking, carrying out and proper disposal. But it also includes helping in the outdoor "kitchen"—peeling potatoes, making salads and washing pots and pans and dishes after meals. Of course, the cooking, the real float trip cooking, belongs to the trip cook. And wisely. You don't put an amateur on a Dutch oven; you don't let a novice broil expensive steaks.

But the camp cook soon figures out who has the ability to do what in the kitchen and those that really want to work there. It is a compliment to be so chosen, but more than that, an opportunity to learn *how* to use a Dutch oven and *how* to broil steaks. Some of the best cook-helper's jobs are out of the kitchen, like maybe catching trout for a breakfast of fresh trout and eggs. On a float trip, jobs that would normally be dull under other conditions are fun. And whether it's a trip through Grand Canyon in Arizona, down the Salmon River in Idaho or even the less glamorous streams of the Midwest, you'll find that you can learn a great deal about outdoor cooking from river runners.

a taste of HONEY

by CHARLES NANSEN

Closeup of the honey bee from whence cometh the most delicious sweet nectar on earth.

ALTHOUGH IT WAS an unseasonably warm afternoon in late October, and time seemed to be passing in slow motion, a faint promise of cold was in the atmosphere. It was hazy rather than sunny bright. And still. The last scarlet leaves of maple and ash trees had blended into brown and now were drifting to earth. Homer Sanderson, who had spent most of the day hunting for squirrels or hickory nuts or fall mushrooms (not in that order, but whichever appeared first), finally sat down beneath a giant oak to rest and savor what was left of a beautiful season. He already had the makings of a delicious dinner in the pockets of a tattered canvas coat. Crisp fried squirrel with shaggy mane mushroom gravy.

Only the hunter didn't rest there very long. A bee buzzed past his face and he flinched at such familiarity. But, being an experienced woodsman, he knew better than to swat at it. Then another bee zoomed close, followed by a third and finally a whole swarm in a single file seemed to inspect him in passing by. All at once Sanderson was on his feet.

"They're trying to tell me something," he muttered to himself—and out loud.

Well . . . not exactly. By lucky accident, my friend had simply stationed himself beneath a bee tree. For uninitiated readers, that means a very old tree containing natural hollows in one of which wild bees have made a home. To many, finding a bee tree may not seem a very important event or maybe even one to be avoided at all costs. But to Homer Sanderson and his like, it was better than striking oil under the back forty, discovering a new Klondike or holding a $100 ticket on the Kentucky Derby winner. Inside that tree was a rare golden treasure which too few know about nowadays.

After etching the exact spot, which was deep in a Kentucky woods, accurately and indelibly in his memory, Sanderson hurried away homeward. He didn't want anyone else to even see him near the spot and thereby arouse suspicions. He wouldn't even tell his wife about it because she had too many gossipy friends. But he did resolve to be back on the spot the first day, come winter, that the temperature dipped well below freezing. And the colder the better.

Now let's skip past Thanksgiving and the deer season. Christmas was only a memory and New Year's Day had slipped by with only a small hangover. According to my notes it was January 22 and the temperature outside was 10 above; I was watching the juncos and chickadees competing with the bluejays around my bird feeder when the phone rang. It was Sanderson and he had a plan which would take me out of that snug and fragrant kitchen.

"I know the whereabouts of this bee tree," he confided and managed to sound like an international spy, "and I'll need your help with it."

An hour later I climbed into Sanderson's pickup which he called his country convertible. Besides his huge bluetick coonhound, Frank, the bed of the pickup contained an axe, assorted ropes, a two-man saw, telephone lineman's climbers, a step ladder, a smoker, several buckets and a sturdy wooden box about the size of two car batteries. What followed was as exciting adventure . . . almost . . . as some hunting and fishing incidents I'll never forget.

At the tree, Sanderson determined that the bee hive was about 15 feet above the ground and at the point where a large limb had died long ago and fallen away, leaving a place for borers to enlarge the hole. Sometime in the past honey bees moved in to set up housekeeping and now the problem was to move them out—part of the hive going into the wooden box to be carried elsewhere so that Sanderson could watch it. Hopefully there would also be enough honey to fill a couple of the buckets for our immediate use.

Fortunately the hive seemed low enough to be within reach of the step ladder. That was an advantage and maybe the first of only two. The other was the intense cold which hopefully would keep the bees fairly dormant while their place was robbed. I didn't like it when my friend handed me a head mask (I already wore gloves), built a smudge fire in his teapot shaped smoker and told me to hold firm to the base of the ladder, NO MATTER WHAT, while he climbed it.

My buddy's first task was to enlarge with his axe the hole into the hive which was practically sealed with wax. That alone was touchy, balanced atop the last ladder rung. It was even touchier when a few bees came out and tried to get under the head net. But on the second try, with a smoker and a bucket in hand instead of the axe, more bees buzzed out in angry defense. If they noticed either the smoke or sub-freezing temperature, it didn't seem to slow the attack. Even *that* wasn't so bad until some hummers focused their attention on me!

"Hold onto that ladder," Sanderson shouted in alarm, as if anticipating that I might defect.

There is no point in describing the incident any further except to say that the hive was successfully robbed with not too much damage to our own hides. Mostly the damage was psychological. One of my wrists was swollen by three bites, but that was a small price to pay for a gallon of aged, dark golden, right-from-the-comb honey. That happened many years ago and was the first chance I'd ever had to taste that wild and cool, tangy nectar. I've enjoyed other honey since, but never ever enough.

Ever since Aristotle, outdoorsmen (as well as scientists) have been as fascinated by the complex society of bees as they have enjoyed eating the honey which is among the most nutritious substances known on earth. It is impossible to spend much time anywhere in the American outdoors without encountering bees, perhaps even frequently or unpleasantly, but few of us really know the remarkable creatures or how they produce honey. Later, as we shall see, wild honey is an extraordinary ingredient which can make just any outdoor cook into a master of cuisine. But that's jumping too far ahead too fast.

Entomologists disagree on the exact number, but about 500 species of bees, alien and native, now inhabit this continent. Most are rare and seldom seen. Probably several times as many live elsewhere around the world. But by far the most common species in the United States is not a native. This main honey-producer is a fuzzy-legged immigrant introduced from Italy sometime before the Civil War. Most live in captive colonies handled by bee-keepers, but the species has also gone wild everywhere and these wild ones are most likely to be encountered by sportsmen. It is also my opinion that the wild ones produce a more delicious, more robust, less bland kind of honey than their domesticated cousins.

Other bees have also been imported, but in modern times bee-keepers or apiarists, have preferred the Italian honeybee because of its sunnier disposition. Sunnier? Some, with bee stings to prove it, would consider that a bad joke.

No matter what its disposition, the honeybee's life history and habits are fascinating. A single colony of either wild or managed-by-human bees—which is really a commune—can contain from 50,000 to 70,000 individuals. Inside the commune are three kinds of bees—drones, workers,

---

Charles Nansen spends most of his waking moments afield. He finds renewal in nature and writes about it for Field & Stream. *Honey is a subject close to his heart. He feels it is better than apples in promoting good health and he has 20 years of illnessless to prove it.*

On warmer fall days afield in an eastern or southern deciduous forest is a good time to spot bee trees.

and the queen. The sole function of the queen is to lay eggs, as many as 2,000 a day for as long as five years or until a younger queen comes along and drives her away. If she hasn't completely run out of gas, the deposed queen may lead a swarm of bees to organize a new commune elsewhere.

The drones, or males, have it made. They do nothing much except live the easy life and impose on the workers. One drone mates with the queen, but death is his reward for the fling. Most bees in any hive are workers, underprivileged females that work nonstop from birth until death. No liberation there.

The worker's first chore is to feed the larvae in the hive, a demanding job since larvae eat continually. After several days on the nursery assignment, the worker stands guard at the hive's entrance, keeps the hive clean, and helps aircondition it by constantly beating her wings. On her final assignment the worker at least gets a change of scenery. She hauls nectar and pollen from source to hive, flying between 10 and 20 mph depending on wind direction, until her wings wear out or she is speared by some bee-eating bird.

The value of bees to conservation is impossible to comprehend. Pollinating activities vastly increase the productivity of fields and forests so that more birds and animals can live there. The number of squirrels in any given woods, for example, might drop to less than half if all the resident bees were suddenly eliminated.

Not too long ago, hunting wild honey was a lively and important event on many a sportsman's calendar. It was a splendid opportunity—and excuse—to spend spare winter hours, or maybe a weekend, vagabonding in the woods after hunting seasons closed and before fishing seasons opened. Of course, it's less hazardous in winter since the bees are dormant, and it seems appropriate then. Sadly, though, wild-honey hunting is rapidly becoming a lost art.

The first step in any honey hunt is to locate a wild beehive, and oldtimers used many ingenious methods. Among the most interesting techniques is one that employs a honey box, a container with a sliding glass top in which a comb of honey is placed. The hunter takes the box afield, looks for a worker bee hovering over a flower somewhere, and tries to trap or maneuver the bee into the box. The theory is that the bee will find the honey inside, load up, and then, when the glass lid is opened, fly back to the hive.

Most of the time, if the hunter stays in the same place, the worker will return with a convoy of other workers from the commune. He gradually follows the course of the bees back to the hive, never moving so far or so fast that contact is lost with refueling bees. This method works well in the late summer and early fall.

As any outdoorsman may suspect, however, there are some pitfalls. Once Homer Sanderson and I "tracked" a whole swarm of worker bees right to a neighbor's backyard hive. With that lesson learned, we concentrated our efforts in Homer's own large woodlot. Here the trail *did* lead to a hive in the hollow of a huge, partially dead beech tree, which we felled, and after considerable aggressiveness on the part of the bees, extracted two gallons of deep brown honey. Luckily we had the sense to wear masks and gloves, which left no bare skin exposed.

Ordinarily Homer prefers to hunt honey another way. On hazy summer or autumn evenings, when the sun is quite low, he walks into the woods, sometimes to hunt squirrels or groundhogs, sometimes for a leisurely stroll. But he always keeps looking directly into the sun. Curiously, the

Homer Sanderson extracts hive and honey from fallen dead maple tree.

back lighting provides the best chance to spot the whirring wings of insects in flight.

Eventually Homer discovers bees moving or converging in a particular direction, and still using the back light to advantage, he follows slowly. It may take more than one evening of following, but soon he finds the bee tree and marks it in his memory for harvesting later on.

One day recently with the mercury around zero, Homer called. "Let's go check the tree that I spotted last September," he suggested.

It was a sugar maple with a hole only an inch or so in diameter about 20 feet above the ground. Since Homer was selectively cutting his timber and this tree was obviously hollow anyway, he didn't hesitate to chop it down. Then with a two-man buck saw, we cut a large V-notch at the hive's entrance. The rich cache of golden honey we found brightened the bitter, snowy day. There was far more than we could carry in two large glass jars, but neither of us minded the mile hike back to a farmhouse for larger containers. Nor were we bothered this time by angry bees swarming to defend the hive.

Humans aren't the only wild honey hunters. Raccoons and opossums occasionally make a fast raid on a hive, and once an active hive is located, black bears simply cannot resist harvesting both the honey and the plump young larvae. Bruins will endure no end of stinging and pure torture to rob a hive.

There have been many instances in the Southeast where bears have ignored electric fences, barbed wire concertinas, and constant stinging just for the ecstasy of tearing commercial hives to splinters. Once in Michigan a bear climbed a power pole and was electrocuted, having mistaken the hissing lines above for the buzzing of bees entering and leaving a hive.

Recently a south Georgia sportsman blamed a swarm of wild bees for completely destroying his weekend fishing camp. The bees found an entrance to the camp under an eave and quickly set up a hive there. This was the beginning of a chain reaction. Soon a bear found the hive and forced his way inside to gobble the contents. He also found other assorted goodies—a sack of sugar, a can of molasses, dried prunes, and several capsules of worm medicine meant for the owner's dogs. When the bear finally left, the cabin was a scene of utter devastation.

The honeybee is a formidable defender. I once saw, for example, a bee maneuver a young attacking sparrow hawk to a standstill. Stinging insects, including all bees (and not honeybees alone), cause more disability and deaths in the United States than venomous reptiles or any other critters, wild or domestic. Two principal reactions come from bee stings. The first is merely an unpleasant swelling plus redness, which usually disappears with time or the application of ice cubes. A series of bee stings at any one time may induce shock. The other reaction, which is allergic, is more

◀ While honey gathering demands a certain degree of knowledge and caution, it is always an adventure with the end justifying whatever you may have to go through to get the honey.

Rich golden brown honey is highly nutritious and can be substituted for sugar or syrup in almost any recipe.

Here wild bees have built a hive in a multiflora rose hedge rather than inside a hollow tree.

places far more numerous than any other trees, are thickly branched with sturdy gray brown trunks and dark green glossy leaves. They seem to be everywhere—tender slips at the water's edge, thick bushy younglings mingled with the forest growth on the low shore, mature trees standing in the still backwaters and lagoons. This is the tupelo gum tree of the southern rich muckland.

From its branches in the springtime depend thousands upon thousands of small fuzzy balls or blooms, on long stems and in thick clusters. The blossoms are usually borne on separate trees, the male in dense round clusters and the female alone on long slender stems. The male tupelo bloom resembles a black clove and is said to contain more honey dew than the female bloom, which is a small fuzzy ball.

Each of the blooms secretes nectar constantly and profusely for two or three weeks, and bees return again and again to the same blossoms for nectar, which often gathers so thickly that it could be scraped off with a knife. It is said that under favorable conditions a honey bee can gather a "load" of honey from just one of the little round balls which are the male or staminate flowers. The nectar is gathered from the surface of the tupelo blossoms instead of the inside of the flowers as is found in other plants.

Following are several recipes especially for wild tupelo honey (but any wild honey would be great) and guaranteed to make any outdoor cook a living legend in his own time.

Wild honey varies in taste and color from region to region, depending on which plants are used by bees to gather nectar.

serious. It increases the pulse rate, produces coughing, and may lead to convulsions or even death. If you tend to have allergies, don't take any unnecessary chances with bees.

Wild honey can be used instead of sugar or any kind of syrup in a recipe and be vastly better than the original ingredient. Just for starters, try it for breakfast on hotcakes or oatmeal or waffles or French toast. Not only will it transform the least inspired batch of blah pancakes into a pure delight, but it will also give a man a lot more energy to venture out and do good deeds.

On the other hand, suppose it's the end of the day. You just came in from following beagle hounds after cottontails in a snowstorm. Or maybe you're half congealed from sitting too long in a duck blind. No matter which because here comes honey to the rescue. Into a pot of hot tea or strong coffee, add a couple of plugs of light rum (or bourbon or brandy if you're highfalutin). Next stir in a generous amount of honey, keeping sure that the brew does not cool off. This simple formula is guaranteed to restore anybody's confidence, as well as his general outlook on life, immediately.

Wild honey varies in taste and color from region to region, differing mostly according to which plants are used by bees to gather nectar. One rare and exquisite honey comes from the nectar of the white tupelo trees found in the coastal regions of the southeast, especially in the river swamps of north Florida where there are sufficient numbers to produce a pure strain of tupelo honey. Along the banks of these rivers and their sloughs the tupelo trees, in many

The complex society of bees is as fascinating as the honey it produces is delectable.

HONEY PINEAPPLE BAKED HAM
1 10-12 pound cured ham
1 cup pineapple juice
2 tablespoons lemon juice
1 cup tupelo honey
1 tablespoon whole cloves
5 pineapple slices

Wipe ham with damp cloth. Place ham in uncovered shallow roasting pan, fat side up. Then bake in a slow oven, (325°F.), allowing about 20 minutes per pound of ham. About 45 minutes before ham has finished baking, remove from oven. Skin, score fat and dot with whole cloves. Combine pineapple juice, lemon juice and honey. Heat to boiling point. Remove from heat immediately and pour over the ham. Return to oven and bake approximately 45 minutes or until interior temperature is 170°F. To serve: Garnish with sautéed pineapple slices and fresh mint.

CANTONESE CHICKEN
2 frying chickens, disjointed
¼ cup tupelo honey
¼ cup soy sauce
½ cup catsup
¼ cup lemon juice

Arrange chicken pieces in single layer in large baking pan. Mix honey, soy sauce, catsup and lemon juice. Pour over chicken pieces. Allow chicken to stand in marinade several hours or over night. Cover pan with foil and bake in 325° (slow) oven 1 hour. Remove foil, baste with sauce. Return to oven and bake uncovered until tender. If a thick sauce is desired, add 1 tablespoon cornstarch, moistened to smooth paste in cold water. Wonderful over cooked rice.

ORANGE MARMALADE
2 large oranges
1 lemon
2 cups orange pulp and
  juice of 2 large oranges
  pulp and juice of 1 lemon
1 cup tupelo honey

Slice unpeeled fruit very thin. Combine pulp, juices and add Tupelo honey and boil 15 minutes or until syrupy and clear. Pour into sterilized glasses. Cover with parifin when cold.

HONEY SALAD DRESSING
1 teaspoon paprika
½ teaspoon powdered dry mustard
½ teaspoon salt
½ teaspoon celery salt
⅓ cup liquid tupelo honey
3 tablespoons lemon juice
1 cup salad oil
¼ cup vinegar

Mix the dry ingredients. Add the honey, lemon juice, and vinegar. Slowly add the salad oil, beating until well blended. Makes about 2 cups.

HONEY NUT BRAN MUFFINS
1 cup sifted flour
¼ to ½ teaspoon soda
¼ teaspoon salt
1 cup bran flakes
¾ cup finely chopped pecans
1 cup melted butter
½ cup milk
½ cup tupelo honey

1. Sift together the dry ingredients and mix with the bran flakes and pecans.
2. Add milk and melted butter and honey.
3. Pour into muffin tins.
4. Bake at 400° F. for 25 minutes.

Unfortunately this otherwise happy piece about food must be ended on a sad or pessimistic note. In the past decade honeybees have been threatened by the evil that is endangering other forms of life today, including human beings—pesticides. The same poisonous mist that may temporarily eliminate mosquitoes also has a lethal effect on honeybees and on the birds that eat them. Recently DDT residues were discovered in Adelie penguins and seals as far away as Antarctica, so it shouldn't surprise anyone if bees suddenly vanish from hives on the edge of anybody's town and the honey they leave behind tastes peculiar.

Honeybees are too valuable to lose. We enjoy their honey, and their pollen-spreading activities are more important than we realize. Even their semi-ominous buzzing would be sorely missed in the great outdoors.

BACKPACK FOODS CAN BE GOOD!

Many supermarkets, aside from their normal selection of dehydrated and freeze-dried foods, carry foods prepared especially for outdoor persons. Some stores even have special pack food sections where a camper has a choice of meals ranging from beef stroganoff to lasagna and meat balls.

by CHARLES J. FARMER

"LET'S SEE . . .," my wife, Kathy murmured as she stared into the bed of cooking coals that I had been pampering for almost an hour. "We can start with a sip of wine from the bota. Top that off with lasagna and meatballs. And finish with pineapple cheese cake.

"How's that sound for dinner?" she asked confidently. "Great," I said. "Reminds me of Antonio's Pizza . . . uh, without the cheese cake, of course."

We were 11,290 feet high, at timberline in Wyoming's Bridger Wilderness fishing for golden trout. And, by rough estimate, I figured we were at least 280 miles from the closest, good Italian restaurant. But that evening, after wetting our appetites on dry, red wine from the skin, we dug into some respectable lasagna and meatballs. The red checked table cloth was missing, so was the mandolin music. But the Italian flavor was there, despite the fact that we ate off a log table of lodgepole pine and listened to a crooning coyote, rather than Dean Martin. And the pineapple cheese cake? Not as good as Mama used to make . . . but a satisfying dessert nonetheless.

We had roamed the Bridger Wilderness for six days. Fishing was good. Wildlife abundant. And the very pleasure of exercising the senses to the wonders of alpine meadows, wild flowers, shimmering lakes and mountain cirques, was invigorating.

And the food was good. That is important to us because neither Kathy or I are spartans when it comes to eating . . . whether we are at home in our log cabin in Jackson Hole, Wyoming, or on top of a wilderness mountain—we enjoy good food. And I believe our experiences in the back country are directly related to the taste, variety and nutritional value of the food we eat.

An unemotional diet of beans, bread, fish and water in the back country excites me as much as the C-rations I was sometimes forced to eat in the Army. Yet, I have several backpacker friends, who not only fit under the beans and bread . . . mountainman plan, but even go so far as to pack souvenir army ration cans into the woods. They tell me they dine elegantly on *Meal, Combat, Individual* (the boxes are labeled that way) "Chicken, boned"; "turkey loaf"; "chopped ham and eggs"; and "ham and lima beans." I don't believe them. Either their taste buds are warped or they are gluttons for punishment. Besides, C-ration meal units and cans border on being too heavy for backpacking. "A can or two of sardines in mustard sauce, and some pickled Vienna sausage, along with some rations does me just fine," one friend says. I shake my head.

So, the meat (and also the potatoes, vegetables, soups, eggs and snacks) of this article is geared to those backpack readers who not only are interested in nutrition, but also enjoy good taste and pleasant eating experiences.

I should set one point straight right here. Rather than excite you into thinking that freeze-dried or dehydrated backpack foods will taste homemade, or nearly so, I will stop long enough to say that they do not. I have personally tested just about every type of commercially prepared pack food, and have found they fall short of home cooking. This is not so bad if you are not used to home cooking. Those who enjoy good, home-cooked meals can prepare themselves for the biggest letdown of all. And the pack food manufacturers who claim that their dehydrated or freeze-dried meals taste as good as "Mother used to make" have had mothers who fell short in the cooking category . . . way short.

Most foods can be cooked easily and quickly with hot or boiling water.

Backpack foods are lightweight and compact easily.

There is no spaghetti or stew on the backpack market today that even comes close to my mother's. Nor is there a beef stroganoff or western omelette that can share a table with Kathy's. But I believe that once a backpacker realizes that commercially prepared foods cannot taste like home cooked dinners, a more objective evaluation can be made of modern trail foods. It is somewhat unfair to put the pack food manufacturers down without comparing their efforts to those of the "TV Dinner" producers. Even with a weight and size advantage, TV dinners still do not qualify for home-cooked status. And in my opinion, no commercially prepared foods do (with some restaurants being an exception).

For the most part, knowing full well that commercially prepared backpack foods do not rival their home cooked cousins, I still evaluate the taste of most foods as good. But, there are variations of good taste . . . some foods dip slightly under the good rating; others rank high on the good level. As a lover of the outdoors, foods and tastes, honestly I cannot rank any freeze-dried or dehydrated meal or snack as excellent . . . or very good for that matter.

Fortunately, there are only a few foods that I rate as poor. And I find little difference in quality among different brands. The poor ones fall under the heading of desserts. Not all are poor, but a hiker would be better off with a candy bar, or food stick than spending the time to prepare some desserts. The cobblers, berry flavors, are the worst backpack foods I have eaten. But I do not consider the elimination of cobblers from my back country meals a disaster because there are too many other fine desserts to take their place. The puddings and pies, for example, are good.

The degree of good, in evaluating the taste of backpack

For the fisherman, a day sack can carry a good supply of pack foods and snacks.

foods, is a variable that coincides, I believe, with the variable degree of hunger. And food manufacturers have a very strong point in their favor. That is, outdoor air and exercise, stimulate appetites and hunger, more than normal. What would taste fair at home, after a normal day at the office, or school, might taste good after a day of hiking.

The degree of hunger also varies from day to day on a backpack trip. So on some days, certain foods may taste better than the same foods eaten on other days. It is my opinion that because the taste of these foods cannot be honestly rated as excellent, the degree of hunger is the most important factor in evaluating true taste. You can test this theory at home. Commercially prepared backpack or trail foods, or their boxed, household counterparts (freeze-dried or dehydrated) can be bought at most supermarkets throughout the country.

Prepare one or several dried or dehydrated meals at home. Evaluate taste. Then on your next camping trip, prepare the same meals and evaluate taste again. I believe you will find a significant difference. To complete the taste course, prepare, within a reasonable span of time from your camping trip, the same meals at home again. Use only the ingredients, or extra spices you would use on a camping trip. Any taste difference?

One of the more important points about trail foods is that I have found little or no taste difference between brands of backpack foods. Quantity and variety differ somewhat, but not enough to make a significant comparison.

Probably the most important reason that most trail foods taste the same is because of the very processes in which they are prepared. Methods of dehydration and freeze-drying are universal. The processes will be explained later in this article. It all freezes down, or is dried out to the point that, although there may be a difference in quality of the original foods before processing, methods of freeze-drying and dehydration tend to equalize tastes and make them uniform. But there is a distinct difference between the two processes (explained later) that have an effect on taste.

Aside from backpacking, many conventional camp meals are built around and spiced by dehydrated and freeze-dried foods.

Food manufacturers even have a wide variety of desserts.

Freeze-dried meats are especially handy for that craving for something "solid."

Pack foods are also handy for canoe and kayak trips where space and weight are factors.

Taste is personal. True. There are some outside factors, both real, like price; and psychological, like appearance, that influence taste.

One of the more commonly heard remarks about the appearance of trail meals is that they are mushy looking and mushy tasting. One packer I know refers to the numerous noodle dishes as "globs." But he eats them nevertheless. Prescribed cooking times, variable due to altitude and the heat source, can be at their best, rough estimates. Overcooking predominates at times because of erratic and irregular open fire heat. Mush is often the result. But not all the blame can be heaped onto the manufacturer's plate. My wife and I have found that careful watch over boiling and standard "low simmer" starch foods can guard against overcooking. And we prefer the slightly chewy vegetables and noodles to the mashed potato type. As Kathy puts it, "There is a certain type of good, wholesome aggressive energy expended in the chewing process...especially when foods *have* to be chewed. A constant barrage of overcooked, mushy meals are not good for the mind and body." Kathy has a Master's degree in Clinical Psychology. So there is some basis for her remark.

Price affects taste. The general concensus among backpackers is that food prepared and packaged especially for backpacking is expensive; while dehydrated and freeze-dried food, prepared and packaged for the general consumer, and found on supermarket shelves, costs about half the price. The big difference in the two is variety. Certain dehydrated foods are available in supermarkets. But the choice is not a large one. That's the reason why trail food manufacturers have arrived on the scene. They offer variety . . . everything from complete beef dinners and dumplings to freeze-dried neapolitan ice cream. Packers pay for variety. They also pay for the freeze-dried and dehydration processes. And they pay for the handy, individual, compactable and (mostly) biodegradable packaging that holds their dinners, lunches, fruits, salads, snacks and drinks.

When a person pays $1.50 for a 3-ounce, pre-fried bacon bar, it's gotta taste good! Although hikers and campers may moan a little about the cost of specialized trail foods, more than once I've heard them say . . . "Anything that expensive is good—whether it's good or not."

How many times have you been at a fancy restaurant, paid 6 or 7 dollars for a small, tough steak, and because

Bike camping has about the same weight limitations as backpacking and for that reason, lightweight foods are essential and practical for the cyclist.

you have paid that much say, "It was good." We like to get what we pay for. And sometimes when we don't, we make excuses for it or rationalize that it was "good."

The Best Buys and Eating in Trail Food

In my findings, a hiker can duplicate, and improve on most of the soups, fruits, desserts, beverages and snacks sold specifically and primarily as trail food. All of these items are available in the supermarket, at just about half the price. Do your own packaging with plastic bags. Just the right portions can be bagged before the trip. It's fun and easy.

The real values (and not necessarily because of low price) are found in the basics of breakfast, lunch and dinner. Availability has a great deal to do with value. And because it is extremely difficult and impractical these days to hunt up powdered eggs, freeze-dried meats of all sorts and dried vegetables, the backpacker is better off spending a little extra on the foundation meals and forgetting about how to skimp on or replace eggs, meat and vegetables.

The above staples, individually or combined, complete dinners, are worth their money because they are handy, good tasting, relatively lightweight and easy to pack. There is nothing a backpack camper can do right now to equal or better those convenience meals.

Adding Zest to Pack Meals

For around two dollars I can add enough zip to my wilderness meals to make me think I was in Mexico . . . or Italy. The secret is spices. And even the blandest, or mushiest of trail meals can be given a shot of life—that is if you like taste and spices and zip.

Good tasting trail foods can be made to taste better. Note that I did not say great—better is more accurate. In the food bag of my pack I insure taste zing, regardless of the meal, by carrying containers of oregano, poultry seasoning, cinnamon (for breakfast foods), garlic salt and Italian (or Spanish) spices. Salt and pepper are standard equipment. They all can be purchased at the supermarket. And they definitely lend themselves to certain meals, depending on the tastes of the campers. There is enough variety there to make any meal interesting, and equally as important is the fact that they take up little room, and depending on their containers, usually weigh less than half a pound. It is only fair to say, that backpack food manufacturers gear their processing to the norm or average tastes of consumers. I'm sure that they would be highly criticized, just as some restaurants are, for spicing their foods too much. So they stick to the middle of the road in the taste category, figuring if persons want more spice, they can add their own . . . which I usually do.

I liken the situation to many high school, college or hospital cafeterias. Food is commonly bland. Institutional cooks gear their menus to the persons who like neither salt nor pepper (and the family of spices), thinking those that like zip will add their own. Of course it goes without saying that foods prepared (cooked) with a sensible array of spices will be tastier.

Here's What the Experts Say

I contacted home economists and nutrition experts from ten leading universities to find out their opinions of trail foods and nutrition. Most of us have a pretty good idea by now, of what many of the meals taste like.

Christine R. Peters, Division of Foods and Nutrition, at the University of Illinois had this to say: "I feel that modern freeze-dried and dehydrated foods are just as capable of providing adequate calories, protein, fat and carbohydrates as the unprocessed foods. The fulfillment of these nutrients

Backpack foods fill a definite need —for the mobile, limited space, back woods traveler.

For ski touring, pack foods and snacks fit easily into day packs and add enjoyment to the trip and scenery.

does, however, depend on two factors. The first factor is the selection of foods that the person chooses to consume. Even at home, one does not always wisely choose the correct foods to provide adequate amounts of these nutrients. Therefore, the backpacker's choice of dried foods, and the amounts he or she consumes, will have a direct relationship with the quantity of calories, protein, fat and carbohydrates provided by the outdoor diet. With this factor taken into consideration, if the person chooses a well balanced selection of dried foods comparable to their fresh counterparts, there should be no problem in achieving adequate levels of these nutrients."

Miss Peters continued, "The second factor concerns proper processing techniques before the foods reach the consumer. Methods of dehydration vary from product to product. That is, before any food product can be successfully dehydrated or freeze-dried, the method of processing which provides the best quality must first be developed. When the method is carefully adjusted to each food product, the availability of fats, proteins and other essentials remains comparable to that of fresh food. It is my understanding that today's industry has extensively researched all methods of preserving food and that the freeze-dried and dehydrated foods available on the market are indeed of high quality."

In regards to taste and processing methods Christine said, "I would rate the taste of most dehydrated foods as fair and most freeze-dried foods as good. I have found that dehydrated foods have a less natural taste due to the scorched flavors imparted by the high heat treatment involved in the dehydration process.

"Freeze-dried foods, on the other hand," continued Miss Peters, "appears more natural in taste as the low temperature of processing helps to inhibit protein denaturation and adverse bacterial or chemical reactions and minimize the loss of flavorful, volatile components."

Evelyn J. Gray, Extension Nutritionist at Ohio State University in Columbus said, "Freeze-dried food is basically good food. But there is some loss of nutrients as is the case of any method which requires processing and storage." She added, "The quality has improved."

In regards to dehydrated foods, Mrs. Gray said, "They were developed to meet a specific need. The quality is good . . . and improving. But," she warns, "some camping food may be beyond its shelf life. And as of yet, there has been no attempt to let the consumer know how old, or how fresh the foods are."

Evelyn Gray rates both freeze-dried and dehydrated foods good in taste, but says, "Variety is important, and the backpacker should use some discrimination in choice of food and the combinations purchased."

Jane A. Bowers, Ph.D., Associate Professor of the Department of Foods and Nutrition at Kansas State University, in Manhattan, Kansas suggested the following references for campers desiring detailed information on the freeze-drying and dehydration processes. Although numerous references were cited, campers might be interested in:

Ballemtyne, R.M., 1958, Dehydrated cooked meat products. *Food Technology,* 12, 398.

Bird, Kermit. *Selected writings on freeze-drying of foods.* U.S. Department of Agriculture, ERS-147 (code description).

Goldblith, Samuel, 1963. The role of food science and technology in the freeze dehydration of foods. *Food Technology.*

The references can be obtained by writing to the U.S. Department of Agriculture, Washington, D.C. 20000. Further information about dehydration and freeze-drying of foods may also be available at this time.

The remaining nutritionists and home economists, agreed in one way or another with those mentioned. It was their consensus that although freeze-dried and dehydrated foods fell a little short in the taste department, nutrition essentials were being realized. "Balanced meals, even in the field, are the key," said Monica Ratone, New York nutritionist. "The foods certainly fill the needs of hikers and campers . . . the energy producing proteins are there," she added.

The best trail foods manufacturers offer the camper a complete menu planner and nutritional guide. Some of the guides are available at supermarkets and sporting goods stores where the foods are sold. If the guides are not available there, ask your grocer to furnish you with the address of the processor. Write for the nutritional guides and suggest that your grocer stock them near the foods being sold. Those trail foods manufacturers who fail to send you the requested information can be checked off your list. There are good ones processing and packaging food for you. And they will be more than happy to tell you about their foods.

Fresh caught lake trout make a perfect shore lunch in Canada's Northwest Territories. Even if you bring lake trout fillets home with you, they'll never taste the same.

FIELD TASTING

by MARK SOSIN

TIME WAS PRECIOUS to us, but a few minutes on that gravel bar to pacify cramped and aching muscles seemed a necessity. Five of us in two freighter canoes were on a scouting mission, and it hadn't been easy. After dragging those heavy canoes over three miles of glacial eskers, we finally reached the Pepeshquasati River above the point where it empties into Quebec's famed Lake Mistassini. We had six hours to fish our way down 14 miles of river and reach the pickup point before dark. Of course, there were rapids to shoot, spots so wild that the canoes had to be tracked downstream, and trophy brook trout to keep us busy.

Gathering some driftwood, we hastily built a small fire to combat the mist that had made things uncomfortable since early morning. Although it was well past noon, the thought of food was a luxury we couldn't afford, since there wasn't time to make a shore lunch. However, Renald Guay pulled an old pot out of his pack and promptly brewed some tea. Then, almost miraculously, he unveiled a loaf of home-baked bread and a wheel of cheese.

The only recollection I have of the entire episode is that the hunks of bread we pulled off the loaf were the best I have ever tasted and the cheese had a delicate flavor that gave it legendary qualities. To this day, I would be hard

---

Mark Sosin has earned his reputation as a respected outdoor writer and photographer through his dedication, knowledge and skill of fishing. With his home base in Highland Park, New Jersey, he has traveled around the globe in search of new and exciting fishing adventures.

pressed to remember a better piece of cheese or a more appetizing meal.

Too often, many of us who have enjoyed foods at streamside, around a campfire, or in an outdoor setting, attempt to relive those moments by collecting recipes and then duplicating the culinary masterpieces in the comfort of our kitchens. Sometimes the food is equally palatable, but in the majority of experiments, the recipe doesn't turn out the same way as you remember it.

Initially, one mentally reviews the ratio of ingredients and then questions the cooking time. Perhaps something was omitted. Try this often enough and you will eventually discover that it is not always what you eat that makes the difference, but where you eat it. That bread and cheese on a gravel bar had a special meaning because we were hungry

Often overlooked by saltwater anglers, the lookdown is a member of the pompano family and boasts a uniquely delicate flavor.

and tired, and the surprise of even a snack was a delightful treat. Who knows how good that cheese really was if one were to place it on a tray at a cocktail party and it could be compared to other cheeses.

Any angler who has traveled the bush country knows that a shore lunch of fresh fish is a gourmet's delight. You've never tasted fish like that and the standard reason is the fish are super fresh. They just came out of the water and are being cooked on the spot. I'm not convinced that's the sole ingredient of such a sumptuous repast. To my thinking, it's being at lakeside away from the comforts of civilization and eating a hearty meal in the open air when your appetite is at its peak and your taste buds can easily be fooled.

Eight thousand miles south of the Pepeshquasati River, the Chilean Lake Region is laced with swift flowing glacial streams that tumble out of the lofty Andes. Rainbows and brown trout quickly become heavyweights in these waters and, as a general rule, the bigger rivers yield huskier fish. They are too deep and far to swift to wade, so most of the fishing is done from small brightly colored rowboats that are used to float downstream.

Shore lunch is a tradition in Chile and the relaxing experience is one you will never forget. About noon, the boat is beached and your guide builds a fire. A couple of trout from the morning's fishing are cleaned and a rack of young lamb is skewered on a green stick and suspended above the fire. Chilean wine is chilled in the river, while fresh vegetables are washed for the salad. Fruits are spread out and there is the typical Chilean bread.

Known locally as an *asado*, this type of shore lunch is a full course meal in which you simply serve yourself from all of the various foods. A sharp knife is carefully placed near the lamb and you cut pieces off as you want them. When you've feasted on the varied menu and enjoyed the local wine, it's time for a siesta before continuing the fishing. The wine, coupled with the warm noonday sun and the mountain air, make this relaxed atmosphere a welcome addition to the journey.

Lamb has never been a favorite of mine at home or in any restaurant, yet on the banks of the Rio Fui in Chile, it had a flavor that defies the printed word, proving once again that it's not what you eat, but where you eat it that can make food so delicious.

Every fishing camp in the world has its culinary specialties. If your palate is even the least bit adventuresome, that's

You can often preserve the flavor of most fish by cleaning them immediately after they are caught and keeping them cool. Here, noted fly-tyer Bub Church deftly cleans an eating size brown trout at streamside.

the time to try many of the exotic dishes and even the more mundane items on the menu. They'll never taste better than they do in the remote atmosphere. Anglers who must watch their diets back home, suddenly discover that they can eat almost anything without ill effects in the pleasurable surroundings of a fishing or hunting lodge.

It's no different on the saltwater scene where such delicacies as conch fritters, crayfish (or lobster), shrimp dishes, and dolphin or snapper fingers boast an unbelievable freshness and a unique flavor. In Angola, shrimp are cooked in the local piri piri sauce. Piri piri is a type of pepper that is allowed to ferment somewhat in its own juice and some versions are strong enough to siphon your breath away.

Cross the Atlantic to the Western shore and the same large shrimp are stuffed with crabmeat, while the crabs are

While we cast around a rocky shoreline, the mate donned flippers and snorkel and probed the rocky outcroppings. In a matter of minutes, he had enough crayfish for dinner and they were by far the best I have ever eaten. When you consider that they were cooked on a Coleman stove, that's going some, but in spite of the limited kitchen (or galley) facilities, it's not everyday that one can dine on lobster aboard a boat riding at anchor along a jungle shoreline.

On the same trip, we would even get selective about the species of fish to have for dinner. At one point, we probed some very deep water for the elusive silky snapper which is acclaimed for its very delicate flavor. And, all of us suddenly became obsessed with catching silky snapper while ignoring prime gamefish.

There have been other journeys where fishing suddenly

In Chile, the typical lunch or *asado* consists of fresh caught trout and a rack of lamb roasted slowly over the embers of a fire. This menu is supplemented with fruits, vegetables, and Chilean wine.

prepared with hot pepper. Around Chesapeake Bay, crabs are served on newspapers and the aficionado enjoys the rigors of breaking the crab open with hammer and nut cracker.

One of the most memorable trips I have ever made was an excursion on the Pacific side of Panama to the islands of Montuosa and Coiba. We had left the base camp on the mainland aboard a 32-foot Prowler and would stay out for four days before returning to refuel and try another four days on the water. The boat was stocked with plenty of staples, but in addition to sportfishing, we had the responsibility of putting fish on the table.

After a couple of days of fresh fish, we were searching for variations to the menu. Capt. Don McGuinness suggested local crayfish and it didn't take long to convince us.

became more than sport. On a fly-in junket to a cabin on Bearpaw Lake in Northern Ontario, we suddenly discovered that provisions were at a low ebb. A fresh walleye could make the difference between a tasty supper and a can of beans. The two walleye I caught weren't big, but I don't think I was ever under more pressure to catch fish. Darkness was closing in over the tops of the pines and there wasn't much time to put supper in the fish box. The lake was noted for its northern pike and trying to seduce a pair of walleyes was a herculean job.

On the way to Columbia's Amazon Basin, our plane experienced some mechanical difficulties and we had to change aircraft. In the process, someone forget to transfer the supplies and we arrived in camp minus the tender steaks and poultry that we were bringing in from Bogota. For-

The best waterfowl recipe I have ever found came from Helen Webster of Remington Farms where cooking ducks and geese is a way of life.

tunately, the waters at El Dorado abound with peacock bass, a delicately flavored cousin of our own largemouth, and some of us hastily went fishing to insure an adequate supply to go along with the rice for supper.

In the outdoor world, each meal seems to take on special meaning and memories are crowded with spreads fit for royalty. Usually, if you walk away from the table with even a wisp of appetite left, it's your own fault. Often, food is served family style and you just keep piling it on your plate until a brisk walk is the only thing you have room for.

At a tiny farmhouse on the banks of one of Iceland's most famous salmon rivers, each spread was an adventure in eating. There were always enough appetizers to make you shudder when the main courses (and I emphasize the plural) were squeezed on the already crowded table. Meals in Greenland were similar and I also vividly recall sailing on some of the fjords while fresh caught Arctic char was boiling in a giant pot along with vegetables.

Aboard a houseboat on a Brazilian tributary of the Amazon, the specialty of one evening was broiled caiman tail. The caiman, of course, is a relative of our own alligator.

It was my first experience with this delicacy and it tasted more like beef than anything. You could also supplement the caiman diet with some pieces of giant catfish. Amazonian catfish come in a variety of species that grow from an inch or two in length to a few species that can weigh up to 800 pounds. It dosen't taste anything like the catfish in Tennessee and there are no hush puppies to go with it, but its an adventure in dining.

One time at a hunting camp in Mozambique, we were treated to roast warthog. In Africa, most visitors have more than ample opportunity to sample many forms of wild game, yet a warthog banquet, properly prepared, is an experience that will linger. At Camp Zinave, Baron Werner von Alvensleben sent one of his hunters out in the morning to bring back a warthog. It was as if the hunter went to the local supermarket, because he was back in half an hour with one of the right size. All day, that animal was slowly roasted over the embers of a fire, and as I reflect on it, the time spent in savoring the meal added to the intrigue.

When darkness enveloped the plains and the sounds of the African bush inundated the air, the warthog was ready. Sitting outdoors and eating by firelight provided the perfect setting and I still recall that the warthog prepared in that manner was among the tenderest and most delicious meat I have ever eaten. There were other goodies on the menu, but I can't help remembering cutting up some home grown watermelons for dessert.

Since I have learned a long time ago that spectacular

In the Bahamas, the conch is a tasty delicacy that is prepared in many ways. The most common is conch chowder and conch fritters.

It's surprising how great some freshly fried fish and heated vegetables can taste when cooked over an open fire on the shore of a remote lake.

meals in the outdoors can seldom be duplicated at home, I stopped collecting recipes. The same menu might be prepared in your own kitchen, but I honestly believe it loses something if you don't eat the meal in the surroundings of the outdoors.

There's an exception to every rule and the one recipe I did bring home came from Helen Webster at Remington Farms in Maryland. Helen and her husband manage that spacious waterfowl refuge and when I coaxed her out of that old family secret, I knew it could be duplicated in any kitchen. Normally, I would tell you that it's not what you eat, but where you eat it that counts. However, if you've been looking for a waterfowl recipe, try this one:

Place the duck (or geese) in a pan breast up. Sprinkle each bird with one tablespoon of cooking sherry. Then, season each duck with ½-teaspoon of celery salt; ½-teaspoon of onion salt; ½-teaspoon of celery seed; ¼-teaspoon of curry; ¼-teaspoon of pepper; and 1 teaspoon of salt.

Allow the birds to sit in the pan for ½-hour to an hour.

Chop one small onion and one stalk of celery and place them in the pan with the ducks. Add ¼- to a ½-inch of water. Bake at 500 degrees until the breast is brown (about 20 minutes). Turn the birds and bake until the backs are brown. Cover and cook for one more hour at 300 degrees. Total cooking time is about 2 hours. Of course, if you enjoy dressing, add your favorite.

Jack Dennis, well-known fishing guide, fixes feast for lunch of cutthroat trout, freshly caught, salad and baked beans and potatoes. (Jack Dennis has the patterned shirt on and is by the fire. Author Dan Abrams has the cowboy hat on.)

Secrets of Streamside Cooking

by Dan Abrams

"TIME FOR one more cast before lunch."

These were the words of our guide, Jack Dennis, as he nosed the 14-foot neoprene rubber boat toward one of the many small islands dotting the Snake River which braids its multi-channeled course southward through the Jackson Hole Country of Wyoming.

My fishing partner, Chuck Wilson, and I made our "one

Dan Abrams, pastor of the First Baptist Church in Jackson, Wyoming, finds enjoyment in writing about his favorite pastime—fishing, especially dry-fly fishing for cutthroat trout. He has sold articles to Field & Stream *and* Sports Afield. *He, his wife Claire and their two sons thrive on the rigors of Wyoming outdoors.*

more cast" and had just completed unproductive retrieves when our boat touched against the bank of the little island. Both of us jumped ashore and helped Jack pull the boat up on the river-smoothed stones and out of the force of the current.

As Chuck and I stretched the kinks out of our legs, I began to realize how hungry I was. My hunger pangs triggered the recollection of overhearing someone state that the only thing better than catching cutthroat trout on a Snake River float trip was eating Jack Dennis' streamside lunch.

Well it was going to have to be *some* lunch if it were to vie with the fishing experience of that particular morning! Casting Muddler Minnow steamers tight against the undercut banks of the Snake had provided just about all the ac-

171

All the ingredients for an unforgettable streamside banquet. The best place to store these is in a cooler, which fits nicely into a fishing boat. All the chef needs is a little know-how and a pinch of imagination.

tion Chuck and I were able to handle. Each of us had landed more than a dozen trout. We kept four of the beautifully-marked cutthroats of about 15 inches for our lunch and the rest we returned to the water.

Jack Dennis is one of Wyoming's best-known fishing guides and professional fly-tiers. His base of operations is centered around his well-stocked tackle shop in the town of Jackson. Chuck and I were about to find out that Jack was also an outdoor chef of no ordinary ability.

About ten minutes after we landed on the island we were joined by Tony Kirkpatrick, one of Jack's guides, and the two fishermen in his boat. The arrival of the other boat touched off a flurry of lunch-making activity.

Tony drew the fish-cleaning detail while Chuck, the other two fishermen and I gathered dry driftwood for a fire. Jack hauled an ice chest from his boat and went to work.

As soon as the fire was blazing, Jack took a pound of sliced bacon from the ice chest and wrapped it in heavy duty aluminum foil, making sure all seams were tightly sealed by folding them over and pinching them closed. He set that aside until the fire had a chance to burn down a little.

Meanwhile, he emptied a large can of baked beans into another piece of heavy duty foil which had turned-up edges to keep everything from overflowing. He stirred a small bottle of barbecue sauce through the beans and brought all edges of the foil together and pinched the seams tightly, forming a leak-proof cooking container.

On yet another piece of aluminum foil he emptied a package of bite-sized potato puffs (with the brand name of Tater-Tots) which he had picked up from the frozen food department of the local super market. A couple of good-sized chunks of margarine (equal to about three or four healthy tablespoonfuls) went in with the Tater-Tots. Salt, pepper and a couple of onion slices added a touch of seasoning. Like the beans, the potatoes were sealed in a little foil tent.

By this time the fire had burned down to a nice bed of hot coals and Jack carefully placed all three foil packages—bacon, beans and potatoes—right on the coals.

I was interested in this, because for some reason or another I had always been nervous about placing even well-buttered, foil-protected food directly on hot coals that way. Call it lack of faith or whatever you will, I had always suspected that anything I dared seal in those neat little foil packages would be instantly incinerated as soon as I put them even *near* a hot coal. I mean I'm the kind of guy who has trouble keeping bacon from sticking in a teflon-coated skillet over low heat on the kitchen range. But without a twitch of fear or trembling, Jack placed those three packages smack dab on the hot coals.

Then he went back to the ice chest and got a head of lettuce which he shredded on a sheet of that ubiquitous aluminum foil—a piece about three feet long. He chunked up a couple of small tomatoes, added three or four onion slices, scrambled this around with a fork, and the salad was just about ready.

It was at that moment Tony appeared with the trout. Jack tore off a two-foot length of aluminum foil for each fish. He thoroughly salted and peppered the trout inside and out, and then generously dusted each fish with Lawry's Seasoned Salt. After that, he placed a couple of thin slices of onion inside the cavity of each fish.

By that time the bacon had been sputtering in the fire for

Heavy duty foil is the only cookware needed. Foil can be pan, plate and bowl all wrapped into one. Here the lunch's three courses are put securely in foil while the fire burns down to embers.

about eight minutes. Jack removed the package with a pair of tongs and peeled back the foil. He put one slice of bacon inside the cavity of each trout and also placed a slice of bacon along the flanks of each fish. After a tablespoon-size chunk of margarine was added to each package, the fish were tightly sealed by crimping the foil edges together, and all were carefully placed on the hot coals of the fire.

Jack then announced, "Today, you will also sample one of the specialties of the house—'Trout à la Green Goddess.'" And having said that, he took two trout (which had been set aside without my noticing), laid each one on a two-foot length of foil, took a bottle of Seven Seas Green Goddess salad dressing, smeared some inside the cavity of the trout, poured a generous covering of it over the entire fish, sealed the foil, and placed them on the hot coals, too.

"I've got to tell you how this little delicacy was discovered," grinned Jack. "One day one of my guides forgot to take along any bacon or margarine on the float trip. When it came time to prepare the fish, he knew he was in trouble. He had a bottle of Green Goddess salad dressing in the ice chest, and it was only as an act of desperation that he plastered the fish with the stuff to keep them from burning or sticking to the foil. He didn't let on that anything was wrong. He just went about it as if this were the way he *usually* prepared his trout for the streamside lunch. Much to his surprise (and relief), everyone loved it! And since then it has been one of the most popular variations in the preparation of our trout."

When the trout had been on the coals for five minutes, Jack flipped them over. He gave us each a paper plate and a

Placed right on the coals, the fish in their aluminum foil cocoons are scrumptiously baked in 10 to 15 minutes. The aroma alone primes the appetite.

Believing that fishermen need to be in top physical condition with energy to spare, Jack Dennis sees to it that his clients get a well-balanced meal, including salad and the trimmings. No better place to eat royally than at streamside.

fork and told us to help ourselves to the salad. We had our choice of three kinds of salad dressing.

When the fish had cooked for five minutes after they had been flipped, they were removed from the coals and served. The potatoes and beans (which, at this point, had been on the coals for a total of 20 minutes) were also ready. In spite of my worry and concern, nothing was burned—not even slightly scorched. The salad was great! The beans and potatoes—delicious! The bacon-flavored trout—superb! The Trout à la Green Goddess—fantastic! It was a time to enjoy, and enjoy we did!

I asked Jack if he ever brought any hot dogs along—just in case there was a streak of poor fishing. Or, did he ever come to the lunch hour without the main ingredients for the meal—a mess of trout?

He laughed as he replied, "Let me put it this way . . . once or twice lunch has been mighty late . . . and a couple of times when some visiting fishermen just couldn't get the hang of fishing these big Western waters, I have had to take rod in hand myself to help things along . . . but the old Snake River hasn't let me down yet. Because of that, I don't even think of bringing any provisional substitutes along. If for some reason a person cannot eat fish we take along some ground beef or something, but the fish are always there if you want them."

Later, I learned from Jack that beginning with the 1973 season, new regulations stipulated there were to be no open fires along the Snake River within the boundaries of Grand Teton National Park (just a few miles north of the section we were floating that day). At first he was concerned that this might have a detrimental effect on the quality of the streamside lunch he would provide his fishermen when he

In some National Parks, fires are prohibited. Then, a Kangaroo Kitchen, a self-contained, propane cooking unit, is a must for hungry fishermen.

floated the Park section of the Snake. But then he happened upon one of the handiest self-contained cooking units I have ever seen. It's called a Kangaroo Kitchen, and with it you can roast, toast, broil, boil, bake, fry, steam, smoke fish or fowl, and even do some pressure cooking (thanks to its unique clamping cover).

The Kangaroo Kitchen is fueled by a standard propane cartridge and has a clam shell style cover which enhances its cooking efficiency. Inside, it holds a removable griddle surface and wire grill which adds to its versatility. For picnickers, boaters, campers, and backyard chefs, this is one piece of equipment well worth considering. This outfit closes to a compact 5 inches x 14 inches x 16 inches travel or storage unit, and only weighs 12 lbs. (including fuel cartridge). At this writing the Kangaroo Kitchen was priced around 40 bucks.

When using the Kangaroo Kitchen, Jack prepares his streamside lunches exactly as he does for the open fire cooking (including all the aluminum foil). He says everything turns out tasting every bit as delicious as when cooked on the coals of an open fire.

After we had all helped ourselves to second (and for a couple of us, third) servings of everything, a box of chocolate chip cookies which had been baked by Jack's charming wife, Sandra, were quickly dispatched by the six of us.

As we were cleaning up all the litter, Tony asked us if we had enjoyed our lunch.

"Lunch,," someone retorted, "why, I've been to twenty-dollar-a-plate banquets which couldn't hold a candle to this feast!"

Someone else added, "Yes, and I've never been in a better banquet hall than this, either."

With the beautiful snow-topped Teton Mountains north and west of us, the Gros Ventre range to the east, the hills above the Hoback River to the south, and with all this under the intense blue of a Wyoming August sky, none of us were about to dispute that point.

As Chuck and I got back in the boat to resume our fishing, he turned to me and said, "You know, Dan . . . I've always declared that I'd rather fish than eat. But after this meal, I just might have to reconsider my position on that statement."

Knowing how much Chuck Wilson enjoys fishing, I consider that to be the ultimate testimonial to a riverside banquet prepared by a real pro.

When using the Kangaroo Kitchen, prepare steamside lunches in the same way you would for the open fire cooking. The trout are just as delicious.

Anyone who can cook on gas at home can prepare a meal in a RV.

the RV galley

by JACK SEVILLE

RECREATIONAL VEHICLES (or RVs) as we use the term here, refers to *camping* vehicles and not snowmobiles, all-terrain vehicles, dune buggies or off-road vehicles. RVs combine the facilities for both living and traveling. They can be either self-propelled or carried or towed by another vehicle. They vary in size (and interior space) as well as in the comfort features they provide. But size itself is a poor criterion.

Anyone unfamiliar with the phenomenon might be puzzled by the ability of an entire family to actually live in a RV which contains far less space than one room of their home—until they see the vehicle reach its campsite and disgorge mom, pop, kids and dogs. Those who camp by RV avoid claustrophobia and escape the tangle of knees and elbows by spending as much time as possible outside. They soon learn that days of travel and periods of rain provide all the togetherness they require.

Much more significant than size is the degree of self-containment—a term which means it contains heat, light and plumbing to sustain its occupants in relative comfort for a period of time without resort to stationary facilities. Fully self-contained, the vehicle will have a refrigerator, a cooking range with oven, space heater and water heater, electric lights, sink, lavatory and bathing facilities and accommodations for sleeping and dining. There will also be a fresh water storage tank and a separate tank for holding waste until it can be disposed of.

Liquid petroleum (LP) gas, stored in refillable tanks outside the vehicle, provides fuel for operation of the gas-fired appliances. Electricity is supplied by 12-volt batteries or by a gasoline-powered generator.

At full-service campgrounds, hookups are available to supply fresh water, 110-volt electricity and sewage disposal.

While there is some variation in size and quality of the equipment RVs contain, basically it is all the same—and not a whole lot different from their counterparts at home.

Minimum kitchen equipment will include an icebox, two-burner LP gas stove, sink and fresh-water tank with manual pump. In more luxurious RVs, the refrigerator with freezer compartment is mechanical and can be operated selectively off LP gas, 12-volt battery or 110-volt AC current. A four-burner cook stove and full-size oven will be fueled by LP gas. The water system will be electrically pressurized and will include an automatic LP gas-fired water heater.

There are really only a few compromises made and these are for the sake of conserving space and maintaining maximum mobility. On delivery of a new vehicle, it takes only minutes for the dealer to acquaint the new owner with the operation of appliances.

It's the very compactness that takes getting used to, but

Favorite electrical appliances, like coffee makers and toasters, can be taken along for use when hooked up to 110-volt electricity in campgrounds or if the RV is equipped with a gasoline-powered electric generator.

that might be said to be a blessing in disguise. Recognizing that RVs are just another means of escape, the effort should be to break the routines, spending minimum time on chores, leaving maximum time for the pleasures. Most will agree that means a limit on K.P. duty for everyone, and that has to include Mom.

Besides its obvious pleasures, spending more time outdoors will reduce confusion and clean-up time in the RV. Weather and insects permitting, most of us would rather be outdoors anyway. By cooking outside, the heat, grease, odors and mess are kept out of the confined area of the RV which can better serve as the living/sleeping area.

Advance planning and good organization are the keys to smooth RVacationing—and that applies particularly to providing for the three-squares with the least amount of muss and fuss. Meal planning should anticipate bigger appetites.

Because the equipment is similar, anyone competent enough to produce a meal in the kitchen can produce equally well in a RV. To do as well out-of-doors does often require some improvisation, but that can be a rewarding

There is no "roughing it" in the larger, full-equipped RVs.

Weather and insects permitting, a RV vacation emphasizes outdoor living.

pursuit and is thoroughly delineated elsewhere in this publication.

To be a successful cook away from home calls for planning and the ability to improvise. During the early part of the trip, you can rely on ham, beef or chicken that has been cooked at home. You can go a step farther and portion it into individual meals and freeze it. Kept refrigerated in the RV and then reheated, meals are available with little effort for several days.

Simplicity, emphasizing one-pot meals and casseroles, should be the keynote, but that is not to say gourmet meals are out of place. Indeed, they can be the highlight of any trip—when planned that way.

Since dishwashing is no one's favorite pastime, use your ingenuity to limit the number of pots and pans needed. Substitute aluminum foil or disposable foil pans. They are available in most supermarkets as pie pans, cake pans or loaf pans and you can save those supplied with oven-ready packaged rolls. If handled with care they are good for several trips to the oven before they acquire pin holes. Use disposable paper plates, napkins and cups.

While traveling or when camping at unimproved sites, and relying on self-containment, conservation measures are important, to stay within the limits of supply—fresh water and ice perhaps being the most precious.

I've found it reassuring to take along extras of both. We supplement our drinking water with an insulated jug which can be kept handy in the towing vehicle or, in a motor home, it travels well in the sink. Extra ice cubes in a plastic bag and canned soft drinks can be kept in a styrofoam ice chest. This can be kept out of the way in the shower compartment. A block of ice will keep longer than cubes but is not as convenient to use in drinks or to pack around other items. Dry ice is a still less versatile substitute.

By keeping ice cubes in a plastic bag, you can contain the water as they melt and keep from drowning food stored with them in the ice chest. An alternative is to freeze your drinking water in empty milk cartons before leaving home and use these to chill the ice chest. When the ice melts, you have clean drinking water from your home tap.

Even when water supply is limited, don't be careless about getting dishes and cooking utensils washed. Boil some water for rinsing them well to avoid contamination. Another good reason, incidentally, for using disposables.

Don't allow your sink waste water to run on the ground. On most RVs, only waste from the hopper is piped to the holding tank. Sink water, if drained into the holding tank, would soon fill it. Therefore, a bypass is provided. When hooked up to the sewer system in an improved campground, there is no problem. But when operating "self-contained," that sink water could back up through the shower drain. For this reason, it should be drained into a separate closed

With a RV, the traveler has a choice. He can enjoy the comforts of a home-away-from-home in the RV or venture into the outdoors.

container placed at the outlet. This container then must be dumped where it will not cause pollution or contamination. Laws are now being enacted which prohibit draining this sink waste water directly on the ground.

To aid in the conservation of your water supply, use covered pots for cooking and only small amounts of water to cook vegetables. If refrigerator space permits, save the water they were cooked in and any liquids from canned vegetables to use in gravy or sauces or adding to condensed soup.

The mark of an experienced camper is his ability to go light. With the weight of his mistakes on his back, the backpacker soon learns the tricks of substitution and improvisation to lighten the load. The camper who travels on wheels is inclined to take an impersonal view of his load, and is often blissfully ignorant of the dangers of overloading—until his equipment breaks down.

Every vehicle has a gross vehicle weight (GVW) rating, and the manufacturer is required to post it on a permanent plate on the vehicle. Subtracting the curb weight from GVW gives the maximum safe payload, and this must include total weight of passengers, personal equipment, sports gear, bedding, food, utensils, etc., etc. Too often the RV camper overlooks the basic necessities and neglects to make allowances for their weight.

It could be the straw that breaks the camel's back if you fail to take into account that 20 gallons of gasoline adds 120 pounds to the load; 50 gallons of water adds 420 pounds; a carton of soft drinks, 38 pounds; a small block of ice, 50 pounds and a bag of groceries might add 30 pounds.

Just as important as the total weight is its distribution. The manufacturer takes this into account by balancing the weight of built-in equipment, from side to side as well as fore and aft, and the user should maintain the balance with the items he puts aboard.

Trailers tow best when slightly tongue heavy, with approximately 15 percent of total weight on the tongue. Pickup campers usually carry a third of their total weight on the front axle and two-thirds on the rear axle. And those balances should be maintained without exceeding axle ratings.

Heavy equipment added by the user should be placed as near as possible over the axle and low. Items that can shift should be secured.

No less important is the way in which food and cooking utensils are loaded. Better to have heavy cans on the floor than in overhead cabinets which should be reserved for the lightweight items. While traveling, all loose articles are going to shift. Pack them snugly, cushioning the rigid ones with soft packages of paper towels and paper napkins.

Keep breakables to an absolute minimum, protecting those you must take with pillows, blankets and linens.

Repackaging foodstuffs in polyethylene bags and plastic boxes often eliminates awkward shapes and oversize containers.

Don't go overboard when stocking the cupboard and refrigerator with food and beverages. Remember you can replenish the larder enroute. Leisurely shopping in a strange town can be a pleasant change of pace.

When provisioning an RV, you learn to avoid the breakables and the odd shaped items. You buy your milk in waxed cartons instead of glass bottles, and use plastic containers for repackaging those items which are marketed in fragile, breakable or crushable packages.

Depending on season, count on roadside produce stands to supply such treats as luscious tree-ripened fruit, vine-ripened vegetables and sun-sweetened melons. As any angler will attest, you can't count on the fish to cooperate, but there is always a chance you can put on the table a mess of fresh-caught fish.

If you can't be separated from one or two favorite electrical utensils, there is no reason why they can't be taken along. Store them in cardboard cartons cut to proper size for a snug fit and wedge them into a lower locker so they won't shift, rattle or break. When camping with full-service hookup everyone will welcome a familiar electric coffee maker, toaster or frypan.

There is no point in detailing favorite recipes here. Cook books are readily available and home recipes are easy to adapt. Time savers, however, are vital, and here are a few:

Experiment at home and try out new packaged foods and new recipes before hitting the road.

Wash vegetables at home and store in a plastic bag to keep them clean and crisp. That way you will also conserve the RV water supply.

Use undiluted cream of mushroom, celery or chicken soups in place of cream sauce.

Save your bacon drippings for use in frying.

When reconstituting the dehydrated foods, you'll usually get best results by pre-soaking them and simmering over low heat rather than dumping them into rapidly boiling water and trying to cook them fast. And remember that at higher altitudes, it will take longer to boil water.

Most important of all, as a time-saver, is familiarity with the kitchen equipment for trouble-free operation.

Refrigeration. Most RV refrigerators are gas-operated or three-way (gas, 12-volt, 110-volt). 12-volt is the least satisfactory because of battery drain. 110-volt requires that the RV be connected by power cord to a 110-volt source or served by a gasoline-powered electric generator which is less than an ideal source because of its added weight, expense, noise and fuel consumption.

Gas, therefore, is preferred. It too has its drawbacks. It is a slower process and the vehicle must be level. Because it is slower, the refrigerator should be turned on and chilled in advance and when possible foods to be stored in it should be pre-chilled.

Stoves. Standard equipment for RVs will include a gas stove. On small camping trailers it might be a two-burner or three-burner job which can be swung out or carried outside when weather permits. Size is important only in that burner size and distance between burners will determine size of pots you can use, and whether or not you can add a stove-top oven.

Larger vehicles will have built-in gas stoves with three or four burners and a combination broiler/oven. Anyone accustomed to cooking with gas at home will find very little different about cooking in a RV.

Because the vapors are heavier than air, leaking LP gas will settle to the floor or on the bottom of compartments where stored. For safety's sake, it has been odorized so

Even the smallest tent trailers have complete kitchen equipment, usually arranged so the stove can be swung out or carried outside.

By cooking outdoors, the cook gets a break by keeping the muss and fuss out of the RV. A small hibachi or charcoal grill and a bag of charcoal briquets can be taken along for picnics. Some campgrounds provide outdoor fireplaces too.

leaks can be detected. Any compartments for LP gas containers should be isolated and ventilated to the outside to allow the escape of leaking gas.

Joints and connections in the gas line can vibrate loose, and they should be checked frequently for tightness. Avoid excessive tightening which can damage threads. To check for leaks, brush valves and connections with detergent. Bubbles will indicate a leak is present.

Many RV stoves are equipped with pilot lights for the oven; some with pilot lights for the top burners. Care must be taken that pilots are lighted when gas lines are open. There should be shut-off valves on all feed lines immediately ahead of each gas appliance. These should be turned off when the appliance is not about to be used.

Fresh Water Supply. The most critical convenience is the fresh water supply which might be a jug, a portable container which feeds by hand pump into a sink, or a large built-in tank filled from the outside and pumped electrically under pressure to kitchen sink and bathroom fixtures. Whatever the system, both quality and quantity are critical.

Quantity will be limited unless you are camping where you have ready access to water, or where you can hook the RV directly to a pressurized system. Quality is always going to vary and may depend upon a very personal taste (or distaste) for excessive salt or sulfur common in some parts of the country. Before you fill your tank, taste the water. If there is any doubt about purity of your drinking water, boil it for 10 minutes or add Halazone tablets according to directions.

To assure good taste, there are available various types of purifiers and odorless/tasteless hoses for connecting and filling the storage tank.

THE LONG & SHORT OF FINNY DELICACIES

Thick meat of a fresh chinook salmon comes off as Bill prepares to ice it down before immersing slabs in brine. Meat handles better if ribs are severed and left on fillets until after smoking.

by JAMES F. DAUBEL

DESPITE their obvious size differences, inland king salmon and farm pond bluegills have a lot in common.

Pound-for-pound, for example—or ounce-for-ounce in the case of bluegills—both species are among the fightin'est fish in fresh water.

Both are feloniously underrated as food fish by many anglers, and consequently many are wasted. Either they end up in the garbage can or, potentially worse, salmon are released to die and perhaps rot on a stream bank someplace, and bluegills are returned to help overpopulate farm ponds.

It took much trial and error following the introduction of salmon to the Great Lakes in the 1960s before I finally concluded that you can have my share of fried, baked,

Stubby rod and trolling reel are not preferred salmon gear as this fisherman learned when the reel jammed and he lost the fish seen splashing at left.

The very first chinook I ever hooked made a believer of me. It was in the Muskegon River in Michigan that I repeatedly cast a wobbly red and white spoon into a deep pool I knew held salmon. A fish finally struck and, as if fired from an underwater cannon, shot through the surface and into fast current.

You don't play a freshly hooked chinook. You hang on and hope for the best. My drag whined in distress as the "heavy" 20-pound mono peeled from the open face reel. Seconds later the acrobatic fish broke water three more times, stripped my spool clean, snapped the line and made his escape downstream.

I respooled with heavier line and eventually landed three chinook, one 24-pounder, one of 16 pounds and an immature 9-pound male. Determined to experiment further with the edibility question, I noted that the larger fish was freshest, still retaining a slightly silver hue denoting recent entry into the stream. The other two were a brownish red, indicating they had been in the river for some time.

I cooked portions of the chinook differently and made two discoveries: first, all else being equal, the chinook is a better eating fish than the coho; and, second, the more deteriorated a salmon is the less edible it is.

Salmon live according to specified life cycles. A chinook, for example, is a three or four-year fish. It lives in streams of its birth for a time, migrates to open water

pickled, broiled or boiled salmon if only you'll promise me your allotment of properly smoked chinook.

I emphasize the word "properly."

As for members of the sunfish family, there are dozens of recipes for preparing the tasty panfish but only one "bluegill cocktail," an iced variation which even experienced palates often mistake for crab or other fresh seafood.

Regardless of how you prepare them, the cleaning of 'gills is a bore that dissuades many fishermen from using them. If only there were a quickie method of getting the job done, I often thought, until an expert in the field, Bill Gressard, a fishing buddy of mine, asked me one day, "Would you believe I can clean three per minute?"

But first the salmon.

I beat a hot trail to Michigan's West Coast in the late 1960s when the first coho salmon began returning to their home streams to make history in that spectacularly successful fisheries experiment. Even then a debate was on over the question: Is the salmon a good eating fish?

Before I had even seen a fish caught, I encountered an angler and his wife and a woman friend at a campground near Honor, Mich., birthplace of the Great Lakes coho program.

"Trash fish," sneered one of the women. "Don't bother keeping any: you can't eat them," she advised me.

"I'll tell you what," countered the other woman, "I'll take any you catch if you don't want them. You just have to know how to fix them."

When later I did catch three coho, all dark and deteriorating, I prepared them different ways but was dissatisfied. It wasn't until a year after that, however, that I became convinced that both women were correct: To my taste, coho are inferior eating fish, but properly cooked, they are not bad, though not as good as the chinook, or king, salmon.

The chinook is the real prize of the inland salmon story. They grow bigger—topping 40 pounds—fight harder and taste considerably better regardless of how they're done, and that includes smoking.

Salmon cartwheels on the surface as angler plays the stubborn fish in Michigan's Muskegon River.

182

then returns three or four years later to spawn and die.

As a rule, once salmon enter the streams they feed little, if at all. Preoccupied with the spawning urge, they begin to deteriorate before ascending the rivers. From a glistening silver in the big lakes, they turn a dull gray, then a flat brownish gray-green to a dark brown, a reddish brown to black and, finally, to a black with white fungus patches before death comes.

In the last several Octobers that Bill Gressard and I have fished seriously for chinook in Michigan streams, we have concentrated on fish that are reasonably fresh run. Once they turn black they are too far gone for anything but smoking and even then the flesh is apt to be mushy, which in my view spoils an otherwise tasty fish.

Bill and I fish as often as possible in the fall to catch our limits of five each to smoke and freeze for winter consumption. It is possible to freeze fresh salmon fillets, thaw them for smoking then refreeze them. That approach allows us to accumulate the salmon and smoke it all at once, thereby saving time.

Contrary to popular notion, the smoking of fish is not difficult. For years I shied away from it in the mistaken belief that all manner of culinary expertise and sophisticated equipment were involved. Bill convinced me otherwise.

Smokers come in more shapes and sizes than people. Essentially, however, a smoker is nothing more than an

A fresh caught salmon goes on the stringer, destined for the smoker then into the freezer for keeping til winter.

enclosed device in which to trap smoke. It should contain shelves on which to place the meat and it should be vented on top for good circulation. A smoker can be anything from a custom made brick extravaganza in your back yard to a simple hinged metal box that can be folded and carted along on the family camping trip.

Gressard converted an abandoned upright refrigerator by gutting it, cutting a vent in the top, and installing horizontal metal rods to hold wire mesh shelves. The bottomless smoker is positioned atop a cinder block fireplace and we're in business.

The process begins a day before the actual smoking when we immerse the salmon fillets in a brine solution of about three cups common table salt to one gallon of water. The salmon, incidentally, should be skinned. In filleting the fish, sever the ribs and leave them on the fillet. They help keep the flesh together and are easily removed after smoking.

Keep the salmon completely covered with brine overnight. Rinse the fish thoroughly in fresh water before smoking or it will retail a strong salty flavor.

After having experimented for years with different woods, Gressard uses a combination of apple and maple. Many so-called experts have their own favorites. Personally, I'm not sure there is as much difference between woods as the debating implies.

I do know that I've never tasted better salmon than the fish we smoke so there must be something to the apple-maple blend. The fruitwood gives off a sweet smoke and the maple burns well (apple, unless thoroughly dried, leaves something to be desired as a fire wood).

The real secret to the success of our salmon, I believe, is the maple syrup basting it receives four or five times during the smoking. We simply brush the syrup on alternate sides, covering the fillets but not excessively, every two or three hours early in the smoking. Whenever the syrup is thoroughly absorbed on one side, it's time to flip it over and brush the other side.

The syrup gives the fish a moderately sweet flavor that complements the smoky taste. Moreover, it gives the sal-

Battling chinook splashes in a swirl as angler plays the fish in the shallows of the Muskegon River.

Two-man limit of chinook salmon caught by Bill Gressard (shown) and author from AuSable River in Michigan.

Slabs of chinook salmon meat are turned by Bill prior to basting with maple syrup. Smoker in background was made from abandoned refrigerator.

Bill returns salmon to smoker for more curing during 24-hour process.

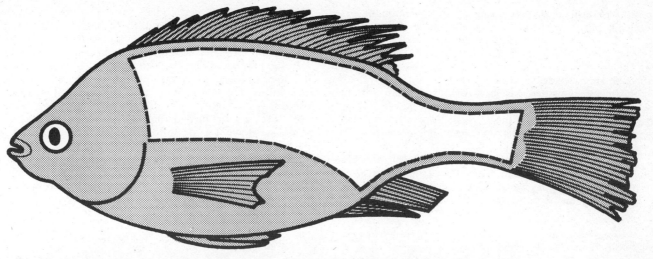

For fast filleting of bluegills, start with a cut behind the gill plate, extending from the backbone to the top of the rib cage. With one stroke of the knife, separate back flesh from bones, from gills to tail. Ignore the side and belly meat.

Strips of bluegill meat look mighty small but it's the taste that counts. Cleaning the fish is quick and easy if you ignore meat on the rib cage.

mon a reddish glaze that positively invites sampling.

Be prepared to spend time on the smoking. It takes us all of 24 hours to smoke thick salmon fillets. A small fire is preferred and it is essential to maintain a constant flow of heat—between 100 and 150 degrees—and smoke through the smoker.

Sufficient moisture has been removed from the fish when the fillet is firm. Squeeze it gently between thumb and index finger. If the meat feels moist, soft or mushy, smoke it longer. The thickest slices should be firm but not hard. Thinner fillets may have to be removed sooner.

The other half of this pair of underused fish, the bluegill, is another species that I plead guilty of once having freely returned to the water or discarded.

Like most members of the sunfish family, bluegills are

Cleaning the fish is a chore, but one considerably simplified by Bill Gressard's fast fillet technique. Bill harvests bluegills by hook-and-line and with traps from a small lake on his farm. He sells the fillets to a local restaurant.

In the process of cleaning thousands of bluegills, redears and hybrids over the years, he has developed shortcuts. He's got the procedure down to three fish a minute and he insists that anybody can do likewise with a little practice.

Bill uses a short-bladed fillet knife sharpened to a razor edge. As shown by the dotted line in the accompanying diagram, start with a cut behind the gill plate, extending from the backbone to the top of the rib cage. With one stroke of the knife, separate back flesh from the bones, from gills to tail and from backbone to the rib cage. Ignore the side and belly meat by simply severing the strip

Late evening fly-rodding for bluegills is a fast way of filling the stringer. A rubber spider, dry fly or small popper can be relied on to provide the action.

highly prolific. Unless their numbers are held in proper balance, they can quickly overpopulate a small lake or pond, placing such an overload on the available food supply that all species sharing the water are stunted.

That's why it is a good idea to remove all sunfish, even the little runts, from small lakes. Resisting the temptation to throw the tiny fish away is an even better idea. In the spring when they spawn I fish hard for bluegills and I keep every one I catch.

Good numbers of bass and bluegills share a shallow lake near my home. In May I canoe the lake to locate bedding 'gills in water less than two feet deep. A long limber fly rod and a sparsely dressed, home-tied gray wet fly are the combination with which I could fill the boat with bluegills if I tried.

of meat off at the top of the ribs. (Because you get more bones than meat, trying to salvage meat on the ribs is a waste of time). Skin the fillets.

The bluegill cocktail, a snap to make, is a veritable gourmet delicacy.

Merely put the strips of bluegill meat in a wire basket and hold over rapidly boiling water for about a minute, steaming the fillets until they turn a delicate white. Do not oversteam or the meat gets mushy.

Ice the steamed fish well and serve as you would shrimp or crab, with a red sauce of horseradish and chili sauce.

Bluegill cocktail is the poor man's crab but it's surprising how many people mistake the bounty of an ordinary farm pond with the high priced produce of the sea.

Off-Beat Stuff I Have Et

by BARNEY PETERS

Never pass up any meat because of reputation or prejudice. Try it and then decide.

SOME YEARS AGO in the Midwest where I lived, there existed an informal club of outdoorsmen and conservationists who paid no dues, elected no officers and had no prestigious name. They met only twice each year and on one of these occasions just to go fishing together in Lake Erie. At the time Erie was still pure enough so that the fish could be eaten without fear. Or at least it wasn't yet discovered that most of the edible species were contaminated with mercury which was being dumped into the lake, courtesy of Big Industry.

Without exception members of the club were hard core environmentalists—wildlife biologists, writers, newspapermen—who deplored what was happening to the air, water and soils of the Buckeye State. The second annual meeting—the non-fishing winter one—was always held at Winous Point Marsh, a waterfowl shooting club near Port Clinton. The host for the meeting was marsh manager John "Frosty" Anderson, perhaps the hardest of the hard cores. Thanks to his preparations (which included sipping the best aged sour mash obtainable), members often were able to forget their problems. At least temporarily.

Being a vast area of open marshland, Winous Point was the home of several thousand muskrats and each fall a lot of them were "harvested" by professional trappers. The silky brown pelts then as now were quite valuable. But unlike other places where muskrats are trapped, the carcasses were not thrown away or sold to mink farms. Here each one was as carefully dressed as are frying chickens for a supermarket sale and put aside in a deep freeze. On the morning of the annual meeting, Frosty Anderson thawed them out for the big game dinner to follow.

Cut in half, the 1-to-1½-pound animals were browned in large iron skillets of peanut or vegetable oil. That done, all were drained and transferred into cast iron Dutch ovens containing water laced with dry red wine. There all were steamed for about an hour when a robust barbecue sauce was added. Then 15 or 20 more minutes of cooking and the entree was ready. What followed was a feast to be long remembered by everyone on hand. The muskrat vanished like magic. Most new members attending for the first time thought they were eating rabbit—or even lamb or veal. Maybe it can be blamed on the sour mash, but I can't recall seeing anyone ever refuse a second helping.

But eating muskrat? Isn't that a bit . . . well, unusual?

Absolutely not. Too often nowadays, for reasons which are not really clear, we pass up foods (especially wild foods) which are nutritious or delicious and often both. We pass them off as being "gamey" or simply not fit for human consumption. But far closer to the truth is that too many of us have become much too fastidious, too sophisticated, for our own good and well-being. But I suppose that isn't all bad; as it stands, more delicious wild edibles exist for those of us who remain unreconstructed and (as one lady editorial writer suggested recently) "uncivilized."

In a career spent largely vagabonding around the outdoors, I have sampled more than my share of off-beat

Barney Peters is a travel and outdoor writer who has traveled the globe. He continues to travel because he falls in love with each place he visits. He is a connoisseur of unusual cities and the food that made them that way.

How about crayfish from the local creek as a handy substitute for shirmp? Author et them and survived.

matter how you cook it. The easiest way is to batter and deep fry it a la Colonel Sanders and serve it with collard greens, buttered hominy and hush puppies. But the best turtle I ever ate too much of was another of Frank Sayers' concoctions.

For several years my friend was chairman of the food committee of the Riverside Liars Club, a loose association of sportsmen in Upper Arlington, Ohio. They sponsored a wild game banquet every winter which became celebrated because the lying took a distant second place to the eating. Blame that on the snapper soup—or stew, which probably was a more appropriate name. Before ladling it out however, Frank usually provided some strange, *very* strange hors d'oeuvres such as rattlesnake or smoked grasshoppers. The rattler was tasteless, but I recall the latter as being like roasted, very salty peanuts. Since the banquet was held in a Methodist church basement, there were no great reservoirs of distilled products flowing to jade a liar's taste buds. We tasted the food like it was. And it was fine.

Anyhow, here is how Frank's snapper stew recipe could be adapted/cooked in an outdoor camp, or even at home if (unfortunately) you're stuck there. Remove all the meat

things. Some were good, some so-so and some not so good, which is about the way that chain store groceries run. But let me recall here without any apologies some of the good things I have et.

Long ago I was lucky enough to encounter one Frank Sayers, a kindred spirit who would rather go fishing in a snowstorm or score a double on grouse than be a millionaire. Frank was always game to try anything and no pun is intended. Because our wanderings in time took us from the limestone streams of southern Ohio to the Alberta Rockies, to British Columbia's Cassiars and eventually to Africa, we cooked up everything from bullfrogs to warthogs and elephant and some off-beat stuff in between.

OK, so there's nothing unusual about spearing a sack full of bullfrogs on a warm August night because aren't they the same as the ones listed on chic restaurant menus? Indeed they are. But what restaurant is able to serve them when they are best—just an hour or so out of the water? The best handling calls for skinning the frogs' (take only the biggest, leave the smallest to grow up) body and legs immediately, dry dip in a light beer and pancake flour batter, and fry quickly in hot peanut oil. Do it right on the river or pond bank, don't even bother to take the catch home. Serve it with watercress and mushrooms if you can find them.

Slightly more on the exotic side are two other critters which share most fresh warm waters of North America with bullfrogs: common crayfish and snapping turtles. Both are easy to catch and for complete details on taking the turtles see page 238, "In Summertime Try Snappers," *Hunter's Digest* (Digest Books, Inc., Northfield, Ill.).

Crayfish are utilized almost nowhere except in Louisiana and lower Mississippi where they go into bayou jambalaya. But large crayfish taken *anywhere* can be treated, cooked and even substituted for saltwater shrimp, from which many find them indistinguishable. In fact, I once saw a bettor lose his $20 bill when he could not tell the difference between a Kentucky River crayfish cocktail and a Gulf shrimp cocktail.

Snapping turtle doesn't resemble anything else (at least nothing I've tried) but it is delicious mild meat almost no

Frosty Anderson hangs muskrat pelts to cure at Winous Point. But meat is not thrown away. Instead it serves delicious conservation banquet.

Too often deer hunters discard heart and liver of deer and other big game. It's a terrible waste. Author et both and relished same.

from a five to ten pound snapper and cut it into small pieces, say ½-inch square. Or you may prefer to put it through a meat grinder. Either way, brown it well in bacon fat and put it aside.

Next dice up a couple of pounds of mixed vegetables and you can go heavy on those you like best. Frank used carrots, turnips, okra, onions, celery, parsley and peas. The meat and vegetables were placed in a large kettle or Dutch oven, covered with a can of tomato paste and water—or a can of V-8 juice. That much was simmered slowly all day before the big banquet. During the simmering, salt, pepper and taco sauce (Victoria brand) were added for seasoning. But soy sauce, tabasco or Worcestershire sauce might suit other palates better. They might even make a person tell more preposterous lies.

It is no lie, however (as anyone who knows Frank will testify), that during one pack trip in the Hummingbird Creek Country of Alberta, Frank cooked up the chops of a mountain lion which somebody had bagged. In all truth I faced those on my plate with some prejudice and except for that would have considered them as good as any Illinois or Indiana corn-fed pork chops of the past.

A year later we were hunting along the Spatzizi River in British Columbia and during the trip, Frank collected a fine grizzly bear. Beside the silvertipped pelt, he packed a couple of huge ham loins and ribs back to camp. Some of this was smoked (see page 268, "How I Preserve Meat in Camp," *Hunter's Digest*). But Frank broiled the ribs over a low birch and willow fire. Dipped in hot piquant sauce these rivaled the finest barbecued pork ribs and that is no exaggeration. We even enjoyed these as cold trail lunches during the next few days.

One other of Frank's adventures into exotic game cookery didn't turn out quite so well, but he couldn't be faulted for lack of originality or ingenuity. The time was 1966 and we were hunting near Rhino Camp along the Upper Nile in Uganda. However it wasn't a tusker hunt in the usual sense because we traveled mostly by outboard boat, scanning both papyrus-fringed banks for game. One day a fine big bull was bagged and as so often happens, natives suddenly, unaccountably, swarmed out of the dense bush from all directions to cut up and carry away the meat. They came on foot and on bicycles. Nothing was wasted. Some even set up camp on the spot and smoked the meat as they hacked off huge strips of the elephant.

"If they can eat it," Frank said, " why can't we try it, too."

"Suit yourself," outfitter Brian Herne answered without enthusiasm or encouragement.

It is true that Frank had little opportunity to be selective. Most of the best "cuts" had already vanished down forest trails or into hungry stomachs. But no matter; carefully my old hunting buddy carved out a section of trunk, skinned it and cut it into circular steaks. I must admit that these looked fine and choice. But even though broiled on fragrant hardwood coals, the elephant was as tough as steel-belted rubber tires and probably just as tasty.

"You win some," Frank said philosophically, "and you lose some."

I have always been sorry that Frank was not a member of a certain expedition made in 1967 to Colombia. The object of the trip was a jaguar, but almost everything else that happened seemed to overshadow the main event, as I'll try to illustrate.

Specifically Lew Baker and I were to travel from Maracaibo upstream on the Magdalena River for about 200 miles, past some of the oldest European settlements in the New World, to a then jungle region where the big spotted cats were said to be numerous. Our guide was one Saloman Baragan, a pleasant and sincere man perplexed by river navigation in an unfamiliar houseboat with an unfamiliar, but willing crew. Somehow we made it safely up the muddy and sometimes swift current to a place where the river widened into a vast shallow lake called Cienaga de Zapotsa. We moored finally against an island in the lake which at first seem uninhabited. But on jumping ashore we were greeted by two men who might have been Robinson Crusoe and his twin, plus several thin dogs of no distinguishable ancestry.

"Welcome señors," said one man in good English. "I'm Perfecto Sanchez and that fellow there is my helper, Macedonio Polo."

What followed is certain to sound fictional to many readers, which is understandable, but except for some slight lapses in my memory is probably all true. Sanchez welcomed us into his house which was hidden in dense vegetation and fairly modern. By that I mean it had some plumbing. He explained that he had learned to speak English while once working at the Chrysler plant in Detroit—long enough to save enough money to return to South America and buy his island hideaway. Macedonio was a hired man—hunting guide, cook, caretaker, the works.

"Why don't you stay for dinner, señors?" Perfecto asked. "Macedonio can go out and get it ready."

"Why not," Lew answered.

Viewed in retrospect, it was a very good dinner: first chicken soup followed by roast chicken which tasted something like the "char-broiled" stuff one sees advertised along the U.S. highways. Only I hadn't seen any chickens around the house and so commented.

"We need none here, señor," our host grinned, "we only eat wild food. That was parrot in the soup and snake bird (actually anhinga, I later learned) from the grill."

"You could have fooled me," Lew said and I thought he was turning a little green.

Snapping turtle, abundant almost everywhere, is among the most delicious of wild foods.

May look strange, but that tiger-striped catfish of South America was terrific.

And so was the iguana provided fresh out of the Colombian jungle by Macedonio Polo.

Still there is more to this adventure. We spent several days hunting waterfowl around Perfecto's island retreat and it was extremely good. Lots of ducks everywhere. One day Macedonio took his pack of nondescript dogs into the nearest jungle opposite our island, hoping to locate a jaguar. But he had no luck whatsoever with the cats. Instead one evening he returned with other and much more unusual game; one large silvery, tiger-striped, whiskery catfish of about ten pounds and a pair of tree iguanas which together weighed about the same. The fish looked like it might have swam out of a science fiction movie.

"Tonight señors," Perfecto promised, "we really have big feast." Our host's smile, I thought, was almost a leer.

Well, that was a feast to match the best at Winous Point or the Riverside Liar's Club. No, that's understatement.

The catfish, which was cooked whole in a shallow pit over ruby coals and basted with spiced oils, was wonderfully tender, flaky and good. I couldn't then and still cannot recall any better catfish ever—not even in the southern United States where skilled catfish cooks are (and should be) honored citizens.

Then followed the iguana tails, pure white, mild and also flaky, basted in olive oil and baked in a stone-lined oven with plantains and vegetables. It is lucky for iguanas, I decided, that they live so far from so many human beings like Frank Sayers. Otherwise they would soon be candidates for the growing list of endangered species.

Put them, in fact, atop the list of most off-beat stuff I have ever et. And hope to eat again.

Home on the Campfire Range

Cooking utensils help make campfire cooking predictable and delicious. These heavy iron, long-handled skillets promote evenness of heat and assist the chefs with frying these trout to perfection.

by NORMAN STRUNG

LITERALLY AND FIGURATIVELY, there's nothing that captures the flavor of the outdoors quite like a meal cooked in the open. The hint of woodsmoke, and a sprinkling of fly ash add up to heady flavors and unique spices that will never come out of a kitchen.

There is nothing difficult or magical about cooking over an open fire; in fact, the "cooking" is the same as on a kitchen stove. Heat is heat, whether its source is glowing embers or electric coils, and it is heat which cooks food.

The real difference between indoor and outdoor cooking lies 1) in your ability to control that heat without the ease of calibrated dials (be sure to read "Campfire Magic" elsewhere in this book), and 2) in the equipment you choose and how you use it. Cooking utensils must bridge the gap between glowing embers as a heat-source and the sophistication of a modern range.

To see what I mean, let's take a look at the stove in your kitchen by the numbers. First there are the burners.

Burners are easy to cook over not only because they have a wide and exact range of heating capacity, but because they give off even heat; heat that's equally distributed in intensity across the bottom of your pot and pan.

Evenness of heat is to some extent, a function of the fire you build, but you'll increase the effect by using heavy iron skillets. This excess of iron tends to feather out hot spots so the entire bottom of the pan is roughly the same temperature. In addition, heavy skillets warm and cool slowly. This too, evens out the rise and fall in temperature as you add more coals to your fire, and they gradually burn low. This kind of continuity will make cooking fried foods and pancakes as easy as at home because of its predictability.

Just how much of this type of cookware you should bring is only limited by the weight and space you can afford. I try to tote along at least one 12-inch skillet, a 12-inch Dutch oven for frying and baking, and a 12-inch by 18-inch "cake griddle" for eggs, pancakes and the like. This might seem like a lot of weight, but it isn't by some campfire/gourmet standards.

Dave Wolny, my partner in the guiding business, once was a railroad man and came away from that calling several "rail-crew" frying pans richer. These are huge things, fully two feet across with a three- or four-foot handle, and a second ring-type handle opposite the long handle for leverage, when the pan is full and cool enough to touch. The skillet weighs around 20 pounds, and he always brings it along when we horse-pack.

It has cooked up onion-laced hash browns and fried trout for a dozen men, and to such a golden-brown perfection that the mere memory of those meals nearly brings tears to my eyes.

Any pots, pans or hand utensils that will be used for campfire cooking will be most satisfactory if they have a long, unburnable handle. Heat from the fire works outward fast, and unless handles are long enough to dissipate that heat, you'll burn your fingers at every meal.

There are times when this caveat about heavy skillets is unworkable. When you're backpacking you can't afford to carry a #7 skillet around. In this situation, you'll have to opt for aluminum, and the best arrangement here is the "nesting mess kit." This is an integrated set of aluminum utensils that finds plates and cups fitting inside one another, the whole assortment "nesting" inside a large pot-and-frying pan that doubles as a cover.

Aside from the heat distribution problems, aluminum will burn in a very hot fire, and food sticks badly to it when you fry.

Boiling foods raises no such problems, since the water in the vessel acts both as a heat distributor, and puts a limit on the temperature inside. Unless it's under pressure, water will get no hotter than 212 degrees at sea-level, its boiling point. This boiling point does drop as you climb however. When you're in the mountains over 5,000 feet, food takes longer to cook because the boiling point is lower, and the cooking temperature cooler. At these elevations, a three-minute egg takes five minutes, and a cake requires additional flour and water and will take one-fourth more time to bake than the recipe will indicate. As you go even higher, cooking times stretch out even more.

When cooking by boiling, don't overlook two variations on the theme; a good survival tactic is to heat up rocks in your cooking coals. The rocks can then be dumped into water to make it boil. This is how American Indians managed to cook in leathern and wooden vessels before the coming of white men and steel. Food can also be steamed by elevating some sort of rack above the boiling water, and cooking food on the rack. This is an especially good practice in the preparation of fresh vegetables since their flavors and juices stay with the food, and are not drawn off into the boiling water.

The broiler on your "stove" comes next. The principal difference between broiling outdoors and indoors is that campfire heat comes from under the food being cooked. This makes it cook much faster, searing the outside of a steak or chop as well as heating its insides. This is one reason why coal-broiled foods taste so very good.

The other reason they taste good is the splattering fire that bounces back in response to dripped fats. There is a limit to how much of this yellow-flame you should allow to lick at the meat, but an occasional flare-up is what imparts some of the bittersweet charcoal flavor.

Beyond those factors, frying, broiling or boiling foods over an open fire is a matter of attention on your part. Water boils over wood just as it does on a range, fried foods

A griddle and spatula are two of the handiest items for fixing chow on the range as well as in a camp.

splatter and smoke wildly if they're too hot and close to burning, and a broiled steak responds to the same tests for doneness you'd make in your own kitchen. Baking however, requires the touch of light education.

There are three types of baking possible over a campfire; oven baking, reflector baking and foil baking.

Oven baking requires that you have or make some sort of oven. Several camping-equipment companies (Coleman is one that immediately comes to mind) make campfire ovens, but it's just as easy to put one together yourself.

You must suspend whatever it is to be baked in a heated environment. The most professional way to achieve this effect is via the deep, covered skillet known as a Dutch oven. You either make or buy a legged grate that fits inside the oven, and bake on top of the grate. You can create this same situation with a large covered pot. Place three rocks inside the pot, then a metal plate on top of the rocks. I have also seen strictly homemade but efficient Dutch ovens made from two hubcaps and a grate. In transit they nest; in use, they oppose each other with the grate in between.

To bake in this type of oven, scrape out a hollow in your bed of coals, then bury the covered pot in the hole. Baking will be the slowest and best if you have no coals under the oven, and lots on top. Timing is tricky here, as you have no oven thermometer or adjustment. In general, I've found coal-baking to cut normal baking times by 25 per cent, but I make a check on the progress of things halfway through the cooking span required for kitchen baking. Realize too, that timing will be a function of the heat of your fire, which in turn is dependent on draft, wood type and size.

Reflector baking is a much slower process, and requires a different kind of oven. The heat for this kind of cooking comes directly from the fire rather than coals. The reflector oven is a little like a mini-lean-to, placed close to the fire, that traps and concentrates ambient heat.

Reflector ovens are most efficient when made of shiny sheet metal. These can be made along lean-to lines so they fold up into a flat package. Remember that the more heat you trap, the better they'll cook, so sides on the "lean-to" and a lip on the top edge improve their performance. A reflector oven can be constructed of a twig frame and aluminum foil, but I've got misgivings about ecology and my common sense whenever I start messing with green wood, crotched willows and make-do engineering. They can be made to work but it requires so much hassling that in the end you really have some searching questions about whether it was indeed worth the effort.

Foil baking is, by far, the easiest of all cooking methods. When one meal is done, you can eat out of the foil. After dinner fold the foil and pack it out. There's no clean-up. But remember, foil does not burn up in a campfire. Because of its durability, foil can be reused.

However, it does raise a question of cooking semantics. Cooking with foil isn't really baking, it's a cross between poaching and steaming whereby foods cook in their own juices, or in moisture that you provide; water, wine, beer, bouillon or butter.

Whatever *you* call it, it is a delicious way to prepare food. Just make sure you wrap the food securely in the foil. There should be no hole in the foil under the package for the moisture to drain out, and there should be one

The cleaning up after a meal is simplified by planning ahead. By cooking over a low-flamed or coal fire, by filling pots with water after they are emptied of cooked food and by soaping pots before placed on the fire, dishwashing will be a breeze.

The cookware you can bring along is limited only by the weight and space you can afford. A horse-pack trip gives you more leeway than a backpack outing does.

small hole in the top so steam can escape. If you don't make that hole, the package will either unravel or worse, explode. Foil-cooked foods can either be placed on top of a grate or put into the coals. Coals will cook the contents much faster.

Clean-up of the inside of utensils should begin before you sit down to eat. Fill any pot used for cooking with water, set it on the fire, and by the time you're finished the water will have softened stuck foods, making washing little more than a quick wipe.

Iron skillets should not be washed, but rather wiped clean of excess grease and foodstuffs with a paper towel. If you've cooked in them properly, no food will stick, and they'll come clean, shiny and black quite easily. If food has stuck to them, they must be scoured with soap and water, and then re-cured. This heavy iron cookware actually has pores, and the pores must be filled with grease at extremely high temperatures if food is not to stick. To cure a skillet, heat it to near the blue range (500 to 600 degrees) and sprinkle a pinch of salt in it. Next, drop a teaspoonful of high-grade vegetable oil in the middle of the pan. If it disperses immediately, like a sunburst, the pan is cured. Let it cool and swab it with a paper towel.

Plates are most easily cleaned if you don't have to clean them at all. I always use paper plates while camping, except when I have food that requires a lot of cutting, like steak. Paper plates can drive you mad by collapsing, but you'll avoid that possibility if you'll use them on top of regular dishes or, better yet, metal camping plates.

Cleaning the outside of pots and pans should begin before you start cooking. There is no work so mean and monotonous as scrubbing lampblack from the sides of pots and pans. You'll make the job a lot easier if you'll first give your pot a rub-down with liquid soap. That way there will be a detergent *under* the accumulation.

For the actual cleaning chore, nothing beats Brillo or a similar soaped metal scouring pad. Grass and sand will work in a pinch, but you're getting into the jerry-rigged realm of dingle sticks again.

Of course, if you've built and used your cooking fire correctly, clean-up won't be much of a chore. Cooking over coals doesn't produce lampblack; it's the smoky, uncontrolled, yellow-flame fire that creates that monster.

So in a way, clean-up is a good test of your abilities as a campfire chef. When it's a pleasant task, I'll bet my last book of matches that the meal you've cooked will be one your mouth will remember long after your campfire is out and your sleeping bag rolled away for another day.

This sheepherder uses his Dutch oven for all kinds of cooking—boiling, baking, frying, roasting. Its usefulness can not be overrated in the outdoors.

My wife Sil and I have many such memories and meals under our respective belts; feasts of wonderful food we've found particularly well-suited to campfire cooking. Here's a sampling of some of the best.

SHISH KEBABS

½ slices of bacon, folded
Whole mushroom caps
Onion chunks
Small potatoes, cooked
Green pepper chunks
1½-inch chunks of sirloin, veal, lamb or pork
Salt and pepper to taste
quartered tomatoes

Assemble kabobs by alternating bacon, mushroom, onions, peppers, tomatoes and meat on 12-inch to 24-inch skewers. Grill over coals until done. To serve: rest end of skewer on plate; with knife, push food off skewer.

For the extra flavor, first marinade the meat before cooking in a Soy Marinade and use the marinade for basting as the kabobs are grilled.

SOY MARINADE FOR SHISH KEBABS

¾-cup soy sauce
¼-teaspoon powdered ginger
½-cup red wine
1 tablespoon curry powder
1 clove minced garlic

Combine ingredients. Pour over boneless cubes of meat and let stand in refrigerator overnight.

FOIL-BAKED TROUT

2½-pound trout, dressed
⅛-pound butter or margarine
1 cup dry red wine, bouillon or soup
1 large green pepper, sliced crosswise
1 large onion, sliced
1 large tomato, sliced
Salt and pepper to taste
Paprika to taste

Place each fish in aluminum foil, dot with butter or margarine, and pour desired liquid over it. Cover with green pepper, onion, and tomato slices. Sprinkle with salt, pepper, and paprika and seal. Bury in campfire coals. Test for doneness in 15 minutes. The flesh should flake off the bone when touched with a fork.

Here is a recipe that's good for a quick dessert that will keep the children busy while you do the dishes.

DOUGHBOYS

1 cup Bisquick mix
¼-cup milk
2 to 4 tablespoons jelly

Place Bisquick mix in bowl, add milk, and stir. (Should make a soft dough). Divide the dough into a portion for each eater and roll each portion between floured hands onto a smooth stick. Pinch one end of dough tight to hold it on the stick. Have the children cook the dough over coals, turning it frequently until lightly browned and cooked through. Remove from stick and pour jelly into the hole that's left.

Baked potatoes are admittedly a simple dish, but here's a way to make them cook twice as fast without burning their delicious skins.

MICKEY'S POTATOES

Pierce each potato to be served on two sides with the tines of a fork. Nest them in individual squares of heavy-duty aluminum foil. Add one teaspoon of water. Wrap, seal, and bury the potatoes in the coals of your cooking fire. It should take from 30 to 40 minutes for a large potato to bake. They're done when you can pierce them to the center, then easily remove the knife blade or fork.

If you need to prepare a hearty campfire meal in a hurry, this is the recipe for you.

SHEEPHERDER'S STEW

Prepare the following for each person who will be eating.
½-pound diced meat (substitute hamburger or other ground meat)
1 small carrot cut in thin slices
1 small potato cut in thin slices
½-teaspoon dried minced onion
1 square foot heavy aluminum foil
1 bouillon cube dissolved in ½-cup hot water.
Salt and pepper to taste

Combine meat, carrot, potato, and onion in center square of foil and sprinkle with seasonings. Pour bouillon broth over mixture, fold foil around it, seal loosely, leaving some space for steam expansion, and bury package in coals. Cook 20 to 30 minutes in hot coals. Pour juices into cup and drink as a hot broth; eat stew directly out of foil package. The broth can be thickened with flour and used as a gravy.

BARBECUED ONIONS

1 medium sized onion per person
1 tablespoon barbecue sauce (prepared)
1 tablespoon honey
Aluminum foil squares
Salt and pepper to taste

Place onion in aluminum foil package and pour honey and barbecue sauce over top. Wrap, seal, and bury the onions in the coals of your cooking fire. It should take from 30 to 40 minutes for the onion to bake. They're done when you can pierce them to the center with fork.

For some reason barbecue sauce and camp-fire cooking go hand in hand. The combination of charcoal flavor and barbecue sauce leaves a taste treat that is almost sinful.

I've learned the hard way that the best barbecue sauce combines prepared convenience with a homemade twist.

BARBECUE SAUCE

1 cup prepared barbecue sauce
¼-cup brown sugar
Salt and pepper to taste

Wipe meat or fowl with damp cloth and rub with salt and pepper. Combine barbecue sauce and brown sugar, and baste meat with it. Place on grill or on skewer for spit. Turn frequently and keep basting till meat is done to your liking.

BARBECUED PORK CHOPS IN MUSHROOM SAUCE

6 pork chops
½-cup water
1 10½-ounce can undiluted cream of mushroom soup
Salt and pepper to taste

Arrange chops on grill, sprinkle with salt and pepper, and cook 4 to 6 inches above coals for 15 minutes to a side or until nicely browned and almost cooked. Remove from grill, lay chops on sheets of heavy-duty aluminum foil, two to a sheet. Add ½-cup of water to mushroom soup, stir until smooth, and spread over chops. Wrap and seal chops with the foil and lay packages on grill 4 to 6 inches above coals. Cook for 20 minutes, turning over after 15 minutes. Serves 4 to 6.

MUSHROOM

by JANE BARR

GROWING UP IN Buffalo, N.Y. wasn't so bad. As far as the winters went, we believed that it was the same all over the country and automatically walked to school, built igloos, skated and tobogganed, made ice slides while hanging onto the school fence and in general loved every day of it. The clank of chains on tires in the brown sugar-like snow was one of my favorite sounds.

But in March, even though there usually was a blizzard, that marvelous feeling of anticipation started. Sometimes, walking home from school with the piles of snow making a canyon, I'd wonder why there were butterflies in my stomach and I was so happy. Then I'd remember. When this winter was over, we would be at "The Beach."

It was then that winter lost its fun and a feeling that the snow would never melt would scare and overwhelm me and my annual Spring prayer would pop into my head. "Dear Lord, please let the snow melt so we can move to The Beach." It seemed forever, but the day finally would come when we'd pack the car with linens, pillows, large bottles of city water and clothes. The great exodus was always some time in May and it took more than one trip across the Niagara River on the ferry boat to Canada to get every necessity over.

Most of the time it was still mighty chilly and our only heat in the old brick farmhouse was a giant pot-bellied stove, but no one cared. We had five months of being there to look forward to. Our house was only seven miles and a ferry ride to Buffalo but it was a different world.

School wasn't finished until late in June so the mothers took turns taking us to Fort Erie to catch the ferry and then the streetcar which stopped right at the school. With lunch bag in hand and 16 cents for the round trip ferry and streetcar ride, we couldn't have been happier.

It would still be light by the time we got home from school and we would go out to pick the wild strawberries with which Mother would make the most divine jam, or that job done, we would race to the water to test it with wintertender toes. Decoration Day was the first day for swimming regardless and anyone who chickened out by not getting completely wet carried a stigma the rest of the summer. We had the world by the tail and we knew it.

Each year would bring something new. Swimming to the pier some 300 yards out; building diving boards and tripods to dive, jump or fall from; tennis on a clay court which seemed to produce more weeds than good tennis; the horses which we brought over on the ferry and rode pridefully up the road to the barn; "borrowing" a family car; and finally golf.

Mushrooms and golf are synonymous to me as I think back on those "Olden Days." There were seven or eight of

Where there is no insecticide, fungicide or fertilizer used, mushrooms can be found in great numbers.

Jane Barr is an outdoor writer for The Hudson Hub in Hudson, Ohio. She and her husband Cy travel extensively, always with an eye towards the novel, such as riding the parakite at Mazatlan, Mexico. She is a very young grandmother of three.

MUNCHING

us who took up golf at the same time and in those days we pretty much could play any time of day, as long as we observed the niceties of the golf course and let grown-ups go through and raked our footprints out of the sand traps which seemed to have a magnetic attraction for our erratic shots.

We must have behaved ourselves because the adult members asked us to be partners in Scotch foursomes. I thought it must be our charm, but looking at it now from a distance, I'm pretty sure it was our high handicaps.

The club manager was "Mr. Charles." Someone must have known his last name. I never did. But it was Mr. Charles who started me on the mushroom trail. He met us one day with paper bags in hand and a meadow mushroom which he had just picked. After showing us the smooth white top and the pink gills, he sent us off carrying our clubs and a paper bag.

This being the olden days, there was no insecticide, fungicide or fertilizer used on the course and there were mushrooms by the thousands all over the course. We never had picked them (as a matter of fact I shudder when I remember how many practice swings I took at those white toadstools) because a cardinal rule in our house and at those of our friends was never, but never touch anything like that.

The golf game that first time has been long forgotten but the overflowing mushroom bags never will be. We had picked so many, that we had put some in the pockets of our golf bags.

Mr. Charles was waiting for us and very carefully looked at each and every mushroom we had found. In one bag, he found a Destroying Angel, white top and white gills. Then and there, the whole bag of good mushrooms was thrown out because someone had forgotten to look at the gill color. We all shared our treasures with the unfortunate kid and that was the beginning of a mushroom hunter. It also was almost the end, too, because I forgot those extras I had put into the seldom used pocket of the golf bag. How well I remember coming down for breakfast and seeing Mother sniffing around in the kitchen. There was a pretty deadly odor near the pantry. Before I even started to help sniff, I saw my golf bag and I knew what I had done. Grabbing the bag, I ran out the door to the nice fresh air and opened the pocket. The sight and the smell were almost unbearable but the cleaning out was even worse. I certainly didn't have any friends that day, even my mother whose pantry was her pride and joy, wasn't very fond of me.

But we learned and by the end of the season Mr. Charles had graduated us as button, field (also called pinkie or meadow) mushroom and puffball pickers.

We all grew up, went to college, got jobs or married or both and now we're scattered all over the world. It's hard to tell about the rest, but I have hunted my three kinds in Illinois, Wisconsin, Michigan, New York, New Jersey and Ohio. Wherever my husband was transferred, the kids and I would try to spot something white in fields, lawns and on our many camping trips out west.

It wasn't until about 5 years ago that I was introduced personally to the morel. Having read stories about the great competition in Michigan where the women actually have a morel tournament and scatter and disappear to their carefully guarded secret morel territory, I was fascinated but never expected to see any growing.

It happened that I was in the right place at the right time and for once used my eyes for something other than blinking. Walking along a road made on an old railroad bed. I saw something I had never seen before. A tan spongy cone about 4″ on a stem about the same length. Pretty sure I had practically stumbled on a morel, I was a little afraid I might be wrong. It's hard to admit, but I'm not always right.

As I stood there looking around, something seemed to click and instead of uninteresting weeds and thorny bushes, I could see tiny black growths along with all sizes of tan, yellow and brownish mushrooms. There was no question about it. The fishing would have to give way to identifying my find.

Marking the spot with my rod and reel, I cut the large sponge with my fish knife and ran as fast as the aging legs would take me to the owner of the land, hoping against hope that I wouldn't get the disgusted look I'd seen so many times before when I thought I was pretty smart and turned out to be a real dum-dum.

Panting heavily as I looked in the barn, then running down a small hill to the workshop, I was greeted by the question, "What's the matter? Did a snake scare you?"

Annoyed at the question and breathing so hard, all I could do was hold up my find. First, the startled expression; then the questions, no waiting for answers; a terse, "Get in the truck," and we were roaring up the dirt road to the railroad bank. Finally there was enough breath to say that I had marked the spot with my favorite rod and please do not run over it. Just in time too.

We had hit a bonanza. They were really morels and eventually our eyes were accustomed to finding them large and small and it was beautiful but unreal. A few growing by the road but mostly on the slopes of the bank. Over fallen logs, through stick tights and thorny bushes, (hang the hair done just that morning) crawling on hands and knees on mud and gravel to reach a cluster growing surreptitiously under the brush and dead elm logs.

We didn't pick them all and we kept discovering more as we clawed through growth no one but dedicated mushroomers would combat without a machete. What a day that was and the next year was just as great. However, something has happened to our weather for the past two years and the morels, although there have been a few, haven't had a chance to give us the spectacular show we have come to expect.

Cooking and Recipes

In every case of readying morels for a meal, it's best to soak them in cold water for at least an hour. Like the clown fish's protection to the sea anemone, small black bugs are found in the ridges of the morel. The soaking will bring

If there are too many mushrooms for one meal, the best way to preserve them is through drying.

To prepare morels for a meal, it is best to soak them in cold water for at least an hour.

Morels have an entirely different taste than white field mushrooms. But they complement any meal.

most of them to the surface and a quick glance while preparing will make sure there are no intruders left.

Morels have an entirely different taste and chewability from those white field mushrooms. They are a little tougher but so tasty that it's worth a tad more jaw usage.

We always wash our morels immediately and slice depending on size into a frying pan with butter or margarine. Turning often and testing only because of greed, we cook them over a medium fire for about 10 minutes. They brown up a little and are ready.

If there are too many for one meal, dry off excess water on paper towels, put in a bowl and keep in the cooler. They will last for a week this way, but usually if they are available, the lucky camper will eat them with eggs, cream them for lunch or put into soup, then fry them at night to go with the fish he's caught for dinner (or the beans if the fish weren't biting).

In trying to keep morels for a rainy day, I've found that they don't freeze well but drying is another matter. Some people string them up like popcorn chains, others have them spread out in a warm dry place and turn them each day. A rather long process and a space-user, but who cares if the kitchen counter is covered with drying morels when she knows next winter, after being soaked, they can be used in everything a canned mushroom goes into?

Unfortunately, they don't compare to a crisp morel fried in butter, but a turkey stuffing made with revitalized dried morels is still a conversation piece among the people who were our dinner guests one evening this winter.

Walking along a road made on an old railroad bed, one is very likely to discover a mushroom patch.

Because the morel mushroom has such a distinctive appearance, there is no danger of mistaking it for a toadstool.

SEAFOOD SOUTHERN

by MARVIN TYE

A STRONG FISH hit my lure with a sturdy jolt that put a deep bend in my trolling rod. I smiled, knowing that the hard fighting Spanish mackerel at the other end of the line would provide a tasty meal as well as fine fishing action. One of the finer things about living in the southeastern United States is the abundance of a wide variety of tasty salt-water game fish in the Atlantic and Gulf of Mexico.

Spanish mackerel are one of the most plentiful species and are a particular favorite as a food fish. Mackerel can be baked, broiled or fried. My favorite recipe for the spirited Spanish is one taught to me by a native Floridian after a successful fishing trip out of Destin, Florida. The necessary ingredients to serve six people consist of two pounds of Spanish mackerel fillets, eight ounces of mushrooms (sliced), ¼-cup cooking oil, one teaspoon salt, a dash of pepper and one cup grated cheddar cheese. The fillets should be skinned and cut into serving size portions. Combine salt, pepper and oil and spoon or brush over mackerel. Broil on a well-greased broiler pan about three inches from the heat for three to four minutes, then turn over and broil three to four minutes on the other side until

The author lands a tasty Spanish mackerel.

The South offers abundant salt water game fish in the Atlantic and Gulf of Mexico.

STYLE

fish flakes easily when touched with a fork. Spread mushrooms and cheese on the fish and broil approximately three minutes longer. One serving of this delicacy will make you a confirmed mackerel fan.

The larger king mackerel is nearly as abundant as the Spanish. They can be cooked with this same recipe or broiled in a slightly different manner. Ingredients for this recipe are two pounds of king mackerel fillets, one clove finely chopped garlic, ¼-cup orange juice, ¼-cup soy sauce, two tablespoons catsup, two tablespoons cooking oil, one tablespoon lemon juice, ½-teaspoon oregano, ½-teaspoon pepper. The fish should be placed in a single layer in a shallow dish. The remaining ingredients and sauce should be poured over the fish and left to stand for 30 minutes turning once. Remove the fish and place on a well-greased broiler pan. Broil about three inches from source of heat for four to five minutes. Turn carefully and baste with sauce left in the dish, broil on that side for an additional four to five minutes.

In cooking mackerel at a beach side campsite, fillets can be dipped in seasoned flour, crumbs or corn meal and placed in ¼-inch of hot fat or oil and cooked over medium high heat until golden brown on both sides. This usually takes about four to six minutes on each side.

Mackerel fillets can be deep fried by submerging them in hot fat or oil, approximately 375 degrees F., and cooked over high heat for approximately four to six minutes. The fillets should be placed on absorbent paper to remove the excess oil.

It seems that I am always discovering a new species of fish to be cooked or new ways to prepare familiar species. Not long ago I attended a South Georgia fish fry. I was surprised to learn that we would be eating fried mullet. Mullet is generally used as bait for channel bass, tarpon and a number of other species. It is sold in fish markets but I had never sampled it before. Somehow the idea of eating mullet had never appealed to me. Figuring that these people probably knew what they were doing, I almost reluctantly sampled the mullet which were fried in deep fat. They were delicious.

Since that time I have sampled mullet cooked in a variety of ways. Not long after this cookout at a meeting in Florida I was served mullet which had been sliced open on the underside, the entrails removed, and the fish cooked on a grill over an open fire with the skin still on. It was also surprisingly good.

Mullet can also be prepared in a tasty dish that serves six. Ingredients are two pounds of mullet fillets, 1½ cups crushed cheese crackers, ½-cup French dressing and two tablespoons melted fat or oil. Fillets should be cut into serving size portions and skinned. Dip fish in dressing and roll in cracker crumbs. Place on a well-greased flat oven

The author's favorite recipe for Spanish mackerel begins with two pounds of fillets and sliced mushrooms . . .

Then cheddar cheese is grated to provide additional flavor for this dish . . .

pan. Drip fat or cooking oil over the fish; bake at 500 degrees F. for ten to 12 minutes. This meal should convince almost anybody that the lowly bait fish mullet is indeed table fare.

Mullet should be cooked or frozen soon after being caught. Fishermen sometimes catch mullet in brackish water while fishing for panfish with live worms. They can also be collected with a cast net. The latter method is the most common way to pick up a mess of mullet.

Oysters and shrimp can be purchased at a reasonable cost on any trip to the coast. During one hunting trip in Florida my hunting partner picked up some of this delectable food and prepared it almost every night while we were in camp. We would simply boil the shrimp and flavor it with tabasco sauce. The oysters were left in their shells and placed in the coals of the campfire until the steaming juices would bubble out. We would retrieve the oysters from the coals, pry them open, season them and enjoy a treat. We usually had a broiled steak, garlic bread and canned soft drinks, tea or coffee to drink with these meals. This was a so-called primitive camping area on a national wildlife refuge. The camping facilities may have been primitive because of a lack of running water and other facilities but our food and the hunting were strictly first class.

A tasty method of preparing shrimp salad is the well-known Florida recipe for shrimp tropicana. We use one pound of boiled shrimp, one cup creamed cottage cheese, ½-cup drained crushed pineapple, ⅓-cup mayonnaise, two teaspoons lemon juice and ½-teaspoon of salt. The shrimp is chopped and the cottage cheese drained and all the ingredients combined and chilled. This can be placed in a salad bowl over lettuce leaves or placed on slices of wheat bread with lettuce for a tasty sandwich. Either way it provides a delicious treat.

Fried oysters or oysters cooked over coals are well-known delicacies. Another method of preparing this shellfish is not so well-known but is equally delicious. Ingredients are 12 ounces of oysters, 12 slices of bacon, one cup dry bread crumbs, one cup flour, one beaten egg, one tablespoon milk, ½-teaspoon salt, a bit of pepper, 18 slices of buttered toast, ¼-cup mayonnaise, six lettuce leaves and two sliced tomatoes. Begin by frying the bacon and draining it on absorbent paper. Combine crumbs and flour and roll oysters in this mixture. Combine egg, milk, salt and pepper and dip the oysters in this mixture and fry in hot bacon fat at moderate heat until brown on one side. Then turn and brown on the other side. Cook for approximately five to seven minutes. Drain on absorbent paper. Spread six slices of toast with mayonnaise, arrange lettuce and tomatoes on top, cover with second slice of toast and then put bacon and oysters on top of this. Cover this with the remaining slices of toast, secure with toothpicks and cut in quarters.

Grouper can be combined with Parmesan cheese and other ingredients to make a tasty meal. Start with two pounds of skinned grouper fillets, one cup sour cream, ¼-cup grated Parmesan cheese, one tablespoon lemon juice, one teaspoon grated onion, ½-teaspoon salt, a dash of liquid hot pepper sauce, paprika and chopped parsley. Place fillets in a single layer in a well-greased baking dish. Mix Parmesan cheese, lemon juice, grated onion, salt and pepper sauce and spread the mixture over the fish. Sprin-

Shrimp tropicana is synonymous with Florida sunshine. Begin with sliced, boiled shrimp . . .

The grated cheese and sliced mushrooms are placed on mackerel fillets and broiled. This gourmet seafood is ideal for a recreational vehicle or houseboat chef who has a well-equipped kitchen...

The completed meal, a specialty of Florida fishermen, broiled mackerel ready to eat. Easy and good to fix after a full day of fishing.

kle with paprika and bake at 350 degrees F. for 25 to 30 minutes. Then garnish with parsley.

The red snapper is one of the South's favorite saltwater food fishes. One tasty way to prepare this fish is to assemble two pounds of fillets, three tablespoons oil, two tablespoons orange juice, two teaspoons grated orange rind, one teaspoon salt and a dash of nutmeg and pepper. Cut the fish into serving size portions, place in a single layer in a well-greased baking dish. Combine the other ingredients, pour over the fish and bake at 350 degrees F. for 25 to 30 minutes.

Red snapper can also be baked with a sour cream stuffing. In order to do this you must clean, wash and dry the fish, sprinkle inside and out with salt, stuff loosely with sour cream, close opening with toothpicks, bake on a well-greased pan at 350 degrees F. for 40 to 60 minutes. These instructions are for the preparations of a three- to four-pound fish. The fish should be basted occasionally with oil while cooking. Baking time can be varied for a larger or smaller fish.

Just over a year ago I caught my first cobia while fishing off the coast of Alabama. This new species fought savagely and was quite thrilling to catch. When fried it had a unique taste that I enjoyed. This whetted my desire to catch more specimens of this fine game species and to experiment in cooking it in various ways.

A couple of years ago, my wife and I enjoyed a different method of preparing seafood in Mazatlan, Mexico. At the Camino Real we were served jumbo shrimp, snapper, oysters and scallops broiled on a hibachi grill. The hibachi grill with the seafood still on top of it was placed on the table to keep the meat warm.

As stated earlier we are always discovering new species of fish and new ways of preparing familiar species. Perhaps that is why we are such seafood fans and perhaps that is why we love to fish.

The shrimp is then combined with cottage cheese, spices and crushed pineapple to make an out-of-this world salad. Refreshing for a hot, day-in-the-sun lunch...

The author's wife Mary Elizabeth beams over the dish. It is tasty as well as low in fattening calories.

...JUST COOKING

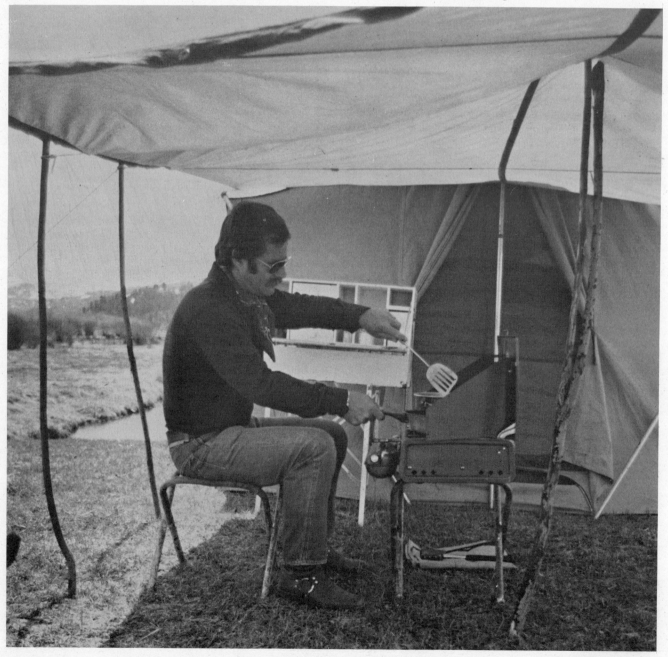

Overhead tarp provides protection from rain and room for cooking.

IN THE RAIN

by CHARLES J. FARMER

"MY GAWD, Johnnie, if it doesn't stop raining, I'm ready to head home." Sheet rain bathed the canvas tent. An aerosol mist made the inside of the tent look like a foggy day in London. A damp chill crept into every corner of the mountain retreat and Johnnie Stewart was beginning to think that his brother Jeff had a good point when he suggested heading home.

It had been raining off and on for two days. Between cloud bursts, the two men had enjoyed good fishing for bullheads and chunky bluegill. But as far as they were concerned, if they couldn't fish, they did not want to be stuck up in the hills peering from mosquito netting and watching pond-like puddles fill the stone fire circle—a fireplace they had not yet used because their firewood was spongy wet.

Huddled in the umbrella tent, their spirits ebbed. A good, hot meal would have cheered them up. The men were hungry. But they were not prepared for rain—and the relentless showers were getting the best of them (as they often do to campers who damn drizzly nature as a scourge, rather than a fact of camping life).

There was a time when I cussed rain that invaded a camping or fishing trip as vehemently as I do the doorstop that seldom missed snagging my big toe during a midnight trip to the bathroom. I still berate the doorstop on occasion but I have learned to control my disappointment over a rain soaked campout to the point where my wife, Kathy, and I try to make the best out of it.

Provided you have the proper equipment to keep you comfortable and dry inside, the biggest rainy day obstacle you face as adults, or camping with children, is boredom. The state of being bored during a rained out camping day is natural. Rain shuts off many camp activities. During a limited-time camping vacation or weekend trip, impatience fuels boredom which usually results in a restlessness unequaled by most fidgetiness experienced during normal, everyday routine. And the rain keeps coming. To make matters worse, kids often feel the pangs created by soggy nature far worse than adults do. So the quickest, easiest next step is to pack up the saturated, leaden, mud-floored tent—corral the mucky-pawed hound who is dripping with a bad case of doggie odor—and head back to the comforts of civilization (at least back in town you don't have to be out in that wet stuff). That is the easy way out. There is a better way to handle inevitable rain!

Waterproof Rainy Day Kitchens

I'll never forget standing under a huge, canvas tarp during a three-day squall while on maneuvers in the Army at Fort Polk, Louisiana. Most of you would assume, and with good reason, that this would be a rather dreary predicament in more ways than one. And in many ways it was. But there were some good things that happened under that rain-thumped tarp. The memories, smells, flavors, good food (I never had any complaints about most GI cooking) and good comradeship made me feel there was always hope for rain-filled camping trips. If you can have fun under soggy, olive-drab, you can have fun anytime.

The most important, maneuver-saving element of that Army bivouac centered around the mess truck. Hot food and drink (plenty of it) turned combat boot monotony into near-delight. There we were munching fresh-fried, early-morning donuts and sipping hot, black coffee while the drill instructors (DIs) turned red in the neck because the rain put a halt to our drill and ceremonies (better known as D&C) exhibition. We enlisted men chuckled heartily under our dog tags as the rain fell harder and some of the bayou creeks jumped their banks.

We spent three days under that tarp, literally camped in that comfortable outdoor kitchen. Our ears were tuned to the sound of kitchen helpers snapping the lids on fresh coffee—or noses alert to kitchen patrol (KP) surprises like donuts, muffins and, get this, fresh-baked apple strudel (we were blessed with imaginative cooks)—our tastes geared to hot, wholesome food. The three days zoomed by. We missed the smell of the hissing field stoves and the wonders they turned out. Most of us gained weight. But the DIs took care of that as soon as the sun worked its way back into the sky. The culinary bivouac, not specifically stated in the *Standard Operating Procedure* (SOP), was one of the best things the army taught me. Many a rainy camp has been salvaged by the camp kitchen theory.

It is important to prepare for rain even though the sky may be cloudless blue. Forget long range weather reports. Think rain. When you do your at-home planning and packing, the gear that can rainproof your camp will not be forgotten.

The Cooking Tarp

Many tents have doorway awnings that add a measure of rain protection to the tent and the immediate area. Some cooking can be done under this awning during light rainfall with little or no accompanying wind.

Nylon tarp additions to the basic doorway awning prove their worth quickly during a moderate or heavy rain with gusty wind. Tarps can be purchased with grommets, or a grommet tool (an extremely handy camper's tool) can be used to punch heavy duty grommets where they are

207

needed. Tarps can be tailored to fit tents with awnings. Or they can be modified so they can be attached to standard, awning-less tents or small mountain tents. In any case, the cooking tarp—often roomier and higher than the tent itself—offers a new dimension to rainy day cooking, eating and just plain waiting out the storm.

My wife Kathy and I witnessed a good example of smart camping recently on a backpack trip into Wyoming's Bridger Wilderness. We had just broken a two-day camp at a developed campsite at lower Green River Lake. Rain had been with us off and on but the promise of good fishing lured us into making a backpack, side trip to upper Green River Lake. We left in the rain, ponchos over our packs.

A deceiving sky had led us to believe the rain would let up. It didn't. The spray came in sheets, sometimes so hard that we sought the broad, taupe trunks of the Douglas firs along the trail. The southern exposures of the trees were dry, or nearly so and afforded some protection. "Maybe this wasn't such a good idea," I whispered to Kathy. "Sure is miserable," she added. Since the hike was a relatively short three miles, we agreed that if the rain continued, we would fish the upper lake for a while, then, instead of setting camp, return to the car. Both of us knew we were not equipped for rain.

After a stop-and-go hike in the downpour, we made it to the Upper Green River Lake. It was there that we came across Florence and Jack Weiss from LaCrosse, Wisconsin. Their camp was like an oasis for us. The blaze orange color of their cozy, dry mountain shelter had drawn us to them. And the middle aged couple welcomed Kathy and me.

Grill and open fire can be used under tarp and campers can eat under protection of canopy.

Homemade tarp addition to tent is good for shade and cooking and eating in bad weather. Guy ropes secure tarp so that it handles most winds.

Some public and private campgrounds feature build-in rain protection.

Smoke curled from the soothing flames. Although the rain had not let up, the auxiliary shelter provided cozy, dry comfort. "If we have to be cooped up in that mountain tent all day, or any tent for that matter, both of us go bananas," Florence grinned. "Rarely do we set a camp without a shelter like this one. Sometimes we even sleep under it. It is ideal for cooking since the sides are open and there is no problem of inadequate ventilation. When it's raining real hard (like yesterday), we use our little single burner stove to cook on," Jack added.

In a way, the little shelter with the aroma of fresh coffee and the smell of pan fried Indian bread, reminded me of the Fort Polk bivouac. Florence served hot chocolate in heavy, plastic cups. The steam that rose from the cups felt good on my icy cheeks.

"What depresses most people about camping in the rain," Jack said, "is that they are confined to one small tent. Sometimes it is hard enough for some people to sleep in a tent. But when it's raining, and they have to spend the day inside four canvas walls without seeing anything new . . . well that can get pretty depressing. A shelter like this one, sort of opens the sky (and the mind) a bit. We can stand up and stretch . . . walk outside and not worry about coming in and getting the sleeping bags wet. We can have a small fire going—cook and eat when we want to. Sure, I'd rather be out on that lake fishing for brook trout right now, but we have camped too many times to fight the rain or let it beat us."

A second cup of hot chocolate and 15 minutes had passed when we first realized that patches of blue were appearing in the north. "Hey, that's a great sign," Jack beamed.

Small, pack stoves are used for cooking within small tents or low tarps. Adequate ventilation is a must however.

We each sipped a cup of mellow, white wine from the bottle that the couple packed in. The liquid warmed our insides. "I'll get some hot chocolate going," Florence volunteered.

The Weiss's camp setup was a simple one, but an arrangement that stuck in my mind. Aside from their two-place backpack tent, a large, orange nylon tarp was slung over an area perhaps 15 feet by 15 feet. The shelter was drawn tight by nylon rope tied to trees and boughs. Heavy duty grommets added to the tarp's durability and snugness. The shelter had a slight pitch in the middle created by a nylon rope that was strung through the center of it. The front and back of the tarp sloped just enough to shed rain and prevent puddle pockets from forming.

Near one end of the shelter a small but efficient fire cradled a bubbling, charred coffee pot. Florence had hunted up a flat "griddle rock" that she was particularly proud of. It was flat enough and fit the fire so well, that Jack told me they had fried eggs on it that morning. "That rock holds its heat for a long time," Florence chipped in. "After the coffee perks on the open fire, we leave the pot on the griddle rock and it stays hot for a couple of hours." Jack fueled the fire and the rock with small chunks of deadfall pine. He found enough dry wood near the base of the tall pines to keep the fire going for hours.

When there is lack of dry firewood, small propane stove is handy.

"Maybe we will catch some fish yet. We have had three solid days of rain up here."

After we said goodbye to Jack and Florence and thanked them for their warmth, I could not help but be impressed with the couple's good spirits. They had traveled a long way from Wisconsin to Wyoming. Besieged by rain for three days, their comfortable, waterproof camp rewarded them with a unique experience. They had joined nature, rather than try and fight her. Their lesson has been a standard for Kathy and me.

The rainy day kitchen tarp is a simple affair. It can be strung with nylon rope to trees. Or in treeless areas can be supported by wood, metal or fiberglass poles. When used with poles, additional guy ropes give extra stability during high wind. In setting the tarp, remember that although it can be used for shade and a quiet place to nap, its main function is to keep you warm, dry, happy and full during storms. It should be pitched with bad weather in mind, so that it weathers the storm.

Some commercially manufactured shelter additions can be purchased as options with various brands of tents. If they are made from good materials; can be rigged so they are stable during high winds; and are reasonably priced, they are worthwhile additions. If you cannot find one for your tent, custom tailor a tarp that will work just as well. With the extra shelter, you will find that rainy camping days are

Space blankets provide protection for these campers under rainy skies.

It is a good idea to give the cook plenty of cooking light—whether under dark sky or at night.

not as long and boring as when you were confined to the four canvas walls. Here are some other tips for camping and cooking in the rain:

Cooking Inside a Tent

An important safety hint to remember is that your tent may "breathe" due to the material from which it is constructed, but when cooking inside, additional ventilation (completely open a window or door flap) is recommended. The same type of ventilation should also be utilized for catalytic heaters.

With proper ventilation, it is practical to cook inside an average size wall tent, say ten feet by eight feet. This size tent usually insures adequate head room, anywhere from five feet-five inches to six feet-five inches, so there is a sufficient heat (or flame) space from the stove to the roof of the tent. There is also enough room for standard size gas stoves and even table and stools if desired.

Cooking *is* possible inside low profile backpack or mountain tents although more care is needed. Many mountain tents, especially those with rain flies, are practically air tight. Adequate ventilation is a must and this outside air should come in from the front and rear of the tent.

Since there may be only a three- to five-foot floor-to-roof clearance in the backpack tent, small propane or gas pack stoves, can be used. With care, complete meals can be fixed on such stoves without scorching the sidewall or roof of the tent. Due to the limited space inside such tents however, eating and cooking is sometimes cramped. Every move has to be in slow motion in order to avoid tipping the stove or spilling food items. I highly recommend the use of a cook tarp for eating and food preparation during periods of bad weather—any sort of flame in a tent can be hazardous.

To this day, I have never built an open fire in a canvas or nylon shelter. And I doubt if I ever will. Even with the floorless models, there is just too much likelihood of sparks catching the tent, sleeping bags or gear on fire. Again, an additional kitchen tarp would serve the need handily.

Tents as small as ten feet by eight feet have been successfully equipped with wood burning heat and cook stoves. With proper installation, asbestos pipe liner and sufficient stove pipe clearance above the highest part of the tent, the portable wood cook stove can be a delight. Hunting and fishing camp operators have used them with great success. As reason would dictate, they are more suitable to permanent or semi-permanent camp setups where assembly and take down chores are worth the efforts. Certain conditions make them valuable even for a week-long camp life. Fall and winter camping in certain cold climates, for instance, can warrant the heating and cooking pleasure of a wood burning stove. For most campers and outdoor chefs though, the wood stove is impractical. Modern, lightweight gas and propane models are better suited for the mobile camper.

Fuel for Rainy Days

Gas or propane stoves are always handy during long periods of rain when wood is soggy wet. There are ways though of finding dry fuel.

The last resort in finding dry wood (at least for me) is to purchase it from a campground wood vendor or from a wood vending machine. And in case you haven't noticed, both are steadily creeping into our campgrounds. The day I yield to the vendor or the machine for obtaining wood, will be the day I cease camping. Despite the so-called scarcity of wood in our busy campgrounds (as we hear the buzz of the logging company's "quick-kill" tree harvester down the road) I cannot find it in my stomach to purchase wood from anybody or anything.

When it is wet, think small. Tiny "twiggies" growing near bottom tree limbs or boughs (commonly on the south exposure) are usually dry enough for use as quick-lighting tinder. Long, wooden "strike anywhere" matches are best for starting flame. Once the tinder is dancing, add small twigs slowly. Let the fire breathe. Slowly build it up until you can add larger twigs and branches. Some fuel will be damp. But a small, hot fire will eventually dry damp wood and it will burn. Arrange several damp pieces near the fire so they can dry.

Dry tree lichen, pitch, dead (rusty brown) pine needles and the powdery inside "sawdust" of some rotted logs can also serve as efficient fire starters. Patience is a prime requisite. For those cooks who lack it, commercially sold charcoal lighter, fire ribbon or lighter fluid can be sprinkled or pasted on wet wood for faster, surer results. A mixture of kerosene and sawdust works well. Poof! Flames.

The rainy days at camp are times for good food. Eating days. Slow and easy. With some advance planning and a good overhead shelter, the next rain storm may be the most pleasant you have ever experienced.

This old time camping scene was re-created, with permission from the Coleman Co., Wichita, Kansas, by artist, Gail M. Farmer (sister of the editor). It shows one of the very first Coleman stoves in use by this "modern" motor-camping outdoor family. Note that the Grand-Daddy of 'Em All, the Coleman stove, has changed very little over the years.

the Grand~Daddy of 'em all

by SHELDON COLEMAN

TWO YEARS BEFORE I was born—that's close to 74 years ago; how time flies—Pop started the Coleman Furnace Company. He cared about protecting people from cold temperatures and windy weather. Picnicking and camping were for the rich who had nothing better to do with their time.

Fishing was how I got involved with the outdoors. I've never seen an ugly trout stream and I've never met a fisherman I didn't like—at least a little. I spent more time fishing than I did anything else. Playing hooky to fish seemed a matter of common sense to me. Pop predicted I'd ruin my life if I didn't cut down on my fishing. But I was hooked—literally—and I decided to make the most of it.

Pop's main gripe about camping was the inconvenience. Who wants to scorch the hair off his arm just to fry some bacon and eggs? True, the food once cooked did take on a special flavor. But the actual cooking belonged to prehistoric times. As I grew a little older, "roughing it" became less fun to me too. And I joined Pop in seeking ways of making camping—a necessary "evil" when fishing isolated, virginal streams—more comfortable.

Pop's first invention, the gasoline hot plate, was introduced to the public in 1911. It appealed to more homebodies than it did to outdoorsmen but that was because there were more of them around. Even though I was only nine, I was as proud of it as he was; inside I felt I had something to do with it. I took it along on fishing trips and let him sample the delicious walleye fillets that were fried crispy brown on it. Before I came along, he considered fishing something you did when you went to the market on River Front Street.

Once Pop began thinking of camping as something desirable, he suddenly realized what a wide open field it was. Camping had not yet been discovered by most people. Recreation to them was basking in the more civilized pastimes, such as, plays, parties, Sunday baseball games with the neighborhood guys. The streetcar was the most common means of transportation and that was not conducive to exploring unknown, untamed areas.

But with the advent of the family automobile, one's horizons broadened. A person could bounce and bump his way in a Model T to wilderness' edge and camp and fish to his heart's content. It's funny, the more technologically advanced our society becomes, the more social beings strive for the primitive. Once again proving, the grass is always greener . . .

Next to fixing hot meals without too much fuss and mess, the main problem facing campers was how to see in the dark without carrying a kerosene or oil lamp around with you. The Coleman Lamp Company rose to the occasion, originating the Coleman Quick-Lite Lamp and Lantern, fueled by gasoline. By the early 1920's, we had become the largest manufacturer of pressure type gasoline lamps and lanterns. In fact, in 1965 we sold the 15-millionth Coleman lantern. As a tribute, I was presented a gold-plated one. It was truly a heartfelt experience for me. Wish Pop could have been there to share the glow of a job well done. He died in 1957 but he knew then that his small furnace business was blossoming into a leading designer and manufacturer of camping equipment.

Sheldon Coleman is first a fly fisherman. He travels worldwide introducing himself to new streams and rivers. He is Chairman of the board of the Coleman Company. He personally tests most new products before they are put on the market.

This is Sheldon Coleman, Chairman of the board of the Coleman Co., an avid outdoorsman and fly fisherman. He field tests all of the company's new products personally on his many fishing and camping trips. Sheldon Coleman is 72 years old.

Here is the modern version of the Coleman, two-burner camp stove . . . ready to do what it does best—fry freshly caught fish.

Looking back on it, the camp stove appears to be another one of those American inventions whose time had come. After the first World War, Americans took to the highways on the wheels of low-priced, mass-produced automobiles. Added to the attraction of relatively low cost "touring cars" was the emergence of marked highways and eventually the development of federal and state highway systems. Concurrently, there was considerable expansion in the National Park System.

In short, the time was right for the Coleman Camp Stove, the Grand-Daddy of camping and modern outdoor cookery. The very first Coleman camp stoves, appropriately designated "Model No. 1," were produced in February, 1923. In that month, twelve units with a folding oven as an integral part of the stove were produced. We also built six stoves without ovens. According to Herb Ebendorf, historian for the Coleman Company, by the end of 1923 we had built 11,510 with ovens and 1,508 without ovens.

The camp stove was originally called the "camp cooker" and since its arrival on the marketing scene, it has been an important part of the Coleman line of gasoline appliances. In the "Directions for Operating the Coleman Camp Stove" which accompanied each new stove in 1923, the Coleman Cooker offered special features, such as:

A Built-in Air Pump . . . "It's 'just the thing' for campers, autotourists, hunters, fishermen. No chance to lose or damage pump. It's always ready for use. Carry it anywhere, in any kind of weather."

Wind Baffles . . . "Raise the hinged sides of the lid to an upright position and pull them forward until they rest on the ends of the stove cabinet, at about a 30-degree angle, thus providing plenty of protection for the burners against the wind."

Sturdy Construction . . .

Fuel Tank Mounted on Swivel Joints . . . "Could be neatly dumped inside of the casing without the necessity of disengaging nuts and bolts. Is always connected with burners—can't get loose—lays inside when cabinet is closed; one turn swings it outside for operation where it is always handy and cool."

Simple, Practical Way of Lighting Stove . . . "The lighting mechanism is simply a burner cup. Pour a tablespoon of flammable liquid—wood alcohol or gasoline are good—into the burner cup. Light the liquid. In about a minute, the heat of the idle flame from the cup will warm up the generator tube and thus partially vaporize the gasoline in it."

You can find all these features in our 1974 Coleman Stoves, except for the method of lighting. We now have instant lighting, which was added in 1929. After 51 years of usage, the Coleman stoves are fundamentally the same. Remarkable, even if I do say so myself.

As for the built-in oven, it was then, and in my opinion still remains, an outstanding example of sound engineering and manufacturing techniques. Eventually, the oven was dropped but for the first two or three years the camp stove was in production, the oven-equipped models outsold the models without ovens. Why? We don't know for sure. Maybe people felt they were getting more for their money by buying an oven with a stove. And I think they were. But most outdoorsmen did not want to bother with an oven. And we were primarily concerned with a simple, long-lasting, sturdy stove. An oven seemed too much of a

A casual check of campgrounds, anywhere in the world shows the Grand-Daddy of 'Em All at home in the outdoors. Nesting pots and pans aid in outdoor cooking efforts.

luxury for campers. Who knows, maybe we will re-invent the oven to complement the Coleman stove.

No one, until now, has ever asked me how many camp stoves the Coleman Company has made since February, 1923. To be on the safe side, I am certain the number is at least 5 million. How's that? I'm sure this is a conservative estimate because, as I mentioned before, one of my dedicated employees counted 15 million lanterns that we have manufactured since the early 1900's. Maybe I should say we have made between 5 and 15 million Coleman stoves. That will leave me plenty of error room.

I would also guess for the record that a majority of all these Coleman stoves are in use today or else should be. There is simply not much to wear out, unless it be the generator or the pump leather; and even then, these parts are easily replaced. In a sense, the Grand-Daddy Coleman Stove is nearly immortal. He is still around today to watch his grandchildren grow old and yet can keep up with them. He works as well today as he did in the glorious twenties. Sometimes, I dream of being a Coleman Stove.

In 1926, three years after the Coleman Stove made its debut to the buying public, we brainstormed a new campaign: Teach the American people how to camp with a motorcar and enjoy it. In many ways it was a novel concept: Use a machine to see the country yet sleep under the stars, eat among the squirrels and drink from a gurgling stream. By means of a horseless carriage, get closer to nature. To many, the idea was a contradiction. "If you can afford a car, why pretend you are destitute by camping out. Why try to fool people?" Others considered camping a sacrifice. "When we go on vacation, why skimp? Stay in a hotel. Live it up!" Some thought we were secretly against hotels and trying to drive them out of business.

Eventually, we contacted Frank Brimmer to write a booklet for campers. An experienced "autocamper," he agreed to share with novice campers his experiences and tips about camping that he had learned the "hard way." We published his *Motor Campers Manual* in 1926. I believe he set the stage for modern camping. Many people followed his example when they had questions or doubts about what to take along on camping trips, how to choose

The complete outdoor camp and kitchen—roughing it, with all the conveniences of home.

Here is a good combination—the tent and motorhome for the ultimate in camping.

a campsite, how to select tents and camp beds and where to camp.

Brimmer's writing was straight forward. Today it might be judged "hokey." But then, he mixed a good deal of knowledge, wisdom and foresight into his book. He predicted the present firewood crunch and society's emphatic concern abont conservation. He suggested certain camping rules of etiquette, particularly applicable now in many overcrowded campgrounds. Here is what he had to say about the "Ethics of Camping":

Playing the game is one of the most important earmarks of a real motor camper. Play square with the campground. Clean it up after you have enjoyed it. Play safe with your open fire, if you have one. Cover the ashes or coals with sand or soil. Be sure that all duff and dead twigs are raked well back away from the place where an open fire is to be started in the woods.

Somebody has pointed out that a match has a head—but you have to *think* for it. A match may be the millionth part of the other wood where it is carelessly thrown; but it may burn a billion feet of valuable growing lumber.

The loss of lumber is only a small part of the terrible rape of nature caused by forest fire. More awful are the arid streams that result in the region; no fishing there! And a nude barren tract is no place for game birds and animals to live; hunting has gone, likely forever!

Play fair with the other fellow. Burn the rubbish. Bury the tin cans and garbage, unless the city in which the camp is located has a garbage disposal system in operation. Don't cut or bark trees. Don't dig holes and leave them unfilled. Don't allow oil and grease from the motor to soil the grass. Don't pollute the water. Be human!

Autocamp upon others as you would have others autocamp upon you. Thoughtlessness on the part of campers will result in laws restricting the sport. For example, in Minnesota recently we saw a sign: 'No Fires Allowed.'

And that was back in 1926. Outdoor writers tell us the same things today about camping. Of course, not so bluntly . . . but the principles of ethical camping with conservation being the camper's foremost goal, these have not changed for 48 years.

At that time, tents were simple; sleeping bags, nonexistent. Equipment and accessories were necessary, of course, but campers had no specially designed gear. Each camper had to make do with what he brought from home. Being more of a camping pro than the average person,

The cook stove is a good addition to open fire cooking.

Brimmer spoke with authority when he listed the necessities for a camping party of four.

- Autotent size 9x11, Coleman Camp Stove on high stand
- One double spring bed, two single folding cots
- Three wool blankets for each person
- Camp bed mattress or air mattress
- Coleman Camp Lantern, four-party cooking and eating utensil set
- Folding table and chairs, luggage carrier
- Ice basket or chest, thermal jug or bottle
- Accessories for the automobile
- Miscellaneous equipment such as fishing tackle, camera, outboard motor, camp axe and hunting knife in sheath, flashlight, first-aid kit, field glasses, water bag, auxiliary tank, radio, phonograph.

A tenter had to be dedicated to haul a double spring bed around in a car and actually like it.

Not meant to be bragging, exactly, but there was one aspect of camping which was as easy then as it is now—outdoor cooking. Don't take my word. Listen to what Brimmer has to say:

Usually the women folks in the family go motor camping, which is one reason why this new sport is so popular, for it is equally enjoyed by both sides of the family, as well as children of all ages and sizes; hence the matter of camp cookery is greatly simplified with the cook right along.

For all practical purposes camp cookery, with food carried in the portable ice basket (made of reed with a metal lining), and with the Coleman Camp Stove over which to work, is exactly like it is at home.

I don't agree completely with the chauvinistic attitude that women should be the cooks of a camping group. But I do support Brimmer 100 percent with his description of the Coleman Camp Stove. It really does make outdoor cooking as predictable, fast and uncomplicated as indoor cooking. It gives the chef time and energy to exercise creativity, originality and daring. Drive through a large campground around 5:00 pm and you will see that 99 out of 100 campers think I'm right. So you see, I'm not biased. Can I help it if I am Chairman of the board of a company who has produced a true-grit camping stove that will probably outlast most of us?

I call an ace, an ace. And I call the Coleman Camp Stove, Grand-Daddy.

Berries for the Picking

Wild plums, fresh and sweet, hang temptingly in morning's dew.

by BRADFORD ANGIER

IT'S DIFFICULT to travel across a corner of North America, from the very deserts to the glittering ice cakes of the Arctic Ocean, that doesn't regularly yield wholesome and often delectable wild berries.

Besides the numerous common grapes, cherries, and plums, the uniquely flavored little wintergreens and the mulberries, there are startlingly red but less familiar berries of the staghorn sumac that, crushed in water and sweetened, give a drink like lemonade. Also not to be overlooked are the sustaining red berries of the kinnikinic, whose leaves are still a familiar backwoods tobacco substitute.

It's not hard to find the common blueberries, gooseberries, cranberries, and their ilk that every year fill out by the thousands of tons. And there are such abounding members of the rose family as strawberries, blackberries, and raspberries whose young stems and stalks are also tasty and whose leaves can be profitably steeped for tea.

Delicious wild foods grow everywhere. For example, there is a familiar berry that, although you've maybe never sampled it, has the flavor of fresh apples. More important, its juice is from six to 24 times richer in Vitamin C than even orange juice. Throughout much of the continent you can pick all you want the greater part of the year, even when temperatures fall a booming 60 degrees below zero. As for recognizing the fruit, no one with a respect for brambles and a modicum of outdoor knowledge is going to get the wrong thing by mistake. It is the rose hip, the ordinary seed pod of roses everywhere.

Some 35 or more varieties of wild roses *(Rosa)* thrive throughout the United States, especially along streams, roadsides, fences, open roads, and in meadows, often forming briary thickets. The hips or haws, somewhat roundly smooth and contracted to a neck on top, grow from characteristically fragrant flowers, usually pink, white, or red. Remaining on the shrubs throughout the winter and into the following spring, they are available for food in the North when other sources of nourishment are covered with snow.

These rose hips have a delicate flavor that's delectable. They're free. They're strong medicine, to boot. Studies in Idaho found the scurvy-preventing vitamin in the raw pulp running from 4,500 to nearly 7,000 milligrams a pound. Daily human requirements, estimated to be 60 to 75 milligrams, provide a yardstick for this astonishing abundance.

Three rose hips, the food experts say, have as much Vitamin C as an orange. We don't pay much attention to these gratuitous vitamins in the United States and Canada. But in England during World War II, some five million pounds of rose hips were gathered from the roadsides and put up to take the place of the then scarce citrus fruits. Dried and powdered, rose hips are sold in Scandinavian countries for use in soups, for mixing with milk or water to make hot and cold drinks, for sprinkling over cereals, etc., all of which they do admirably.

Even the seeds are valuable, being rich in Vitamin E. Some backwoods wives grind them, boil in a small amount of water, and then strain through a cloth. The resulting vitamin-rich fluid is used in place of the water called for in recipes for syrups, jams, and jellies.

Despite the name of highbush cranberry, this shrub of the *Viburnum* family, some 20 species of which occur in the U.S., is not a cranberry. A lot of people, too, object to its distinctively sweetish-sour odor and flavor. They do at first, that is. It has become one of my favorite berries, especially when I let a few frozen fruit melt on my tongue like sherbet in late fall and winter. I wouldn't swap the provocatively different jelly it makes for any other.

Wild berries are fine, extra food addition to any camp.

Kathy Farmer plucks fresh, clear-stream, watercress from brook.

The juicy red highbush cranberries, which often have an attractive orange hue, are also sometimes called squash berries and mooseberries. They are at their best for cooking just before the first softening frost, although they continue to cling to their stems throughout the winter and are thus one of the more useful emergency foods in Alaska, Canada, and the northern states, where they are to be found usually the year around. Even when soft and shriveled in the spring, they are particularly thirst-quenching, and once you get to recognize the clean but somewhat musty odor, you're never going to get the wrong berry by mistake.

Highbush cranberries grow as straggly or erect shrubs whose slender grey branches are generally all within reach of the average adult. The usually three-lobed leaves, whose edges are toothed, resemble those of the maple. Like those of that familiar tree, they become brilliant in the fall. The berries which are actually drupes, each enclosing a large flattened seed, appear in easily picked groups whose flavor becomes milder as they age.

Now for that beautifully sparkling, salmonish-red jelly of perfect texture and unique flavor! This latter will be improved if the still firm berries are picked before the first freeze, while about half ripe. Bring each 2 cups of these to a boil in 3 cups of water. Mashing them as they cook, simmer for 5 minutes. Then strain. Add ⅔-cup sugar to each cup of resulting juice and bring to a bubble. Then pour into hot, sterilized glasses and seal immediately. A lot of people don't care for this at first, but with repeated samplings many of them come to agree that there's no other jelly quite as good.

Also known as juneberries, the numerous members of the serviceberry (*Amalanchier*) family are used like the blueberries they resemble. Millions were once gathered to flavor pemmican. Four or five species of serviceberries, which are primarily North American shrubs and trees, are native in the East and up to about 20 in the West. Bearing delicious fruit from Alaska to Newfoundland and south to California and the Gulf of Mexico, they thrive in such habitats as open woods, rocky slopes and banks, and in swamps. Various other common names include saskatoon, shadbush, shadblow, shadberry, sugar pear, and Indian pear. Incidentally, some frontiersmen still make an eyewash from the boiled green inner bark.

The daintily conspicuous white, longish, five-petaled blossoms appear while the leaves are just expanding and are among the first spring flowers of our native woody plants. They cover the tough, flexible shrubs and small trees which have small alternate leaves, varying from elliptical to almost round and being at least partially toothed. These change from green to a beautiful rusty red in autumn. The loose bunches of berries, whose five-toothed summits cause them to resemble large blueberries, are red when young, becoming purplish or almost black.

The sweet juicy pulp surrounds ten large seeds, which add to the flavor when the fruit is cooked. As a matter of fact, although for years I have lived in our British Columbia log cabin within a few feet of enough serviceberries to supply a good-sized restaurant, I have never much cared for the fruit raw. Cooked, though, especially when the then mild sweetness is enlivened with acid, that's another story. Too, the cooked seeds become softer and impart an almond-like piquancy to the fruit.

Drying also considerably alters the otherwise rather insipid taste for the better. The serviceberries thus treated can be substituted in recipes for currants and raisins. The Indians used to preserve them this way by the thousands of bushels, spreading them in the sun and later beating some of them into a mash which was molded into cakes and dried. The dried berries were also used in puddings and in the famous pemmican which, if you want, you can duplicate today. Essentially, this most nourishing and notable of concentrated outdoor foods is, by weight, ½ well-dried lean meat and ½ rendered fat, both pounded together. Dried serviceberries are mixed in for flavoring.

Spicy little red wintergreen berries, which, when very young, I used to pick and eat on a New Hampshire slope slick with pine needles, are the first wild fruit I remember gathering. I still enjoy both them and the wintergreenish leaves of this small evergreen plant (Gaultheria) which is one of the most widely known of all the wild North American edibles. The some 25 names accorded it, including teaberry and checkerberry, support this conclusion.

The familiar wintergreen flavor, though, so common to drugstores and markets, is no longer made from this plant but, when not obtained synthetically, from the distilled twigs and sometimes shreds of bark of the black birch. In older times, quantities of wintergreen were gathered around October, dried, and then packed for shipping. Before the volatile oil was distilled off, they were soaked in water for about 24 hours, which will give you an idea if you ever want to make any of your own.

Wintergreens are diminutive members of the heath family, often thriving in the shade of evergreens. A pleasant part of the woods of the Northeast, this midget relative of the salas of the Pacific Coast grows in forests and clearings from eastern Canada to the Gulf States and as far west as the Great Lakes. Western wintergreen, *Gaultheria shallon,* grows on the other side of the continent from California to British Columbia. Although less spicy than the eastern species, the larger and still esteemed berries were highly regarded by the Indians.

The firm berrylike fruit of the wintergreens, which is inconspicuous though bright red, can be an important emergency food when found in great enough quantities,

Ah, fresh mint! Just right for tea or Juleps—mint is common find.

Hunting various kinds of berries can be fun for picker . . . and hound.

as it clings to the stems all winter. It is sometimes seen in the eastern markets and is often turned into pies. The only use I have ever made of these sweetly dry berries, though, has been to enjoy them while hunting, fishing, hiking, or just plain relaxing in the wilderness.

You can use the flowers of the common elderberry *(Sambucus)* in your cooking, feast on the berries, and make flutes from the limbs. As a matter of fact, some Indians knew this member of the honeysuckle family as "the tree of music" because of the way they made wind instruments from the straight stems. These were cut in the spring, dried with the leaves on, and then the soft and incidentally poisonous pith of their interiors was poked out with hot sticks. In fact, this is a way to make spouts for gathering sap from the maples, birches, and other trees.

The common or American elderberry, sometimes known as the sweet elder, is a shrub growing from 4 to 12 feet high and occasionally in the South reaching the proportions of a small tree. The stems often spring in erect groups from tangled roots in moist, fertile soil along fences, walls, roadsides, ditches, banks, streams, and in fields from the Maritime Provinces to Manitoba and south to Florida and the Gulf of Mexico.

Creamy flat clusters of blossoms, which decorate and pleasantly scent the *Sambucus canadensis* in June and July, are made up of dozens of tiny star-shaped flowers. In late summer and early fall these become juicy, round berries, each with three or four rough seeds.

Quantities of these purplish black berries can be picked in a hurry. But even when at their ripest, they are none too palatable. However, there's an easy way to improve the flavor. Just pick and clean the mature berries as usual. Then dry them on trays in the sun or oven or on outspread newspapers in a hot, dry attic. The difference will be astonishing, and this way they will keep well, too.

Partridgeberries *(Mitchella)* are so easily recognizable that they make a good emergency food. Too, they are available from autumn to spring, clinging conspicuously to the trailing evergreen shrubs throughout the winter. You will find them in moist woodlands and clearings from Nova Scotia and New Brunswick to Florida, west to Minnesota, Arkansas, and Texas. Other names include twin berries and checkerberries.

We have a single species of partridgeberry on this continent. Another grows in Japan. Ours is a slender, creeping vine, six to 12 inches long, putting down new roots along its prostrate stem. The small, shiny, smooth-edged leaves grow on short stems in opposite pairs. Dark green and sometimes white-veined, they are oval or heart-shaped and usually no more than ½-inch long on the average, although they run closer to ¾-inch in some sections.

The June flowers burst out in pairs, often with the past year's coral red berries. These fragrant pairs of ½-inch blossoms, each with four pinkish or white petals, grow together at their bases in such a way that it takes two blooms to make one berry. The fruit, too, has a Siamese-twin aspect.

It ripens during the usual fall hunting season, and I often enjoy its aromatic pleasantness while wandering through the woods. Although seedy and on the dry side, it will take the edge off hunger. Ruffed grouse, bobwhite, wild turkey, and small animals including the red fox like it, too.

As for kinnikinic *(Arctostaphylos)*, after you have filled up on the sustaining if blandly dry berries, you can make yourself a smoke with the leaves. Dried and pulverized, these have been a frontier tobacco substitute for centuries. They are both mixed with dwindling supplies of regular tobacco and smoked alone.

Dandelion greens, before the weed flowers, are good in salads or cooked.

Berries are found in many thickets throughout the country.

The widely distributed and easily recognizable kinnikinic should be better known, if only for possible use as a sustaining emergency food. Some of the other names that have become attached to it are mealberry, hog cranberry, upland cranberry, arberry, and especially bearberry. In fact, one of the best places to look for black bear after they have roused from their northern sleep in the spring is on a sunny hillside patch of kinnikinic.

Berry hunting in late summer, in combination with camping and cycling, adds an extra dimension to the outdoors.

Some berries can be picked fresh that morning and eaten for breakfast.

Kinnikinic is luxuriant across Canada, Alaska, and the tops of Asia and Europe. Preferring a sandy or gravelly upland habitat, this member of the heath family is found south to Virginia, New Mexico, and California. Grouse and other game birds pick its small fat berries. Deer browse extensively on its green, leathery foliage.

Chinook-bared hills around our log-cabin home are green in the very early spring, while snow is still deep in the woods, because of kinnikinic. This trailing perennial shrub with its long fibrous root forms a dense, matlike, evergreen carpet. The alternate egg-shaped leaves are short-stemmed, small, thick, and tough. The pink flowers, which are inconspicuous, grow like tiny bells that sway in terminal clusters. The sometimes pink berries, which are more often dull red with an orange cast, ripen in the fall.

One of the important things about these berries, especially when considered as potentially important emergency food, is that, hard or dry, they cling resolutely to the prostrate shrubs all winter. Otherwise, although mealy, they are rather tasteless. Cooking improves them considerably, however. Too, people depending on wild fruit sometimes gather them in poor berry years and mix them with blueberries.

Sumac "lemonade" is just the thing to take the edges off a hard afternoon. Pick over a generous handful of the red berries, drop them into a pan and mash them slightly, cover with boiling water, and allow to steep away from any heat until this is well colored. Then strain through two thicknesses of cloth to remove the fine hairs. Sweeten to taste, and serve either hot or cold.

Some Indian tribes liked this acid drink so much that they dried the small one-seeded berries and stored them for winter use. Many settlers learned from them and followed suit.

The rapidly growing staghorn sumac (*Rhus*), also called the lemonade tree and the vinegar tree, is one of the largest species of the cashew family, commonly reaching 10 to 20 feet in height. It is easily recognized at any season because of the close resemblance of its stout and velvety twigs to deer antlers while these are still in velvet. It ranges from the Maritime Provinces to Ontario, south to Georgia and Missouri.

The tiny, tawnily green flowers grow in loosely stemmed clusters, one sex to a shrub or tree. The male clusters are occasionally ten to 12 inches long. The female blossoms are smaller and extremely dense, producing compact bunches of berries. These are erect and so startlingly red that sometimes I've come upon a lone cluster suddenly in the woods and thought it was a scarlet tanager perched on a branch.

The hard red fruits are thickly covered with bright red hairs. These hairs are tart with malic acid, the same flavorsome ingredient found in grapes. Since this is readily soluble in water, the berries should be gathered for beverage purposes before any heavy storms if possible.

Incidentally, the berries of the poisonous sumacs are white. However, there are other sumacs in the United States and Canada with similar red berries that provide a refreshing substitute for pink lemonade. All these red-fruited species are harmless.

One of them is the smooth or scarlet sumac, *Rhus glabra*, which grows from the Maritimes to Minnesota, south to Florida and Louisiana. This closely resembles the staghorn sumac except that it is entirely smooth, with a pale bluish or whitish bloom coating the plump twigs.

Another is the dwarf, shining, or mountain sumac, *Rhus copallina*, which grows from New England and Ontario to Florida and Texas. Although similar to the aforementioned species, it can be distinguished from all other sumacs because of peculiar winklike projections along the leaf stems between the leaflets.

Indians made a poultice of the bruised leaves and fruit of the red-berried sumacs and applied it to irritated skin. An astringent gargle, made by boiling the crushed red berries in a small amount of water, is still used for sore throats.

Sashimi is produced from fresh caught fish by charter boat crew member.

FISH BONES NEED LOVE

by HELEN "TIGER" MARTIN

A SHARP FILLET KNIFE and a lineup of internationally proven recipes play key roles in my efforts to prepare fish. Husband Jim graciously assumes the cutting and cleaning duties, with our son, Jim, often a willing helper. Both males, however, tend to handle their knives as if they were machetes. Yet a bit of extra meat clinging to a fish carcass, fits into my culinary plans quite nicely.

Comedians who poke fun at fish-head soup would perhaps dance to a different tune if they had ever eaten a stew prepared from fish backbones. Should the idea make you feel squeamish, simply be Continental and call the concoction a *bouillabaisse* as they do in France. Chowders can also be prepared from the leavings of a fillet knife. Although both soups are delicious, I'm surprised at the many cooks who fail to utilize fish trimmings for this purpose.

Here's a technique I use to make chowder from striped bass.

After my two Jims have hacked off the fillets, they cut the carcass into manageable pieces—say about 8 inches long. The chunks are packaged into plastic sacks for the freezer. When in the mood for a fresh chowder, I thaw a package and proceed as follows:

FISH CHOWDER

1 package striped bass backbones (approx. one pound)
1 onion
2 potatoes
4 tablespoons butter
1 quart milk

I start each fish chowder by covering the bottom of a large soup kettle with about an inch of water. Into the pot goes a trivet, or small rack, upon which the pieces of fish carcass are placed. Do not allow the water to rise high enough to touch the fish and bones.

After inserting the fish, cover the kettle and bring the water to boil. Reduce heat and allow to steam for about 10 minutes. Be careful to "steam," not boil the fish. As the carcass steams, the juices will drip down into the water to become a delicious soup stock. Be careful not to steam so long that the water boils away.

Remove the steamed carcass from the water, allow to cool, then pick fish flakes from the bones. Set them aside in a bowl for later use. Striped bass have a tendency to be a bit "fatty" around the backbone, so this portion, which is easy to recognize, should be discarded.

In a soup kettle, melt four tablespoons of butter. Add the minced onion and diced raw potatoes. Cook until onion turns a light gold in color.

Strain the striped bass broth to remove any small bones, then add the liquid to the onion/potato mixture. Cook until potatoes are tender. Add fish flakes and one quart of milk. Heat until the mixture simmers and season with salt and pepper to taste. Do not allow to boil. If you are calorie conscious, low fat or powdered milk can be substituted, however the flavor will not be as rich.

One reason I don't mind the fact that the menfolk are not too delicate when wielding their fillet knives is that I prefer having a large quantity of fish flakes with which to work. After allowing enough fish for the chowder, I serve the rest as a fish cocktail. When dished up with a blending of chili sauce, Worcestershire sauce and lemon juice, it is every bit as delicious as crab, and quite similar in taste.

One of our favorite hors d'oeuvres is raw fish, or *sashimi*, which is so popular with Japanese connoisseurs. Striped bass is delicious when served in this fashion. It's an elegant tidbit that belongs in the "don't knock it until you try it" category. Actually, sashimi is not raw fish, but rather fish that has been quickly pickled in soy sauce and powdered hot radish called *wasabe*. It can be purchased at most oriental food

These small grayling can be fried crispy so there is no waste.

Proper filleting techniques mean enjoyable eating and little waste.

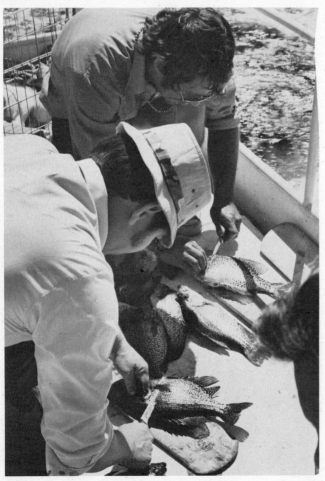

Lots of action here . . . and some of the best is yet to follow at camp.

shops; but if not, our dry mustard will give you a similar result.

Any firm, closely grained white fish makes excellent sashimi, but the striped bass is unsurpassed. I slice the fillets into paper thin pieces, which are then attractively arranged on a bed of finely shredded lettuce. Before eating, each piece should be dipped in the sauce, which makes for instant pickling.

Striped bass fillets can be prepared in a number of ways. Fried, baked or barbecued—all are delicious. Yet the real challenge and enjoyment comes when making full use of all portions of this excellent gamefish.

If striped bass are not available in your part of the country, you can make delicious soups with either lake trout or salmon. These pink-fleshed fish blend well with a vegetable soup base. Proceed with the steaming process as outlined. Strain this broth and add enough water to equal approximately 2 quarts. Into the kettle add onion slices, fresh or canned stewed tomatoes, green beans, sliced carrots and shredded cabbage. Simmer until the vegetables are tender. Add the boneless fish flakes and season with salt and

Flat, hard surface and sharp knife are keys to good filleting.

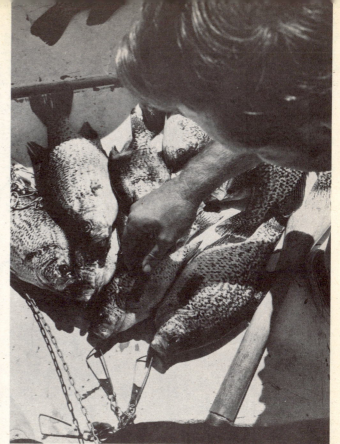

Even, thin slabbed crappie can be great eating when cleaned properly.

Largemouth bass from clear, clean waters make excellent table fare.

pepper to taste. A long-slow simmering process greatly enhances the flavor.

The beauty of these soups is that the variety is only limited by your imagination. Sometimes I add a clove or two of garlic, maybe some chopped parsley. If I have celery on hand, I'll chop up a stalk or two and add that. Try a bottle of clam broth in the soup for added flavor.

The same Dutch oven that performs yeoman's service on so many of our camping trips makes a practical fish pot for a bouillabaisse. Here you need the following ingredients.

1 large fish (3 to 5 pounds dressed weight)
2 large onions
½ head cabbage
4 fresh tomatoes
4 large potatoes
   seasoning—salt, pepper and thyme

Fillet and skin the fish. Cut fish into small chunks. Peel and slice the onions, potatoes and tomatoes. Shred the cabbage coarsely.

Oil the bottom and sides of the Dutch oven. Then alternate layers of ingredients. First fish, then potatoes, onions,

Just about every part of that large trout can be used.

cabbage and top with tomatoes. Sprinkle each layer with a scant amount of salt, pepper and a sprinkle of thyme. Repeat the layering and seasoning until all the ingredients have been used up or the kettle is full.

Cover the bottom of the kettle with approximately 2 inches of water, then cover and place in a 375-degree oven until the casserole commences to bubble. Reduce heat, then allow to simmer for 45 minutes. The bulk in the casserole will cook down to form a delicious stew.

If you wish to take the additional time to first steam the backbone, this strained broth can be used in the place of water to make a richer flavor.

COOKING MY MOTHER NEVER TOLD ME ABOUT

by VICKI TALLON

Sometimes our outdoor cooking is done inside and eaten outdoors. Learn to utilize storage space in campers.

MOTHER TAUGHT ME how to use ovens, stove burners, pressure cookers, rotisseries, broilers and barbecuers, but mother never told me about camp cooking and white gas stoves. I had seen the stoves in the sporting goods sections of department stores, but never realized that one day they would become an important part of my life. That era began when I married my husband, Jim, a man bent on life in the outdoors. On our first camping trip together—actually a fishing trip—he pulled a white gas stove from a burlap sack like a pearl from a soft, felt bag; I didn't have the slightest idea of how to light it. Jim twisted a knob and pulled on it to reveal it internally linked to the stove by a long rod. He pumped about 20 times, turned a lever up, and the stove hissed. Jim struck a match to a burner and BINGO, we had fire. Jim did the cooking too, and he made me feel a bit jealous by the delicious camp meals he turned out.

On our second trip together, we arrived at our Lee's Ferry campsite in northern Arizona in late afternoon, and Jim cooked dinner on the white gas stove. The following morning we crawled from our sleeping bags before daylight with plans to cruise our boat up the Colorado River to fish for rainbow trout. The campground at Lee's Ferry is maintained by the National Park Service and provides modern washrooms. Jim headed for one to shave.

I eyed the two-burner, white gas stove as if it were a bomb to be treated with respect. Then I took the bull by the horns, and twisted and pumped and turned and lit. The stove hissed and burned cheerily in the darkness of predawn. I was delighted. So was Jim. When he returned I had hot tea ready, and bacon, eggs, and potatoes cooking. And I had burned only one finger.

When we returned to Phoenix, use of the white gas stove still turned over in my mind. Despite the fact we ate well off of it, our present cooking arrangements left a lot to be desired. So I made some changes. Jim had somehow accumulated a bunch of old pots and pans, and skillets that were out-sized for the little stove and two-people cooking. I stored Jim's old utensils, and bought some new, smaller but deeper pots and pans, and two small skillets. Now I could use both burners on the stove and keep a third pot or pan between the two, literally giving me the near-efficiency of a three-burner stove. While cooking dinner, for example, I could fry pork chops in a skillet, perhaps potatoes in a second skillet, and heat up vegetables or soup in a pot between the burners. And I learned about lids, too.

At home I sometimes cook without lids. But one night cooking beneath a white gas lantern, various insects flew into the lamp to commit suicide, making doubly sure they got the job done by falling into hot mushroom soup and a skillet full of hamburger steaks. I understand that insects represent a certain amount of protein and that trout love them, but not me. After that, *all* open cooking utensils were covered. I also learned that lids can serve another purpose, warming foil-wrapped rolls.

Well, Mother had told me about pots and pans, and skillets and skewers, but Mother never told me about foil cooking. With our two-burner white gas stove, for instance, I asked myself how in the world do I bake biscuits on it. Foil, of course. I popped open a container of biscuits and folded them in foil, but not so tightly that steam couldn't escape, then put them in a skillet. After 10 minutes over a low flame, I turned the package over for another 10

On one of our first trips, with Steve Frank along, I learned about too-big-skillets and that husbands are likely to invite fishing friends to dinner.

minutes. Certainly this was slower than baking store-bought biscuits at home, but they came out just as delicious. Maybe more. After that, foil became just as important as pots and pans, and skillets in our camp cooking; and its use is limited only by your imagination.

One of our foil favorites is trout and corn on the cob. Husk the corn carefully so you don't tear up the husks, placing them aside to be used again. Remove all the cornsilk, then butter the cobs liberally and salt and pepper. Now rewrap in the husks and foil, and cook over coals for 20 to 30 minutes. For the trout, you can use fillets or whole, cleaned fish. Simply butter, salt, pepper and squeeze on some lemon juice, then bake over coals about 15 minutes. Of course, put the longer-to-cook corn on first and turn both corn and trout frequently. You may have to make some time variations because of the heat of your particular fire. But when properly cooked—delicious!

Mother taught me how to make jerky, can pickles and preserve peaches, but mother never told me about plastic food bags. I owe that one to my brother, who gave Jim and me one of those heat-sealing devices and a supply of plastic bags for Christmas. With this clever gadget I can cook up camp meals ahead of time, seal them in plastic, freeze them, then take them with us for simple camp cooking. We use the heat-sealer to package dishes such as casseroles, beef stroganoff, lasagna, and chili, and also frozen desserts. Before you seal the bags and freeze their contents, remember to squeeze out as much air as possible. This makes the package more compact and stores better; it should be no more than one-inch thick. This permits it to freeze fast and to thaw quickly when needed. Next to ice in your camp cooler, these packages will stay frozen for days. You can slip them into hot water to hasten thawing, but the bags are not designed for cooking. The food should be removed from them for re-heating. After fishing or hunting all day, then returning to camp after dark, these plastic-packaged meals are prizes for tired outdoor people.

I was raised in the Rocky Mountains of central Utah, and camping for our family meant a trip from our farm in the valley to our grandfather's homestead in the mountains at round-up time. We could load a pickup truck with bedding, saddles, and boxes of food then drive the zig-zagging road to the ranch. There we "camped" in a log cabin with a bunkhouse large enough to house a dozen of us. We cooked over a wood-burning stove and had to get water from a pump outside. After rounding up cattle and horses, the men would come back to camp for dinner of

(Facing page). In the mountains of Idaho, we camp by tent and cook outside. By now I have learned a lot of things that Mother never told me.

In the National Park Service Campground at Lee's Ferry, Arizona, my husband and I look down on the Colorado River after breakfast. It was here I first learned to camp.

the likes of stew, corn on the cob and fresh pie, baked from berries my cousins and I had gathered that afternoon. When dinner was over, a fire would be built outside where we could roast marshmallows; there was always a grate over the fire and camp coffee percolating on it. We would listen, shuddering, to the ghost stories my uncles would tell. All this gave me an affinity for camping, while my mother was teaching me how to feed large numbers of people. She also taught me about chokecherries, gooseberries, acorns and pinyon nuts, but Mother never told me about fishing nuts, or what to expect from them.

In the beginning I planned meals for two people, Jim and I, and maybe packed enough to camp one extra day. We wanted to travel light. But my husband is likely to invite numerous people he has met on the stream, or beach or lake, or the lonely guy in the next campsite, for dinner or breakfast the next day, on the spur of the moment. To compensate for this, I have learned to make a checklist, shop carefully, and carry more and a greater variety of food. In the process, we eat more balanced meals and can change our pre-planned menu if we like. In my childhood days, we ate the same delicious food up on the homestead in the mountains that we did at home, and on our present-day camp trips, Jim and I apply the same theory: a well-fed person will get by better mentally and physically, especially while camping. If you try to prove how tough you are by neglecting proper diet, then you may wreck your whole camp trip. More than once we have literally shocked our camping friends, who expected little more than cold meat and bread for dinner, by serving meals comparable to posh restaurants, complete with wine in chilled wine glasses; and real dishes, not paper plates. This has converted a number of our friends to our style of camp cooking. Some of these meals are prepared with two-burner, white gas stoves, but we now carry a hibachi for the more sophisticated cooking of meats and other foods as well. This applies when we are over-night camping in a parking lot on a San Diego wharf prior to a long-range fishing trip; at the Outdoor Writers Conferences—which may be tent-camping; and on the beaches of Mexico as well.

Mother taught me how to shop for home use, what to store in cabinets and cupboards, but Mother never told me what goes in the storage compartments of a cab-over camper. One of my first lessons came when Jim spotted a herd of antelope in the backcountry of northern Arizona; my husband makes part of our living through wildlife photography and on sight of the antelope, we spent an extra, unplanned, day shooting, and trying to shoot, pictures of the spooky animals. My food supply didn't include lunch or dinner for a day of chasing antelope. However, I found some C-ration cookies beneath a seat compartment in the camper, and with hot tea they didn't taste too bad. After that, though, I made sure the camper always contained a certain amount of "emergency" foodstuffs.

First, I appraised the space available for food storage, considering the fishing rods, chestwaders, jacks and other tools, and camping and fishing gear already in them. I then fitted some cardboard boxes into the spaces, cutting out the tops or sides for access. Inside these boxes I grouped our foodstuffs, i.e. tea, coffee, hot chocolate, instant soups and cream, and salt and pepper; biscuit mix, instant dinners, crackers and cookies in a second; canned fruits and vegetables in a third, and so on. This beat letting these items bounce around loose in the compartments, having the labels torn off by jack handles or having glass bottles and jars broken, or losing some only to have them reappear weeks later in the foot of the chestwaders.

Of course I give much thought to the selection of foods, especially those relatively easy to prepare without adding other ingredients, such as macaroni, and canned foods that need only to be heated. With part of the emphasis on space, we have compacted foods that came in bulky cartons. For example, we buy teabags in 100-bag boxes; we cut this back to 25 for storing in the camper, sufficient to last six or eight camping trips. I make regular checks of the quantity of food in our compartments so that we don't run short in any category. If you don't have adequate space to store a goodly supply of necessities, you might consider the following list as an emergency package to be carried in your vehicle at all times, along with your campstove:

2 Cans of stew, chili, or chunky-style soups
2 Cans of prepared dessert such as tapioca
2 Cans of vegetables such as peas or corn
Cookies and crackers
Canned pop

The above require no extra water and fit neatly into a

Our first enclosed camper. Here I learned to compact supplies, and to do all our cooking outdoors. The campsite is Organ Pipe National Monument in southern Arizona.

Sometimes simple outdoor meals are the best. We stop for a picnic lunch in the southern Arizona desert.

small cardboard box. If you have more adults to feed, you will need to proportionately increase your food supply. In a real emergency, you can get by without a stove, building a small fire and heating the food in their own cans. Be sure to open the can, though, to allow steam to escape.

Mother taught me about refrigerators and freezers, but mother never told me about camp iceboxes. If you like fresh foods, then the camp icebox rates as the most important "appliance" on the trip. We prefer fresh and fresh-frozen foods over canned and freeze-dried. We also like to keep a large supply of fresh meats on hand during our camp trips. In winter we get by on one icebox; the colder temperatures outside the box help prolong the ice inside and subsequently keep frozen foods longer. In summer we use two iceboxes. We store food for the first part of the trip in icebox number one, and food for the second part in icebox number two. The latter is not opened until absolutely needed. If the outing is to be an extended one, then we'll wrap icebox number two in a dacron sleeping bag or a couple of blankets for additional insulation. Without dry ice, we have managed to keep our steaks and other meats, and frozen packages of fruits and vegetables solidly frozen for many days. Most campers we know tend to ignore an icebox that has suddenly been exposed to the sun; and children may fan the top, or get into it for a soft drink then walk away, leaving the top open. Ice goes in a hurry under this kind of treatment. On our trips we have an "icebox guard" who explains that the icebox must be kept in the shade and closed as much as possible. Never, never do we put warm items in the boxes, such as six-packs of beer or pop. We buy these things already chilled or chill them ourselves *before* stocking in the boxes.

Mother taught me a lot of things. Some of the things she never told me about weren't even invented when I was a child at home. Of course the white gas camp stove has been around for a long time, but Mother was never a camper. That is, until today. In the past few years she has sampled the outdoors, camp style; and it has opened a whole new world for her. She knows how to get the most from camp stoves, how to use foil, and freezing with plastic bags. She knows what gets stocked for camping and her emergency supply in the back of her station-wagon would impress the most discriminating gourmet. And she has camp iceboxes of her own. Mother has learned a lot of new things herself in the past few years, and I imagine that she will be only too happy to tell me about them.

Hiking across Rocky Mountain meadows will lead any outdoorsman to countless plants which are edible and suitable for Rocky Mountain salads.

ROCKY MOUNTAIN

SALADS

by JENNY REID

THE MISERABLE TRUTH of the Salad Matter is that most of them aren't worth the trouble and cost of putting them on the table. The ordinary salad is served for one or more of several reasons: it looks refreshing, the salad course is traditional and/or greens are good for you. Well, supermarket greens probably don't do much, if anything, for your nutrition. Often one-third of the vitamins and minerals have departed within one hour of the picking. Habit (tradition) is not a good reason for doing anything; and although the crisp leaves may look good, chances are they are utterly devoid of taste. Any pleasurable sensation at all is due to a fine dressing or added delights such as avocado slices, bacon bits or grated cheese.

May I, at this dismal point, interject a note of hope?

Consider Rocky Mountain Salads. Tender, young greens full of healthful nutrients growing in shades of green from the palest chartreuse to emerald, abundant, and in most cases free for the picking. These savory morsels do not rely on extras; they're delicious with almost no kitchen treatment. If proof is needed, may I point out that every one of the usable greens is robust enough to be excellent steamed and buttered in a casserole or to give extra flavor to a stew. Commercial salad ingredients cannot equal their fresh wild cousins in any area. So whether you live in our Rocky Mountain West or will only be able to visit us, give our way a try. You may never be satisfied with a cardboard and tissue paper salad again.

By Rocky Mountain Region, I refer to the northern areas of Arizona and New Mexico northward through the mountainous regions of Colorado and Utah, most of Wyoming, western Montana, eastern Washington and Oregon and the whole of Idaho. As in all mountainous regions the vegetation encountered depends more on the altitude of the area than its latitudinal distance from the equator. However, even when the altitude favored by a particular plant is mentioned, be flexible. This can, and often is, further influenced by whether you find yourself (or the plant finds itself) on the sunny side of the slope or not, whether in or near a damp gully, the prevailing winds and a host of other considerations.

No one need concern himself with altitude, slope or much of anything else when collecting one of the most abundant edibles in nature—the dandelion. We all know this one and can recognize its leaves and flowers instantly. The dandelion is a native of Eurasia, but it has colonized almost universally to the regret of those who work toward a "weed"-free lawn.

For the best salads the leaves should be gathered before —repeat *before*—the flower stalks appear, from rich moist areas where the leaves grow rapidly. Tender young dandelions can be found almost any time during the summer. Conservative botanists count about 50 varieties and of these, six grow in the Rocky Mountain Region. The outdoor cook/salad maker need not distinguish between them; all varieties make a fine dish. Fresh, young greens are delicious with a mild dressing, with chopped hard-cooked egg and mixed with other greens. Later in the season when the buds and flowers appear, the leaves have become bitter and are best passed over.

Consider a hot dandelion salad delicious with rabbit or squirrel dishes. Pick more leaves than you think you could possibly use; the smaller, the better. Wash and pat dry. Make the dressing using a half cup of slightly thinned evaporated milk, two eggs, one tablespoon sugar, one teaspoon salt, four tablespoons vinegar, butter the size of an egg, paprika and salt and black pepper to taste. Beat the ingredients and cube and fry four thick slices of bacon.

The edges of beaver ponds, which provide plenty of moisture, nourishment and let the sun shine through to growing plants, is where dandelions and wild lettuce and other leafy greens flourish.

Slowly pour the dressing into the fat, stirring constantly. This soon thickens and at this point remove from the heat and stir in onion rings cut from two medium onions. Now pour over the dandelions and toss thoroughly. Serve hot to a band of smiling outdoorsmen.

Another familiar leafy green for a salad is watercress. This plant will be best known to two very distinct groups; the social-group-afternoon-tea type lady, who may have nibbled literally hundreds of tiny sandwiches filled with the leaves over the years, and the trout fisherman. Watercress grows in floating mats in cold water. These form excellent cover for young fish and at the same time harbor fresh-water shrimp, snails, and numerous aquatic insects upon which trout feed. Watercress grows from the lowest elevations to about 8000 feet. All but the toughest stems are chopped and used alone as a delightful, tangy salad or in combination with other greens, shredded raw carrot, diced celery or chopped cucumber. Americans are certainly not the first to recognize the fine qualities of watercress. It has been cultivated in Europe where it originated for centuries. Xenophon highly recommended it to the Persians; the Romans considered it a good food for the insane and in western India it is prized by the Mohammedans.

Watercress prefers clean cold waters, but is rather more tolerant than some other plants and can also be found in free flowing springs, ranch drainage ditches, roadside wet areas and pools. Unfortunately, with civilization growing and polluting our environment as it is, it would be well to be quite certain of the purity of the water before serving the salad. If there is any doubt, soak the cress for half an hour in water in which a halazone tablet has been dissolved. These little white discs can be obtained at almost every drug or sporting goods store and are very inexpensive. Every outdoor cook should have a bottle of these tablets anyway to drop into any water whose purity is in question.

Having said unkind (but true!) things about commercial lettuces, I must now endeavor to direct the Rocky Mountain outdoor cook toward better things. The best of the wild lettuces may well be *Lactuca scariola,* and if that sounds like more than it's worth to say, try some of the common names—prickly lettuce, blue-flowered lettuce or chicory lettuce. The leaves resemble dandelion leaves, but are more sharply toothed. They grow from two to 12 inches long and later in the season produce lovely blue composite flowers on a single stem one to four feet tall. Please don't wait until the leaves are a foot long, though, or until the flowers appear; gather the young leaves and new shoots when they first appear, the latter part of June. Look for this lettuce in medium dry to moist soil to 7000 feet. In general, milky-juiced plants should not be eaten, but this plant like Pink Milkweed and Salsify, which we will get to shortly, is an exception.

To make a salad difficult to surpass, gather enough tender young wild lettuce for four, which will be at least four cups. Wash them gently, dry with the same care and keep in a cool place. Mix together a little celery salt, ½-teaspoon dry mustard, fresh ground pepper to taste and a minced clove of garlic. While stirring add ¼-cup lemon juice, and then a teaspoon of finely chopped pickles. Gradually mix in ¾-cup salad oil. Meanwhile fry eight slices of bacon until crisp, toss the greens with the dressing and with two tablespoons of the hot bacon fat. Garnish with crumbled bacon. Superb.

Another good ingredient is dock or curley dock which is grown in or infests, depending on your vantage point, much of the temperate areas of the world. It is a smooth-leaved, dark green plant with curly or wavy leaf margins. The flowers are inconspicuous, but you may identify this plant when you know that in the fall tiny reddish-brown grains appear which resemble coffee grains. Look for it in moist areas to 6000 feet. The early spring leaves mixed with dandelion leaves or mustard or watercress make an excellent salad. Because of its somewhat lemonish flavor, you may prefer to skip the vinegar in the dressing, using oil only. This may be the time for that first-press olive oil plus salt and pepper. Dock has a more sturdy flavor than most other leaves and with that bit of tartness, a dressing with a hardy flavor is called for.

Milkweed is familiar to everyone and the young shoots are delicious before they reach eight inches in height. After that, but before the flower buds have formed, use the top leaves in salad either alone or with other varieties of greens. Later in the season the young pods are delicious. Be sure they're very firm to the touch or you may end up with a mouthful of what feels like feathers.

The young shoots from wild cucumber are good too. Pick them in the very early spring. Do you know them as twisted-stalk, or liver-berry? Shred lots of the tender young wild cucumber shoots into very small pieces to fill a medium sized bowl. Cover with slices of an onion and pour over all a heaping cup of sugar. Stir the whole works well and let it sit in a cool place. Then add a ¼-cup of mild vinegar plus salt and pepper and enjoy. This plant

Spiny and prickly on the outside, the core of this elk thistle is tasty cooked as a vegetable or in a crisp salad.

A Rocky Mountain trout fisherman uses his net to gather morel mushrooms.

grows in wet and boggy areas higher by two or three thousand feet than the other edibles mentioned and by fortunate chance nodding (or wild) onion grows here too. Why not go really wild and use those instead of the cultivated variety? There are more than 50 different species of onions in the Rocky Mountains. Surely you can find one!

And still there are many more ingredients for wild salads: the leaves of sow thistle, when young, are tasty with an oil and vinegar dressing with a little crumbled Roquefort cheese added. Purslane or spring beauty is a native to India and Persia where it has been a food for 2000 years. It spread to Europe and was an early arrival

Snow mushrooms appear immediately following the receding snows and are wonderfully edible.

in the New World. Since colonial times it has distributed itself to almost every area in America. In Massachusetts someone wrote, "I learned that a man may use as simple a diet as the animals, and yet retain health and strength. I have made a satisfactory dinner off a dish of purslane which I gathered and boiled. Yet men have come to such a pass that they frequently starve, not for want of necessaries, but for want of luxuries." The author is Thoreau and the date was over a century ago.

The roots of knotweed (snakeweed or bistort), silverweed (tansy) and fireweed are all fine salads when chopped if young, or boiled, cooled and sliced when older.

Wild celery stalks are honestly better than any you can buy in a store. This is also called angelica and grows in damp shady spots from sea level to 8500 feet. We often pick off a piece and chew on it while hiking mountain trails. The stem is juicy, cool and delicious. Look for the large coarse leaves and flat umbel of white flowers atop this tall plant. This, like all members of the parsley family, should be identified with certainty before eating as a few members of the family are poisonous.

No study of Rocky Mountain Salads is complete without mention of salsify (also known as meadow salsify, goatsbeard and oysterplant). The stem grows from one to four feet in height with yellow, single flowers two to three inches across. The leaves look like grass and clasp the stem. Salsify carpets Jackson Hole, Wyoming, and thrives along fence rows and in waste areas across most of the U.S. to 7000 feet. Probably the most distinctive feature of the salsify is the huge, globular seed head which resembles a dandelion seed-head. When young the tops are fine in salads and as cooked greens. The root is the most often used part, however. Boiled, it tastes to some like parsnip and to others like oysters. Cool the simmered (young) product, slice it and toss with a watercress dressing for a remarkably zesty salad, all the better garnished with bacon.

As we have said, mixing varieties of salad greens and adding any of the edible roots can make a fine and interesting dish. We also mentioned the wild onion family which is familiar to almost everyone and adds tang, but there is one thing we have not gone into—mushrooms. And for obvious reason. Although unsurpassed either raw

One of the few common plants of the high West without known uses is the beautiful green gentian.

or cooked when properly chosen, they can be dangerous or even fatal if incorrectly identified and eaten.

Mushrooms are a fungi, as is generally known. Usually the edible varieties are called mushrooms and the inedible, toadstools. These members of "The Third Kingdom" are not plants as they have no chlorophyll, no roots, or stems or leaves. Common tests for safety are useless—the silver spoon test, the bread-crumb and the clove of garlic. Feeding a doubtful specimen to a dog or cat is cruel and besides their reaction may very well differ from yours. Even when a mushroom is correctly identified as harmless (even delicious), it can become poisonous as a result of deterioration. Frost, for example, can make the most desirable fungi dangerous. And ptomaine poisons—similar to those produced by the putrefaction of food in general—will occur in over-ripe fungi.

However, here in the Rocky Mountains, there are three varieties which we identify, pick and eat with great pleasure. There's the snow mushroom, which looks for all the world like a mahogany-colored, wrinkled brain. It grows just at the edge of the melting snow mass and is unsurpassed in a salad with watercress which is just then emerging, chopped hard-cooked egg and either an oil and vinegar dressing or something cheesy.

Another of our "absolutely-identifieds" is the morel. Although not plentiful in the Rocky Mountain region, it is found here and there. I suspect that there are those who know where they grow in abundance but just aren't telling. The third type is the well-known puffball. We find them rather frequently and they range in size from tennisball diameter to volley-ball size. Those smaller we leave, hoping to return later to reap a larger fruit.

A great deal of knowledge about wild edibles came to us from the Indians. Most of us think of Indians eating mainly meat—deer, sheep (remember the Sheepeaters?), bear, buffalo, etc. But the fact is that these animals were constantly on the move and that they could only be brought down by fairly sophisticated methods. Therefore, there were many, many times when the tribes subsisted entirely on plant matter. Indians were fine botanists and few plants grew in their territories which they couldn't identify and put to use either as food or for medicinal purposes. A vast lore was passed down through the generations and this knowledge accounts for their very survival. The white man learned from the Indians as he moved westward. Lewis and Clark's expedition traded trinkets for plant food. Others, such as John Colter, Truman Everts and Hugh Glass who played major roles in early Western history, owed their lives to their familiarity with wild, emergency foods. Such knowledge was the difference between success and disaster.

Today, less than 150 years later, we have seen the Indians confined to reservations; farmers have plowed the prairies; loggers have changed the face of our forests and only a pitifully few wild streams remain unchained. The buffalo herds are no more and we draw lots to harvest a moose or antelope. Very little of the primitive West remains except the plants. They are no longer vital to survival as they once were, but are instead a luxury; a tangible and delicious reminder of a way of life gone forever.

Fresh trout and a fresh Rocky Mountain salad are sufficient excuse to make a backpacking trip.

MENU

Cooking and eating fish right where you caught them rounds out a fishing day and prepares you for tomorrow's adventures.

COOK YOUR FISH WHERE YOU CATCH THEM

by DICK KOTIS

IT'S NO BIG THING to prepare and cook delicious fish dinners on the lake shore, the ocean beaches or even on the ice.

Here are several ways I have found to come up with outdoor cooked fish that rival the best restaurant or home cooked recipes.

A small grub box can easily be stowed in the boat, the camper or back in the tent. In it are all the equipment and ingredients needed to produce memorable outdoor fish feasts.

For fish cook-outs I carry the following:

Supplies
  Vegetable-base cooking oil in plastic jug
  Box of prepared pancake mix
  Beer in cans
  Eggs
  Salt
  Butter
  Onions
  Lemon—whole
  Chili sauce
  Horseradish

Equipment
  Two burner propane or white gas stove
  Filleting knife
  Frying pan
  Deep pan
  Mixing bowl
  Silverware
  Spatula
  Strainer spoon
  Roll paper towels
  Roll aluminum foil
  Very Important—Deep frying thermometer

Using the above ingredients and equipment a day's catch may be prepared in at least six different ways. By bringing in four or five species of fish at least 30 varied tastes and textures are available. It's pretty hard to get tired of fish when offered this many choices.

Some of my favorite fish dishes are:

1. Deep fried fish chunks in beer batter

Use a gas camp stove. Almost any salt or fresh water fish is fine. Slice off the fillets and skin them. Cut along the top of the rib bones and discard bony piece. Cut the fillets into one by two inch rectangles. In a bowl mix the following:
  1 cup prepared pancake mix
  1 cup beer
  1 egg
  Salt to taste

Drop fish chunks into batter. Using the deep frying thermometer bring two inches of cooking oil in deep pan to 375 degrees F. Drop no more than five chunks of battered fish into hot oil. (Too many chunks will excessively cool the oil.) Very important—maintain 375 degree oil temperature by regulating the stove's burner. Turn the chunks over once in the oil. When they turn golden brown they are done.

Remove fish with large strainer spoon. Place them on several thicknesses of paper towel to remove excess oil. Sprinkle with lemon juice and eat happily.

Dick Kotis, president of the Fred Arbogast Company, designs, manufactures, and tests all kinds of fishing lures. A master fisherman, he knows what he is talking about when he speaks about the best ways of preparing fish.

The super-fresh fish makes one feel like royalty in spite of blue-jeans, waders and your favorite fishing hat.

Note—when you are finished and the oil is still warm, strain it and replace in container for next time.

I've used this recipe for everything from bluegills to Chinook salmon and bluefish to sharks. The pancake flour-beer combination produces a very light crisp coating.

2. Sautéed fish fillets

Use either the camp stove or hardwood fire coals. Melt a chunk of butter in frying pan over low heat. Cook skinned and deboned fillets very slowly—butter should barely bubble. When meat flakes easily, drain on paper towels, salt to taste and serve. For best results fillets for sautéing should not be over one-half inch thick.

3. Fish in foil

Build a hardwood fire and burn down to coals. Scale, behead and eviscerate the fish. Medium size fish such as trout or bass can be used whole. Larger fish such as salmon should be cut vertically into two or three chunks.

Place chunks of butter and onion in cavity and wrap fish in aluminum foil—air tight. Bony fish such as pike are more enjoyable to eat if you use only the tail section from the vent back. Place the packages right on the coals and turn every five minutes. In 25 minutes the fish should

By taking time out to fry, bake or boil fish your "secret" way, your fishing buddies can't help but be impressed.

be done. The flaky white meat cooked in its own juices plus butter is hard to equal. We eat our foiled fish right out of the aluminum wrapper.

4. Roasted fish on a stick

Build a hardwood fire and burn down to coals. Wash and eviscerate the fish. Do not scale and leave the head on.

Push a sharpened ½-inch diameter peeled stick lengthwise through the fish from head to near the tail. Salt lightly and roast the fish over coals like you would a hot dog. When you can easily stick a fork or twig through the fish it is ready to eat.

5. Fish baked in clay

Build a hardwood fire and burn down to coals. This Indian cooking method is sure to impress your companions. First find a seep or spring and dig up a few handfuls of blue or grey clay. It should be the consistency of putty. Scale, behead and eviscerate the fish, place chunks of butter inside. Form a one-inch thick clay coating over the entire fish. Wet your hands and smooth over the surface of the messy glob. Place the glob in the coals, cover with more coals and cook for about 20 minutes. Break open the hard shell lengthwise and eat the steamy white meat right out of the hardened clay dish.

6. Fish cocktail

Here is a sleeper which can be served as a main course or appetizer.

Fillet, skin, cut off and discard the rib bone section of any salt or fresh water fish. Flounder or bluegills are great. Cut larger fish into chunks. Half-fill the deep pan with lightly salted water and bring to a boil over the camp stove. Drop the small fillets or chunks into boiling water. When water returns to boil, cook for two or three minutes.

Quickly remove fish from water and drain. If you have ice, chill fish quickly; if not, cool by spreading out on paper plates. Prepare a dip from chili sauce and horseradish. Dip the pieces of fish in hot sauce and compare the results with those expensive shrimp or crabmeat cocktails.

Of course the old standby shore lunch method of dust-

Roast fish melts in your mouth. You have a hard time not making a glutton out of yourself.

ing fish fillets with flour and frying them in bacon grease or cooking oil makes good eating, however, if you are watching that cholesterol count or those extra pounds several of the above recipes will serve you better.

Like those ever-present breakfast grits south of the Mason-Dixon, it is almost automatic to dip a fish fillet in egg and corn meal for a southern fish fry. They taste pretty good but remind me slightly of chewing on sandpaper. My Cracker friends will climb on me for this statement.

Here is a tip on preparing fish that will make you an instant expert. If you have 110 volts available in your camper or at the campground use a regular electric carving knife to zip off and skin your fillets. It does a neat job everytime.

A new 12-volt electric knife has just come on the market. This one can be clamped to your car, camper or boat battery.

To keep your fish ultra-fresh and at their very best, carry a well-iced insulated cooler while fishing. Place the fish you decide to eat in a heavy-duty plastic bag and put them on top of the ice. Fish which contact water, even cold melted ice, for any length of time lose something taste-wise.

If no ice is available remove the gills and entrails. Wipe fish clean inside and out with paper towels. Wrap the fish in moss, ferns or other leafy vegetation and keep in the shade until ready to cook.

An evaporator cooler can be made using an open wooden box covered with frequently wetted down burlap. Hang it in the shade.

Another way to keep perishables cool if you run out of ice is to place them in a heavy-duty plastic bag. Tie a stout line to the neck of the bag. Add a weight to the line (not the bag) and drop the whole thing into deep water near the campsite. Don't forget to tie a float to the upper end of the line. It's cold down there even on the hottest days. Butter, bacon, fish and eggs will keep fresh for days.

If your fishing buddies don't come back for seconds of your outdoor culinary endeavors prepared according to one of the above suggestions, fry your fish in bacon grease and pass the baking soda.

The Cree Indians of Saskatchewan, Canada "Ponass" fish. The same result may be obtained by roasting the fish on a stick, much the way you roast hotdogs.

Moods and spirits are bright during Christmas tree hunt in Wyoming as chestnuts roast over open fire.

CHESTNUTS ROASTIN' ON AN OPEN FIRE

by CHARLES J. FARMER

Chestnuts are split to keep them from exploding off the grill.

Hotdogs and sausage are grilled over fire with green sticks.

JACK FROST WAS NIPPING at our noses and for good reason. It was 15 degrees on that icy December morning in Wyoming and a stiff wind was blowing in from the north.

"What a day to cut Christmas trees," I muttered to my wife, Kathy, as she huddled alongside me in our four-wheel-drive vehicle. "Wonder how the boys will take it?" she questioned as we came to a halt at the first of four houses along our pickup route. "Don't worry about them," I quipped. "They'll be bouncing around like rabbits."

Kathy and I had decided to do something different that year in hopes of elevating the Christmas spirit somewhat. As a clinical psychologist in Cheyenne, Wyoming, two years ago, she came in contact with several boys, whose ages ran from 11 to 14. The boys were having some trouble at school ... and at home. Nothing serious. They were just a bit mixed up and my wife and I teamed up to see if we couldn't get them on the outdoor track. A December Christmas tree hunt in the Medicine Bow National Forest, west of Laramie, would give the boys a good taste of the snow laden pine forests. The U.S. Forest Service encouraged tree harvesting in designated areas and we were looking forward to hand picking the trees that would cradle tree top angels, strings of popcorn and cranberries and twinkling lights.

The tree cutters were eager and ready too. It wasn't long before we were on Interstate 80 heading west.

Near the entrance to the tree cutting area we purchased tree cutting permits from the ranger. He headed us in the right direction and within 10 minutes, wood saws, rope and two rucksacks were unloaded. The boys buckled their rubber boots and pulled their woolen stocking caps down over their heads. We looked like a band of lumberjacks as we powdered through the deep snow. There would be good, full trees about a quarter of a mile off the road.

Nearly two hours passed before all the trees had been selected and cut. Each boy sawed down his own pine. We then collected boughs for wreaths and decorations. A couple of large, plastic garbage bags proved handy for collecting pine cones. Left as is, or painted, the cones would make great tree decorations and could be wired on to the natural pine wreaths.

The boys were really soaking up the snow when Kathy asked if anyone was hungry. A unanimous "yes" boomed through the forest and eager eyes were glued on my wife as she unpacked the ingredients of a winter outdoor feast from the two rucksacks.

Kathy and I, after many winter camping experiences,

have discovered that snowtime food has to be something special. Sure it has to taste good and be nourishing at the same time. But it has to have a warm, psychological flavor that is good for mind and body both. We gear our menu planning by the length of the trip and how much weight we can carry. That day we decided on a Christmas "mini-feast" that most of the boys probably had never sampled.

I started a small pine wood fire from dead, dry twigs and branches. The boys helped me collect the tinder for our blaze. Then they watched as I held a wooden match under the mound of "twiggies." The wood was dry enough so that it ignited on the first match and the boys cheered. Then we added bigger twigs and soon had a good fire going.

"We will build a good bed of coals with some bigger branches," I told the boys. They promptly gathered enough wood to last for two days. While the flames were still licking the frosty air, Kathy laid our backpack grill over the fire bed and on top of the grill placed a two-quart kettle filled with apple cider. "I even remembered the cinnamon sticks," she boasted.

"How many of you guys ever had chestnuts roasted over an open fire?" I asked. No one had. "How many of you have ever had chestnuts?" No one. "Okay, you are in for a treat."

Chestnuts, usually the Italian variety, can commonly be purchased in most large supermarkets during the fall and early winter. In the eastern states, some small groceries often carry them loose in vegetable or nut bins. Most often, they are packaged in plastic bags. They are relatively popular around Thanksgiving time when used for chestnut gravy and dressing. But many persons, including a good share of adults, have never sunk their teeth into a steamy, delectable chestnut. The flavor is different . . . often taking some time to get used to. But once you do, you get hooked.

With my pocket knife, I made a quarter-inch slit in each chestnut. This prevents them from popping (exploding is a more accurate word) off the grill and sinking in the snow. With the grill directly on top of the coals, I positioned the nuts on top of the embers. As hot as those coals were, the chestnuts would still take about 20 or 30 minutes to roast. When the outer skin or shell of the chestnut cracks or peels back where the knife cut was made, that is usually a good enough indication that it is hot and steamy and well done.

Kathy poured generous servings of hot cider and added a cinnamon stick in each cup as we waited for the chestnuts to roast. Already the aroma of the roasting morsels was catching the attention of the boys. "Hope they taste as good as they smell," little Jimmie Smith bubbled. "Don't worry about that."

After the cider was consumed, Kathy filled the kettle with snow and melted it over the fire. She readied packets of instant hot chocolate. Essential ingredients to winter outings are plenty of hot drinks. Hot chocolate is a real energy and morale builder. Ready to serve packs are handy. Or you can mix your own instant drink by adding instant milk (and sometimes sugar) to powdered cocoa. Servings of instant chocolate can then be packaged in plastic baggies, and stored in a rucksack or food bag.

The chestnuts were done. I slid the grill off the coals and put it and the nuts on the snow. "They're hot boys. Let's let them cool for a minute."

The minute had barely passed before the aroma of crispy-shelled chestnuts finally got the best of us. We dug in . . . peeling the shell and plunking the nut sections into our mouths. The nuts were hot and we held them on our tongues to cool. Kathy nibbled at hers gingerly as she held it in her gloved fingers. The chestnut has a dry, somewhat chewy taste and the boys reacted differently. "Man, I need something to drink". Or, "Not bad . . . not bad." "Wait 'till

My wife Kathy samples steamy, full-bodied chestnut during Christmas tree hunt.

I tell Mom I had roasted chestnuts . . . I know she has never had them."

The chestnuts must have made a hit because the entire two-pound package ended up in our stomachs. It was pure delight to watch the boys peeling the nuts and popping them into their mouths. I knew there was more to roasted chestnuts than a Christmas song. They had been the highlight of our winter feast . . . one that did not end with chestnuts.

Hot dogs were next on the menu. Each boy cut his own green roasting stick. I built up the coals so they burst into flames and there was ample flame room for three grillers at a time.

Elaborate winter menus are not really necessary. In fact, many of them make cooking during the cold, or when snow lays on the ground, a long, drawn-out affair. Nutritious, tasty foods like chestnuts, hot dogs, hamburgers and plenty of hot drinks, make cooking and eating fun.

Hamburgers, for instance, can be pre-shaped and even pre-cooked—wrapped in foil and ready for cooking or warming over an open fire.

The boys elected to roast their hot dogs crispy so that the outer skins split. Kathy had packed about two-dozen flour tortilla shells which we have found to be easier to keep than

Part of our harvest of trees and boughs during December hunt and cookout.

We head through pine forests in Medicine Bow National Forest.

bread, just as tasty and a treat for most persons. When the hot dogs were just about ready, I placed the grill over the fire. Kathy sliced some Colby cheese in thin slices and placed the tortillas and cheese on the grill. In a few minutes the cheese melted. We spread it over the entire tortilla. The boys wrapped their hot dogs in the semi-crisp shells, added a squirt of mustard that we had packed in a squeeze tube and feasted on these different hot dogs. Although some of them may have had a few doubts about the chestnuts, the hot dogs disappeared fast. With the dogs, we sipped more cupfuls of hot chocolate.

Topping off the winter feast were marshmallows. The favorite ending of summertime picnics is also a delight when snow lays on the ground. The marshmallows are good, sweet morale boosters when toes are beginning to feel a little cold and the wind starts to howl through the pines.

With the feast completed, we gathered trees, boughs and cones and shuffled our way through the deep snow back to the car. I tied our prizes on the luggage rack. The boys chattered vigorously for ten minutes or so, but then an almost spontaneous silence fell upon the back seat. Kathy and I glanced around to see all of them snoozing soundly. They appeared extremely contented and it made us feel good. The cold, the snow . . . food and plenty of it, and thoughts of the best Christmas trees ever, had put their minds and bodies at ease.

And we made the drive back to Cheyenne . . . happy.

Simple cooking. Simple eating. Mini-feasts I call them. Nothing complicated at all. But in the outdoors, food never tasted so good.

About a month after our Christmas tree outing Kathy received a phone call from the mother of one of the boys on the trip. She said that Terry has not stopped talking about chestnuts and the way "Mrs. Farmer" fixed hot dogs. My wife beamed. It is amazing . . . the power of food when it is cooked outdoors.

You can't get shrimp fresher than these. This shrimp trawler was working off of Biloxi, Mississippi and we obtained a pail full of the tasty crustaceans, which we prepared right on board, for a tasty treat I'll long remember. A packet of Crab Boil was used to give the sea water an added flavor.

Coastal Smorgasbord

by MILT ROSKO

THE SUN WAS just lifting off the horizon in the eastern sky as we approached the stern of a shrimp trawler that had been dragging its nets through the night. The boat was now anchored with the crew busy at work culling their catch. They discarded crabs, squid, trash fish and crushed or damaged shrimp overboard. Then sorted the good shrimp, packing it between layers of crushed ice in the hold of the trawler. We knew that a wide variety of game fish, including bonito, cobia, king mackerel, jack crevalle, dolphin and a host of other species would take advantage of the chum line of trash being discarded overboard. By tying up to the trawler, we would enjoy some exciting sport.

As is usually the case when you find a shrimp trawler offshore, the fishing is superb, especially just after daybreak, when the fish are still hungry. But, as the sun rose high into the sky over the Gulf of Mexico off Biloxi, Mis-

A photo/journalist specializing in fresh and salt water fishing, Milt Rosko writes outdoor columns for several publications. He has authored a variety of fishing booklets and books. He also is a sport fishing consultant to industry.

sissippi, the fish became disinterested in our offerings. They had been gorging themselves for hours. We had become a bit tired too. In fact, our arms ached from tangling with the variety of tough adversaries that weighed from eight to over 30 pounds!

"Gosh, I hadn't realized how hungry I am," I said turning to Captain Lionel Holley, skipper of the charter boat *Quicksilver*. "It was three in the morning when I ate breakfast and it's past ten now. I think I'll have a sandwich."

"The heck you will," replied the good skipper. "When we took aboard some of that trash for chum this morning I passed the crew of the trawler a couple of six packs of beer. And in return got that bucket of shrimp that's sitting in the ice box. When you taste them you won't be much interested in your dry sandwiches."

With that, Lionel placed a huge kettle of sea water fresh from the Gulf on the stove and in short order it was boiling. He then deposited a package of "Crab Boil" into the water. The Crab Boil was a three by four inch cloth bag, sort of a miniature pillow case, which was filled with herbs and spices. The cloth packet allowed the flavor of the herbs and spices—both delicately blended to offer just the right amount of seasoning—to seep through and prevented a lot of powder and leaves floating around in the water. After the seafood was boiled or steamed, the packet was discarded.

While the Crab Boil is used primarily along the Gulf coast for steaming crabs, it is also used for shrimp. Lionel deposited handfuls of shrimp into the boiling sea water and Crab Boil, which in itself gave off an aroma that made your mouth water.

"You've got to be careful and not cook 'em too long. Just as soon as they're pink they're ready," tutored the skipper as I tended the pot.

That day I enjoyed a feast that I never experienced before but have experienced many times since. Luscious shrimp just hours from the sea prepared in a way far superior to any gourmet recipe I have tried. Lionel even had horseradish and ketchup on board and made a delicious sauce. There we sat: a bucketful of fresh shrimp, some fresh Louisiana tomatoes, a couple of ice cold cans of beer. We never did touch those sandwiches!

Food fresh from the sea is without question among the tastiest food there is. Unfortunately, few people get the opportunity to eat truly fresh seafood simply because of geographic location. However, even along the seacoast, some restauranteurs and gourmet chefs sometimes mask the natural flavors of the fish under sauces and garnishments.

My wife June and I like seafood for what it is—fresh and flavorful. Neither of us hesitate to prepare a fresh fish dinner on the beach, aboard boat or at home, even though prime steaks or chops are sitting in the freezer.

Mention of the shrimp trawlers in the Gulf of Mexico brings to mind another type of trawler. In the open reaches of the Atlantic Ocean off Ocean City, Maryland, June and I were fishing with George Seemann aboard his charter boat *Mitchell II*. We had hooked and released a beautiful white marlin at boatside and had several fine dolphin and bonito in the fish box. Late in the day the fishing slowed and George turned the bow westward to complete the 60 mile trek to shore. It was then he spotted a scalloper. The scallop trawlers drag the ocean floor for the tasty bivalve mollusks. As scallops are hauled onto the deck, teams of crew members stand along tables built the length of the boat and shuck the scallops, discarding the shells overboard. They save the single large adductor muscle, which is the scallop you may be accustomed to eating.

"We're having scallops for dinner tonight," Seemann beamed.

With that he swung the bow of the *Mitchell II* to bring

Aluminum foil pans, such as this disposable model, are ideal when you've got to prepare fish in a hurry. As you can see here, it's dark out already, and we're still cooking. These steaked salmon were caught just hours before being baked. June Rosko feels a minimum of sauces and garnishments make for better fish dinners.

her abreast of the scalloper. The skipper of the scalloper knew what George wanted. After several days at sea, the crew was pleased to see us. We traded for a sackful of scallops.

George is no gourmet. But he knows how to cook seafood. Relinquishing the helm to the mate for the long ride back to port, George went down to his galley and heated vegetable oil in an electric fry pan. In less time than it takes to tell about it, the oil was at just the right temperature. And he was rolling the scallops in the thin layer of oil covering the bottom of the pan. The scallops were cooked delicately and quickly to prevent moisture and flavor loss.

Veteran beach buggy angler and Cape Cod fisherman Frank Woolner spends a lot of time on the beach, and has his stove built right into his four wheel drive vehicle.

Along the seacoast you can often catch the makings of a fine meal with a crab trap such as this. The trap is baited with a piece of dead fish, and when the crabs enter you pull the trap shut, trapping the crab.

As I watched George it reaffirmed my conviction that seafood tastes best when simply prepared. He placed the golden brown scallops on our plates. Dusted with paprika, they were so juicy and full of flavor that we filled ourselves and returned for seconds. Pickles and tomatoes left over from lunch and a can of succotash rounded out the scrumptious, unexpected dinner.

Months later George's electric skillet was brought into play again with another mouth-watering treat. June and I and friends chartered with George at the Chub Cay Club in the Bahamas. Most of our time was occupied with fishing for blue and white marlin, dolphin, king mackerel and other tropical exotics. But one afternoon George commented that he was getting tired of frozen beef. He uses only Pfaelzer's prime Chicago beef and tiring of that takes some doing. That afternoon we stopped over a patch of coral bottom along the edge of the dropoff at the Tongue of the Ocean. We baited with pilchards. I decided to use a bucktail jig to probe the depths above the coral.

Almost simultaneously, all of us were hooked up. After a good fight on the light outfits we were using, we brought beautiful red snappers, yellowtail snappers and Nassau groupers to the surface. The snappers were from one to four pounds and the groupers, to 20 pounds plus. Within a half-hour the live fish well was filled with enough fresh reef fish to last us the better part of a week.

When we reached the dock at Chub Cay, George filleted several small snappers and one grouper. He announced, "Better have cocktails now because we eat in half an hour."

While I made tall drinks, George diced a fillet of grouper into bite size pieces and pan fried the "grouper fingers" in deep fat. He drained them on paper towels. What a great appetizer before dinner—just minutes from the sea!

Deftly, George cleaned the fry pan with toweling. He salted and peppered the snapper fillets and the remaining grouper fillet. Placing them in the skillet, he smothered the fish with canned stewing tomatoes and placed canned Irish potatoes around the fish. He added another can of whole kernel corn to a corner of the fry pan, reserved for that purpose.

Placing the cover on the fry pan, the skipper announced, "Now this is the way to cook dinner for five with a minimum of fuss . . . a point the distaff members of our party should note!"

Minimum of fuss it was, but maximum five-star rating when we ate. The snapper and grouper were delicately

You just can't beat the delicious flavor of fresh caught fish cooked over a charcoal fire. Here June Rosko checks the fish as Gladys Gray watches. Sizes best suited to cooking like this are fish weighing from 1 to 2 pounds.

steamed so that the white meat literally fell apart as you cut it with your fork. But all the juices of the fish were retained and it was moist and tasty. This is an extremely important consideration. For nothing will ruin even the freshest fish more than overcooking and in turn drying the fish out.

Countless cookbooks have been written on ways of preparing fish. But some of the ways in which we prepare our fish are so simple that they can hardly be classified as recipes.

While fishing with Art Lavalee in Narragansett Bay, Rhode Island, back when our children Linda and Bob were youngster, we had a rewarding evening of bluefishing. Fishing later than we had anticipated, we had not provided for dinner. And because we all were tired, cooking a big meal would be too bothersome. I remedied the situation in part by filleting a stringer of one- to two-pound bluefish we had landed.

Everybody's cooking out here. The scene is the beach at Cape Cod, where hundreds of beach buggy fishermen fish for stripers, blues and other species, and enjoy their dinner in the evening, prepared right on the beach, in as picturesque a setting as you could ever ask for.

Placing the bluefish fillets on a disposable aluminum pan, June dabbed butter and sliced onions on the fish. Popping the fillets into the broiler of the small oven we had in the camper, dinner took just about five minutes. We had the makings of a delicious meal. The broiler crisped the onions and melted the butter over the fish to keep it moist. Fresh Rhode Island lettuce and tomatoes topped off a dinner that had to be eaten to be appreciated.

Wherever we travel, whether in a pickup camper or motorhome, we always carry a charcoal grill. Even in a remote wilderness area along the coast we can quickly use it to whip up a delightful meal in a hurry. I recall one evening when we scored a bonanza while fishing for sea trout in Virginia. It was hot and June did not want to compound the problem by cooking in the motorhome. So I filled the grill with charcoal, added Sterno cubes to get the fire going in a hurry and then began filleting sea trout.

We placed the sea trout fillets on foil, covered them lightly with mayonnaise and placed them on the grill. Along the edge of the grill we roasted several ears of fresh Virginia sweet corn that had been pulled that afternoon. The mayonnaise melted and smothered the fillets. June sprinkled on salt and pepper. That night we had a repast of mouth-watering sea trout, fresh corn and a tossed salad of lettuce, tomatoes and peppers. A simple outdoor meal but a delectable one.

The grill has also been used to cook American shad. As many of you are no doubt aware, shad are very bony and it takes a bit of skill to fillet them. But an old-timer along the seacoast once showed me how to solve the problem. He simply splits the shad; wraps several pieces of smoked bacon around the fish; butters the stomach cavity and then double wraps it in aluminum foil. The double wrap is important as this ensures that juices will not escape from the fish.

The shad is then placed on the glowing coals and left there for a full five or six hours. Yes, five or six hours! This causes the bones in the shad to become so soft you can even eat right through the backbone. The butter and bacon help maintain a good moisture level in the foil and the result is a tasty spring fishing treat without annoying bones.

Of course, many times we have prepared fish simply by placing them right on the grill. This can be done with bluefish, mackerel, sea trout, flounder and most small fish that weight a pound or two. Simply clean out the stomach cavity, leaving the head on the fish. This helps hold it together as it cooks. There is no need to remove the scales and fins. Once the fish is cooked you peel the skin away and discard it, enjoying the piping hot fish. The skin retains the delicious juices of the fish.

Another popular way of preparing small fish when fishing or camping along the seacoast is to plank them. This method is especially popular with summer and winter flounder, southern flounder and small halibut. The flatfish is secured to a plank and placed very close to an open fire. The heat of the fire is directed on the fish and will cook it through surprisingly fast.

A variation of this is commonplace at campgrounds along the seacoast. It essentially consists of baking small fish, such as spot, sea trout, bluefish, kingfish or mackerel, on sticks of green wood over an open fire. First, build a fire in a shallow hole in the sand lined with small rocks. Then, clean the fish and skewer a green stick through the mouth and body. Stand the twig in the sand so that the fish is positioned above and off to the side of the fire. They will get done in short order. Much like roasting hot dogs!

Crustaceans, such as blue crabs, lobsters and crayfish, are available along many sections of seacoast. Blue crabs can be easily collected by baiting a line with a piece of fish and then slowly drawing it to the surface. The crab latches onto the fish so it can be scooped up with a crab net. Crabs can also be netted along bulkheads and bridge pilings or in marsh grass. I have observed times when you could wade along the beach and by using a long-handled net simply capture free-swimming blue crabs.

If you are a skin diving buff you can obtain crayfish in southern waters and in the Bahamas. In the case of lobsters, if you are staying in an area for a few days you can set out a couple of lobster pots and obtain enough for the table. If this proves too much of a chore, along many areas of seacoast you can fish the local seafood cooperative and purchase a couple of lobsters at a lower price than you are accustomed to paying inland.

In any case, make certain to check state laws when col-

Here we're camping on the seacoast overlooking Casco Bay in Maine. We caught and planked winter flounders from the waters down the bluff, and enjoyed as delicious a seafood treat as you could ever ask for. The flounders were so plentiful you could catch them until arm-weary.

Blue crabs are easy to obtain and are delicious. These bathers are using long handled crab nets and are dipping free-swimming blue crabs from the surf at Point Pleasant, New Jersey.

Cleaning the fish promptly and properly is the key to retaining their flavor. Here George Seemann immediately dresses some dolphin, tuna and bonito caught aboard his *Mitchell II* just hours earlier.

There's no nicer setting for outdoor cooking along the seacoast but to pull your camper into a stand of pines and set out your charcoal grill and prepare the fish you caught that day. The fresher the fish the finer the flavor, especially if you cook them for just a short period of time.

lecting crustaceans. There are restrictions governing seasons and the size of crabs, crayfish and lobsters.

There are several ways to prepare crustaceans: boiled, broiled and steamed. I have tried them all and prefer mine steamed. Broiling generally dries out crayfish and lobsters. Boiling, because the crustaceans are immersed in water, tends to rob them of flavor. Steaming, however, retains the full flavor of lobsters, crayfish and blue crabs.

Steaming is easily accomplished and if you are camping along the seacoast, you can use a charcoal grill and a large, deep pot. Fit the pot with a small wooden rack. Crabs, lobsters and crayfish rest on the rack and not in the water. The pot is filled with water to the top of the rack and brought to a boil. Once boiling, add about two ounces of vinegar and prepared mustard to the water. Place the live lobsters, crabs or crayfish tails on the rack in the pot. They are steamed when they turn bright red.

Many people carry along a package of the Crab Boil I mentioned earlier as they like the flavor that bay leaves and other spices and herbs add to the crustaceans. Oftentimes we eat the hot lobsters and crabs as soon as we can handle them. Both June and I enjoy them with a hot sauce of horseradish and ketchup when the meat is still warm. They can be chilled on ice for a fine treat too. Whatever the case, keep them in a covered container once cooked. This helps to retain moisture and flavor and prevents dryness so often associated with seafood that is old, overcooked or improperly stored.

The best way to eat fresh seafood is promptly after it has been caught. Even though June and I have savored many exotic seafood dishes, we always return to the simple recipes. There is something special about being in the outdoors all day, trolling offshore for big game, probing the depths for reef species or basking in the solitude of a coastal estuary, that results in complete relaxation. There is no finer way to cap such a day than to feast on freshly harvested seafood. Enjoyed in the outdoors, close to the sea, the tang of the salt and the aroma of the seafood combined for a taste treat that lasts forever.

The Rosko clan, June, Linda and Bob, prepare to enjoy some fresh Maine lobsters, purchased from a lobster cooperative, and steamed outside their camper.

Evening comes to Puerto de Lobos, on the Sea of Cortez, and fishermen ask, "What's to eat?"

making the most of a MEXICAN COOKOUT

by VICKI TALLON

YOU'RE PLANNING a five-day outing in Mexico, on the remote Sonoran beaches of the Sea of Cortez (Gulf of California). My husband, Jim, would rather fish here than most anywhere, since he is a far-out surf fishing buff, and probably few places in the world offer better surf fishing. But there is no water but sea water here, no ice, no wood for fuel, no restaurants, no motels, no stores; nothing except small native villages whose people make their living from the sea. "The sea gives us everything but beans and coffee, señor," a Mexican fisherman once told Jim. But even the fisherman had to travel over 60 miles, 45 of them over primitive desert roads to get them. For the average *norteamericano*, the sea is not so generous, nor are his wants so simple.

For us, Mexico represents escape, a chance to "recreate" our spirits and to give our stomachs a break from routine as well. And with the lack of facilities on the Sonoran coast, the success of our trips depend upon what we take with us and how we use it. This starts with checklists. While Jim checks his fishing tackle and other gear, I work on the food and related supplies, and start planning meals.

Winter camping on Sonoran beaches require less effort and checklists are shorter. Sometimes the wind whips cold off the sea and hot meals and drinks cheer up chilled fishermen. Even though some days may be very warm, liquids go farther and ice lasts longer. Since summer trips may deal with temperatures in excess of 100 degrees, I choose a great deal of foods that contain liquids or those that need little or no extra liquids to prepare; this is keyed to avoid dehydration. We double our beverage supply, extra jugs of water, beer, canned pop, milk, non-carbonated drinks, orange juice, a couple of bottles of good wine, and perhaps a bottle of rum for mixing Cuba Libres when the fishing is done for the day and the sea breeze says relax.

Our intention to eat even better than we do at home includes at least one meal cooked over an open fire. And the basis for this is a specific kind of wood for open-fire cooking. From experience we have learned that such desert woods as mesquite and ironwood are excellent. Ironwood is a slow-burning, hot fuel, but our second choice if food is to be cooked directly over the fire. Mesquite burns faster, but it imparts an excellent flavor to meats, and exclusive restaurants in Phoenix and Tucson use it for broiling steaks. You can find these woods for sale in southwestern cities, but we just pick it up in the desert, often enroute to our Sonoran destination.

We usually have our Mexican cook-out dinners after dark since the fishermen like to catch what they call "the evening bite." Once the flames of the evening sun die, our mesquite fire flames and we have shish kebab. Dinner becomes a mouth-watering experience in which everyone participates. Sometimes our shish kebab comes from cans, but no-one ever complains. More often we take such fresh items as mushrooms, onions, potatoes, and pineapple. We prefer chunks of beef, but alternate with pork or hamburger meatballs. What really makes the cook-out a success is a zippy barbecue sauce of my own concoction that is prepared a few hours ahead and let brew. We brush the sauce onto the skewered food just before placing it over the mesquite fire. You will need the following ingredients to make the sauce:

1 tablespoon dry horseradish
1 cup catsup
1 tablespoon lemon juice
1 tablespoon chili powder

Simply mix all the above together and let stand at least one hour before brushing over the shish kebabs.

We know that breakfast is considered the most important meal. But not for us. Dinner, cooked outdoors, or at least eaten outdoors, amid the smell of sea and sounds of surf, and served with a good wine comes pretty close to convincing us that we're in paradise. Some of our favorite outdoor meals come out of our van conversion camper's oven. And it is just a matter of a couple of steps to be outdoors listening to the sea and inhaling salt air now flavored with the savory odor of fine food. One of these meals is corn and sausage casserole. You'll need the following ingredients:

Surf fisherman works the Sea of Cortez at Puerto de Lobos.

Sonoran coast of the Sea of Cortez (Gulf of California).

Heading for Puerto de Lobos. This fishing village on the Sea of Cortez is 60 miles from the nearest town, 45 miles over desert roads. You must plan meals ahead.

2 cups of corn
½-pound of sausage, link or patties
¾-cup cracker crumbs
2 eggs and 2 cups milk
2 tablespoons butter
½-teaspoon salt

Sometimes we take the corn and sausage to the Sonoran beach in canned form, but prefer fresh-frozen. (We have found that by freezing foods and keeping them next to the ice in a rarely-opened ice box, we can have fresh frozen foods throughout most of our trips.) Cook the corn, and brown the sausage in a skillet. Then beat the eggs and combine them with the corn and salt. Place alternate layers of the corn mixture, sausage and crumbs in a greased baking dish. Save some of the sausage and crumbs for the top layer and dot each layer with butter. Pour the milk over the top

Camping on the Mexican coast insures the best of salt water fishing, primitive beach atmosphere and spicy open-air cooking.

Looks like a good spot to pick up firewood, especially mesquite.

and bake at 350 degrees for about 30 minutes. This will handle three to four hungry fishermen and their spouses.

An alternate, equally looked forward to by salt-air fired appetites, and feeds the same number of people, is apple, sausage and cheese casserole. Here are the ingredients for this one:

    12 pork sausage links or patties
    4 tablespoons flour
    2 cups hot water
    1 tablespoon vinegar
    ½-teaspoon salt
    4 medium apples
    2 tablespoons brown sugar
    ¼-pound sliced cheese

Brown sausages as you would for the corn and sausage casserole, then put them in a casserole dish. Remove all but ¼-cup of the sausage fat from the skillet then add the flour and brown. Pour water in gradually and cook until thickened, then add vinegar and salt. Next, pare and core apples, then slice them and arrange on the sausages; sprinkle with brown sugar and pour the gravy over them. Cover the casserole dish and bake at 350 degrees for 30 minutes, until the apples are tender. Now lay the cheese slices on top and return to the oven uncovered, long enough to melt and brown the cheese.

When your people smell this casserole cooking, you won't have to ring the dinner bell at all; they'll be there waiting for it to be served. The average camper or fisherman does not have nor expect such excellent bill-of-fare and you'll be blushing from the raves. This is not idle chatter, but proven from experience. These meals will be greeted even more enthusiastically if you have the ability to properly cook them in that wonderful utensil, the Dutch oven.

Of course each of our Sonoran-Sea of Cortez fishing outings include at least one fish fry. Corvina, cabrilla, white sea bass, or pintos may provide the fillets, but more often the triggerfish. Waters off Puerto de Lobos and Libertad, two of our favorite places on the Sonoran coast, are congested with triggerfish. This species looks like an overgrown bluegill with buck teeth and some fishermen call it a nuisance and a bait-stealer. But when the fishing is slow in the surf, the men will take a small boat a few hundred yards off shore and load up with triggerfish.

My husband and his friends fillet the triggerfish without opening the body cavity. A sharp knife is used to slit the leather-like skin along the back, belly, sides and around the tail-fin, carefully avoiding penetration of the body cavity. They use pliers to peel off the hide. It's like pulling the sole off an old shoe. Since some of these fish will weigh more than five pounds, the fillets may be too large for the skillet and must be cut down to size.

The triggerfish is fine cooked most anyway, but a beer batter makes fishermen and friends keep coming back for another helping. You simply mix the beer, pancake flour, and one or two eggs to make a gooey batter, and dip the fish into it. You cook them in deep, hot shortening or oil, and season them with salt and pepper as they fry.

Even though we consider dinners to be *our* most important outdoor meal, something should be said for breakfast, especially our favorite whether at home or Sea of Cortez beach. In keeping with the Mexican theme, I'm talking about *chili relleno* (pronounced RE-YEH-NO). When you serve this dish, you'd better make up plenty because the men will eat a lot more breakfast than they normally do. Here are the ingredients:

Author Vicki Tallon with a triggerfish. This fine food fish is excellent in a beer batter.

eggs
whole green chilies, preferably Ortegas
¼-pound of cheese, such as longhorn, per each 3 eggs
¼-cup of milk to each 3 eggs

The recipe is based on a one egg to one chili ratio. To prepare chili rellenos, carefully remove the chilies from the can so you do not tear them. Rinse them in cold water and be sure to remove the oil, seeds and large stringy fibers. A slit in the side lengthwise makes this easy. Now cut the cheese into elongated blocks, about 3 inches long and ½-inch square. Stuff the cheese into the chilies. Put about two tablespoons of bacon drippings in a hot skillet and two or three chilies; the number depends upon the size of the skillet. Pour a mixture of eggs and milk over the chilies and season with salt and pepper. When the egg and milk mixture sets, separate the chilies and flip as you would any hard-fried skillet egg. What you now have are chili and cheese islands in a miniature sea of egg. When the egg is fully

Vicki's husband Jim puts power into a spinrod at the Sea of Cortez while surf fishing.

Bob Hirsch of Phoenix prepares to fillet a four-pound triggerfish.

cooked and the cheese melted, remove from the skillet and serve on a hot plate. A few slices of bacon and tortillas go great with chili rellenos, and garnish with some extra grated cheese. The only trouble with serving this dish is that it makes a fisherman reluctant to leave the breakfast table and delays you from getting to the beach for your suntan. Or doing a little fishing on your own.

Living in the southwest, most soon acquire a taste for Mexican food. We are among those and we have Mexican food at least once a week. Among our favorites is *guacamole* (pronounced WA-CA-MO-LAY). You might call it a luxury item that is super easy to make and super delicious to eat. At one of our fish fries in Phoenix, we served guacamole for a dip, along with several other kinds of dip. One of our guests asked Jim what the "green stuff" *was*.

"Was?" said Jim. "There's a half-a-gallon of it."

"It's all gone now," said the guest.

The other dips were practically untouched, but the bowl of guacamole had been cleaned out.

On the beach, guacamole tastes even better. You can serve it as a dip, make tostados with it, put it on salads and use it as a dressing for other Mexican foods. Here's the ingredients:

2 medium ripe avocados
½-cup of finely chopped onion
½-can of diced green chilies, preferably Ortegas
garlic salt
pepper
lime juice

To prepare, just spoon out the avocados into a mixing bowl. Add the other ingredients, then mash with a hand potato masher or large fork, until you have a thick consistency. Do not put in a blender unless you want a guacamole cocktail. You can make variations to suit your own taste, such as reducing or increasing the amount of garlic salt or lime juice.

My husband and his fishing friends say they love fishing in the salty paradise of the Sonoran coast, but I imagine the smell of salt air, the sounds of the seashore, and certainly eating fine food in the outdoors has a lot to do with it.

A dozen triggerfish and a rockbass. All will be eaten after sunset. The salt air induces unbelievably huge appetites. Fisherman is Frank Johnson of Denver.

John Scott, our Yellowstone Lake guide, makes sure that everyone is happy and full of good food.

CAMP COOKS ARE SOOTHSAYERS

by KATHLEEN FARMER

THE UNKNOWN spurs apprehension, excitement and uneasiness. Doing something you have never done before is always traumatic. Whether it is 6-year-old Samantha waiting for her first school bus ride or 25-year-old Eric watching his girl, dressed traditionally in white, waltz towards him down the aisle or 65-year-old Wilfred waking up to Day One of retirement, each has prepared himself for something new. To calm himself, his mind repeats, "I can handle whatever comes up." He is naturally tense, readying himself for action. This is where habits fail us and often get in the way of learning different ways and adapting to the unfamiliar.

"This is the first day of the rest of your life" has become so commercialized that it sounds trite. But it sums up what each of us experiences when faced with the challenge of the unknown. No longer can routine protect us from the realization that we live only from day to day, hour to hour. There is no guarantee that we will enjoy a long, happy life. The unknown clearly reveals to us that nothing is certain, everything is conditional. Life is more than a steady job, financial security and a Martini when you get home from work.

People react to new situations in various ways. Like Paul, the automobile salesman, who talks incessantly about his past. Everyone he meets reminds him of someone else he used to know. He describes his ancestry grandiosely and even traces one-sixteenth of his blood to the Navajos; to prove it, he says a few words in Navajoan. He has tried everything but humbly admits he can do nothing really well. In this way, he informs those around him not to expect much from him. He sees himself as the clown of the group.

Marjorie, on the other hand, giggles a lot. She stimulates others to talk about themselves and tries to impress on them that she is not important. However, she appeals to her companions for assistance in whatever she does. She comes across as helpless, lame-brained and in need of constant supervision.

And then there is Clyde. He is an expert at most things, including fishing, fire-building, wildflower identification and arrowhead-finding. He advises everyone how to do these things better. He himself has mastered these activities to the extent that he now considers them tedious and trivial. He would rather observe than participate.

The majority of us, though, falls into the "Wait and Watch" category. When confronted with a novel situation, most people wait to see what is expected of them. They discover how they are supposed to act by watching the behavior of those around who are accustomed to the situation. By keeping an open mind and by deciphering what is happening in this new environment without judging it as good or bad, the individual can be flexible enough to adjust and adapt to almost any circumstance. This person can learn to feel comfortable with many types of people in a variety of situations.

Almost any time an outdoorsperson leaves the well-known surroundings of home and penetrates untamed nature, he is putting himself into the unknown. No matter how many

When choosing a guide, his operations, but especially his cook, are important aspects to look into.

times one treks over a trail in the forest near home, each hike is different. Never static, nature is always changing, always presenting another challenge.

The guided outdoor experience is becoming more and more popular. With a limited amount of time to spend in the outdoors, most vacationers do not want to waste much of it scouting the area. They can fly to their chosen vacation spot, be met by the guides and put their well-being and precious work-free days into the hands of the guides. They provide everything except personal gear. Some even furnish sleeping bags, fishing equipment, boats, horses; anything a person may need to explore, enjoy, photograph and fish their chunk of the wilds. A list of fishing, packing and hunting guides may be obtained from the Game and Fish Department of the state you are interested in, or from the National Park or National Forest you plan to discover on your next vacation.

While the guided outdoor adventure can open opportunities that few of us could do on our own, it also puts you in a vulnerable position. If you chose a good guide, fine. But if by chance you happened upon one that is not so good. . . .

I remember a September elk hunt—my first hunt on horseback—where the guide conducted a breath-taking sight-seeing trip of the Swan Mountains in the Bob Marshall Wilderness of western Montana. We heard much shooting on the opening day of the season, but our guide was engrossed in pointing out distant ridges, meadows and canyons, used as landmarks by pioneers, trappers and Indians years ago. We watched hunters loading good bulls onto pack horses but we were busy following our preoccupied guide who was searching for a "secret" trail. It led to a forgotten peak which treated us to a panorama of the Hungry Horse valley.

Our guide obviously knew the country and was an expert wrangler but as far as hunting went, he did not understand the importance of arising early, quiet stalks and to place hunters in areas where they are likely to see elk. Our trip would have been an idyllic two-week pleasure horseback ride. It was a complete outdoor experience; one that taught us much about horses, mountains and Montana folklore. However, we were victims of a hunting guide who did not like to hunt.

The savior of this "hunting" venture was Moseley the

While in camp, the cook can make the difference between a top-notch vacation and a poor one. His attitude, not always his cooking, makes the difference. Here camp cook Simon Trafoya discusses the day's hunt with Mark Haight and the author.

The guided outdoor experience is becoming increasingly popular. Here a group of vacationers are led into the wilderness by pack train.

A river float can be a spectacular wilderness experience with the right outfitter.

cook. He not only supplied us with outstanding elk steak sandwiches for lunch—they were supposed to bring us luck, based on the belief that "like produces like"—but he spent hours baking sourdough breads, cakes and biscuits in the Dutch oven. He cut logs exactly to fit the wood-burning stoves in our tents. But his most important service to us was as a sounding board. He listened patiently to our hunting frustrations. He had never hunted big game. Instead, he had followed the rodeo circuit as a roper. He related our failure to find game with disappointments he experienced with rodeos. Each evening, eating delicious grilled meats, potatoes and cake, soothing away saddle sores, we conducted gab sessions which had a therapeutic effect on us. We will never forget that hunt. Not for the hunting but for the eating and the comradeship.

Moseley, easy to talk with and caring about what you said, helped to whisk away the distaste of the unknown. This is true of most camp cooks I have encountered. They are a different breed. Somehow they feel responsible for those they cook for. Like a mother hen, they worry if you have enough to eat. Does the meal agree with you? And are you having a good time? Watching others devour what they have spent time and effort preparing seems to bring out motherliness in them. They feel like a nurturing figure and usually their sensitivity extends beyond the dining table.

On a wilderness boat expedition not long ago on Yellowstone Lake in Yellowstone National Park, we had a camp cook that tripled as fishing guide and boatman. A 30-foot cabin cruiser with rowboat in tow picked us up at the dock at Lake and dropped us off at the wilderness boundary. We climbed into the rowboat while John loaded our gear into it. He rowed us to his favorite spot, about two miles from the dropoff. He set up camp, built two fires—a cooking one and a "social" one—and fixed fried chicken, mashed potatoes and blueberry pie for supper. For seven days we found ourselves in a wonderland of cutthroat fishing. Every other cast produced 24- to 30-inch trout. At sunrise and dusk, we caught these giants on fly rods. During the heat of the day, we rowed 100 yards from shore and fished deep with spinning gear and silver spoons. At night, we huddled around the fire discussing our chances of rowing out to Pelican Island, about two miles away in the middle of the Southeast Arm of the lake, to photograph hordes of white pelicans. John just happened to bring along a fly tying case, filled with everything needed to invent and experiment with new flies.

I hate to admit it, but the fishing was so good, we tired of it. Not having to do any chores around camp, freeing us for fishing and eating, finally pushed us into searching for something else to do. It was too perfect. Without saying a word, John docked the rowboat one morning on an island. "There's all kinds of arrowheads and pieces of flint scattered all over this island. What the Indians left behind when they summered here." He proceeded to outline the history of the land, Yellowstone Park and what he thought the future should be for this gem of nature. In short, John thought of many things to make our stay exceptional.

In many ways, the camp cook functions much like a manager of a baseball team. He is the organizer, the compromiser, the spirit uplifter of the group. He sees that everyone is happy or at least not sad. He draws the members of the group closer together and feels entitled to do what he wants when he wearies of cooking. Cooking is usually not his chosen profession but represents a change of pace from his customary line of work. Camp can be a refuge from the hard knocks of the outside world. A good cook strives to keep it that way with as few upsets, quarrels and hurts as he can manage. He intuitively appreciates what you are seeking by selecting a guided wilderness vacation and he tries to see that you find it. If you find peace and solitude, adventure and communication with nature, chances are better that he too will discover them. He helps you enjoy your vacation and in turn he reaps benefits as well.

One day I suddenly got the river floating mania. I impulsively signed up for a guided, three-day float trip down the Green River through Dinosaur National Monument. On the advice of a friend, I picked the river float outfitter. She too made reservations on the same trip. In eight-man rubber rafts, we were guaranteed a chance to learn how to maneuver through rapids. I figured that this would be an educational as well as a fun outing.

To save money, the director of the floating company did not hire a cook. Because the group was rather large (21), the guides divided us into Breakfast, Lunch and Supper. Seven individuals were assigned breakfast detail; seven, lunch; and seven, supper. The three river guides ate together but separate from us. As a result, mealtime was chaos. It was every person for himself, grabbing food, pushing for a cooking space around the fire and in general hating to eat yet being hungry enough to engage in such ridiculous roughhousing.

The sleeping bags that we rented from the float company were stored in huge, black plastic bags and placed in the bottom of the rafts along with other supplies. This would insure their being dry at the end of the day when we set camp. Unfortunately, the plastic bags had leaks in them. About two-thirds of the group opened up their plastic bags to find a body of water lying in the sleeping bag. This meant no sleep for 14 of the floaters, unless the fire could dry the bags quickly. Thus the pressure increased around the fire and tempers flared.

Meanwhile, the guides considered the scene comical. They had their own equipment, which was of higher quality than our rentals. They had checked for leaks in their plastic protective bags before the trip and had reinforced the slashes with waterproof tape. The tantalizing aroma of their broiling hamburgers incited several of the group to talk of raiding the guides' camp and robbing them of their food, dry sleeping bags, snug tents (we were expected to sleep "under the stars") and smug attitude. The guides, realizing the folly of their assumed security, safety and comfort, hurriedly ate their dinner, turned off the lantern and pretended to sleep. It is much more difficult to attack a snoring person, even if it is too loud to be authentic, than it is to jump a jeering, snickering one. The talk of "revolt and rebellion" ceased and we once more shoved for a warm spot around the campfire. Making sure no one squeezed you out of your place by the fire heated the body probably more than the fire itself.

The trip was not a complete failure. We learned how to ride the rapids and overcame the initial fear that overwhelms one when he first hears their deafening roar. Also, our struggle for respectful treatment from the river guides

To a camp cook, the camp is a refuge from the hard knocks of the outside world and he strives to keep it that way.

banded the floaters together. At the end of the trip, we still had not determined how to share cooking chores but we had learned to build several small campfires instead of one large bonfire. This way we no longer fought each other.

But without a cook, the trip was an unbelievable hassle. Each person was estranged from everyone else. Even my friend and I spoke little. Because of wet sleeping bags or poorly prepared food, most were edgy and miserable. They were afraid they would expose their bad moods and so they kept to themselves. Each feeling sorrier by the day for himself. This would not have happened if a camp cook accompanied us.

Camp cooks are the backbone to the guided outdoor experience. They not only feed the hungry outdoorspeople but they act as counselors. The unknown is not so frightening. Their supportive attitude gives one the confidence to look for the unknown instead of shrinking from it. In addition, their rustic kitchen is something to look forward to if the day afield was particularly trying. The camp cook influences and affects people in different ways. But one thing is certain, without the wilderness chef, the wilderness vacationer's body and soul might starve.

Tent camping presents a real challenge to the cook. It's tougher to go first class this way but much more satisfying.

IT ALL STARTED with a bologna sandwich.

Pete and Bill and I were on the second day of a three-day fishing trip and it was lunch time. The menu was simple: make-it-yourself bologna sandwiches, potato chips, and a can of beer or pop—with a handful of cookies as an extra treat.

Bill had eaten half his second sandwich when he suddenly stopped and held the remains out at arms length.

"Why am I eating this junk," he asked Pete and I. "If I were home and my wife served me this kind of lunch, I'd revolt."

"Well, at least it's quick and easy," Pete said. "The quicker we eat, the quicker we get back to fishing."

Bill waved the half-devoured sandwich. "An extra half hour for lunch isn't going to make that much difference. I hereby volunteer to be the chef on the next trip—and I guarantee no bologna sandwiches!"

That was the beginning—15 years ago—of a tradition that is still going on. The three of us make at least one annual "big" fishing outing and over the years we've taken turns trying to outdo each other in providing the classiest menus and most unusual food items.

Last year's trip is a good example. We headed for the pine country and some trout fishing. The chef-of-the-year always keeps the menu a secret and most of the fun is in surprising the other two with some new delicacy.

Where breakfast was once a hurried affair—lest we miss some of the early morning action—breaking the fast on the trout trip included a mushroom omelet, a bowl of chilled fruit cocktail and toast with fresh strawberry jam. That was the first morning.

GOING FIRST CLASS

by BOB HIRSCH

Lunches never—but never—include sandwiches, no matter how fancy. Unusual soups are popular, so are big bowls of chili, trout grilled over oak coals, chef salads or platters of assorted cheeses.

The evening meal is the big one. The cook quits fishing early and heads for camp to do his thing. One meal last year began with a cocktail hour which featured tiny bite-sized tacos—heated in the Coleman oven—and wheat crackers covered with a spicy garbanzo bean salad. The main course was noodles Romanoff, complete with sour cream gravy. There was also corn on the cob, biscuits from the Dutch oven, a tossed salad and French style green beans. Naturally service included a robust red wine.

If you're saying about now that you don't even eat that well at home—neither do I. At least not often. But since every trip outdoors is special, why shouldn't the cooking and eating be the same? So the 'going first class' habit developed with Pete and Bill has carried over to all my outdoor eating, especially trips with my wife and children. Mary and I and our five young ones have, for instance, camped out every Thanksgiving for the past ten years or so. We have our traditional turkey dinner at home on Wednesday night and then head for the hills the next morning. The left-over turkey goes along, to form the basis for two or three meals on the long weekend.

A sudden storm caught us one evening, just as the turkey and gravy and dressing and mashed potatoes were ready to

Framed by the tent opening, Mary works on a camping breakfast. Whatever else it is, the meal will not be ordinary.

This campsite had caches, used to store food and gear away from bears. Our kids quickly adopted them as tree houses and lunch was sent up in a bucket that had been lowered from the lofty perch on a rope. Out-of-the-ordinary eating like this can make a trip memorable.

eat. Mary and the kids dashed for the tent and I served dinner—a plate at a time—by ferrying it from the stove to the tent beneath a poncho. In a few minutes we were all sitting cross-legged under the canvas roof, watching the rain come down and enjoying an outdoor meal we'll never forget.

Once, on a motorhome trip to Mexico, we bought a huge selection of cheeses and lunch each day was a happy sampling of all the different brands. One of the kids began to rate the tastes—on a scale of one to ten—and the idea caught on. We enjoyed a series of lively lunches, during which the tads learned something about the cheese and the country where it was made. On the last day a grand champion was elected. I've forgotten the variety that won but I do remember that the mid-day repast was the highlight of the trip. Sure the cheese was expensive, but the experience was priceless.

As you might have guessed by now, 'going first class' is mostly a matter of attitude and a little planning. It does cost more than the beans and wieners route but the extra time and care needed to be an outdoor gourmet also rubs off on the rest of the trip. Every part of the total outing is heightened by the joy of eating well. And this goes for everything from a one day picnic to a two week vacation. It includes hunting and fishing and backpacking. You can use ideas in your camper, your motorhome, your tent or boat. The important step is to determine that meals will not be necessary nuisances but breaks in the routine that will be welcomed by all.

I remember a particular spring turkey hunt in the high country of Arizona. There were eight or nine of us camped together, but on a kind of casual basis. Everybody brought his own chow and picked his own pine tree to shelter his bedroll. Hunting is a great appetite builder anyway and sneaking through the April chill trying to fool a big, wary gobbler is one of the more potent ways to sharpen a dull taste bud.

By some lucky coincidence, that turkey camp brought together some outstanding cooking talent. Norm happened to be a salad freak and his ice chest was loaded with fresh vegetables. Each night he would toss a huge bowl of mixed greens, whomp up a special vinegar and oil dressing and stand back. The result was so cold and crisp I'm surprised we didn't scare all the turkeys in the vicinity when we started munching. That was ten years ago and I still haven't matched the magic taste of those salads—but I try everytime we eat outdoors and if my efforts don't quite measure up to Norm's, at least I've learned that including fresh vegetables on the outdoor shopping list is another way to go first class.

That turkey camp also furnished two other memorable eating experiences. Since the company was all male and all hungry, steak was the main course every night. Someone had brought a big grill and while the drinks and hunting tales flowed freely, a big oak fire was burning down to coals. When the embers were just right, they were transferred with a long-handled shovel and the grill was ready to receive

Tables with stand-up grills, like this one at Organ Pipe National Monument in southern Arizona, help make classy outdoor cooking easy.

steaks. I'm a garlic lover and while garlic salt is OK, nothing beats a fresh bud of garlic rubbed on a steak just before it hits the heat. Walt added another special touch. He sliced an onion, cut small slits in three or four places on his filet and slipped a piece of onion into each. Nifty!

Hy made Dutch oven biscuits the first night and was quickly put in charge of that detail on a permanent basis. He mixed the dough from scratch, with beer instead of milk or water, and used his hands to blend the ingredients. He'd brought along a jar of mesquite honey and when the golden biscuits were scooped out of the oven and spread with honey, none of us even bothered to ask Hy if he'd washed his hands before he mixed them.

Dutch oven cooking spooks many modern campers but if you use the big iron pots for nothing more than biscuits, they should be part of your outdoor gear. And though it takes a bit of practice, you can often let your dinner cook while you're off enjoying some part of the outdoor scene.

We camped one fall in the high pines for a deer hunt and a couple of Dutch ovens were in the gear that bounced around in the back of the pickup on the way in. Squirrel season was also open but we didn't want to take time for them until a deer or two decorated the pole we lashed between two sturdy pines near camp. On the way back into camp early the first afternoon, however, I passed a tree with two bushytails in noisy residence. Back at the pickup I swapped the '06 for a .22 rifle and walked back and collected them both. The next morning, before we left camp for the day, I combined in the Dutch oven: the squirrels, now cut up, with potatoes, onions, carrots, a handful of rice, some water and a couple of cans of vegetable soup for stock. A healthy dose of salt and pepper, a bay leaf and the lid was ready to put on. Then the entire oven was buried in the coals of the morning campfire.

That evening I came back into camp from the downwind side and there was no danger I'd lose my way. The scent of

Small members of the clan can help too. This one is whipping up a special omelet.

Eating well outdoors can be practiced on anything from a one day picnic to a two week vacation.

that delectable squirrel stew wafted through the pines for what seemed like half a mile. The fire had burned down to a pile of white ashes but beneath the cool exterior the pit was still hot and the stew made happy bubbling noises. First class? You'd better believe it!

Sometimes going first class can be deceptively simple. Once I took a buddy on a quicky one-day hunt for javelina in the rolling grassland south of Tucson, Arizona. I'd gotten a pig in the area the week before and felt sure I could find one for him—even on a short hunt. As so often happens on 'sure thing' hunts, we didn't see a thing. We did cover a lot of ground and by lunchtime we were both tired. I'd volunteered to provide the chow and when we stopped at mid-day, in the bottom of a pretty little draw, Stan watched with interest when I opened the little day hiker packsack I'd carried all morning. Out of the small bag came a tin can, two foam cups, a pair of tea bags, a pill bottle full of sugar, a can of corned beef and a package of crackers.

The can became a teapot and the water boiled quickly on the tiny fire. In five minutes we were feasting on beef and crackers washed down with hot, sugared tea. Dessert was a handful of dried apricots and a second cup of tea—followed by half an hour's nap. A month later Stan had forgotten we struck out on javelina but he was still raving about the 'fantastic lunch.'

Simplicity is all right but worthwhile productions on the outdoor eating scale require more effort. A couple of years ago we got an unexpected bonus for an evening meal during a fishing trip. The menu already included a ham with pineapple slices that had been baking all afternoon in the Coleman oven—plus some whipped yams and a Waldorf salad. Then one of the kids discovered the lake was full of freshwater clams. We gathered half a bucket of the small bites of heaven, washed them thoroughly—made a steamer from a one-gallon can and some rocks and began the first class meal with steamed clams on the half shell. They were served —along with the ham that followed—on a rough wood table by the light of a lantern but no fancy restaurant ever equaled the quality of the food we ate that night.

Pete and Bill and I still go on our annual fishing trip, though our wives now accuse us of using the jaunt only as an excuse to eat. It does seem to get fancier every year. Inevitably, a few years ago, one of us came up with an evening meal of steak, baked potato, tossed salad, asparagus tips and imported wine—all served on a sparkling white table cloth and lighted by tall candelabra.

It's my turn to be chef again this year and I'm going to serve duck breasts in wine sauce, sprinkled with sliced almonds. We'll be trout fishing in the pines and I'm toying with the idea of hiring a violinist and stashing him in the trees. I'll serve the meal with a flourish and then—just as I strike the match to light the candles—he will come strolling forth, playing gypsy music.

Top that, fellow first class addicts!

Bill and Pete getting ready for a go at trout. You can bet the pickup is loaded with goodies, as part of our avowed plan to really go first class when it comes to outdoor eating.

"YOU AIN'T gunna convince me no dif'rant. Campin's dirty, pure 'n simple. All started with those for'in gypsies. Gallivant'n across this country when honest folk had their nose to the grindstone tryin' to eek a livin' out of the no-feelin' soil. Campin's built on dirt. That's all there is to it."

That is Big Red Flicker for you. All 402 pounds worth. She was only four when her folks brought her in a covered wagon from St. Louis to western Kansas. They worked the land through drought, dust storms, epidemics, hail, frost, plagues of insects. The strain killed her father at 38 and nearly broke her mother. Three of the six children died of smallpox. The wilderness meant work, sorrow, tragedy. For Big Red, the untamed wilds was anything but romantic.

"No, sir. I got this fur by breakin' my back and drippin' bar'ls of sweat. No polecat's gunna catch me in no tent. That's goin' backwards fur as I see. I had enuf of that years ago. Now's time for shag carpet and a shot or two of VO 'fore a spread of roast pork. That's livin' for me. Clean, uplift'd, firs' class."

Cleanliness has been nearly an obsession with Americans since the early 1900's. Daily bathing; deodorants designed to annihilate perspiration; perfumed soaps, lotions, salves; manicured half-mooned fingernails; gleaming teeth; hairlessness. These smack of sterility, of wiping out what is human. What is wrong with dirt underneath the fingernails, the lusty smell of a hard day's work, beads of perspiration along the upper lip? These are reminders of how hard life used to be. Concern with where the next meal will come from is clearly low class. Financially secure people could spend hours pampering the body and not bother about the baseness of man—about his hunger, thirst and need for shelter.

Camping then was an activity engaged in by two divergent groups: the eccentric well-to-do who wanted to see how the other half lived and the nomadic outcasts of society, who failed at respectability and were rejected as undesirable. As leisure time, salaries and inflation in-

SQUEAKY CLEAN

by KATHLEEN FARMER

A clean camp is a healthy one. Flies and odors can be kept to a minimum by prompt, thorough washing of dishes and garbage removal.

Most fry pans can be "boiled" and wiped clean. Washing in heavy suds, with inadequate rinsing cause stomach problems.

creased, a return-to-nature craze was popularized as a temporary refuge from the many worries and anxieties of the work-a-day world.

Recreation specialty manufacturers read the market well. Tents, camp stoves, lanterns, recreation vehicles were massively produced. Consumers responded, purchasing new and better equipment. Besides the essentials, such as sleeping bags and tents, campers clamored for convenience gadgets, like air mattresses and rain flies. They wanted to venture into the outdoors while retaining the level of comfort to which they were accustomed.

As a result, motorhomes, fifth-wheelers and trailers were huge successes almost overnight. With hot and cold running water, a 10 to 40 gallon hot water tank, gas-or-electric refrigerator, gas stove and oven, the camper was fundamentally hauling or driving a miniaturized, compact version of his own house. "A home away from home," was more than an advertising slogan. It was the truth.

Cleanliness is no problem to owners of recreational vehicles as long as plumbing, electrical and gas systems are in working order. The cleansing rituals of home can simply and effectively be carried over. Most conveniences are available in recreational vehicles. Few sacrifices in daily routine are demanded.

In comparison, tent or backpack camping is truly a primitive experience. Water must be found, judged safe or treated and then hauled to camp. The absence of kitchen cabinets requires campers to establish order, ideally in the form of a food bag or grub box. How to wash dishes without a sink? What about baths or showers? Should hands be scrubbed before each meal? Despite Big Red's disparaging remarks, cleanliness is easy to achieve while camping. But camp cleanliness differs from the stringent standards in the home. Mainly because of the limitations of water and fuel, conservation rather than sterilization is the ruling theme behind life in the outdoors.

Too much soap is the most common error. If soap residue is not completely rinsed from dishes and cookware, diarrhea will most likely strike the unsuspecting campers. A long-established custom has equated mounds of suds with spotlessness. But frequently the corollary that every speck of soap should be rinsed away with hot water or else suffer the consequences, has not been properly emphasized.

Surprising as it might sound, boiling water kills bacteria. Soap does not. Suds loosen dirt and food particles and break down grease to hasten cleansing. But bacteria still remains. Only boiling water destroys "germs." In fact, by smothering eating and cooking utensils in boiling water, suds are unnecessary and actually wasteful if the water supply is limited and rationing is called for.

A pot of boiling water is so useful and versatile, it is wise always to have one on the stove or over the fire. Boiling water mixed with instant hot chocolate, tea or coffee, produces hunger-alleviating, before-dinner drinks. It activates dehydrated and freeze-dried food. It sterilizes cooking utensils before they are used. After plates are heaped with steaming Chicken with Rice or Chili Mexicali, pots can be filled with boiling water to disengage stuck-on food. This facilitates cleaning up after dinner.

For skillets and griddles, pots and pans, boiling water can be poured over them to release caked on food and eliminate bacteria. Then, after throwing away the water, the skillet or griddle can be wiped clean with paper towels. Paper towels are the second important tool for maintaining a neat, clean camp.

Boiling water is the first line of defense, disarming potentially harmful substances. Paper towels do the rest,

Cups should be thoroughly sterilized with boiling water and wiped clean.

Paper towels are big aid in camp cleanliness and they should be used liberally for dishes and utensils.

A mixture of mud and grit (gravel, pebbles) will cut grease and remove sticky food. After the mud treatment, rinse thoroughly in hot or boiling water.

removing food specks and grease. Soaking may be mandatory, especially when a thick layer of cooked-on food lines the pot. For burned-on food, the pot with boiling water can be heated on the stove or over the fire, simultaneously being scraped clean with a wooden spoon. The action of water boiling agitates most scorched particles free from the pot.

Prevention, however, is the best way to solve cleaning problems. For example, food is not as likely to stick to Teflon-coated pots and pans. Cooking meals over low heat or glowing coals and frequent stirring likewise will insure flavorful dishes without tasting mushy or overdone.

For personal cleanliness, a heavy-duty plastic wash basin is handy. From this, the camper can freshen up by washing hands and face or shaving without polluting streams or lakes. Bathing in rivers or natural waterways violates respect for the outdoors. Showers and baths are not vital to the camper and should be attempted only at campgrounds that offer such convenience. Once the camper decides that "roughing it" will be fun and adventuresome, being away from a shower for a week or two will be part of the total experience and not that much of a hardship. Being "uncivilized" will help the camper appreciate the niceties of civilization much more.

Hands seem to accumulate grime more readily than any other part of the body. To combat dirty hands, Wet Ones in the pop-up container are at your fingertips whenever they are needed. This way the camping party need not bother with soap, water and towels just to wash the hands.

Litter, empty cans and wrappers around camp draw insects and wild animals. Keep the area clean around the campsite too.

Personal hygiene is a matter of personal habit. But there is no need for feeling "grubby" if you don't want to. Shaving can be practical with a small mirror and supply of hot water. Washing hands before eating should be a must, especially when camping. Plastic wash basin is handy for keeping clean.

Scrape food from fry pan immediately after use. Pan will be easier to clean later and prevent insects from feasting on particles.

Children like to use Wet Ones and then they do not have to interrupt mother. This feeling of independence and self-sufficiency makes them feel almost grown-up. Wet Ones may also be used to wash the face without the trouble of warming water, pouring it into a bowl and using a bar of soap with rinsing and drying necessary.

When it comes to a clean camp kitchen, food should be protected by covers of aluminum foil or plastic bags. Insects, like flies, ants, mosquitoes, and birds like the Gray Jay are especially bold and seem to find their way into everything. This is relatively easy for backpackers since pre-packaging most items into plastic bags is usually necessary before stuffing the food into a sack. For the family tenter in an organized campground, guarding the food against invasion by foreign organisms can be a challenge. For simplicity's sake, remove only the food needed for the current meal from its cooler, box or bag. As soon as ingredients are used, repack them into containers and store them in their proper place. This will aid organization as well as promote cleanliness.

What to do with food scraps, wash water and grease can be a problem. Most organized campgrounds have facilities for disposal of garbage and grease.

When in the wilderness, burning the scraps in the fire is best. Wash water and grease should be poured into a hole about four to six inches deep and covered with soil. Burying garbage is not a good idea since animals will dig it up and scatter what they do not eat. It is best to pack unburnable trash out with you in plastic bags.

Camping is not what it used to be—it is much better. With specialized equipment and improved facilities, campers never had it so good. Now all campers have to do is to keep the goal of camping in mind: fun, rejuvenating the spirit and exploring the unknown.

Cleanliness is important and may be easily achieved. But cleanliness is not sterilization. Spotless hands and soil-free faces are beneficial for morale as well as for good hygiene. Besides, a few pine needles or wood ash flakes in the soup may add some zip to the dish. That reminds me of a pine cone stew I once made . . .

Take along plenty of water. Make sure it is good water. Boil it. And keep the use of soaps to a minimum.

GOOD FIELD CARE MEANS GOOD EATIN'

by MONTE SAGGE

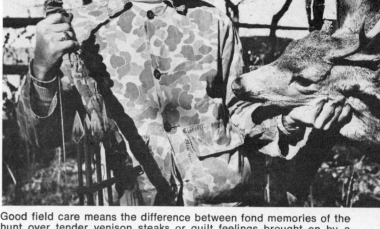

Good field care means the difference between fond memories of the hunt over tender venison steaks or guilt feelings brought on by a tough, gamy piece of meat. This archer is hanging the deer to cool. He can look forward to gourmet venison dishes.

Proper and careful field attention is especially important with antelope since the temperatures are usually warm and the hunting area is often void of trees and water.

SOME OF THE BEST MEALS I can remember around a campfire were the venison or elk chops and steaks fresh from the fall hunts. In fact, beef was a rare treat, and still is. Being from British Columbia, my wife and I live on game meat as do a lot of folks up this way. That doesn't mean a hamburger or fried chicken is not welcome once in a while—because it is. Tastes good. But the meat is a valuable bonus for the table and I handle it with care.

Monte Sagge is a hunting and fishing outfitter in British Columbia. He is inclined to regard wildlife with the highest respect. Once in awhile, he witnesses a hunter neglecting his duty towards the game he is hunting. At these times, Monte is pushed into putting his thoughts down in an article.

A successful antelope hunter is preparing the liver of the antelope, considered by some to be the prime part of the animal. Indians ate it raw when it was still warm to give them the speed and agility of the antelope, according to ancient custom.

Antelope archers Al Carly and Dan Broyles (eating) enjoy their first taste of antelope after each shot a respectable buck.

For the past 20 years, I have run hunting and fishing camps in Wyoming and British Columbia. During that time, numerous tales about the good meat and the bad meat have passed over the lantern-lit camp table.

"Shot an antelope in Wyoming last year," one 30-year old advertising executive told me. "And that old buck was the worst piece of eating I ever had in my life. Why, my dog wouldn't even touch those steaks. And the smell of that stuff cooking was enough to drive me, the wife and kids right out of the kitchen."

I should point out at this break in the story that before moving to British Columbia, each fall in Wyoming my wife and I shot a buck pronghorn each—for 11 straight years. We never ate a "bad" piece of antelope meat. Some were a bit stronger than others; some cuts more tender (just like beef) but never bad. Originally from the city, we were not born with a taste for game meat. It was not hard to acquire a taste for it either. Having hunted birds and small game as a boy, my dad was a stickler for taking care of the quail and rabbits we shot. This indoctrination, plus my wife's skill in the kitchen, carried over to our first years of hunting big game in Wyoming. We handled the meat with care in the field—and cooked it with care in the kitchen. (Most novices cook game meat so long that it has the consistency of shoe leather.) Our initial switch to game meat was a pleasant one. We enjoyed new and different flavors from beef, pork or lamb. And usually the tenderness of game cuts far surpasses that of domestic meat when properly cooked.

There was a time when I would ignore the comments of some hunters about the quality of various game animals they shot. But now I rarely let a remark go by, without asking a few questions on field care, transportation time and how the meat was taken care of when it reached the processors. My advertising executive client, at my camp for a 10-day moose and bear hunt, had some interesting facts on his Wyoming antelope hunt.

"We hunted near Douglas," he told me over a mugful of hot coffee. "On the second day out I shot a pretty good 14-inch buck. It took me a while to gut him out because I had forgotten my folding saw. Getting through the pelvic and brisket bones was tough. My knife got dull quick and I didn't have a sharpening stone. There was no water nearby so I couldn't wash the body cavity out. And to top that off, I had to drag the animal nearly two miles back to the vehicle by myself."

As it turned out the hunter's friends were out doing their own hunting. The antelope lay in the September, Wyoming heat for nearly four hours before it could be washed and hung in the shade. It took the hunting party three days to fill out their numbers with five respectable heads. In the meantime, the animals were subjected to 75-degree heat, little shade and possible spoilage.

Instead of quartering the antelope for better cooling during their long drive back to Pennsylvania, the five animals were tied to the top of the station wagon luggage carrier—whole (heads and all) and endured more heat in the next two days of driving.

The meat processor, my friend told me, had reservations about accepting the antelope, but did so when one of the hunters said . . . "What do you mean you can't take them in—we drove all the way to Wyoming for these animals."

Enough said. It is poor field care—little or no field care—that turns the majority of noses up at game meat. And, nonresident hunters are not the only ones guilty of poor game meat handling practices. Resident hunters, some of whom forget about the game after the excitement of the stalk and kill, often have only themselves to blame for strong, tough game meat.

I feel that all big game meat, regardless of the species, sex, and age is potentially tender and good tasting. The quality variable is the care that meat receives before it reaches the table. Some persons I know have never had a good moose roast. They will not eat venison. And feel that the tender juicy, flanks of Rocky Mountain goat are better left in the rocky crags where the animal was shot. It is a matter of good taste. When it comes to insuring high quality game meat for your next fall or summer camp, here are tips that have proven themselves reliable and consistent over 20 years.

Field Care Equipment

Even under the most strenuous of hunting conditions there are handy little items that can be packed on the belt, in a small pack or in saddle bags. Among the basics for good field care are a good sharp sheath or folding hunting knife; a sharpening stone; small belt hatchet or

GOOD FIELD CARE—GOOD MEAT!
How to take care of your kill.

I. Bleed promptly. Cut throat at point A. Or if head is to be mounted for trophy, insert knife at point B cutting deeply until blood flows freely. In case of wound that bleeds freely or internally, bleeding may not be necessary.

II. Remove genitals or udder. Prop carcass belly up—rocks or brush may be used for support—and cut circular area shown in illustration. Musk glands at points A & B MAY be removed to avoid tainting meat. Glands cease to function at time of death.

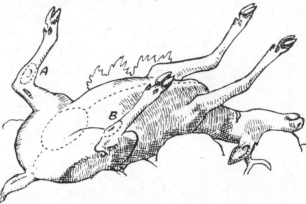

III. Split hide from tail to throat. Insert knife point under skin but do not cut into body cavity. Hide may be peeled back several inches on each side to keep hair out of meat.

IV. Cut through pelvic bone. Turning carcass down hill will cause viscera to sag into rib cavity. This will decrease the chance of puncturing viscera while cutting or chopping through bone. Large intestine can then be cut free from pelvic cavity but not severed from viscera.

V. Open carcass by cutting thru length of breast bone and neck into exposed wind pipe.

VI. Turn carcass, head uphill. Free gullet and pull viscera toward rear. An alternate method is to leave head down hill and strip viscera from rear out over the head.

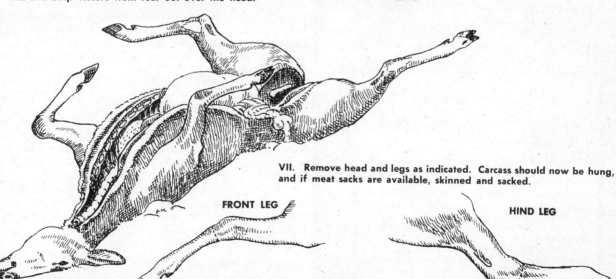

VII. Remove head and legs as indicated. Carcass should now be hung, and if meat sacks are available, skinned and sacked.

FRONT LEG   **HIND LEG**

VIII. Allow carcass to cool before transporting if conditions permit. A cooling time of 6 hours before transportation is recommended by many hunters.

IX. Attach the proper tag as required by law.

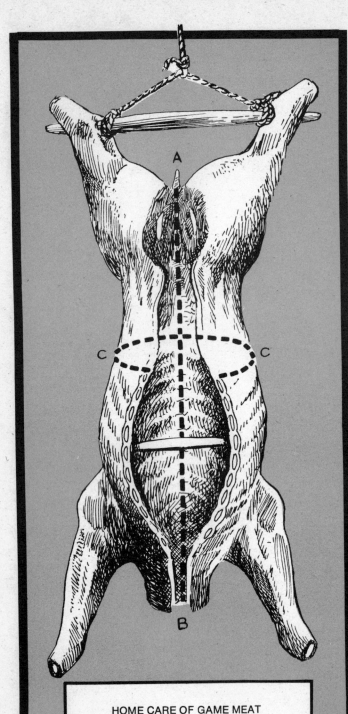

HOME CARE OF GAME MEAT

Hanging the carcass for aging at least 36 hours.

Carcass, skinned and wiped free of hair with damp cloth, should be hung in a cool place for aging—at least 36 hours. Gambrel, inserted through rear hock tendons, should spread hindquarters. Insert stick in rib cage as shown. Wrapping or sacking in cheesecloth or other loosely woven material offers protection from flies. Excess fat and bloodshot parts should be cut away. To start cutting process, split down length of backbone, from "A" to "B," and separate front and hind quarters at points "C-C."

folding game saw (I carry both) and a 30-foot length of half-inch braided nylon rope.

By packing these items, regardless of whether you are hunting "just for a couple of hours" alone, or with a guide, you are insuring yourself of being able to open up the animal you have killed. Whether the cleaning operation be one of surgeon's skill and delicacy or a job of novice, rough quality—the most important thing you can do is remove all the organs, entrails and blood. Some hunters I know place great importance on not letting any of the internal organ fluids touch the meat. Depending on where and what the bullet hit, that is an often impossible goal. More important than operating room slowness and care, is getting all the insides *out* and then washing the body cavity as soon as possible. With the above mentioned equipment, all but the washing operation can be performed quickly which means the "switch" has been thrown for the meat cooling process to begin. This basic procedure, with the simple, but *sharp* tools listed, is the foundation to good eating later. The faster the hunter can get to the downed animal and perform this field dressing, the better the chances of good meat flavor.

In many situations, water will be nearby for washing the body cavity. However, some hunters foresake this step because they lack a water holding vessel in which they can bring water to the animal. It is often impossible, for example, to drag even a field dressed elk or moose to water.

One way to solve the water problem is to pack a canteen for such a purpose. With the palm of your hand and a canteenful of water you can thoroughly wash an elk cavity.

In areas where there is plenty of water, pack a folding, rubber or plastic water container (the kind backpackers use) in your day pack. They weigh only a few ounces empty. But filled at a nearby brook, they will hold as much as a gallon of water . . . more than enough to wash out blood and body fluids from the animal.

Antelope hunting, often in dry, semi-arid sagebrush prairies and deserts, presents special water problems. Aside from drinking, cooking and wash water for an antelope hunt (and depending on the number of hunters) I usually take along five extra gallons of water for washing game meat. A canteenful of water will wash out a lot of blood at the kill site. But a thorough washing is needed for antelope because of the warm weather and tendency for the hollow, fragile hairs to fall into the body cavity during field dressing. Back at camp, with the extra water, wash, drain and dry the cavity. I have found this procedure directly relates to the eating flavor of the antelope, more so than whether or not to skin the animal. More will be said later on skinning and cooling.

Field care gear is simple. A game hanging tripod with meat hook (easily made at home) is very handy when hunting treeless antelope areas. It's also great for fast cooling when a tarp is draped or rigged over the animal and tripod.

For timber areas a 30-foot length of rope when slung over a limb can get most animals up off the ground for cooling, either whole, halves or quarters. For large game like elk, moose and caribou, rope pulleys are essential for hanging meat.

Protecting the Meat at Camp

One guide I know made the mistake of taking his client's game meat too casually. After the meat was packed into camp on horseback from the kill site, it was carelessly thrown on the ground in quarters. There it stayed for two days until the hunter discovered it. Understandably, the

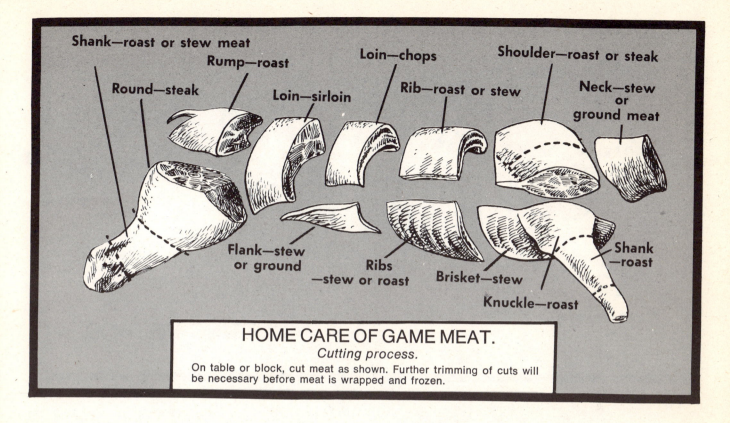

HOME CARE OF GAME MEAT.
Cutting process.
On table or block, cut meat as shown. Further trimming of cuts will be necessary before meat is wrapped and frozen.

hunter chewed out the guide . . . made him erect a game pole and the quarters (saved by a snap of below-freezing temperatures) were hung. That particular guide lost one hunter's business . . . and probably others warned by word-of-mouth.

Fortunately most outfitters are extremely careful about protecting game meat at camp. Game poles, sometimes 15 feet high, keep meat away from intruding bears. More important, meat is hung in the shade and kept as cool as possible. Some hunters drape sheets over whole animals or quarters for shade and protection from birds and insects.

I prefer commercially manufactured game sacks made from lightweight, airy, cotton mesh (like cheesecloth). Air is allowed to circulate, yet the game cover is woven tight enough to keep out dirt, insects and most birds.

Care of meat is important at camp for two solid reasons. The meat should be properly cooled in one or two days. Hanging helps cooling. And after the initial cooling process takes place, aging begins. This is a breakdown of some meat and muscle fibers that, when done right, adds to flavor and tenderness. Most experts agree that the aging process progresses at a good rate when the temperature is

The immense size of the moose demands planning and cooperation from other hunters to gut and pack out the animal.

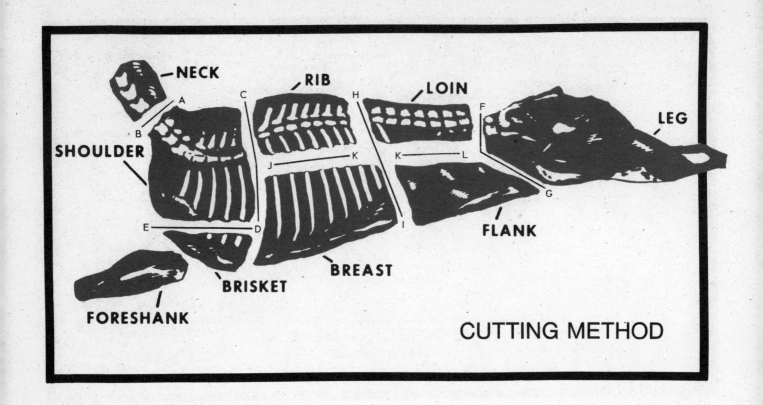

DO-IT-YOURSELF BUTCHER

40 degrees, or in that immediate neighborhood. Warmer temperatures increase the rate to the point where spoilage becomes a factor. Flies, especially, are attracted to meat at this stage. Colder temperatures (near or below freezing) decelerate the aging process to the point where it is virtually nonexistent or nearly so.

It has been my experience that game meat which is thoroughly cooled for one or two days can stand some high temperatures (without affecting tenderness and flavor) during hanging, aging and transportation; whereas meat not immediately cooled, or not cooled thoroughly, breaks down quicker under those same extremes.

Aging

The question of aging is as debatable as religion and politics in some big game hunting circles. I have had back strap cuts off a freshly killed whitetail, that when eaten in camp that evening, were as delectable as any I have tasted. But then again, the outdoors . . . and a Dutch oven or open fire have a tendency to make fresh cuts a delight. The same holds true for livers and hearts. I'll be the first to admit I like 'em when they are still "steaming."

But the rest of the animal, I like aged before the cuts are frozen. And this aging holds true for all big game. Only the length of the period varies. Depending on how long an animal has hung in camp, the meat processor and myself usually come up with an agreeable aging period. Once I shot an old bull moose (age judged by the wear of his teeth) that smelled strongly of sagebrush and the rut. After two days of packing him out on two horses and a mule, I got him to the locker plant where the processor grimaced and pinched his nose with his fingers. "How long you want him to hang . . . a year?" he quipped. "Not quite," I grinned back.

We decided that moose should hang for at least eight days. Which he did. About two weeks later, when nearly 600 pounds of cuts were packaged and ready for eating, my wife and I got the surprise of our lives. There was no strong smell coming from the first moose roast in the

Many residents of the northern Rockies live on elk year round from the elk they shoot during hunting season. While not as big as the moose, an average size elk can feed two adults for about eight months. From the practical, money-saving aspect, it pays to take good care of an elk carcass.

oven. The pink-centered, four-pound chunk of meat when done, sliced as easily as a seven-dollar supermarket tenderloin. When topped with pan gravy, accompanied by oven-browned potatoes, freshly gathered watercress and a dry, red wine, we "um-umed", "wowed" and gorged our way through a wonderful piece of eating. The remainder of those cuts (although we gave away a good share of the meat so it would not outlive its freezer life) were equally good. And I will always have fond memories of that old, love-sick bull.

Here is my standard for aging in a temperature controlled processing plant. Antelope, four days. Deer, five or six days. Elk, six days. Moose anywhere from six to nine days. This guide is set up for animals that have hung anywhere from two to five days, under cool or cold conditions, in camp. I have not been disappointed yet. But there are those among you, I know, who have your own thoughts.

To Skin or Not

One fact is certain. An animal's skin is an insulator against cold and heat. So whether the skin is left on or removed does have an effect on flavor, regardless of how insignificant. And, compared to quick evisceration, thorough washing, and hanging; skinning, in my opinion, is insignificant.

Now, many governmental meat care guides recommend skinning if the temperature is above 40 degrees and the carcass cannot be taken directly to a cooler.

Since it takes some hunters a considerable length of time to skin an animal I would say that it is more important to hang it in a cool place first rather than subject it to the direct rays of the sun, dirt and insects. If skinning is convenient, do it. It is most convenient when the animal is hanging from a tripod or game pole and the hide (especially within two hours after killing) can be pulled off.

I cannot argue the biological evidence that meat cools a little faster with the skin off. The only thing I can say is that I rarely skin any game animal, antelope included.

The Bighorn Sheep of the Rockies presents a problem to the hunter of how to get the trophy back to camp. Because of the sheep's rugged, rocky habitat, the hunter has to work extra hard at packing the animal.

Once the hunter gets the big game meat back to camp, he should hang it on a game pole to cool and protect it from dirt, insects and birds.

Somehow I like the protection the hide gives the meat when I quarter or pack it. And I know that the processor will skin the animal when it can be aged under proper temperature with little worry about dirt and insects.

Field Cutting

Rarely do I leave elk camp without quartering my animal (with the hide on). It is easier to pack and transport that way. Game sacks keep the quarters dirt and insect free. Meat is cooled more efficiently, when cut in fourths.

If the weather turns warm during an early elk hunting season, and a meat processor won't be reached for a while, animals will be quartered and hung. Sometimes, they will be halved down the backbone using a saw for a neat job and less waste. A hatchet or ax does a rough cutting job when splitting a big game animal down the backbone and some of the best meat is wasted. Yet it has been my experience that most guides use an ax for splitting the backbone for halving and quartering.

Another important part of the cutting procedure is to trim off all fat, bloodshot and inedible areas from the carcass. This will help reduce spoilage and the number of insects attracted to the animal.

The final step of cutting, if you elect to do so, is butchering the animal into freezer and eating cuts. This is a great experience. One that you may not want for every big game you shoot, but certainly worth a try. Most state game and fish departments offer handy, do-it-yourself meat butchering guides. They are easy to follow.

With the right meat saw, cleaver and good, sharp knives, you can have the satisfaction of the complete big game hunt—from the stalk to meat in the freezer. A good, solid work table for cutting; and good quality freezer paper insures a clean job that will mean professional looking cuts.

Transporting Meat

Most of us are tired of hearing about the eastern dudes who draped their deer over the hood of their car only to have the engine heat ripen the carcasses to the point of spoiling. An over-used story. And I feel few hunters go that far in trying to ruin game meat. The more common, but equally serious mistakes, are leaving game animals on top of a vehicle, unattended, for long periods of time, during the trip back home. Or the transportation of game, whole or quartered, inside the vehicle or trunk where the heater may be going full blast and little or no air is circulated around the meat. Some spoilage and bad flavor is bound to result.

Spoilage can be reduced and even eliminated on long return trips (at a sacrifice to showing off game) by packing quarters in cartons or coolers filled with dry ice; by shielding game meat from direct sun with loosely draped tarps when stopping to eat or at a motel; or by shipping game meat home separately by air in dry ice containers. At first glance, the cost of shipping is expensive. But in comparison to wasting meat by letting it spoil, the extra money is worth it.

It is a good idea to hunt in a party, not only for safety's sake but also to assist each other in field care, packing the animal back to camp and hanging the carcass to cool on a game pole.

Some hunters are lucky enough to shoot a good buck only one or two miles from the road. Several hunters can help drag the animal that far without much strain to any one hunter.

During cool or cold weather, meat can be safely transported in a utility trailer or on luggage or boat racks on the vehicle. Game sacks, double or triple bagged, will let air circulate for good cooling, and yet protect against dirt.

The Most Common Mistakes in Game Cookery

1. Overcooking! Most cooks feel that wild game is truly wild and all the bad things have to be cooked out. Chances are, game meat is the purest meat, the most untainted by chemicals and preservatives, you will ever eat. Cook game meat like you would a good roast beef, or the best beef steaks and chops you can buy. Take the advice of many restaurant managers who say, "We are not responsible for steaks ordered well-done."

2. Flavor Disguise! More good game meat is wasted under globs of sour cream and orange glaze than by misplaced bullets. Exotic sauces, bastes and marinades are fine once in a while. But the pure, simple untainted flavor of game meat is best by far. Stick with your favorite simple recipes that you use for expensive roasts and steaks. Guess I will never get used to people slapping ketchup over an eight-dollar Kansas City sirloin . . . nor will I accept "candied" game meat.

There is a fine feeling of satisfaction on a fishing, camping or hunting trip to cook wild game—in the wilds. It makes me feel like a trapper, a pioneer. A good feeling, especially when the meat has been taken care of in the field and it darn near melts in my mouth.

The luau is as Hawaiian as grass skirts, pineapple and these wood carved images of the gods.

YOUR OWN HONEST-TO-GOODNESS LUAU

by PEGGY PETERS

THE KONA COAST or western shore of the island of Hawaii has a long and colorful history. King Kamehameha the Great was born here; ancient temples, caves and stone carvings are found along the tide line and just a few miles to the north, at Kealakekua Bay, Captain Cook in 1779 landed to mark the beginning of western influence on the islands. But the best discovery for any outdoor cook is doubtless the Hawaiian luau which I found on this, the Big Island.

Mostly on solid ground, but partially cantilevered over the sea lies Island Holidays Resorts' Keauhou Beach Hotel which treats its guests to a sumptuous, traditional Hawaiian feast which could be duplicated easily here on the mainland. The main course and central figure in the luau is a whole pig roasted half a day in a shallow pit dug in the ground.

The preparation of the ground, the pig itself, and its internment has become an island rite which I recently witnessed. It is the Imu Ceremony which takes place at a special area on the hotel grounds. First, about nine in the morning, a hole about five feet in diameter and slightly less than three feet deep is dug. Keawe (hard) wood is placed in its center and lit. When the chunks of wood are burning well, smooth rounded stones (iliili rocks) about one foot across are added; the rocks are left to absorb the heat until noon when the pit and everything in it is so hot even the mynas who contantly walk the lawns keep a safe distance.

It is now time for the second act in the ritual. A "mainland" pig, dressed, but complete with looped tail and head arrives on a litter carried by several husky Hawaiian lads and is respectfully laid on its back, feet spread-eagled on a wire mesh blanket. Then the rocks are removed from the pit with tongs and the ashes carefully brushed from them with a broom of banana leaves. The hot stones are placed in the cavity of the pig with handfuls of rock salt. Wire bracelets encircle each of the porker's ankles and when the cavity is full the front feet are drawn together as are the rear.

Now steam rolls into the air as the mesh sheet is drawn firmly around the pig and folded along the mid-line. At this point the pig is ready for the pit which still contains a few hot rocks. These rocks along with the wood ash are smoothed to an even bed in the now two-foot-deep depression and covered with stumps and curved staves of banana wood, all thoroughly dampened. Banana wood is preferred because it contains a great deal of natural moisture and will steam the pig well during the cooking process. The

A whole pig is the central figure of the luau. Here hot stones are placed in the cavity of the pig with handfuls of rock salt.

The pig is then tied to a pole and lowered into the cooking pit which has been smoldering from hard wood coals all morning.

staves are placed curved side up to collect the dripping juices.

Over this base the Hawaiians place a layer of ti (pronounced tea) leaves which keeps the meat clean and imparts no flavor of its own. Finally the prepared pig is carried to its waiting "oven" hanging downward from a pipe slipped under the wired feet. The pig is placed on the leaves, the pipe is removed and another layer of ti leaves covers the pig. The leaves are three-foot long, glossy ovals with short stems which are placed upward, the greenery fanning down and outward completely covering the pig. Quickly now wet burlap sacks are added to the mound about four deep. Steam slowly rises from several crevices and, as the final layer, four Hawaiians clad only in bright print sarongs hastily shovel damp loose earth over the dark mound to a depth of about two feet. It is now up to Madam Pele, the fire goddess who seems to be in charge of about everything, to see that the meat roasts and steams to a tender, delicious perfection.

The mainland outdoor chef will obviously have to make a few improvisations in his own Imu Ceremony but most traditions like the luau do survive because the rules are flexible enough to bend to necessity.

You might say that changing the rules not only is permissible, but traditional. First is the size of the roast. At the Keauhou Beach the pig weighs 160 pounds and the chef figures about one-quarter to one-half pound per person. You may wish to figure much more than this unless the accompanying dishes are as large and numerous as his. On the other hand your guests will probably number fewer than 80. I would estimate a pig just under 50 pounds would amply feed 35 guests. The cooking time would be correspondingly shorter than the five hours allowed at the Keauhou. In place of the ti leaves, use two clean tarpaulins.

The Hawaiians themselves have changed the old recipe somewhat by cooking a "mainland" pig rather than the traditional Hawaiian pig. The mainland variety which is commercially grown on the island is taller, longer and far leaner than its Polynesian cousin. This, of course, is the type you will buy.

The outdoor cook should take a tip from the traditionalists and do some carving before the entombment. I noted that deep slices an inch or two wide had been made in the hams of our pig and the larger ribs were separated. This would allow for more even cooking and easier carving later. Extra seasoning might add to the flavor, too. Say a few bay leaves in the cavity or garlic cloves in the slices. Whole peppercorns would be good.

All other dishes of the luau are prepared apart from the pig except sweet potatoes which, if your animal is much smaller than theirs, could be wrapped in aluminum foil and buried in the "oven" right with the pig.

While Madam Pele watches over the entree, the mortal chef should look into the other dishes which he might serve. At our luau everyone particularly enjoyed the lomi, a traditional cold salmon accompaniment. Here (and at

Ti leaves insulate the pig to steam it and keep the meat clean without imparting any flavor.

A native sounds the beginning of the end of the Imu Ceremony, that is, the preparation of the pig. The pig, after five hours of cooking, is uncovered and removed from the underground oven. Let the luau begin!

Hot, moist, tender, the meat can be eaten right from the bone—delicious.

onions. You might wish to make mahi-mahi, medium sized fish fillets of whatever variety was caught that day dipped in batter and deep fried at the very last minute.

Two other delicious and different treats were lau-lau and chicken and long rice. Lau-lau looks like a strip of knotted seaweed on the plate! Not so; the seaweed is in fact a strip of ti leaf (the same leaf that is covering our pig now steaming away underground) knotted around a tiny chunk of pork or fish and a crumpled taro leaf which gives it a spinach flavor. These morsels are boiled until tender. The diner discards the outer ti leaf and devours the rest.

The chicken with long rice looks Chinese, with cubes of chicken combined in a clear sauce with what appears to be short pieces of transparent macaroni. Poi with chicken and long rice were the hands-down favorites of our Hawaiian friend George Ahuna. There must be something nutritious here—George is built like a linebacker, smiles like a Polynesian and sings like a bird.

Beginning about 4:30 in the afternoon the Keauhou Beach hotel guests began to gather at the Imu area to witness the final act in the ceremony. The few benches surrounding the mound were filled and standees in the back jockied for better positions as promptly at five the Hawaiian boys dug away the earth exposing the steaming burlap layer. This gone, the wilted ti leaves molded to the shape of the pig were in sight. I had heard rumors from the rear ranks that during the afternoon someone had made off with our prize, leaving volcanic rocks in its place, so it was with some relief that I saw that it was indeed our pig which was gingerly lifted from its earthen oven to the litter. The meat was well done, in fact, falling from the bone in places and the aroma which arose brought a collective sigh from the group. Some rich, brown shreds of pork stuck to the wire mesh while the main portion had uniformly shrunk away. We were all invited to take a piece for ourselves "to test for doneness." It was hot, moist and absolutely delicious. I can attest to that.

Now you would think that a whole roasted pig, strips of steak, chicken, salads, fruits, vegetables and poi would make a matchless luau—and it did, but there was one more thing: dessert. For the perfect last Hawaiian touch—haupia, an inch and one half cube of rich, smooth coconut pudding.

Your own outdoor luau could be as delicious with a smaller pig, as we have mentioned. For the cocktail preceding dinner the mai tai is the usual choice made with rum and fruit juice. Perhaps instead of haupia for dessert, a square of white cake topped with a coconut frosting that is served frequently in our fiftieth state.

To be really authentic you might follow the Hawaiian decorating scheme. Most dining areas, either indoors or out, feature huge bouquets of flowers: red lobster claws, sprays of red ginger and a few spectacular bird of paradise flowers. If these aren't available in your area you might substitute hydrangea blossoms, rhododendron or Joe-Pye-weed. Anything large and strong and in great profusion. For the absolute ultimate—a lei for each. Any good size flower will do, daisy (put them back to back), zinnia, marigold if the odor isn't too strong, snapdragon, or any combination strung on dental floss or nylon fishing line with a carpet needle. Sprinkle each lei with water and place them in a plastic bag in the refrigerator until needed. Each gentleman receives his lei from his hostess with a kiss on the cheek and an "aloha" and each lady in the same fashion from her host as she arrives.

Along with all the Hawaiians who helped me learn the lessons of luau I wish you "ono kapuu", or good appetite. Aloha.

home) salt salmon is soaked in several changes of water, drained, and combined with chopped fresh tomato and chopped onion all in approximately equal amounts.

Almost everyone has heard of poi, the Hawaiian staple made of the ground taro root. It is smooth and creamy and has the same consistency as applesauce. "One finger" poi is thicker than "two finger" poi. In color it is rather gray with perhaps a shade of violet and in taste is probably the blandest thing I've ever eaten. Hawaiians really don't expect the visitor to like it, but they do feel it should be tried. Almost apologetically it is explained that even tiny babies and those with stomach ailments can tolerate it. Probably not a necessity at your luau, but interesting if obtainable.

Other dishes for the long luau table include thin strips of teriyaki steak, sliced hot sweet potatoes, sliced (or diced or crushed) pineapple, and a platter of tomatoes and

SUPPERTIME & ALL IS WELL

At the end of a good day, outdoors, there is nothing like a relaxing, hearty supper.

by KATHLEEN FARMER

"CHARLIE, my waders are leaking! I think a couple of small fry trout are trapped in them too. I feel a wiggly sensation around my ankles."

We were fly fishing the Green River north of Cora, Wyoming, about five miles from the head waters. We had driven all day to reach this spot. While elk hunting here last fall, we promised ourselves to return first thing in the spring to fish for rainbow trout and grayling. "Nothing will stop us," we vowed. Neither rain nor snow; neither tornado nor blizzard. "No matter what, we will wade that section of river and fish."

"Right," I agreed enthusiastically. Having received a spin-fly combination backpack rod for my birthday, I was anxious to try it out on the stream. I had grown tired of wrapping the fly line around the rafters of our high-ceilinged garage during practice sessions.

When we left our home in Jackson, Wyoming, the day looked beautiful. "I guess Nature does not plan to test our dedication as dyed-in-the-wool fishermen. Even the fair-weather fishers will be out on such a glorious day."

The 100 miles passed slowly. As we drove by the inviting emerald fishing holes of the Hoback River, our fishing fever rose. We nibbled on sandwiches made from last night's sirloin elk roast. We decided what flies to use first. Charlie had created several different versions of old standbys, like the Caddis, Montana nymph and the Stone Fly nymph. We were eager to experiment with them. "Nymphing" was how we planned to fish the days away.

A dirt road about 40 miles long connects the town of Cora with the Lower Green River Lake campground and parallels the Green River the entire way. Periodically we stopped to watch fishermen catch respectable rainbows. "Should we try a few casts here?"

"No, let's go on to our special place." That was approximately 1½ miles south of the campground, where the road ended. Here we would set up camp and spend about five days soaking up the country.

We finally arrived. "No mistaking it. I'd recognize that curve in the river, with the riffle in the middle and two deep holes on each side, anywhere."

Pulling on the waders, we plotted how to work the river. We had just rigged up our rods when the thunderstorm began. Fumbling for raingear, we silently resolved not to allow the rain to dampen our fishing fervor. We proudly walked down to the river pretending not to notice the cold, wet and the wind.

Charlie headed towards the edge of the riffle. Whipping his fly line as he waded. The chest waders permitted him to tackle relatively deep water. Suddenly I saw him floating upright down the river, as if a submerged St. Christopher was carrying him across.

"Charlie!" His feet touched down on firm ground about 50 yards downstream from me. Shaking his head, he splashed through the water and dropped on the bank. "What happened?"

"An undercurrent swept me off my feet in slow motion. It doesn't look that deep and swift but, believe me, it is. I'm glad I had this belt snugly around my waders. Otherwise, they could have filled with water and I'd be on the bottom of the river right now."

I shivered thinking about it. The wind played havoc with my fly line, once winding it completely around me. I was discouraged, wet and disappointed. "Let's build a fire, dry out and fix supper." Last January while whitefishing in the Snake River, my waders kept me bone dry. Now every step I took swished water. Realizing I had brought along no extra socks nor jeans, I figured I better begin drying my clothes soon or else look forward to a drenched five days.

"I'm going to fish a little longer. Can't have that river thinking it got the best of me. The way the rain's coming down, I probably won't fish that much longer."

I sloshed up the bank, crossed the road and searched for a sheltered campsite. I found one on top of a hill over-

Pre-cooked meats can be plopped in fry pan and served up in no time.

Supper can be as simple as hamburgers or fancy as fresh lobster tails.

This family decides it's time to beach canoes for the day and concentrate on pitching camp and getting supper ready.

looking the Green. With a lovely view and a circle of cottonwoods, aspens and Douglas firs, there also were a homespun corral, horse hitching rail, game pole, fireplace and table. "An outfitter must use this area for a camp during hunting season," I said to our beagle hounds Radar and Sonar. They gazed at me as if to agree.

I gathered enough firewood for the night and started a fire. The large number of trees protected the deadfall from becoming soaked with rain. But most of the wood was damp.

I unpacked the cooking gear from the Blazer. Despite the steady drizzle, the flames of the fire dissolved the chill and bleakness which blanketed the campsite minutes before. In fact, it was downright homey.

Charlie would set up the canvas tent when he returned. I arranged the cook stove on its stand, got out the five-gallon jug of water, the cooler and the food bag. I checked over the supplies. "Even if we are short on sunshine, we have plenty of food to keep our spirits up." The dogs made a bed out of dry pine needles underneath a tree and curled up. As good a spot as any to relax and take a nap.

Charlie was disheartened when he arrived at camp after sundown. "I had a good one but he snapped the fly off before I had a chance to catch a glimpse of him. A guy fishing not 75 yards away caught a grayling and threw it back, shouting, 'You no good trash whitefish.' The fish are in there. We have to figure out how to catch them."

Hamburgers being Charlie's second favorite meal (spaghetti is number one on his list of preferences), I had pre-cooked six of them before we left on the trip. Now, all I had to do was to heat them and cook a package of dehydrated hash brown potatoes.

When planning meals for supper, the cook should be easy on herself. One-dish meals are nourishing and inviting, especially if they are spicy and tasty. These can be pre-cooked at home, packaged in plastic containers or empty coffee cans and warmed up at camp when needed. Chili, spaghetti or any type of casserole can be prepared at home, instilled with home-cooked flavor. For extended trips, they can be frozen and packed on ice in the cooler.

After a strenuous day of hiking, supper is a welcome treat.

There is the hope . . . for every camp supper, that the fisherman can provide some fresh fare.

Pre-cooked meats, such as, hamburgers, steaks, pork chops and chicken, are excellent when wrapped in aluminum foil and heated in camp. This requires extra work before the vacation but allows more time for the chef to relax during the action-filled days. Also, when pre-cooked meat is stored in aluminum foil and one-dish concoctions are brought along in throw-away containers, dish washing is nearly uncalled for. An empty coffee can may double as both a storage and cooking pot and then be thrown away or packed out.

Dehydrated and freeze-dried meals, such as, Beef Stroganoff, Shrimp Creole and Ham Cheddarton, always come in handy for a particularly busy day when supper falls late at night. They are nutritious, filling and flavorful. They can be ready in 10 to 20 minutes. When a body needs sleep more than food, the only-add-water-and-heat dinners enable a person to eat quickly before he hits the sack.

Pre-planning is vital for a camp cook. Otherwise, camping will be just an extension of household duties and chores. For instance, the camp cook and bottle-washer should plan on bringing only one skillet, one kettle and two pots (a four-quart size and another one with a two-quart capacity). These should be sufficient for a family of four. That is, if each supper is carefully outlined before the vacation. Pre-cooking a portion of each supper is helpful too. By limiting the number of pots and pans and by using paper plates and cups and plastic eating utensils, dish washing will be cut down considerably. Even in the well-equipped kitchens of recreational vehicles and houseboats, the chef will be smart to concentrate on the plain and simple—things that are easy to fix and clean up after and have proven to be delectable by all family members.

An effective way to formulate supper menus for one or two weeks is to ask each member of the family to suggest two or three dishes. The cook could take this one step further and request that the person who wanted a certain meal should assist in preparing it. This would spread responsibility for supper to everyone in the party.

For example, a dish that Charlie looks forward to preparing and one that both of us are fond of is Italian

A brace of nice fat trout will be a nice addition to the evening meal.

sausage sandwiches. Saute sliced green peppers with Italian sausage in three tablespoons of oil. Serve on hot dog buns or hoogie rolls with tomato sauce and Parmesan cheese. Simple but stimulating to the palate.

Suppertime represents the satisfying glow of a day well done. It is the chance to sit back and talk over the day's happenings, interjecting humor into what was trying or aggravating. At this time, hurt feelings bounce back, wet clothes dry out and sore feet can soak. It is recess from the demands inherent in camping. Here you discover how lucky you are.

Good food makes suppertime even better. When peppered with home-cooked flavor, it is the best time of the day.

Trail bike camp at Wyoming's famous Atlantic City ghost town.

During snowtime hunting seasons . . . or any fall camping, nothing beats coming back to a hot supper.

After supper, there is nothing like a good snooze before evening fishing begins.

Just as supper tops off the daylight hours, dessert highlights supper. As long as desserts are sweet, there is no need for elaborate preparations. Pudding is excellent. It can be combined with dried fruit that has been rejuvenated by soaking in water. Graham crackers can be crumbled into pudding, very much resembling the taste of dehydrated pies. By adding nuts and M&Ms to pudding, a rustic banana split is created.

Candy bars and cookies are also great desserts. Roasted marshmallows too are traditional climaxes to an outdoor supper. "Some Mores," originated by sweet-toothed Girl Scouts, are an extra special dessert. Melted Hershey Bars and roasted marshmallows sandwiched between two graham crackers induce a craving for "some more"—you can not eat only one (if you somehow possess super-human willpower and manage to consume only one Some More, the Girl Scouts will take away one of your merit badges for discrediting Some Mores' reputation).

Jello, while not sweet enough for some campers, is a respectable dessert candidate. There is one drawback, however. Many can not wait until the Jello coagulates. But liquid Jello is as delightful a dessert as hardened Jello—on especially hot nights, it is even better.

After three and a half hamburgers, a heaping mound of hash browns, several cups of instant hot chocolate and a couple of nut-covered candy bars interspersed with chocolate chip cookies, Charlie was beginning to feel like himself again. Already, he was scrutinizing the way he had unsuccessfully fished the Green River. "Tomorrow is another day and those rainbows better watch out. I'll be out there early with new ammunition in my fishing vest."

My clothes were drying out and my socks were toasty warm. Even if the rain continued, it would be of no concern to us. Charlie had set up a tarp, attached it to the top front of the tent. We sat underneath it dry and rested. The campfire was partly underneath the tarp, allowing us to dry clothes over the fire without exposing them to the falling rain. Our raingear had been dried too and was ready for tomorrow's fishing. The dogs had gulped down their dry dog food speckled with a leftover hamburger. We could hear a moose munching on a tender willow not far away.

Rain or no rain, this vacation was worth it. During suppertime we warmed ourselves, wrung out our soaked clothing and were ready for more adventure. After all, nothing but sunshine would be dull, wouldn't it?